Engineering Strategies and Practice

Custom Publication for
University of Toronto

MCGRAW-HILL RYERSON LIMITED

Toronto Montréal Boston Burr Ridge, IL Dubuque, IA Madison, WI New York San Francisco
St. Louis Bangkok Bogotá Caracas Kuala Lumpur Lisbon London Madrid Mexico City Milan
New Delhi Santiago Seoul Singapore Sydney Taipei

Table of Contents

1

THE PRODUCT DESIGN PROCESS

1.1
INTRODUCTION

What is design? If you search the literature for an answer to that question, you will find about as many definitions as there are designs. Perhaps the reason is that the process of design is such a common human experience. Webster's dictionary says that to design is "to fashion after a plan," but that leaves out the essential fact that to design is to create something that has never been. Certainly an engineering designer practices design by that definition, but so does an artist, a sculptor, a composer, a playwright, or many another creative member of our society.

Thus, although engineers are not the only people who design things, it is true that the professional practice of engineering is largely concerned with design; it is frequently said that design is the essence of engineering. To design is to pull together something new or arrange existing things in a new way to satisfy a recognized need of society. An elegant word for "pulling together" is *synthesis*. We shall adopt the following formal definition of design:[1] "Design establishes and defines solutions to and pertinent structures for problems not solved before, or new solutions to problems which have previously been solved in a different way." The ability to design is both a science and an art. The science can be learned through techniques and methods to be covered in this course, but the art is best learned by doing design. It is for this reason that your design experience must involve some realistic project experience.

The emphasis that we have given to the creation of new things in our discussion of design should not unduly alarm you. To become proficient in design is a perfectly attainable goal for an engineering student, but its attainment requires the guided experience that we intend this course to provide. Design should not be confused with discovery. *Discovery* is getting the first sight of, or the first knowledge of something, as

---

1. J. F. Blumrich, *Science,* vol. 168, pp. 1551–1554, 1970.

when Columbus discovered America. We can discover what has already existed but has not been known before. But a *design* is the product of planning and work. We will present a structured design process to assist you in doing design in Sec. 1.5.

We should note that a design may or may not involve *invention*. To obtain a legal patent on an invention requires that the design be a step beyond the limits of the existing knowledge (beyond the state of the art). Some designs are truly inventive, but most are not.

Good design requires both analysis and synthesis. Typically we approach complex problems like design by *decomposing* the problem into manageable parts. Because we need to understand how the part will perform in service we must be able to calculate as much about the part's behavior as possible by using the appropriate disciplines of science and engineering science and the necessary computational tools. This is called *analysis*. It usually involves the simplification of the real world through models. *Synthesis* involves the identification of the design elements that will comprise the product, its decomposition into parts, and the combination of the part solutions into a total workable system.

At your current stage in your engineering education you are much more familiar and comfortable with analysis. You have dealt with courses that were essentially disciplinary. For example, you were not expected to use thermodynamics and fluid mechanics in a course in mechanics of materials. The problems you worked in the course were selected to illustrate and reinforce the principles. If you could construct the appropriate model, you usually could solve the problem. Most of the input data and properties were given, and there usually was a correct answer to the problem. However, real-world problems rarely are that neat and circumscribed. The real problem that your design is expected to solve may not be readily apparent. You may need to draw on many technical disciplines (solid mechanics, fluid mechanics, electromagnetic theory, etc.) for the solution and usually on nonengineering disciplines as well (economics, finance, law, etc.). The input data may be fragmentary at best, and the scope of the project may be so huge that no individual can follow it all. If that is not difficult enough, usually the design must proceed under severe constraints of time and/or money. There may be major societal constraints imposed by environmental or energy regulations. Finally, in the typical design you rarely have a way of knowing the correct answer. Hopefully, your design works, but is it the best, most efficient design that could have been achieved under the conditions? Only time will tell.

We hope that this has given you some idea of the design environment and the design process. One way to summarize the challenges presented by the design environment is to think of the *four C's of design*. One thing that should be clear by now is how engineering design extends well beyond the boundaries of science. The expanded boundaries and responsibilities of engineering create almost unlimited opportunities for you. In your professional career you may have the opportunity to create dozens of designs, and have the satisfaction of seeing them become working realities. "A scientist will be lucky if he makes one creative addition to human knowledge in his whole life, and many never do so. A scientist can discover a new star but he cannot make one. He would have to ask an engineer to do it for him."[1]

---

1. G. L. Glegg, "The Design of Design," Cambridge University Press, New York, 1969.

The Four C's of Design

Creativity
- Requires creation of something that has not existed before or not existed in the designer's mind before

Complexity
- Requires decisions on many variables and parameters

Choice
- Requires making choices between many possible solutions at all levels, from basic concepts to smallest detail of shape

Compromise
- Requires balancing multiple and sometimes conflicting requirements

This long chapter is divided into two parts. Part 1 is an introduction to the engineering design process, with emphasis on product design. It is intended to give you a broad appreciation of all of the elements of design and to orient you to what is covered in much more detail in the subsequent chapters. Part 2 deals with technological innovation and the design process. It is intended to provide motivation for the course by showing the interplay between the advance of technology and what you can do in design. View it as the cultural aspect of this course.

PRODUCT DESIGN PROCESS

1.2
IMPORTANCE OF PRODUCT DESIGN

The engineering design process can be applied to several different ends. One is the design of products, whether they be consumer goods and appliances or highly complex products such as missile systems or jet planes. Another is a complex engineered system such as an electric power generating station or a petrochemical plant, while yet another area is the design of a building or bridge. The principles and methodology of design can be usefully applied in each of these situations. However, the emphasis in this book is on product design because it is the area in which many engineers will apply their design skills. Moreover, examples taken from this area of design are easier to grasp without extensive specialized knowledge.

U.S. manufacturers began to lose their world domination of markets, gained after World War II, in the late 1960s and 1970s as overseas producers entered the large attractive U.S. marketplace. Cameras, typewriters, electronic products (radios, television sets, hi-fi sets), and copiers were the first products to be displaced, but as new products were developed (tape recorder and fax machine) a strong U.S. producer never emerged. In the 1980s Japanese automotive producers gained an appreciable share of the U.S. market, and German companies did the same for the high end of the auto market. Initially the competitive advantage for foreign manufacturers was the much lower manufacturing cost as a result of low local wage rates, so that products could be shipped to the United States and sold more cheaply than locally manufactured products. In addition, U.S. consumers found that in most cases the quality of product was as good as or better than locally made product. Gradually it became clear that we live in a giant global marketplace, where a computer assembled and sold by a U.S. producer may have had its integrated circuit chips made in Taiwan, its disk drive in Malaysia, and its monitor in Singapore.

The initial response of progressive U.S. companies to the world invasion of their home market was to place renewed emphasis on reducing cost of manufacturing through automation and to move plants to lower labor cost regions. Many companies also focused on reducing product defects and enhancing customer acceptance by adopting a system of total quality management (TQM) methods. More recently, and stimulated by a major study of the National Research Council,[1] companies have come to the realization that the real key to world-competitive products lies in high-quality product design. This has stimulated a rash of experimentation and sharing of results about better ways to do product design. What was once a fairly cut-and-dried engineering process has become one of the cutting edges of engineering progress. This text aims at providing you with insight into the current best practices for doing product design.

The importance of design is nicely summed up in Fig. 1.1. This shows that only a small fraction of the cost to produce a product (~ 5 percent) is involved with the product design process, while the other 95 percent of cost is consumed by the material, capital, and labor to manufacture the product. However, the design process consists of the accumulation of many decisions that result in design commitments that affect about 70 to 80 percent of the manufactured cost of the product.[2] In other words,

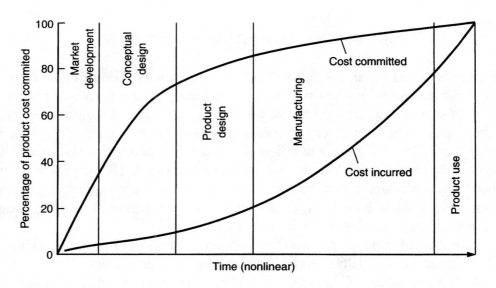

FIGURE 1.1
Product cost commitment during phases of the design process. (*After Ullman.*)

1. "Improving Engineering Design," National Academy Press, Washington, D.C., 1991.
2. "Improving Engineering Design," op. cit.

decisions made beyond the design phase, in manufacturing, can influence only about 25 percent of the final cost of the product. If the design proves to be faulty just before the product goes to market, it will cost a great deal of money to correct the problem. To summarize: *Decisions made in the design process cost very little in terms of the overall product cost but have a major effect on the cost of the product.*

The second major impact of design is on product quality. The old concept of product quality was that it was achieved by inspecting the product as it came off the production line. Today we realize that true quality is designed into the product. Achieving quality through product design will be a theme that pervades this book. For now we point out that one aspect of quality is to incorporate within the product the performance and features that are truly desired by the customer who purchases the product. In addition, the design must be carried out so that the product can be made without defect at a competitive cost. To summarize: *Quality cannot be built into a product unless it is designed into it.*

The third area where product design determines product competitiveness is product cycle time. Cycle time refers to the development time required to bring a new product to market. In many consumer areas the product with the latest "bells and whistles" captures the customers' fancy. The use of new organizational methods, widespread use of computer-aided engineering, and rapid prototyping methods are contributing to reducing product cycle time. Not only does reduced cycle time increase the marketability of a product, but it reduces the cost of product development. To summarize: *The design process should be conducted so as to develop quality cost-competitive products in the shortest time possible.*

1.2.1 Static Products vs. Dynamic Products

Some products are static, in that the changes in their design concept take place over a long time period; rather, incremental changes occur at the subsystem and component levels. Examples of static products are automobiles and most consumer appliances like refrigerators and dishwashers. Others are dynamic products, like telecommunications systems and software, that change the basic design concept fairly frequently as the underlying technology changes.

Static products exist in a market where the customer is not eager to change, and fashion or styling plays little role. These are markets characterized by a stable number of large producers, with high price competition and little market research. There is a mature, stable technology, with competing products similar to each other. The users are generally familiar with the technology and do not demand significant improvement. Industry standards may even restrict change, and parts of the product are assembled from components made by others. Because of the importance of cost, emphasis is more on process research than on product research.

With dynamic products, customers are willing to, and may even drive, change. The market is characterized by many small producers, doing active market research and seeking to reduce product cycle time. Companies actively seek new products employing rapidly advancing technology. There is high product differentiation and low industry standardization. More emphasis is placed on product research than on process research.

A number of factors serve to protect a product from competition. A product which requires high capital investment to manufacture or which requires complex manufacturing processes tends to be resistant to competition. At the other end of the product chain, the need for an extensive distribution system may be a barrier to entry. A strong patent position may keep out competition, as may strong brand identification and loyalty on the part of the customer.

1.3
THE DESIGN PROCESS—A SIMPLIFIED APPROACH

We frequently talk about "designing a system." By a system we mean the entire combination of hardware, information, and people necessary to accomplish some specified mission. A system may be an electric power distribution network for a region of the nation, a complex piece of machinery like a newspaper printing press, or a combination of production steps to produce automobile parts. A large system usually is divided into *subsystems,* which in turn are made up of *components.*

There is no single universally acclaimed sequence of steps that leads to a workable design. Different writers or designers have outlined the design process in as few as 5 steps or as many as 25. One of the first to write introspectively about design was Morris Asimow.[1] He viewed the heart of the design process as consisting of the elements shown in Fig. 1.2. As portrayed there, design is a sequential process consisting of many design operations. Examples of the operations might be (1) exploring the alternative systems that could satisfy the specified need, (2) formulating a mathematical model of the best system concept, (3) specifying specific parts to construct a component of a subsystem, and (4) selecting a material from which to manufacture a part. Each operation requires information, some of it general technical and business information that is expected of the trained professional and some of it very specific

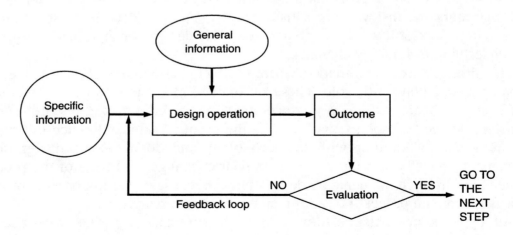

FIGURE 1.2
Basic module in the design process. (*After Asimow.*)

───────────────

1. M. Asimow, "Introduction to Design," Prentice-Hall, Englewood Cliffs, NJ, 1962.

information that is needed to produce a successful outcome. An example of the last kind of information might be (1) a manufacturer's catalog on miniature bearings, (2) handbook data on high-temperature alloys, or (3) personal experience gained from a trip to observe a new manufacturing process. Acquisition of information is a vital and often very difficult step in the design process, but fortunately it is a step that usually becomes easier with time. (We call this process experience.)[1] The importance of developing sources of information is considered more fully in Chap. 4.

Once armed with the necessary information, the design engineer (or design team) carries out the design operation by using the appropriate technical knowledge and computational and/or experimental tools. At this stage it may be necessary to construct a mathematical model and conduct a simulation of the component's performance on a digital computer. Or it may be necessary to construct a full-size prototype model and test it to destruction at a proving ground. Whatever it is, the operation produces a design outcome that, again, may take many forms. It can be a ream of computer printout, a rough sketch with critical dimensions established, or a complete set of engineering drawings. At this stage the design outcome must be evaluated, often by a team of impartial experts, to decide whether it is adequate to meet the need. If so, the designer may go on to the next step. If the evaluation uncovers deficiencies, then the design operation must be repeated. The information from the first design is fed back as input, together with new information that has been developed as a result of questions raised at the evaluation step. We call this *iteration*.

The final result of the chain of design modules, each like Fig. 1.2, is a new working object (often referred to as *hardware*) or a collection of objects that is a new system. However, many design projects do not have as an objective the creation of new hardware or systems. Instead, the objective may be the development of new information that can be used elsewhere in the organization. It should be realized that few system designs are carried through to completion; they are stopped because it has become clear that the objectives of the project are not technically and/or economically feasible. However, they create new information, which, if stored in retrievable form, has future value, since it represents experience.

The simple model shown in Fig. 1.2 illustrates a number of important aspects of the design process. First, even the most complex system can be broken down into a sequence of design objectives. Each objective requires evaluation, and it is common for the decision-making phase to involve repeated trials or iterations. The need to go back and try again should not be considered a personal failure or weakness. Design is a creative process, and all new creations of the mind are the result of trial and error. Of course, the more knowledge we have and can apply to the problem the faster we can arrive at an acceptable solution. This iterative aspect of design may take some getting used to. You will have to acquire a high tolerance for failure and the tenacity and determination to persevere and work the problem out one way or the other.

The iterative nature of design provides an opportunity to improve the design on the basis of a preceding outcome. That, in turn, leads to the search for the best possible technical condition, e.g., maximum performance at minimum weight (or cost).

---

1. Experience has been defined, perhaps a bit lightheartedly, as just a sequence of nonfatal events.

Many techniques for *optimizing* a design have been developed, and some of them are covered in Chap. 12. And although optimization methods are intellectually pleasing and technically interesting, they often have limited application in a complex design situation. In the usual situation the actual design parameters chosen by the engineer are a compromise among several alternatives. There may be too many variables to include all of them in the optimization, or nontechnical considerations like available time or legal constraints may have to be considered, so that trade-offs must be made. The parameters chosen for the design are then close to but not at optimum values. We usually refer to them as *optimal values,* the best that can be achieved within the total constraints of the system.

In your scientific and engineering education you may have heard reference to the scientific method, a logical progression of events that leads to the solution of scientific problems. Percy Hill[1] has diagramed the comparison between the scientific method and the design method (Fig. 1.3).

The scientific method starts with a body of existing knowledge. Scientists have curiosity that causes them to question these laws of science; and as a result of their questioning, they eventually formulate a hypothesis. The hypothesis is subjected to logical analysis that either confirms or denies it. Often the analysis reveals flaws or inconsistencies, so that the hypothesis must be changed in an iterative process.

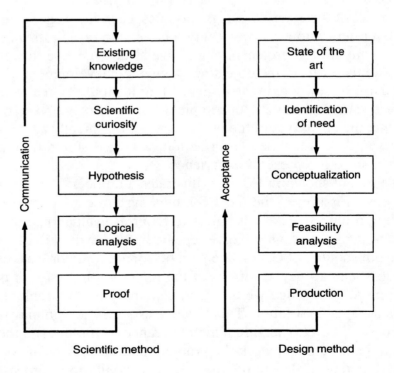

FIGURE 1.3
Comparison between the scientific method and the design method. (*After Percy Hill.*)

1. P. H. Hill, "The Science of Engineering Design," Holt, Rinehart and Winston, New York, 1970.

Finally, when the new idea is confirmed to the satisfaction of its originator, it must be accepted as proof by fellow scientists. Once accepted, it is communicated to the community of scientists and it enlarges the body of existing knowledge. The knowledge loop is completed.

The design method is very similar to the scientific method if we allow for differences in viewpoint and philosophy. The design method starts with knowledge of the state of the art. That includes scientific knowledge, but it also includes devices, components, materials, manufacturing methods, and market and economic conditions. Rather than scientific curiosity, it is really the needs of society (usually expressed through economic factors) that provide the impetus. When a need is identified, it must be conceptualized as some kind of model. The design concept must be subjected to a feasibility analysis, almost always with iteration, until an acceptable product is produced or the project is abandoned. When the design enters the production phase, it begins to compete in the world of technology. The design loop is closed when the product is accepted as part of the current technology and thereby advances the state of the art of the particular field.

In the brief outline of the design method shown above, the identification of a need requires further elaboration. Needs are identified at many points in a business or agency. Most organizations have research or development components whose job it is to create ideas that are relevant to the goals of the organization. A very important avenue for learning about needs is the customers for the product or services that the company sells. Managing this input is usually the job of the marketing organization of the company (see Sec. 1.8). Other needs are generated by government agencies, trade associations, or the attitudes or decisions of the general public. Needs usually arise from dissatisfaction with the existing situation. The need drivers may be to reduce cost, increase reliability or performance, or just change because the public has become bored with the product.

1.3.1 A Problem-Solving Methodology

A problem-solving methodology that is useful in design consists of the following steps:[1]

- Definition of the problem
- Gathering of information
- Generation of alternative solutions
- Evaluation of alternatives
- Communication of the results

This problem-solving method can be used at any point in the design process, whether at the conception of a product or the detailed design of a component.

---

1. A similar process called the guided iteration methodology has been proposed by J. R. Dixon; see J. R. Dixon and C. Poli, "Engineering Design and Design for Manufacturing," Field Stone Publishers, Conway, MA, 1995. A different but very similar problem-solving approach using TQM tools is given in Sec. 3.7.

Definition of the problem

The most critical step in the solution of a problem is the problem definition or formulation. The true problem is not always what it seems at first glance. Because this step seemingly requires such a small part of the total time to reach a solution, its importance is often overlooked. Figure 1.4 illustrates how the final design can differ greatly depending upon how the problem is defined.

The formulation of the problem should start by writing down a *problem statement*. This document should express as specifically as possible what the problem is. It should include objectives and goals, the current state of affairs and the desired state, any constraints placed on solution of the problem, and the definition of any special technical terms. The problem-definition step in a design project is covered in detail in Chap. 2.

Gathering information

Perhaps the greatest frustration you will encounter when you embark on your first design problem will be due to the dearth or plethora of information. No longer will your responsibility stop with the knowledge contained in a few chapters of a text. Your assigned problem may be in a technical area in which you have no previous background, and you may not have even a single basic reference on the subject. At the other extreme you may be presented with a mountain of reports of previous work and

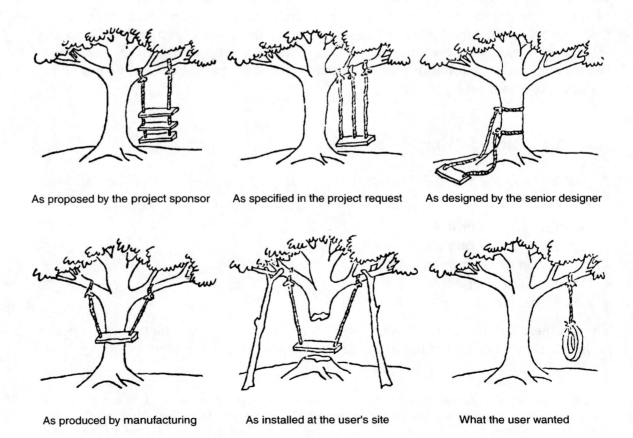

As proposed by the project sponsor As specified in the project request As designed by the senior designer

As produced by manufacturing As installed at the user's site What the user wanted

FIGURE 1.4
Note how the design depends on the viewpoint of the individual who defines the problem.

your task will be to keep from drowning in paper. Whatever the situation, the immediate task is to identify the needed pieces of information and find or develop that information.

An important point to realize is that the information needed in design is different from that usually associated with an academic course. Textbooks and articles published in the scholarly technical journals usually are of lesser importance. The need often is for more specific and current information than is provided by those sources. Technical reports published as a result of government-sponsored R&D, company reports, trade journals, patents, catalogs, and handbooks and literature published by vendors and suppliers of material and equipment are important sources of information. The Internet is becoming a very useful resource, too. Often the missing piece of information can be supplied by a telephone call or an e-mail to a key supplier. Discussions with in-house experts (often in the corporate R&D center) and outside consultants may prove helpful.

The following are some of the questions concerned with obtaining information:

What do I need to find out?
Where can I find it and how can I get it?
How credible and accurate is the information?
How should the information be interpreted for my specific need?
When do I have enough information?
What decisions result from the information?

The topic of information gathering is discussed in Chap. 4.

Generation of alternative solutions

Generating alternative solutions involves the use of creativity stimulation methods, the application of physical principles and qualitative reasoning, and the ability to find and use information. Of course, experience helps greatly in this task. The ability to generate high-quality alternative solutions is vital to a successful design. This important subject is covered in Chap. 5.

Evaluation of alternatives

The evaluation of alternatives involves systematic methods for selecting the best among several designs, often in the face of incomplete information. Engineering analysis procedures provide the basis for making decisions about service performance. Cost estimation (Chap. 14) and design for manufacturing analyses (Chap. 9) provide other important information. Various other types of engineering analysis also provide information. Simulation of performance with computer models is finding wide usage (Sec. 7.8). Simulated service testing of an experimental model and testing of full-sized prototypes often provide critical data. Without this quantitative information, it is not possible to make valid evaluations.

Several methods for evaluating design concepts, or any other problem solution, are given in Chap. 5.

An important consideration at every step in the design, but especially as the design nears completion, is checking. In general, there are two types of checks that can be made: mathematical checks and engineering-sense checks. Mathematical checks are concerned with checking the arithmetic and the equations used in the analytical model. Incidentally, the frequency of careless math errors is a good reason why you should adopt the practice of making all your design calculations in a bound notebook. In that way you won't be missing a vital calculation when you are forced by an error to go back and check things out. Just draw a line through the part in error and continue. It is of special importance to ensure that every equation is dimensionally consistent.

Engineering-sense checks have to do with whether the answers "feel right." Even though the reliability of your feeling of rightness increases with experience, you can now develop the habit of staring at your answer for a full minute, rather than rushing on to do the next calculation. If the calculated stress is 10^6 psi, you know something went wrong! Limit checks are a good form of engineering-sense check. Let a critical parameter in your design approach some limit (zero, infinity, etc.), and observe whether the equation behaves properly.

We have stressed the iterative nature of design. An optimization technique aimed at producing a *robust design* that is resistant to environmental influences (water vapor, temperature, vibration, etc.) most likely will be employed to select the best values of key design parameters (see Chap. 12). The management decision as to when to "freeze the design" will be dictated chiefly by considerations of time and money.

Communication of the results

It must always be kept in mind that the purpose of the design is to satisfy the needs of a customer or client. Therefore, the finalized design must be properly communicated, or it may lose much of its impact or significance. The communication is usually by oral presentation to the sponsor as well as by a written design report. A recent survey showed that design engineers spend 60 percent of their time in discussing designs and preparing written documentation of designs, while only 40 percent of the time is spent in analyzing designs and doing the designing. Detailed engineering drawings, computer programs, and working models are frequently part of the "deliverables" to the customer. It hardly needs to be emphasized that communication is not a one-time occurrence to be carried out at the end of the project. In a well-run design project there is continual oral and written dialog between the project manager and the customer. This extremely important subject is considered in greater depth in Chap. 17.

1.4
CONSIDERATIONS OF A GOOD DESIGN

Design is a multifaceted process. To gain a broader understanding of engineering design, we group various considerations in good design into three categories: (1) design requirements, (2) life-cycle issues, and (3) regulatory and social issues.

1.4.1 Design Requirements

It is obvious that to be satisfactory the design must demonstrate the required performance. Acceptable performance is the first, but far from only, design requirement.

Performance measures both function and behavior of the design, i.e., how well the device does what it is designed to do. Performance requirements can be divided into *functional* performance requirements and *complementary* performance requirements. Functional requirements address such capacity measures as forces, strength, energy or material flows, power, and deflection. They also are concerned with the efficiency of the design, its accuracy and sensitivity. Complementary performance requirements are concerned with the useful life of the design, its robustness to factors in the service environment (see Chap. 11), its reliability (see Chap. 12), and ease, economy, and safety of maintenance. Issues such as built-in safety features and the noise level in operation must be considered. Finally, the design must conform to all legal requirements and design codes (see Chap. 15).

A variety of analysis techniques must be employed in arriving at the *features* of a component in the design. By feature we mean specific physical attributes, such as shape, dimensions, or material properties. The digital computer has had a major impact in this area by providing powerful analytical tools based on finite-element analysis and finite difference. Calculations of stress, temperature, and other field-dependent variables can be made rather handily for complex geometry and loading conditions. When these analytical methods are coupled with interactive computer graphics, we have the exciting capability known as computer-aided engineering (CAE); see Sec. 1.9.

Next to performance requirements we have physical requirements. These pertain to such issues as size, weight, shape, and surface finish.

Environmental requirements deal with two separate aspects. The first concerns the service conditions under which the product must operate. The extremes of temperature, humidity, corrosive conditions, dirt, vibration, noise, etc., must be predicted and allowed for in the design. The second aspect of environmental requirements pertains to how the product will behave with regard to maintaining a safe and clean environment, i.e., green design. Among these issues is the disposal of the product when it reaches its useful life.

Aesthetic requirements refer to "the sense of the beautiful." They are concerned with how the product is perceived by a customer because of its shape, color, surface texture, and also such factors as balance, unity, and interest. This aspect of design usually is the responsibility of the industrial designer, as contrasted with the engineering designer. The industrial designer is an applied artist. Decisions concerning the appearance of the product should be an integral part of the initial design concept.

Manufacturing technology must be intimately connected with product design. There may be restrictions on the manufacturing processes that can be used, because of either selection of material or availability of equipment within the company.

The final major design requirement is cost. Every design has requirements of an economic nature. These include such issues as product development cost, initial product cost, life cycle product cost, tooling cost, and return on investment. In many cases cost is the most important design requirement, for if preliminary estimates of product cost look unfavorable, the design project may never be initiated. Cost enters into every aspect of the design process. Therefore, we have considered the subject of economic decision making (engineering economics) in some detail in Chap. 13. Procedures for estimating costs are considered in Chap. 14.

1.4.2 Total Life Cycle

The total life cycle of a part starts with the conception of a need and ends with the retirement and disposal of the product.

Material selection is a key element in the total life cycle (see Chap. 8). In selecting materials for a given application, the first step is evaluation of the service conditions. Next, the properties of materials that relate most directly to the service requirements must be determined. Except in almost trivial conditions, there is never a simple relation between service performance and material properties. The design may start with the consideration of static yield strength, but properties that are more difficult to evaluate, such as fatigue, creep, toughness, ductility, and corrosion resistance, may have to be considered. We need to know whether the material is stable under the environmental conditions. Does the microstructure change with temperature? Does the material corrode slowly or wear at an unacceptable rate?

Material selection cannot be separated from *producibility* (see Chap. 9). There is an intimate connection between design and material selection and the production processes. The objective in this area is a trade-off between the opposing factors of minimum cost and maximum durability. *Durability* is concerned with the number of cycles of possible operation, i.e., the useful life of the product.

Current societal issues of energy conservation, material conservation, and protection of the environment result in new pressures in selection of materials and manufacturing processes. Energy costs, once nearly totally ignored in design, are now among the most prominent design considerations. Design for materials recycling also is becoming an important consideration.

1.4.3 Regulatory and Social Issues

Specifications and standards have an important influence on design practice (see Chap. 4). The standards produced by such societies as ASTM and ASME represent voluntary agreement among many elements (users and producers) of industry. As such, they often represent minimum or least-common-denominator standards. When good design requires more than that, it may be necessary to develop your own company or agency standards. On the other hand, because of the general nature of most standards, a standard sometimes requires a producer to meet a requirement that is not essential to the particular function of the design.

The code of ethics of all professional engineering societies requires the engineer to protect public health and safety. Increasingly, legislation has been passed to require federal agencies to regulate many aspects of safety and health. The requirements of the Occupational Safety and Health Administration (OSHA), the Consumer Product Safety Commission (CPSC), and the Environmental Protection Agency (EPA) place direct constraints on the designer. Several aspects of the CPSC regulations have far-reaching influence on product design. Although the intended purpose of a particular product normally is quite clear, the unintended uses of that product are not always obvious. Under the CPSC regulations, the designer has the obligation to foresee as many unintended uses as possible, then develop the design in such a way as to prevent hazardous use of the product in an unintended but foreseeable manner. When unintended use cannot be prevented by functional design, clear, complete, unambiguous warnings must be permanently attached to the product. In addition, the designer must be cognizant of all advertising material, owner's manuals, and operating instructions that relate to the product to ensure that the contents of the material are consistent with safe operating procedures and do not promise performance characteristics that are beyond the capability of the design.

An important design consideration is adequate attention to human factors engineering, which uses the sciences of biomechanics, ergonomics, and engineering psychology to assure that the design can be operated efficiently by humans. It applies physiological and anthropometric data to such design features as visual and auditory display of instruments and control systems. It is also concerned with human muscle power and response times. For further information, see Sec. 6.7.

1.5
DETAILED DESCRIPTION OF DESIGN PROCESS

Morris Asimow[1] was among the first to give a detailed description of the complete design process in what he called the *morphology of design.* His seven phases of design are described below, with slight changes of terminology to conform to current practice.

1.5.1 Phase I. Conceptual Design

Conceptual design is the process by which the design is initiated, carried to the point of creating a number of possible solutions, and narrowed down to a single best concept. It is sometimes called the feasibility study. Conceptual design is the phase which requires the greatest creativity, involves the most uncertainty, and requires coordination among many functions in the business organization. The following are the discrete activities that we consider under conceptual design.

- *Identification of customer needs:* The goal of this activity is to completely understand the customers' needs and to communicate them to the design team.
- *Problem definition:* The goal of this activity is to create a statement that describes what has to be accomplished to satisfy the needs of the customer. This involves analysis of competitive products, the establishment of target specifications, and the listing of constraints and trade-offs. Quality function deployment (QFD) is a valuable tool for linking customer needs with design requirements. A detailed listing of the product requirements is called a product design specification (PDS). Problem definition, in its full scope, is treated in Chap. 2.
- *Gathering information:* Engineering design presents special requirements over engineering research in the need to acquire a broad spectrum of information. This subject is covered in Chap. 4.

---

1. M. Asimow, "Introduction to Design," Prentice-Hall, Englewood Cliffs, NJ, 1962.

- *Conceptualization:* Concept generation is involved with creating a broad set of concepts that potentially satisfy the problem statement. Team-based creativity methods, combined with efficient information gathering, are the key activities. This subject is covered in Chap. 5.
- *Concept selection:* Evaluation of the design concepts, modifying and evolving into a single preferred concept, are the activities in this step. The process usually requires several iterations. This is covered in Chap. 5.
- *Refinement of the PDS:* The product design specification is revisited after the concept has been selected. The design team must commit to achieving certain critical values of design parameters and to living with trade-offs between cost and performance.
- *Design review:* Before committing funds to move to the next design phase, a design review will be held. The design review will assure that the design is physically realizable and that it is economically worthwhile. It will also look at a detailed product-development schedule. This is needed so as to devise a strategy to minimize product cycle time and to identify the resources in people, equipment, and money needed to complete the project.

1.5.2 Phase II. Embodiment Design

In this phase a structured development of the design concept takes place. It is the place where flesh is placed on the skeleton of the design concept. An embodiment of all the main functions that must be performed by the product must be undertaken. It is in this design phase that decisions are made on strength, material selection, size, shape, and spatial compatibility. Beyond this design phase major changes become very expensive. This design phase is sometimes called preliminary design. Embodiment design is concerned with three major tasks—product architecture, configuration design, and parametric design.

- *Product architecture:* Product architecture is concerned with dividing the overall design system into subsystems or modules. In this step it is decided how the physical components of the design are to be arranged and combined to carry out the functional duties of the design.
- *Configuration design of parts and components:* Parts are made up of *features* like holes, ribs, splines, and curves. Configuring a part means to determine what features will be present and how those features are to be arranged in space relative to each other. While modeling and simulation may be performed in this stage to check out function and spatial constraints, only approximate sizes are determined to assure that the part satisfies the PDS. Also, more specificity about materials and manufacturing is given here. The generation of a physical model of the part with rapid prototyping processes may be appropriate.
- *Parametric design of parts and components:* Parametric design starts with information on the configuration of the part and aims to establish its exact dimensions and tolerances. Final decisions on the material and manufacturing processes are also established if this has not been done previously. An important aspect of parametric design is to examine the part, assembly, and system for *design robustness*. Robustness refers to how consistently a component performs under variable condi-

tions in its service environment. The methods developed by Dr. Genichi Taguchi for achieving robustness and establishing the optimum tolerance are discussed in Chap. 12. Parametric design also deals with determining the aspects of the design that could lead to failure (see Chap. 11). Another important consideration in parametric design is to design in such a way that manufacturability is enhanced (see Chap. 9).

1.5.3 Phase III. Detail Design

In this phase the design is brought to the stage of a complete engineering description of a tested and producible product. Missing information is added on the arrangement, form, dimensions, tolerances, surface properties, materials, and manufacturing processes of each part. This results in a specification for each special-purpose part and for each standard part to be purchased from suppliers. Detailed engineering drawings suitable for manufacturing are prepared. Frequently these are computer-generated drawings and may include three-dimensional solid models. Assembly drawings and assembly instructions will also be determined. Detail design often includes the building and testing of several preproduction versions of the product. Finally, detail design concludes with a design review before the information is passed on to manufacturing.

The activities described above are displayed in Fig. 1.5. This eight-step process is our representation of the basic design process. The purpose of this graphic is to remind you of the logical sequence of activities that leads from problem definition to the detail design. It constitutes the *primary design.* As we consider various aspects of

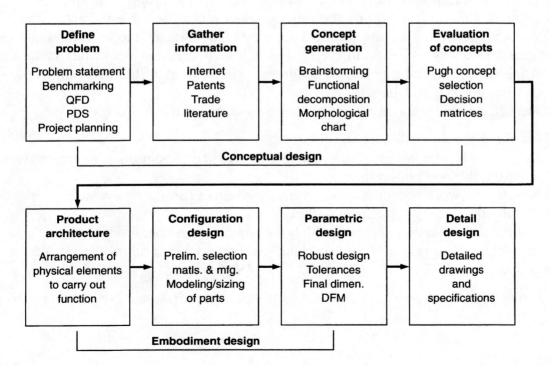

FIGURE 1.5
Discrete steps in engineering design process from problem definition to detail design. The chief tools or techniques applicable in each step are given.

this design process in much more detail as you progress through this text, we shall display this graphic to remind you of where you are in this process. However, remember that design does not normally proceed in a straight-line fashion. Many iterations or branching back (see Fig. 1.1) will be necessary and can be expected for final success.

Phases I, II, and III take the design from the realm of possibility to probability to the real world of practicality. However, the design process is not finished with the delivery of a set of detailed engineering drawings and specifications. Many other technical and business decisions must be made that are really part of the design process. A great deal of thought and planning must go into how the design will be manufactured, how it will be marketed, how it will be maintained during use, and finally, how it will be retired from service and replaced by a new, improved design. Generally these phases of design are carried out elsewhere in the organization than in the engineering department or product development department. As the project proceeds into the new phases, the expenditure of money and personnel time increases greatly.

1.5.4 Phase IV. Planning for Manufacture

A great deal of detailed planning must be done to provide for the production of the design. A method of manufacture must be established for each component in the system. As a usual first step, a *process sheet* is established; it contains a sequential list of manufacturing operations that must be performed on the component. Also, it specifies the form and condition of the material and the tooling and production machines that will be used. The information on the process sheet makes possible the estimation of the production cost of the component.[1] High costs may indicate the need for a change in material or a basic change in the design. Close interaction with manufacturing, industrial, materials, and mechanical engineers is important at this step. This topic is discussed more fully in Chap. 9.

The other important tasks performed in phase IV are the following:

1. Designing specialized tools and fixtures
2. Specifying the production plant that will be used (or designing a new plant) and laying out the production lines
3. Planning the work schedules and inventory controls (production control)
4. Planning the quality assurance system
5. Establishing the standard time and labor costs for each operation
6. Establishing the system of information flow necessary to control the manufacturing operation

All of these tasks are generally considered to fall within industrial or manufacturing engineering.

---

1. Precise calculation of manufacturing cost cannot be made until the process sheet is known. However, reasonable part cost estimates are made in conceptual and embodiment design. These are important elements for decision making at early stages of design. For more detail on costs, see Chap. 14.

1.5.5 Phase V. Planning for Distribution

Important technical and business decisions must be made to provide for the effective distribution to the consumer of the systems that have been produced. In the strict realm of design, the shipping package may be critical. Concepts such as shelf life may also be critical and may need to be addressed in the earlier stages of the design process. A system of warehouses for distributing the product may have to be designed if none exists.

The economic success of the design often depends on the skill exercised in marketing the product. If the product is of the consumer type, the marketing effort is concentrated on advertising and news media techniques, but highly technical products may require that the marketing step be a technical activity supported by specialized sales brochures and performance test data.

1.5.6 Phase VI. Planning for Use

The use of the design by the consumer is all-important, and considerations of how the consumer will react to the product pervade all steps of the design process. The following specific topics can be identified as being important user-oriented concerns in the design process: ease of maintenance, reliability, product safety, convenience in use (human factors engineering), aesthetic appeal, economy of operation, and duration of service.

Obviously, these consumer-oriented issues must be introduced into the design process at the very beginning. Phase VI of design is less well defined than the others, but it is becoming increasingly important with the advent of consumer protection and product safety legislation. More strict interpretation of product liability laws is having a major impact on design.

An important phase VI activity is the acquisition of reliable data on failures, service lives, and consumer complaints and attitudes to provide a basis for product improvement in the next design.

1.5.7 Phase VII. Planning for Retirement of the Product

The final step in the design process is the disposal of the product when it has reached the end of its useful life. *Useful life* may be determined by actual deterioration and wear to the point at which the design can no longer function, or it may be determined by technological obsolescence, in which a competing design performs the function either better or cheaper. In consumer products, it may come about through changes in fashion or taste.

In the past, little attention has been given in the design process to product retirement. This is rapidly changing, as people the world over are becoming concerned about environmental issues. There is concern with depletion of mineral and energy resources, and with pollution of the air, water, and land as a result of manufacturing and technology advancement. This has led to a formal area of study called *industrial ecology*. Design for the environment, also called *green design,* is becoming an important consideration in design (Sec. 6.8). As a result, the design of a product should include a plan for either its disposal in an environmentally safe way or, better, the recycling of its materials or the remanufacture or reuse of its components.

1.6
MARKETING

Marketing is a somewhat foreign concept to many engineers. However, it should whet your appetite to learn more about this mysterious thing called marketing when you learn that inadequate understanding of the market in which they will compete is the number one cause of new product failure. There are two different aspects of marketing. The first, to which we give major attention, deals with the identification of customer needs, product opportunities, and an understanding of market segments. Acquiring this information is often called market research. The second aspect of marketing deals with the introduction of the product into the marketplace and the development of an ongoing relationship with the customer.

The marketing department in a company creates and manages the company's relationship with its customers.[1] It is the company's window on the world with its customers. It translates customer needs into requirements for products and influences the creation of services that support the product and the customer. It is about understanding how people make buying decisions and using this information in the design, building, and selling of products. Marketing does not make sales; that is the responsibility of the sales department.

What is this thing we call the market? Simply stated, a market is a collection of people who refer to each other about their buying decisions. The amount of interaction that occurs will depend on the degree of risk that the buyer perceives in the product. For many purchases we depend on advertising or word of mouth recommendations from friends. For the purchase of major appliances, we may consult references like *Consumer Reports,* but if we are purchasing a major computer system, upon which storage of all company records will depend, we would make a major study and talk with existing users of the product. In this case the market (users group) would be people who use the product to run the same kinds of applications that we expect to run.

The marketing department can be expected to do a number of tasks. First is a preliminary marketing assessment, a quick scoping of the potential sales, competition, and market share at the very early stages of the product development. Then they will do a detailed market study. This involves face-to-face interviews with potential customers to determine their needs, wants, preferences, likes, and dislikes. This will be done before detailed product development is carried out. A common method for doing this is the *focus group.* In this method a group of people with a prescribed knowledge about a product or service is gathered around a table and asked their feelings and attitudes about the product under study. If the group is well selected and the leader is experienced, the sponsor can expect to receive a wealth of opinions and attitudes which can be used to determine important attributes of a potential product. In a vari-

---

1. R. D. Hisrich and M. P. Peters, "Marketing a New Product," Benjamin/Cummins Pub. Co., 1984.

Adam Osborne's Computer

Adam Osborne saw an unfilled need for a portable computer in the embryonic personal computer market. He created a basic computer in 4 months, and within the year had sales of several millions of dollars.

However, he failed to keep in touch with the market, which had been entered by the IBM PC. Failure to achieve IBM compatibility doomed his product, and within 2 years the Osborne computer was history.

An accurate perception of the market made Osborne, but failure to understand a quickly moving market killed his product.

---

ant of this, called *scenario analysis,* persons familiar with a product are asked to write down actual scenarios for the use of the product. Other methods include one-on-one interviews, observing a similar product in use, and detailed examination of competitor's products. Quantitative market research involves careful statistical analysis of customer surveys that are administered by mail, phone interviews, or shopping mall intercepts.[1]

In making a marketing study it is important to understand the various segments of the market. Markets can be segmented with respect to age, sex, race, education, geographic location, and customer income. With technical products there is also a segmentation regarding receptivity to new things. Thus, customers can be classified as:

- *Early adopters:* People who are intrigued by new things and find ways to adopt the product despite the risk.
- *Mainstream adopters:* People who carefully evaluate what their peers in the same market are doing.
- *Laggards:* People who want a product that is low-risk and easy to use. These people do not buy until the product is at the commodity stage at a low price.

Marketing experts also believe that the purchasers of a product are making a statement about their self-images by purchasing a specific brand of a product. Much of this is created by advertising. It is important to have a clear understanding of the market segments your product is targeted to before beginning the product-development activity.

Thus, market research should provide information of the following type:

- Define the market segments
- Identify the early adopters
- Identify competitive products
- Establish the market size ($)
- Determine the breadth of the product line and number of versions
- Determine the product price-volume relationships
- Establish the customer needs and wants

---

1. C. Gevirtz, "Developing New Products with TQM," Chap. 4, McGraw-Hill, New York, 1994.

The marketing department also plays a vital role in assisting with the introduction of the product into the marketplace. They perform such functions as undertaking customer tests or field trials (beta test) of the product, planning for test marketing (sales) in restricted regions, advising on product packaging and warning labels, preparing user instruction manuals and documentation, arranging for user instruction, and advising on advertising. Marketing may also be responsible for providing for a product support system of spare parts, service representatives, and a warranty system.

1.6.1 Classification of Products Based on Market

Implicit in the discussion to this point is that the product is being developed in response to an identified market need, i.e., a *market pull* situation. There are other situations that need to be recognized.[1] The opposite of market pull is *technology push*. This is the situation where the company starts with a new proprietary technology and looks for a market in which to apply this technology. Often successful technology push products involve basic materials or basic process technologies, because these can be deployed in thousands of applications, and the probability of finding successful applications is therefore high. The discovery of nylon by the DuPont Company and its successful incorporation into thousands of new products is a classic example. The development of a technology-push product begins with the assumption that the new technology will be employed. This can entail risk, because unless the new technology offers a clear competitive advantage to the customer the product is not likely to succeed.

A *platform product* is built around a preexisting technological subsystem. Examples of such a platform are the Apple Macintosh operating system or the Black & Decker doubly insulated universal motor.[2] A platform product is similar to a technology-push product in that there is an a priori assumption concerning the technology to be employed. However, it differs in that the technology has already been demonstrated in the marketplace to be useful to a customer, so that the risk for future products is less. Often when a company plans to utilize a new technology in their products they plan to do it as a series of platform products. Obviously, such a strategy helps justify the high cost of developing a new technology.

For certain products the manufacturing process places strict constraints on the properties of the product, so that product design cannot be separated from the design of the production process. Examples of *process-intensive products* are automotive sheet steel, food products, semiconductors, chemicals, and paper. Process-intensive products typically are made in high volume, often with continuous flow processes, as opposed to discrete goods. With such a product, it might be more typical to start with a given process and design the product within the constraints of the process.

Customized products are those in which variations in configuration and content are created in response to a specific order of a customer. Often the customization is with regard to color or choice of materials, but more frequently it is with respect to

---

1. K. T. Ulrich and S. D. Eppinger, "Product Design and Development," McGraw-Hill, New York, 1995, pp. 20–22.
2. M. H. Meyer and A. P. Lehnerd, "The Power of Product Platforms," The Free Press, New York, 1997.

content, as when a person orders a personal computer by phone, or the accessories with a new car. Customization requires consideration of modular design and depends heavily on information technology to convey the customer's wishes to the production line. In a highly competitive marketplace, customization is one of the major trends, so much so that futurists predict that we are moving to a world of *mass customization.*[1]

1.7
ORGANIZATION FOR DESIGN

The organization of a business enterprise can have a major influence on how effectively design and product development is carried out. There are two fundamental ways for arranging the organization: with regard to *function* or with respect to *projects.*

A simple grouping of engineering practice into its various functions is given in Fig. 1.6. We start with research, which is closest to the academic experience; and as we progress downward in the hierarchy, we find that more emphasis on the job is given to financial and administrative matters and less emphasis is given to strictly technical matters.

Research and development (R&D) often is considered the glamour end of the engineering spectrum. We tend to think of research as limited to a scientist isolated in a laboratory and motivated by curiosity to explore nature. But that is basic research of a very pure type. Actually, R&D itself covers quite a spectrum of effort. The Department of Defense (DOD), which sponsors a large amount of R&D, classifies its activities as follows:

6.1 Research

6.2 Exploratory development

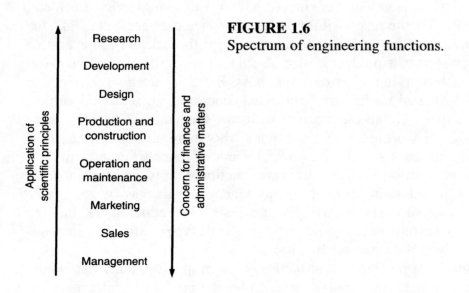

FIGURE 1.6
Spectrum of engineering functions.

---

1. E. B. Magrab, "Integrated Product and Process Design and Development," CRC Press, Boca Raton, FL, 1997, pp. 15–16.

6.3 Advanced development

6.4 Engineering development

6.5 Management and support

With downward progression in this classification, the work becomes more directed (applied) to a specific objective.

A project is a grouping of activities aimed at accomplishing a defined objective, like introducing a particular product into the marketplace. It requires certain activities: identifying customer needs, creating product concepts, building prototypes, designing for manufacture, etc. These tasks require people with different functional specialties. Thus, the two organizational arrangements, by function or project, are at opposite poles of possible organizational structures.

An important aspect of how an enterprise should be organized is concerned with the links between individuals. These links have to do with:

- *Reporting relationships:* A subordinate is concerned about who his or her supervisor is, since the supervisor influences evaluations, salary increases, promotions, work assignments, etc.
- *Financial arrangements:* Another type of link is budgetary. The source of funds to advance the project, and who controls these funds, is a vital consideration.
- *Physical arrangement:* Studies have shown that communication between individuals is enhanced if their offices are within 50 ft. of each other. Thus, physical layout, whether individuals share the same office, floor, or building, can have a major impact on the spontaneous encounters that occur and hence the quality of the communication.

Figure 1.7 shows the organizational chart for a manufacturing company organized along functional lines. All research and engineering reports to a single vice president; all manufacturing activity is the responsibility of another vice president; etc. Take the time to read the many functions under each vice president that are needed even in a manufacturing enterprise that is modest in size. A chief characteristic of a functional organization is that each individual has only one boss. By concentrating activities in units of common professional background, there are economies of scale, opportunities to develop deep expertise, and clear career paths for specialists. Generally, people gain satisfaction from working with colleagues who share similar professional interests. Since the organizational links are primarily among those who perform similar functions, formal interaction between different functional units, e.g., engineering and manufacturing, is forced to the level of the unit manager. This may be acceptable for a business with a narrow and slowly changing set of product lines, but the inevitable slow and bureaucratic decision making which this type of structure imposes can be a problem in a dynamic product situation.

The other extreme in organizational structure is the project organization, where people with the various functional expertise needed for the product development are grouped together to focus on the development of a specific product or product line (Fig. 1.8). Each development group reports to a project manager, who is responsible for overall success of the project, usually the ongoing development of a certain product line. The chief advantage of a project organization is that it focuses the needed

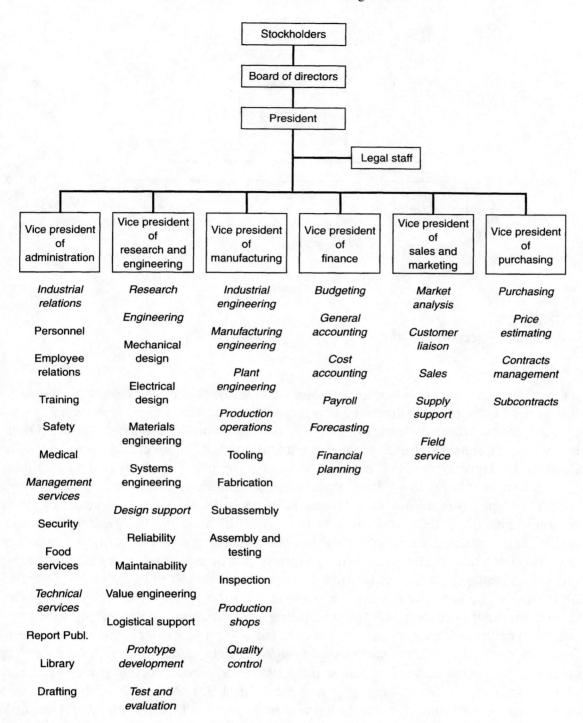

FIGURE 1.7
Example of a functional organization.

specialty talents on the attainment of the goal of the project. Often a project organization is time-limited; once the goal of the project is achieved, the people are reassigned back to functional units. Under this circumstance the organization is usually called a development *team*. This helps to address the chief disadvantage of this type of organization, that technical experts tend to lose their "cutting edge" functional capabilities with such intense focus on the project goal. Another disadvantage is that

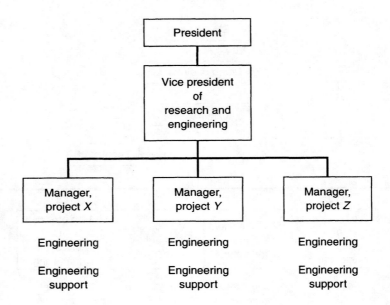

FIGURE 1.8
A simplified project organization.

the project organization is not as economical in utilization of scarce technical expertise as the functional organization. The project organization is very common in start-up companies, where indeed, the project and the company are synonymous. Often large corporations establish project organizations for large critical projects. The Lockheed "skunk works" that developed the U-2 spy plane is a well-known example.

Midway between these two types of organization is the *matrix organization,* which attempts to combine the advantages of each. In the matrix organization each person is linked to others according to both their function and the project they work on. As a consequence, each individual has two supervisors, one a functional manager and the other a project manager. While this may be true in theory, in practice either the functional manager or the project manager predominates.[1] In the *lightweight project organization* the functional links are stronger than the project links (Fig. 1.9*a*). The project manager is responsible for scheduling, coordination, and arranging meetings, but the functional managers are responsible for budgets, personnel matters, and performance evaluations. In the *heavyweight project organization* the project manager has complete budgetary authority, makes most of the resource allocation decisions, and plays a strong role in evaluating personnel (Fig. 1.9*b*). Although each participant belongs to a functional unit, the functional manager has little authority and control. The functional organization or the lightweight project organization works well in a stable business environment, especially one where the product predominates in its market because of technical excellence. A heavyweight project organization has advantages in introducing radically new products, especially where speed is important.

---

1. R. H. Hayes, S. C. Wheelwright, and K. B. Clark, "Dynamic Manufacturing: Creating the Learning Organization," The Free Press, New York, 1988, pp. 319–323.

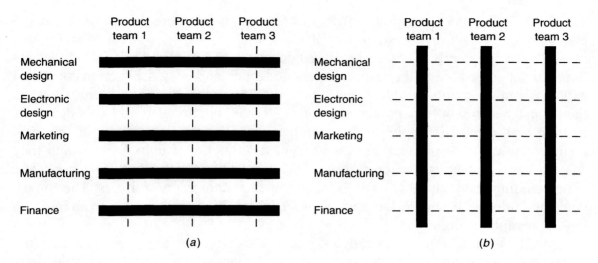

FIGURE 1.9
(*a*) A lightweight project organization; (*b*) a heavyweight project organization.

1.7.1 Concurrent Engineering

The conventional way of doing product design has been to carry out all of the steps serially. Thus, product concept, product design, and product testing have been done prior to process planning, manufacturing system design, and production. Commonly these serial functions have been carried out in distinct and separate organizations with little interaction between them. Thus, it is easy to see how the design team will make decisions, many of which can be changed only at great cost in time and money, without adequate knowledge of the manufacturing process. Refer to Fig. 1.1 to reinforce the concept that a large percentage of a product's cost is committed during the conceptual and embodiment stage of design. Very roughly, if the cost to make a change at the product concept stage is $1, the cost is $10 at the design stage and $100 at the production stage. The use of a serial design process means that as changes become necessary there is a doubling back to pick up the pieces, and the actual process is more in the nature of a spiral.

Starting in the 1980s, as companies met increasing competitive pressure, a new approach to integrated product design evolved, which is called *concurrent engineering*. The impetus came chiefly from the desire to shorten product-development time, but other drivers were the improvement of quality and the reduction of product life-cycle costs. Concurrent engineering is a systematic approach to the integrated concurrent design of products and their related processes, including manufacture and support. With this approach, product developers, from the outset, consider all aspects of the product life cycle, from concept to disposal, including quality, cost, schedule, and user requirements. A main objective is to bring as many viewpoints and talents to bear in the design phase so that these decisions will be valid for downstream parts of the product-development cycle like manufacturing and field service. Toward this end, computer-aided engineering (CAE) tools have been very useful (see Sec. 1.8). Concurrent engineering has three main elements: cross-functional teams, parallel design, and vendor partnering.

Of the various organizational structures for design that were discussed above, the heavyweight project organization, usually called just a *cross-functional design team,* is used most frequently with concurrent engineering. Having the skills from the functional areas embedded in the team provides for quick and easy decision making, and aids in communication with the functional units. For cross-functional teams to work, they must be empowered by the managers of the functional units with decision-making authority. It is important that the team leader engender loyalty of the team members toward the product and away from the functional units from which they came. Functional units and cross-functional teams must build mutual respect and understanding for each other's needs, requirements, and responsibilities. The importance of teams in current design practice is such that Chap. 3 is devoted to an in-depth look at team behavior.

Parallel design, sometimes called simultaneous engineering, refers to each functional area implementing their aspect of the design at the earliest possible time, roughly in parallel. For example, the manufacturing process development group starts its work as soon as the shape and materials for the product are established, and the tooling development group starts its work once the manufacturing process has been selected. These groups have had input to the development of the product design specification and to the early stages of design. Of course, nearly continuous communication between the functional units and the design team is necessary in order to know what the other functional units are doing. This is decidedly different from the old practice of completely finishing a design package of drawings and specifications before transmitting it to the manufacturing department.

Vendor partnering is a form of parallel engineering where the technical expertise of the vendor for certain components is employed as an integral member of the cross-functional design team. Traditionally, vendors have been selected by a bidding process after the design has been finalized. In the concurrent engineering approach, key vendors, known for proficient technology, reliable delivery, and reasonable cost, are selected early in the design process before the parts have been designed. A strategic partnership is developed in which the vendor becomes responsible for both the design and production of parts, in return for a major portion of the business. Vendor partnering has several advantages. It reduces the amount of part design that must be done in-house, it integrates the vendor's manufacturing expertise into the design, and it ensures a degree of allegiance and cooperation that should minimize the time for receipt of parts.

1.8
COMPUTER-AIDED ENGINEERING

The advent of plentiful computing is producing a major change in the way engineering design is practiced. While engineers were one of the first professional groups to adapt the computer to their needs, the early applications chiefly were computationally intensive ones, using a high-level language like FORTRAN. The first computer applications were conducted in batch mode, with the code prepared on punch cards. Overnight turnaround was the norm. Later, remote access to computer mainframes through terminals became common, and the engineer could engage in interactive (if still slow) computation. The development of the microprocessor and the proliferation of personal computers and engineering workstations with computational power equivalent to that of a mainframe ten years ago has created a revolution in the way an engineer approaches and carries out problem solving and design. This great change has not progressed uniformly in all dimensions, but the trend is clear and sure.

The greatest impact of computer-aided engineering to date has been in engineering drawing. The automation of drafting in two dimensions has become commonplace. The ready ability to make changes and to use parts of old designs in new drawings is a great saving in time. Currently, three-dimensional modeling is becoming more prevalent, as it has become available on desktop computers. Three-dimensional solid modeling provides a complete geometric and mathematical description of the part geometry. Solid models can be sectioned to reveal interior details, or they can be readily converted into conventional two-dimensional engineering drawings. Such a model is very rich in intrinsic information so that it can be used not only for physical design but for analysis, design optimization, simulation, rapid prototyping, and manufacturing. For example, geometric three-dimensional modeling ties in nicely with the extensive use of finite-element modeling (FEM) and makes possible interactive simulations in such problems as stress analysis, fluid flow, kinematics of mechanical linkages, and numerically controlled tool-path generation for machining operations. The ultimate computer simulation is *virtual reality,* where the viewer feels a part of the graphical simulation on the computer screen.

The computer extends the designer's capabilities in several ways. First, by organizing and handling time-consuming and repetitive operations, it frees the designer to concentrate on more complex design tasks. Second, it allows the designer to analyze complex problems faster and more completely. Both of these factors make it possible to carry out more iterations of design. Finally, through a computer-based information system the designer can share more information sooner with people in the company, like manufacturing engineers, process planners, tool and die designers, and purchasing agents. The link between computer-aided design (CAD) and computer-aided manufacturing (CAM) is particularly important, and often difficult to achieve.

Concurrent engineering is greatly facilitated by the use of computer-aided engineering (CAE). A computer database in the form of a solid model that can be accessed by all parties of the design team, as in the Boeing 777 example on page 30, is an important method for making sure that everyone is "on the same page." As seen in the example, even teams on different continents can participate. More and more the Internet, with appropriate security, is being used to transmit three-dimensional solid models to tool designers, part vendors, and numerical-control programmers for manufacturing development.

While commercially available database management systems (DBMS) were developed for business users, they can be helpful in many engineering design situations. For example, a designer could ask the DBMS to list all steel beams in a structure where the static load is greater than an allowable maximum load. Commercially DBMS can be used for such purposes as keeping lists of vendors, managing literature references, keeping track of an equipment inventory, or developing a database of material properties. However, engineering database management has several important differences from a business database. Interaction with a business database usually deals with a complete database, one that contains essentially all of the data and does

BOEING 777

The boldest example of the use of CAD is with the Boeing 777 long-range transport. Started in fall 1990 and completed in April 1994, this was the world's first completely paperless transport design. Employing the CATIA 3-D CAD system, it linked all of Boeing's design and manufacturing groups in Washington, as well as suppliers of systems and components worldwide. At its peak, the CAD system served some 7000 workstations spread over 17 time zones.

As many as 238 design teams worked on the project at a single time. Using conventional paper design, this would be expected to lead to numerous potential interferences among hardware systems, requiring costly design changes and revised drawings. This is a major cost factor in designing a complex system. The advantage of being able to see what everyone else was doing, through an integrated solid model and digital data system, saved in excess of 50 percent of the change orders and rework expected for a design of this magnitude.

The Boeing 777 has more than 130,000 unique engineered parts, and when rivets and other fasteners are counted, there are more than 3 million individual parts. The ability of the CAD system to identify interferences eliminated the need to build a physical model (mockup) of the airplane. Nevertheless, those experienced with transport design and construction reported that the parts of the 777 fit better the first time than those of any earlier commercial airliner.

not undergo significant change. Engineering design does not deal with complete databases. A design database starts out nearly empty and is filled up as application programs, specifications, and other constraints generate more data. Only when the design is finished is a complete database achieved.[1]

Spreadsheet programs are useful because of their ability to quickly make multiple calculations without requiring the user to reenter all of the data. Each combination of row and column in the spreadsheet matrix is called a cell. The quantity in each cell can represent either a number entered as input or a number that the spreadsheet program calculates according to a prescribed equation. The power of the spreadsheet is due to its ability to automatically recalculate results when new inputs have been entered in some cells. This can serve as a simple optimization tool as the values of one or two variables are changed and the impact on the output is readily observed. The usefulness of a spreadsheet in cost evaluations is self-evident. Most spreadsheets contain built-in mathematical functions that permit engineering and statistical calculations. It is also possible to use them to solve problems in numerical analysis.[2]

The solution of an equation with a spreadsheet requires that the equation be set up so that the unknown term is on one side of the equal sign. In working with equations it

1. W. J. Rasdorf, "Computers in Mechanical Engineering," March 1987, pp. 62–69; D. N. Chorafas and S. J. Legg, "The Engineering Database," Butterworths, Boston, 1988.
2. S. Jayamaran, "Computer-Aided Problem Solving for Scientists and Engineers," McGraw-Hill, New York, 1991; B.S. Gottfried, "Spreadsheet Tools for Engineers," McGraw-Hill, New York, 1996.

often is useful to be able to solve for any variable. Therefore, a class of equation-solving programs has been developed for small computations on the personal computer. The best-known examples are TK Solver, MathCAD, and Eureka.[1] Another important set of computational tools are the symbolic languages that manipulate the symbols representing the equation. Most common are Mathematica, Maple, and MatLab.

Specialized application programs to support engineering design are appearing at a rapid rate. These include software for finite-element modeling, QFD, creativity enhancement, decision making, and statistical modeling. Useful software packages of this type will be mentioned as these topics are introduced throughout the text.

1.9
DESIGNING TO CODES AND STANDARDS

While we have often talked about design being a creative process, the fact is that much of design is not very different from what has been done in the past. There are obvious benefits in cost and time saved if the best practices are captured and made available for all to use. Designing with codes and standards has two chief aspects: (1) it makes the best practice available to everyone, thereby ensuring efficiency and safety, and (2) it promotes interchangeability and compatibility. With respect to the last point, anyone who has traveled widely in other countries will understand the compatibility problems with connecting plugs and electrical voltage and frequency, when trying to use small appliances.

A code is a collection of laws and rules that assists a government agency in meeting its obligation to protect the general welfare by preventing damage to property or injury or loss of life to persons. A standard is a generally agreed-upon set of procedures, criteria, dimensions, materials, or parts. Engineering standards may describe the dimensions and sizes of small parts like screws and bearings, the minimum properties of materials, or an agreed-upon procedure to measure fracture toughness. Standards and specifications are sometimes used interchangeably. The distinction is that standards refer to generalized situations while specifications refer to specialized situations. Codes tell the engineer what to do and when and under what circumstances to do it. Codes usually are legal requirements, as in the building code or the fire code. Standards tell the engineer how to do it and are usually regarded as recommendations that do not have the force of law. Codes often incorporate national standards into them by reference, and in this way standards become legally enforceable.

There are two broad forms of codes: performance codes and prescriptive codes. Performance codes are stated in terms of the specific requirement that is expected to be achieved. The method to achieve the result is not specified. Prescriptive or specification codes state the requirements in terms of specific details and leave no discretion to the designer. A form of code is government regulations. These are issued by agencies (federal or state) to spell out the details for implementation of vaguely written

---

1. K. R. Foster, *Science*, June 3, 1988, pp. 1353–1358.

laws. An example is the OSHA Regulations developed by the U.S. Department of Labor to implement the Occupational Safety and Health Act (OSHA).

Design standards fall into three categories: performance, test methods, and codes of practice. There are published *performance standards*[1] for many products such as seat belts, lumber, and auto crash safety. Test *method standards* set forth methods for measuring properties such as yield strength, thermal conductivity, or resistivity. Most of these are developed for and published by the American Society for Testing and Materials (ASTM). Another important set of testing standards for products are developed by the Underwriters Laboratories (UL). *Codes of practice* give detailed design methods for a repetitive technical problem, such as the design of piping, heat exchangers, and pressure vessels. Many of these are developed by the American Society of Mechanical Engineers (ASME Boiler and Pressure Vessel Code), the American Nuclear Society, and the Society of Automotive Engineers.

Standards are often prepared by individual companies for their own proprietary use. They address such things as dimensions, tolerances, forms, manufacturing processes, and finishes. In-house standards are often used by the company purchasing department when outsourcing. The next level of standard preparation involves groups of companies in the same industry to arrive at industry consensus standards. Often these are sponsored through an industry trade association, such as the American Institute of Steel Construction (AISC) or the Door and Hardware Institute. Industry standards of this type are usually submitted to the American National Standards Institute (ANSI) for a formal review process, approval, and publication. A similar function is played by the International Organization for Standardization (ISO) in Geneva, Switzerland. Another important set of standards are government (federal, state, and local) specification standards.[2] Because the government is such a large purchaser of goods and services, it is important for the engineer to have access to these standards. Engineers working in high-tech defense areas must be conversant with MIL standards and handbooks in their product line. A more detailed guide to sources of codes and standards is given in Chap. 4.

In addition to protecting the public, standards play an important role in reducing the cost of design and of products. The use of standard components and materials leads to cost reduction in many ways. The use of design standards saves the designer, involved in original design work, from spending time on finding solutions to a multitude of recurring identical problems. Moreover, designs based on standards provide a firm basis for negotiation and better understanding between the buyer and seller of a product. Failure to incorporate up-to-date standards in a design may lead to difficulties with product liability (see Chap. 15). The price that is paid with standards is that they can limit the freedom to incorporate new technology in the design (see box on page 33).

The engineering design process is concerned with balancing four goals: proper function, optimum performance, adequate reliability, and low cost. The greatest cost

1. V. L. Roberts, "Products Standards Index," Pergamon Press, New York, 1986.
2. "Index of Federal Specifications and Standards," Government Printing Office, Washington, D.C.

Standards as a Limit to Technology Advancement

On balance, standards are necessary to advancement of technology, but they can be an inhibiting factor as well. Consider the ASME Boiler and Pressure Vessel Code that has been adopted by all 50 states to regulate machinery using gases or liquids operating under pressure. Formulated during the early 1900s to prevent catastrophic failures and explosions, it spells out in detail the types of material that may be used and the performance specifications a new material must meet.

The materials specifications are nearly the same as they were 50 years ago, despite the fact that much stronger, more fracture-resistant materials are now available. This is because the performance criteria are so stringent that it would take tens of millions of dollars of testing to qualify a new material. No one company can afford to underwrite such costs. But the costs of failure are so high that no one wants to risk changing the code without these tests.

---

saving comes from reusing existing parts in design. The main savings come from eliminating the need for new tooling in production and from a significant reduction in the parts that must be stocked to provide service over the lifetime of the product. In much of new product design only 20 percent of the parts are new, about 40 percent are existing parts used with minor modification, while the other 40 percent are existing parts reused without modification.

Computer-aided design has much to offer in design standardization. A 3D model represents a complete mathematical representation of a part which can be readily modified with little design labor. It is a simple task to make drawings of families of parts which are closely related.

A formal way of recognizing and exploiting similarities in design is through the use of *group technology* (GT). GT is based on similarities in geometrical shape and/or similarities in their manufacturing process. Coding and classification systems[1] are used to identify and understand part similarities. A computerized GT database makes it possible to easily and quickly retrieve designs of existing parts that are similar to the part being designed. This helps combat the tendency toward part proliferation which is encouraged by the ease of use of a CAD system. The installation of a GT system aids in uncovering duplicative designs; it is a strong driver for part standardization. GT may also be used to create standardization in part features. For example, the GT database may reveal that certain hole diameters are used frequently in a certain range of parts while others are infrequently used. By standardizing on the more frequently used design features simplifications and cost savings in tooling can be achieved. Finally the information on manufacturing costs should be fed back to the designer so that high-cost design features are avoided.

---

1. W. F. Hyde, "Improving Productivity by Classification, Coding, and Data Base Standardization," Marcel Dekker, New York, 1981.

An important aspect of standardization in CAD–CAM is in interfacing and communicating information between various computer devices and manufacturing machines. The National Institute of Standards and Technology (NIST) has been instrumental in promulgating the Initial Graphics Exchange Specification (IGES). This is being replaced by the Product Data Exchange Specification (PDES). Both of these represent a neutral data format for transferring geometric data between equipment from different vendors of CAD systems.

1.10
DESIGN REVIEW

The design review is a vital aspect of the design process. It provides an opportunity for specialists from different disciplines to interact with generalists to ask critical questions and exchange vital information. A design review is a retrospective study of the design up to that point in time. It provides a systematic method for identifying problems with the design, aids in determining possible courses of action, and initiates action to correct the problem areas.

To accomplish these objectives the review team should consist of representatives from design, manufacturing, marketing, purchasing, quality control, reliability engineering, and field service. The chairman of the review team is normally a chief engineer or project manager with broad technical background and broad knowledge of the company's products. In order to ensure freedom from bias the chairman of the design review team should not have direct responsibility for the design under review.

Depending on the size and complexity of the product, design reviews should be held from three to six times in the life of the project. The minimum review schedule consists of conceptual, interim, and final reviews. The conceptual review occurs once the conceptual design (Chap. 5) has been established. This review has the greatest impact on the design, since many of the design details are still fluid and changes can be made at this stage with least cost. The interim review occurs when the embodiment design is finalized and the product architecture, subsystems, and performance characteristics are established. It looks critically at the interfaces between the subsystems. The final review takes place at completion of the detail design and establishes whether the design is ready for transfer to manufacturing.

A more sophisticated product would require reviews to assess safety and hazard elimination (Chap. 11), manufacturing issues (Chap. 9), and a review of the performance of the prototype tests.

Each review has two aspects. The first is concerned with elements of the design itself, while the second is concerned with the business aspects of the product. The essence of the technical review of the design is to compare the findings against the detailed *product design specification* (PDS) that is formulated at the problem-definition phase of the project. The PDS is a detailed document that describes what the design must be in terms of performance requirements, the environment in which it must operate, the product life, quality, reliability, cost, and a host of other design requirements (see Sec. 2.7). The PDS is the basic reference document for both the product design and the design review. The business aspect of the review is concerned with tracking the costs incurred in the project, projecting how the design will affect the expected marketing and sales of the product, and maintaining the time schedule. An important outcome of the review is to determine what changes in resources, people, and money are required to produce the appropriate business outcome. It must be realized that a possible outcome of any review is to withdraw the resources and terminate the project.

A formal design review process requires a commitment to good documentation of what has been done, and a willingness to communicate this to all parties involved in the project. The minutes of the review meeting should clearly state what decisions were made and a list of "action items" for future work. Since the PDS is the basic control document, care must be taken to keep it always updated.

1.10.1 Redesign

A common situation is redesign. As a result of decisions made at design reviews the details of the design are changed many times as prototypes are developed and tested. There are two categories of redesigns: *fixes* and *updates*. A fix is a design modification that is required due to less than acceptable performance once the product has been introduced into the marketplace. On the other hand, updates are usually planned as part of the product's life cycle before the product is introduced to the market. An update may add capacity and improve performance to the product or improve its appearance to keep it competitive.

The most common situation in redesign is the modification of an existing product to meet new requirements. For example, the banning of the use of fluorinated hydrocarbon refrigerants because of the "ozone-hole problem" required the extensive redesign of refrigeration systems. Often redesign results from failure of the product in service. A much simpler situation is the case where one or two dimensions of a component must be changed to match some change made by the customer for that part. Yet another situation is the continuous evolution of a design to improve performance. An extreme example of this is shown in Fig. 1.10. The steel railroad wheel has been in its present design for nearly 150 years. In spite of improvements in metallurgy and the understanding of stresses, the wheels still failed at about 200 per year, often causing disastrous derailments. The chief cause of failure is thermal buildup caused by failure of a railcar's braking system. Long-term research by the Association of American Railroads has resulted in the improved design. The chief design change is that the flat plate, the web between the bore and the rim, has been replaced by an S-shaped plate. The curved shape allows the plate to act like a spring, flexing when overheated, avoiding the buildup of stresses that are transmitted through the rigid flat plates. The wheel's tread has also been redesigned to extend the rolling life of the wheel. Car wheels last for about 200,000 miles. Traditionally, when a new wheel was placed in service it lost from 30 to 40 percent of its tread and flange while it wore away to a new shape during the first 25,000 miles of service. After that the accelerated wear stopped and normal wear ensued. In the new design the curve between the

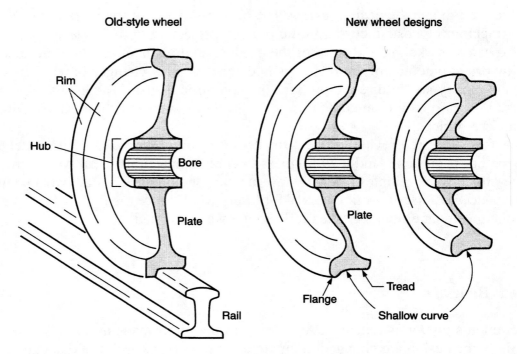

FIGURE 1.10
An example of a design improvement. Old design of railcar wheel vs. improved design.

flange and the tread has been made less concave, more like the profile of a "worn" wheel. The new wheels last for many thousand of miles longer, and the rolling resistance is lower, saving on fuel cost.

TECHNOLOGICAL INNOVATION AND THE DESIGN PROCESS

1.11
TECHNOLOGICAL INNOVATION

The advancement of technology has three phases:

Invention: The creative act whereby an idea is conceived
Innovation: The process by which an invention or idea is brought into successful practice and is utilized by the economy
Diffusion: The successive and widespread initiation of successful innovation

Without question, innovation is the most critical and most difficult of the three phases. Many studies have shown that the ability to introduce and manage technological change is a major factor in a country's leadership in world markets and also a major factor in raising the standard of living at home. Science-based innovation in the United States has spawned such key industries as aircraft, computers, plastics, and television. Relative to other nations, however, the importance of the United States' role in innovation appears to be decreasing. If the trend continues, it will affect our own well-being. Likewise, the nature of innovation has changed with time. Opportunities for the lone inventor and entrepreneur have become relatively more limited. As one indication, independent investigators obtained 82 percent of all U.S. patents in 1901, whereas the corresponding number in 1967 was 24 percent. Nevertheless, small companies do make a major contribution to innovation in this country.

The purpose of this section is to acquaint you with the innovation process and the steps in new product development. Traditionally, engineers play the major role in technological innovation, yet they often do not view themselves in that role. Engineering design and technological innovation are inseparable. It is hoped that you will view your study of design in that spirit so you can make your own strong contribution as an innovator.

The steps in a technological innovation activity can be considered to be:

This model differs from one that would have been drawn in the 1960s, which would have started with basic research in the innovation chain. The research results would have led to research ideas that in turn would have led to commercial development. Although strong basic research obviously is needed to maintain the storehouse of new knowledge and ideas, it has been well established that innovation in response to a market need has greater probability of success than innovation in response to a technological research opportunity. Market pull is far stronger than technology push when it comes to innovation.

The introduction of new products into the marketplace is like a horse race. The odds of picking a winner at the inception of an idea is about 5 or 10 to 1. The failure rate of new products that actually enter the marketplace is around 35 to 50 percent. Most of the products that fail stumble over market obstacles, such as not appreciating the time it takes for customers to accept a new product. The next generic cause is management problems, while technical problems comprise the smallest category for failure.

Studies of successful products delineate four factors that lead to success.[1]

1. *Product planning and research:* Products where adequate time was spent in problem definition (Chap. 2) and concept development (Chap. 5) achieved significantly higher success rate and profitability. These critical "up-front" activities include initial screening of the concept, preliminary market assessment, detailed market research, preliminary technical assessment, and a business and financial review— all before deciding to move to the development phase, i.e., embodiment and detail design.
2. *Product superiority:* Having a superior high-quality product that delivers real value to the customer makes all the difference between winning and losing. Such a product is superior to competing products in meeting customer needs, and these product attributes are easily perceived as being useful by the customer.

---

1. R. G. Cooper, "Winning at New Products," Addison-Wesley, Reading, MA, 1986; R. G. Cooper, "Research Technology Management," July-August, 1994, pp.40–50.

3. *Quality marketing:* High in importance is how well the marketing activities were executed from concept of the idea to the launch of the product in the marketplace (see Sec. 1.6).
4. *Proper organizational design:* Successful products are most often developed by a cross-functional team (Sec. 1.7), led by a strong product champion, supported by top management, and accountable for the entire project from beginning to end.

An approach to business strategy dealing with innovation and investment uses the colorful terminology advanced by the Boston Consulting Group in their portfolio management technique. Business projects are placed in one of four categories:

Star businesses: High growth potential, high market share
Wildcat businesses: High growth potential, low market share
Cash-cow businesses: Low growth potential, high market share
Dog businesses: Low growth potential, low market share

In this context, the break between high and low market share is the point at which a company's share is equal to that of its largest competitor. For a cash-cow business, cash flow should be maximized but investment in R&D and new plant should be kept to a minimum. The cash these businesses generate should be used in star and wildcat businesses. Heavy investment is required in star businesses so they can increase their market share. By pursuing this strategy, a star becomes a cash-cow business and eventually a dog business. Wildcat businesses require generous funding to move into the star category. That only a limited number of wildcats can be funded will bring about the survival of the fittest. Dog businesses receive no investment and are sold or abandoned as soon as possible. This whole approach is artificial and highly stylized, but it is a good characterization of corporate action concerning business investment. Obviously, the innovative engineer should avoid becoming associated with the dogs and cash cows; for there will be little incentive for creative work.

There are other business strategies that can have a major influence on the engineering design. A company that follows a *first in the field* strategy is usually a high-tech innovator. Some may prefer to let others pioneer and develop the market, with the strategy of being a *fast follow on* that is content to have a lower market share at the avoidance of the heavy R&D expense of the pioneer. Other companies may emphasize process development with the goal of becoming the *high-volume, low-cost producer.* Yet other companies adopt the strategy of being the supplier to a few major customers that market the product to the public.

A company with an active research program usually has more potential products than the resources to develop them into marketable products. To be considered for development a product should fill a need that is presently not adequately served, or serve a current market for which the demand exceeds the supply, or has a differential advantage over an existing product (such as better performance, improved features, or lower price). A screening matrix that can be used[1] to select the best prospects for product development is shown in Fig. 1.11 on page 40 and 41. Examine particularly the kind of business criteria that are used to make this decision. The range of expec-

---

1. R. J. Bronikowski, "Managing the Engineering Design Function," Van Nostrand Reinhold, New York, 1986.

tations for each criterion is given in the five columns, from excellent to poor. A weighting factor is applied to certain criteria. In this rating scheme a total of 16 criteria are considered, such that a perfect product would receive a rating of 100 and a poor product would score 20. Most potential products would range from 40 to 80 on this scale, with a rating of 70 typically being required for further consideration. A screening matrix like this should be completed by managers from marketing, product design, R&D, and manufacturing, each working independently.

Studies of the innovation process by Roberts[1] have identified five kinds of people who are needed for technological innovation.

Idea generator: The creative individual

Entrepreneur: The person who "carries the ball" and takes the risks

Gatekeepers: People who provide technical communication from outside to inside the organization

Program manager: The person who manages without inhibiting

Sponsor: The person who provides financial and moral support, often senior management

Roughly 70 to 80 percent of the people in a technical organization are routine problem solvers and are not involved in innovation. Therefore, it is important to be able to identify and nurture the small number who give promise of becoming technical innovators.

Innovators tend to be the people in a technical organization who are most current with technology and who have well-developed contacts with technical people outside the organization.[2] Thus, the innovators receive information directly and then diffuse it to other technical employees. Innovators tend to be predisposed to "do things differently" as contrasted with "doing things better." They are able to deal with unclear or ambiguous situations without feeling uncomfortable. That is because they tend to have a high degree of self-reliance and self-esteem. Age is not an important factor in innovation, nor is experience in an organization so long as it has been sufficient to establish credibility and social relationships. It is important for an organization to identify the true innovators and provide a management structure that helps them develop. Innovators respond well to the challenge of diverse projects and the opportunity to communicate with people of different backgrounds.

A successful innovator is a person who has a coherent picture of what needs to be done, not necessarily a detailed picture. Innovators emphasize goals, not methods of achieving the goal. They can move forward in the face of uncertainty because they do not fear failure. Many times the innovator is a person who has failed in a previous venture—and knows why. The innovator is a person who identifies what he or she needs in the way of information and resources—and gets them. The innovator aggressively overcomes obstacles—by breaking them down, or hurdling over them, or running around them. Frequently the innovator works the elements of the problem in parallel—not serially.

---

1. E. B. Roberts and H. A. Wainer, *IEEE Trans. Eng. Mgt.,* Vol. EM-18, no. 3, pp. 100–109, 1971; E. B. Roberts (ed.), "Generation of Technological Innovation," Oxford University Press, New York, 1987.
2. R. T. Keller, *Chem. Eng.,* Mar. 10, 1980, pp. 155–158.

Considerations	wt. Factor	Excellent 5
Est. gross profit	2	50% and over/yr.
Est. IROI	1	90% and over
Current annual available business	2	$10 million +
Market potential 5 yr.	1	In growth stage. Increasing sales & demand at an increasing rate
Est. market share 1 yr.	1	25% and over
Est. market share 5 yr.	2	50% and over
Stability	1	Product resistant to economic change
Degree of competition	1	No competitive products
Product leadership	1	Fills a need not currently satisfied. Is original
Customer acceptance	1	Readily accepted
Influence on other products	1	Complements and reinforces an otherwise incomplete line
Manufacturing content	1	Completely manufactured in-house
Patent position	1	Impregnable. Exclusive license or rights
Sales force qualification	1	Qualified sales force available
Time to introduction	2	Less than 6 mo.
Technical ability to develop and produce	1	Present technical know-how available and qualified

FIGURE 1.11
Screening matrix for selection of new products (*From R. J. Bronikowski, "Managing the Engineering Design Function," Van Nostrand Reinhold, New York, 1986; reprinted by permission of Carol Bronikowski.*)

Above average 4	Average 3	Below average 2	Poor 1
49–30%/yr	29–20%/yr	19–10%/yr	9% and less/yr
89–75%	74–60%	59–39%	39% and less
$10–$7.5 million	$7.5–$5.million	$5–$2.5 million	Less than $2.5 million
Reaching maturity. Increasing sales but at a decreasing rate	Turning from maturity to saturation. Leveling of sales	Declining sales & Profits	Demand, sales & and profits declining at an increasing rate
24–15%	14–10%	9–5%	4% and less
49–30%	29–20%	19–10%	9% and less
Some resistance to economic change and out of phase	Sensitive to economic change—but out of phase	Sensitive to economic change and in phase	Highly sensitive to economic change and in phase
Only slight competition from alternative	Several competitors to different extents	Many competitors	Firmly entrenched competition
Improvement over existing competition	Some individual appeal, but basically a copy	Barely distinguished from competitors	Copy with no advantages, possibly some disadvantages
Slight resistance	Moderate resistance	Appreciable customer education needed	Extensive customer education need
Easily fits current line, but not necessary	Fits current line, but may compete with it	Competes with, and may decrease sales of current line	Endangers or replaces an otherwise successful line
Partially mfg'd, assembled & packaged in-house	Assembled and packaged in-house	Packaged in-house	No manufacturing content
Some resistance to infringement, few firms with similar patents	Probably not patentable; however, product difficult to duplicate	Not patentable, can be copied	Product may infringe on other patents
Sales force has basic know-how. Minor product orientation required	Sales force has basic know-how, requires product and application education	Sales force requires extensive product and application education	Existing sales force inadequate to handle market and/or product
6-12 mo.	12-24 mo.	24-36 mo.	over 36 mo.
Most technical know-how available	Some know-how available	Extensive technical support required	Ability to develop and produce with present technology questionable

A successful technological innovation requires a good idea or concept that satisfies a societal need. It requires a business champion in the form of supportive top management willing to take the financial risk. The necessary human and technical resources must be assembled. Clear goals and objectives which include milestones for technical accomplishment, and financial and time expenditures, must be established. The final ingredient in a successful innovation is a little bit of luck.

Chief among the factors which lead to failure of a technological innovation are loss of the business champion and/or resources, or oscillation of the commitment to the project. Other factors could be the collapse of the window of opportunity and inadequate attention to technical weaknesses in the concept. Often failure to properly gauge the market is a major contributing factor in failure. Much of the success of the Japanese in world markets is attributed to their overwhelming emphasis in producing the product that is demanded by the market at the price the market is willing to pay, with constant emphasis on raising quality and lowering costs.

1.12
PRODUCT AND PROCESS CYCLES

Every product goes through a cycle from birth, into an initial growth stage, into a relatively stable period, and finally into a declining state that eventually ends in the death of the product (Fig. 1.12).

In the introductory stage the product is new and consumer acceptance is low, so sales are low. In this early stage of the product life cycle the rate of product change is rapid as management tries to maximize performance or product uniqueness in an attempt to enhance customer acceptance. When the product has entered the *growth stage,* knowledge of the product and its capabilities has reached a growing number of customers. There may be an emphasis on custom tailoring the product for slightly different customer needs. At the *maturity stage* the product is widely accepted and sales are stable and are growing at the same rate as the economy as a whole. When the product reaches this stage, attempts should be made to rejuvenate it by incremental innovation or the development of still new applications. Products in the maturity stage usually experience considerable competition. Thus, there is great emphasis on reduc-

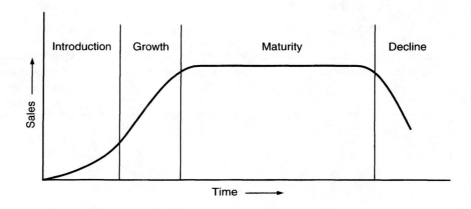

FIGURE 1.12
Product life cycle.

ing the cost of a mature product. At some point the product enters the *decline stage.* Sales decrease because a new and better product has entered the market to fulfill the same societal need.

In the product introduction phase, market uncertainty and the high cost of advanced productivity processes act as barriers to product innovation. Because product volume is low, expensive but flexible manufacturing processes are used and product cost is high. As we move into the period of product market growth, higher volume manufacturing processes reduce the unit cost. In the product maturity stage emphasis is on prolonging the life of the product by product improvement and significant reduction in unit cost. The high investment cost of advanced productivity processes becomes the barrier to further product innovation.

If we look more closely at the product life cycle, we will see that the cycle is made up of many individual processes (Fig. 1.13). In this case the cycle has been divided into the premarket and market phases. The former extends back to the idea concept and includes the research and development and marketing studies needed to bring the product to the market phase. The investment (negative profits) needed to create the product is shown along with the profit. The numbers along the profit vs. time curve correspond to the following processes in the product life cycle. This brief introduction should serve to emphasize that innovation leading to a new product is a complex, costly, and time-consuming process.

Premarket phase	Market phase
1. Idea generation	9. Product introduction
2. Idea evaluation	10. Market development
3. Feasibility analysis	11. Rapid growth
4. Technical R&D	12. Competitive market
5. Product (market) R&D	13. Maturity
6. Preliminary production	14. Decline
7. Market testing	15. Abandonment
8. Commercial production	

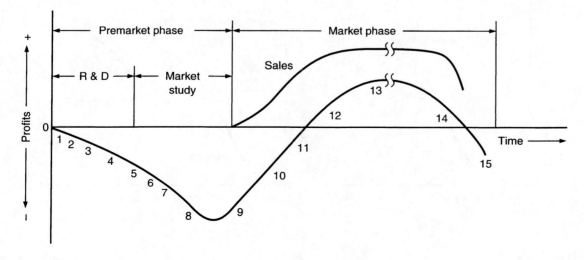

FIGURE 1.13
Expanded product life cycle.

1.12.1 Technology Development Cycle

The development of a new technology follows an S-shaped curve (Fig. 1.14*a*). In its early stage, progress is limited by the lack of ideas. A single good idea can make several other good ideas possible, and the rate of progress becomes exponential. During this period a single individual or a small group of individuals can have a pronounced effect on the direction of the technology. Gradually the growth becomes linear when the fundamental ideas are in place and progress is concerned with filling in the gaps between the key ideas. This is the period when commercial exploitation flourishes. Specific designs, market applications, and manufacturing develop rapidly in a field that has not yet settled down. Smaller entrepreneurial firms can have a large impact and capture a dominant share of the market. However, with time the technology begins to run dry and increased improvements come with greater difficulty. Now the market tends to become stabilized, manufacturing methods become fixed in place, and more capital is expended to reduce the cost of manufacturing. The business becomes capital-intensive; the emphasis is on production know-how and financial expertise rather than scientific and technological expertise. The maturing technology grows slowly, and it approaches a limit asymptotically. The limit may be set by a social consideration, such as the fact that the legal speed of automobiles is set by safety and fuel economy considerations, or it may be a true technological limit, such as the fact the speed of sound defines an upper limit for the speed of a propeller-driven aircraft.

The success of a technology-based company lies in recognizing when the core technology on which the company's products are based is beginning to mature and, through an active R&D program, transferring to another technology growth curve that offers greater possibilities (Fig. 1.14*b*). To do so, the company must manage across a *technological discontinuity*. Past examples of technological discontinuity are the change from vacuum tubes to transistors and from the three- to the two-piece metal can. Changing from one technology to another may be difficult because it requires different kinds of technical skill. Technology usually begins to mature before profits,

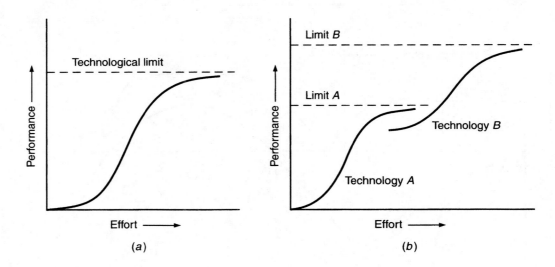

FIGURE 1.14
(*a*) Simple technology development cycle. (*b*) Transfer from one technology growth curve (A) to another developing technology (B).

so that there is a management reluctance to switch to a new technology when business is going so well.

Occasionally a major scientific discovery will open up new opportunities for great advances in performance and reduction in cost. The microcomputer is such an example. However, more frequently small, almost imperceptible improvements will add up to equally great progress. These improvements occur through changes in operating procedures, materials, small variations in manufacturing processes, redesign of products for easier production, or substitution of less expensive components for those used in earlier design. Thus, a great deal of technological innovation is made by incremental advances in cost, performance, and quality improvements.

One can generalize that design and development can be broadly divided into idea dominated design and incremental dominated design. In recent years when the United States has not been competitive in an area of technology we have lost, usually not to radical new technology, but to better incremental improvements. Incremental development is also cyclical. When the current version of the product is in production a development team is working on the next product generation. And, when that next generation goes into production the following generation is started through the development and manufacturing cycle to build a significant product lead and achieve technological leadership.[1]

In highly competitive consumer industries, like personal computers, product cycle time is becoming recognized as a key factor for success.[2] Important in reducing cycle time is a close link between product development and manufacturing. Close ties between design and manufacturing result in early knowledge of technical problems, which when overcome lead to speedy market introduction and higher quality, because the product is easier to manufacture. Because of this cycle, there is a right and a wrong time to introduce new ideas. An idea must be produced at the beginning of the cycle; halfway through is too late because it would cause many changes and delay. Thus, in a technological development there is usually a *window of opportunity* that needs to be recognized. The window of opportunity can have an important pacing function on the development of technology. In areas like consumer electronics, where the development cycle is short, new ideas can be implemented at frequent intervals and the technology develops rapidly. However, in military aircraft, where the cycle time is of the order of 15 years the technology can only advance by large increments. Many of the problems associated with these systems are due to the difficulty of applying incremental developments.

1.12.2 Process Development Cycle

Three stages can be identified[3] in the development of a manufacturing process.

1. *Uncoordinated development:* The process is composed of general-purpose equipment with a high degree of flexibility. Since the product is new and is developing, the process must be kept fluid.

---

1. R. E. Gomory and R. W. Schmitt, *Science,* vol. 240, pp. 1131–1132, 1203–1204, May 27, 1988.
2. S. C. Wheelwright and K. B. Clark, "Revolutionizing Product Development," The Free Press, New York, 1992.
3. E. C. Etienne, *Research Management,* vol. 24, no. 1, pp. 22–27, 1981.

2. *Segmental:* The manufacturing system is designed to achieve higher levels of efficiency in order to take advantage of increasing product standardization. This results in a high level of automation and process control. Some elements of the process are highly integrated; others are still loose and flexible.
3. *Systemic:* The product has reached such a high level of standardization that every process step can be described precisely. Now that there is a high degree of predictability in the product, a very specialized and integrated process can be developed.

Process innovation is emphasized during the maturity stage of the product life cycle. In the earlier stages the major emphasis is on product development, and generally only enough process development is done to support the product. However, when the process development reaches the systemic stage, change is disruptive and costly. Thus, process innovations will be justified only if they offer large economic advantage.

We also need to recognize that process development often is an enabler of new products. Typically, the role of process development is to reduce cost so that a product becomes more competitive in the market. However, revolutionary processes can lead to remarkable products. An outstanding example is the creation of microelectromechanical systems (MEMS) by adapting the fabrication methods from integrated circuits.

1.12.3 Production and Consumption Cycle

The life cycle of production and consumption that is characteristic of all products is illustrated by the *materials cycle* shown in Fig. 1.15. This starts with the mining of a mineral or the drilling for oil or the harvesting of an agricultural fiber such as cotton. These raw materials must be processed to extract or refine bulk material (e.g., an aluminum ingot) that is further processed into a finished engineering material (e.g., an aluminum sheet). At this stage an engineer designs a product that is manufactured from the material, and the part is put into service. Eventually the part wears out or becomes obsolete because a better product comes on the market. At this stage, one option is to junk the part and dispose of it in some way that eventually returns the material to the earth. However, society is becoming increasingly concerned with the depletion of natural resources and the haphazard disposal of solid materials. Thus, we look for economical ways to recycle waste materials (e.g., aluminum beverage cans).

1.13
SOCIETAL CONSIDERATIONS IN ENGINEERING

The first fundamental canon of the ABET Code of Ethics states that "engineers shall hold paramount the safety, health, and welfare of the public in the performance of their profession." A similar statement has been in engineering codes of ethics since the early 1920s, yet there is no question that what society perceives to be proper treatment by the profession has changed greatly in the intervening time. Today's mass communications make the general public, in a matter of hours, aware of events taking place anywhere in the world. That, coupled with a generally much higher standard of

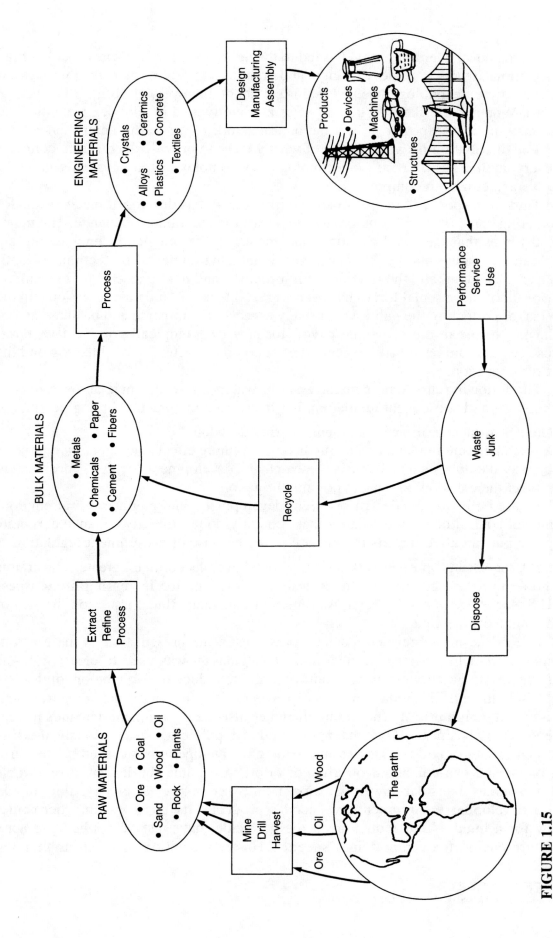

FIGURE 1.15
The total materials cycle. *(Reproduced from "Materials and Man's Needs," National Academy of Sciences, Washington, D.C., 1974.)*

47

education and standard of living, has led to the development of a society that has high expectations, reacts to achieve change, and organizes to protest perceived wrongs. At the same time, technology has had major effects on the everyday life of the average citizen. Whether we like it or not, all of us are intertwined in complex technological systems: an electric power grid, a national network of air traffic controllers, and a gasoline distribution network. Much of what we use to provide the creature comforts in everyday life has become too technologically complex or too physically large for the average citizen to comprehend.

Thus, in response to real or imagined ills, society has developed mechanisms for countering some of the ills and/or slowing down the rate of social change. The major social forces that have had an important impact on the practice of engineering are occupational safety and health, consumer rights, environmental protection, the anti-nuclear movement, and the freedom of information and public disclosure movement. The result of those social forces has been a great increase in federal regulations (in the interest of protecting the public) over many aspects of commerce and business and/or a drastic change in the economic payoff for new technologically oriented ventures. Those new factors have had a profound effect on the practice of engineering and the rate of innovation.

The following are some general ways in which increased societal awareness of technology, and subsequent regulation, has influenced the practice of engineering:

- Greater influence of lawyers on engineering decisions
- More time spent in planning and predicting the future effects of engineering projects
- Increased emphasis on "defensive research and development," which is designed to protect the corporation against possible litigation
- Increased effort expended in research, development, and engineering in environmental control and safety—areas that generally do not directly enhance corporate profit but can affect profits in a negative way because of government regulation

Clearly, the societal pressures described above have placed much greater constraints on how engineers can carry out their designs. Moreover, the increasing litigiousness of U.S. society requires a greater awareness of legal and ethical issues on the part of each engineer (see Chap. 15).

One of the most prevalent societal pressures at the present time is the environmental movement. Originally, governmental regulation was used to clean up rivers and streams, to ameliorate smog conditions, and to reduce the volume of solid waste that is sent to landfills. Today, there is a growing realization that placing environmental issues at a high priority (not doing them because the government demands it) represents smart business.[1] One major oil producer publicly takes seriously the link between carbon dioxide emissions and rising global temperatures caused by the burning of oil and has embarked on a major effort to become the leader in renewable energy sources like solar power. A major chemical company has given major emphasis to developing environmentally friendly products. Its biodegradable herbicides allow for a hundredfold reduction in the herbicide that must be applied per acre, greatly reducing toxic runoff into streams. This reorientation of business thinking

---

1. *Business Week,* Nov. 10, 1997, pp. 98–106.

toward environmental issues is often called *sustainable development,* businesses built on renewable materials and fuels.

The change in thinking, from fixing environmental problems at the discharge end of the pipe or smokestack to sustainable development, places engineering design at the heart of the issue. Environmental issues are given higher priority in design. Products must be designed to make them easier to reuse, recycle, or incinerate—a concept often called *green design.*[1] Green design also involves the detailed understanding of the environmental impact of products and processes over their entire life cycle. For example, life-cycle analysis would be used to determine whether paper or plastic grocery bags are more environmentally benign. Table 1.1 gives the chief aspects of an environmentally responsible design.

It seems clear that the future is likely to involve more technology, not less, so that engineers will face demands for innovation and design of technical systems of unprecedented complexity. While many of these challenges will arise from the requirement to translate new scientific knowledge into hardware, many of these challenges will stem from the need to solve problems in "socialware." By the term socialware is meant the patterns of organization and management instructions necessary to effective functioning of hardware.[2] Such designs will have to deal not only with the limits of hardware, but also with the vulnerability of any system to human ignorance, human error, avarice, and hubris. A good example of this point is the delivery system for civilian air transportation. While the engineer might think of the modern jet transport, with all of its complexity and high technology, as the main focus of concern, such a marvellous piece of hardware only satisfies the needs of society when embedded in an intricate system that includes airports, maintenance facilities, traffic controllers, navigation aids, baggage handling, fuel supply, meal service, bomb detection, air crew training, and weather monitoring. It is important to realize that almost all of these socialware functions are driven by federal or local rules and regulations. Thus, it should be clear that the engineering profession is required to deal with much more

TABLE 1.1
Characteristics of an Environmentally Responsible Design

- Easy to disassemble
- Able to be recycled (see Sec. 8.14)
- Contains recycled materials
- Uses identifiable and recyclable plastics
- Reduces use of energy and natural materials in its manufacture
- Manufactured without producing hazardous waste
- Avoids use of hazardous materials
- Reduces product chemical emissions
- Reduces product energy consumption

1. Office of Technology Assessment, "Green Products by Design: Choices for a Cleaner Environment," OTA-E-541, Government Printing Office, Washington, DC, 1992.
2. E. Wenk, Jr., *Engineering Education,* November 1988, pp. 99–102.

than technology. Techniques for dealing with the complexity of large systems have been developed in the discipline of *systems engineering.*

Another area where the interaction between technical and human networks is becoming stronger is in consideration of risk, reliability, and safety (see Chap. 11). No longer can safety factors simply be looked up in codes or standards. Engineers must recognize that design requirements depend on public policy as much as industry performance requirements. This is an area of design where government influence has become much stronger.

There are five key roles of government in interacting with technology:[1]

- As a stimulus to free enterprise through manipulation of the tax system
- By influencing interest rates and supply of venture capital through changes in fiscal policy to control growth of the economy
- As a major customer for high technology
- As a funding source (patron) for research and development
- As a regulator of technology

Wenk[2] has expanded on the future interactions between engineering and society. The major conclusions of this study are summarized in Table 1.2.

Because of the growing importance of technology to society, a methodology for systematically determining the impact of technology on the social, political, economic, and physical environment is being evolved. It is called technology assessment (TA).[3] Technology assessment is an attempt to determine the benefits and risk inherent in the range of technological alternatives. Its practitioners try to provide an early-warning system for environmental mishaps, define the necessary monitoring and surveillance mechanisms, and provide the decision-making tools for setting technological priorities and allocating resources. Technology assessment, although still an evolving science, already has a number of characteristics that differentiate it from the more traditional methods of engineering analysis.

1. Technology assessment (TA) is mostly concerned with the second-, third-, and higher-order effects or impacts that are rarely considered in engineering analysis. Remote impacts often can be more important than the intended primary variable in social issues.
2. TA considers the needs of a wide range of constituencies.
3. TA is interdisciplinary. There is a need to be able to integrate different intellectual traditions and diverse methods of treating data.
4. TA probably is more closely related to policymaking than to technical problem solving.

Engineering is concerned with problems whose solution is needed and/or desired by society. The purpose of this section was to reinforce that point, and hopefully to show the engineering student how important a broad knowledge of economics and social science is to modern engineering practice.

---

1. E. Wenk, Jr., op. cit.
2. E. Wenk, Jr., "Tradeoffs: Imperatives of Choice in a High-Tech World," The Johns Hopkins University Press, Baltimore, 1986.
3. M. A. Borough, K. Chen, and A. N. Christakis, "Technology Assessment: Creative Futures," North Holland Publishing Co., New York, 1980.

TABLE 1.2
Future trends in interaction of engineering with society

- The future will entail more technology, not less.

- Because all technologies generate side effects, designers of technological delivery systems will be challenged to prevent, or at least mitigate, adverse consequences.

- The capacity to innovate, manage information, and nourish knowledge as a resource will dominate the economic domain as natural resources, capital, and labor once did. This places a high premium on the talent to design not simply hardware, but entire technological delivery systems.

- Cultural preferences and shifts will have more to do with technological choice than elegance, novelty, or virtuosity of the hardware.

- Acting as an organizing force, technology will promote concentration of power and wealth, and tendencies to large, monopolistic enterprises.

- The modern state will increasingly define the political space for technological choice, with trends becoming more pronounced toward the "corporate state." The political-military-industrial complex represents a small-scale model of such evolution.

- Distribution of benefits in society will not be uniform, so disparity will grow between the "haves" and the "have nots."

- Conflicts between winners and losers will become more strenuous as we enter an age of scarcity, global economic competition, higher energy costs, increasing populations, associated political instabilities, and larger-scale threats to human health and the environment.

- Because of technology, we may be moving to "one world," with people, capital, commodities, information, culture, and pollution freely crossing borders. But as economic, social, cultural, and environmental boundaries dissolve, political boundaries will be stubbornly defended. The United States will sense major economic and geopolitical challenges to its position of world leadership in technology.

- Complexity of technological delivery systems will increase, as will interdependencies, requiring management with a capacity for holistic and lateral conceptual thinking for both systems planning and trouble-free, safe operations.

- Decision-making will become more difficult because of increases in the number and diversity of interconnected organizations and their separate motivations, disruptions in historical behavior, and the unpredictability of human institutions.

- Mass media will play an ever more significant role in illuminating controversy and publicizing technological dilemmas, especially where loss of life may be involved. Since only the mass media can keep everyone in the system informed, a special responsibility falls on the "fourth estate" for both objective and courageous inquiry and reporting.

- Amidst this complexity and the apparent domination of decision-making by experts and the commercial or political elite, the general public is likely to feel more vulnerable and impotent. Public interest lobbies will demand to know what is being planned that may affect people's lives and environment, to have estimates of a wide range of impacts, to weigh alternatives, and to have the opportunity to intervene through legitimate processes.

- Given the critical choices ahead, greater emphasis will be placed on moral vision and the exercise of ethical standards in delivering technology to produce socially satisfactory results. Accountability will be demanded more zealously.

From E. Wenk, Jr., "Tradeoffs," Johns Hopkins University Press, 1986. Reprinted with permission from *Engineering Education,* November 1988, p. 101.

1.14
SUMMARY

Engineering design is a challenging activity because it deals with largely unstructured problems that are important to the needs of society. An engineering design creates something that did not exist before, requires choices between many variables and parameters, and often requires balancing multiple and sometimes conflicting requirements. Product design has been identified as the real key to world-competitive business.

The steps in the design process are:

Phase I: Conceptual design
- Recognition of a need
- Definition of the problem
- Gathering of information
- Developing a design concept
- Choosing between competing concepts (evaluation)

Phase II: Embodiment design
- Product architecture—arrangement of the physical functions
- Configuration design—preliminary selection of materials, modeling and sizing of parts
- Parametric design—creating a robust design, and selection of final dimensions and tolerances

Phase III: Detail design—creation of final drawings and specifications

While many consider that the engineering design process ends with detail design, there are many issues that must be resolved before a product can be shipped to the customer. These additional phases of design are often folded into what is called the product development process.

Phase IV: Planning for manufacture—design of tooling and fixtures, designing the process sheet and the production line, planning the work schedules, the quality assurance system, and the system of information flow.

Phase V: Planning for distribution—planning for packaging, shipping, warehousing, and distribution of the product to the customer.

Phase VI: Planning for use—the decisions made in phases I through III will determine such important factors as ease of use, ease of maintenance, reliability, product safety, aesthetic appeal, economy of operation, and product durability.

Phase VII: Planning for product retirement—again, decisions made in phases I through III must provide for safe disposal of the product when it reaches its useful life, or recycling of its materials or reuse or remanufacture.

Engineering design must consider many factors, which are documented in the product design specification (PDS). Among the most important of these factors are required functions with associated performance characteristics, environment in which it must operate, target product cost, service life, provisions for maintenance and logistics, aesthetics, expected market and quantity to be produced, man-machine interface requirements (ergonomics), quality and reliability, safety and environmental concerns, and provision for testing.

BIBLIOGRAPHY

Dixon, J. R., and C. Poli: "Engineering Design and Design for Manufacturing," Field Stone Publishers, Conway, MA, 1995.

Ertas, A., and J. C. Jones: "The Engineering Design Process," 2d ed., Wiley, New York, 1996.

Hales, C.: "Managing Engineering Design," Longman Scientific, Essex, England, 1993.

Magrab, E. B.: "Integrated Product and Process Design and Development," CRC Press, Boca Raton, FL, 1997.

Pahl, G., and W. Beitz: "Engineering Design," 2d ed., Springer-Verlag, New York, 1996.

Pugh, S.: "Total Design," Addison-Wesley, Reading, MA, 1991.

Ullman, D. G.: "The Mechanical Design Process," 2d ed., McGraw-Hill, New York, 1997.

Ulrich, K. T., and S. D. Eppinger: "Product Design and Development," McGraw-Hill, New York, 1995.

PROBLEMS AND EXERCISES

1.1. A major manufacturer of snowmobiles needed to find new products in order to keep the workforce employed all year round. Starting with what you know or can find out about snowmobiles, make reasonable assumptions about the capabilities of the company. Then develop a needs analysis that leads to some suggestions for new products that the company could make and sell. Give the strengths and weaknesses of your suggestions.

1.2. Take a problem from one of your engineering science classes, and add and subtract those things that would frame it more as an engineering design problem.

1.3. There is a need in underdeveloped countries for building materials. One approach is to make building blocks (4 by 6 by 12 in) from highly compacted soil. Your assignment is to design a block-making machine with the capacity for producing 600 blocks per day at a capital cost of less than $300. Develop a needs analysis, a definitive problem statement, and a plan for the information that will be needed to complete the design.

1.4. The need for material conservation and decreased cost has increased the desirability of corrosion-resistant coatings on steel. Develop several design concepts for producing 12-in-wide low-carbon-steel sheet that is coated on one side with a thin layer, e.g., 0.001 in, of nickel.

1.5. The support of thin steel strip on a cushion of air introduces exciting prospects for the processing and handling of coated steel strip. Develop a feasibility analysis for the concept.

1.6. The steel wheel for a freight car has three basic functions: (1) to act as a brake drum, (2) to support the weight of the car and its cargo, and (3) to guide the freight car on the rails. Freight car wheels are produced by either casting or rotary forging. They are subject to complex conditions of dynamic thermal and mechanical stresses. Safety is of great importance, since derailment can cause loss of life and property. Develop a broad systems approach to the design of an improved cast-steel car wheel.

1.7. Consider the design of aluminum bicycle frames. A prototype model failed in fatigue after 1600 km of riding, whereas most steel frames can be ridden for over 60,000 km. Describe a design program that will solve this problem.

1.8. Discuss the spectrum of engineering job functions with regard to such factors as (*a*) need for advanced education, (*b*) intellectual challenge and satisfaction, (*c*) financial reward, (*d*) opportunity for career advancement, and (*e*) people vs. "thing" orientation.

1.9. Strong performance in your engineering discipline ordinarily is one necessary condition for becoming a successful engineering manager. What other conditions are there?

1.10. Discuss the pros and cons of continuing your education for an MS in an engineering discipline or an MBA on your projected career progression.

1.11. Discuss in some detail the relative roles of the project manager and the functional manager in the matrix type of organization.

1.12. List the factors that are important in developing a new technologically oriented product.

1.13. List the key steps in the technology transfer (diffusion) process. What are some of the factors that make technology transfer difficult? What are the forms in which information can be transferred?

1.14. (*a*) Discuss the societal impact of a major national program to develop synthetic fuel (liquid and gaseous) from coal. (It has been estimated that to reach the level of supply equal to the imports from OPEC countries would require over 50 installations, each costing several billion dollars.)

(*b*) Do you feel there is a basic difference in the perception by society of the impact of a synthetic fuel program compared with the impact of nuclear energy? Why?

(*c*) The reason synthetic fuel from coal has not yet become a developed technology is that the cost still exceeds that of comparable natural fuel. What are some of the alternatives to synthetic fuel that may solve our nation's long-term energy problem?

2

NEED IDENTIFICATION AND
PROBLEM DEFINITION

2.1
INTRODUCTION

Of all the steps in the engineering design process, problem definition is the most important. Understanding the problem thoroughly at the beginning aids immeasurably in reaching an outstanding solution. Of course, this axiom holds for all kinds of problem solving, whether it be math problems, production problems, or design problems. However, in product design, where the ultimate test is whether the product sells well in the marketplace, it is vital to work hard to understand and provide what it is that the customer wants. This chapter gives a special emphasis to that aspect of problem definition, an approach not always taken in engineering design.

The information in this chapter draws heavily on developments within the total quality management (TQM) movement, where customer satisfaction is given major emphasis. The TQM tool of *quality function deployment* (QFD) will be presented in detail. The chapter ends with in-depth discussion of the *product design specification* (PDS), which serves as the governing documentation for the product design.

2.2
BEFORE THE PROBLEM-DEFINITION STEP

We start the product design process with problem definition. This is to emphasize the importance of this step, and because it is the logical first step in many situations. Suppose your boss says that your next assignment is to redesign the turboencabulator unit in the M35 system so as to improve thermal efficiency by 20 percent. The assignment would be clear to you, and you would set about defining the problem according to the methods described in this chapter. Or, your design team may have responded to a request for proposal (RFP) from a government agency, and having won the contract, the specifications of what is required are well spelled out. Again, the problem-definition step is the place where the design process begins. However, not all design tasks are as well defined. Often there is development work that precedes the point where problem definition starts. We might call this *planning for the design process* or *new product business development.*

To put this into context, review Sec. 1.11, Technological Innovation, Sec. 1.12, Product and Process Cycles, and Sec. 1.6, Marketing. The chief emphasis is to assemble enough information to decide whether the venture is a good investment for the company, and to decide what time to market and level of resources are required. The documentation might range from a one-page memorandum describing a simple product change to a business plan of several hundred pages giving details on such things as the business objectives, a product description and available technology base, the competition, expected volume of sales, marketing strategy, capital requirements, development cost and time, expected profit over time, and return to the shareholders.

Design projects commonly fall into one of five types:[1]

- *Variation of an existing product:* This involves the change of at most a few parameters, such as the power of a motor or the design of a fastening bracket. The required level of technical expertise is very modest.
- *Improvement of an existing product:* This, more major redesign, can be brought about by the need to improve performance or update features because of competition, the requirement to improve quality or cost in manufacturing, the failure of a vendor to be able to supply specified materials or components, or the development of new technology that allows for an improved product.
- *Development of a new product for a low-volume production run:* Many products are made only a few times in volumes less than 100,000 total units. The prospect of low-quantity production, as opposed to mass production, constrains the selection of manufacturing processes to those with cheaper tooling costs. There is more emphasis on buying off-the-shelf components than in designing special items. Often the first item produced is shipped to the customer; so it is the prototype.
- *Development of a new product for mass production:* This is the category of the automobile, major appliance, or top-of-the-line PC. These design projects allow an engineer flexibility in selecting materials and manufacturing processes, but they require careful planning for manufacture and assembly.
- *One-of-a-kind design:* These design projects can vary from a quick, simple design, using a minimum of analysis, as in the design of a welding fixture to hold parts in assembly, to a large expensive system like a 100-MW steam turbine. In the latter situation, because of the cost and complexity of the product, the testing of prototypes is not very affordable and we must learn as much as possible from analysis and from field experience. Design evolution in situations like this is likely to be incremental. We note that the design of most large buildings, process plants, and power plants is one-of-a-kind design.

Wheelwright and Clark[2] present a model for the product development process that would be applicable for a large technology-oriented company interested in bringing a steady flow of new products quickly to market. They visualize a widemouth

1. D. G. Ullman, "The Mechanical Design Process," 2d ed., McGraw-Hill, New York, 1997, pp. 78–79.
2. S. C. Wheelwright and K. B. Clark, "Revolutionizing Product Development," The Free Press, New York, 1992, pp. 124–127.

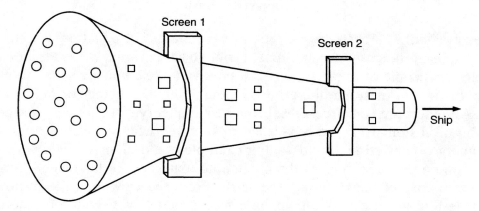

FIGURE 2.1
Wheelwright-Clark model of product development process. (*Reprinted with the permission of The Free Press a Division of Simon and Schuster, Inc., from "Revolutionizing Product Development" by Steven C. Wheelwright and Kim B. Clark, copyright 1992.*)

development funnel (Fig. 2.1). In the first part of the process there is a highly stimulated activity to gather new product ideas from a wide range of sources. These include the R&D division of the corporation but also include employees anywhere in the company, as well as customers, competitors, and suppliers. The first screen, where the funnel narrows down, is not a go-no-go decision point but instead is a review by midlevel managers to determine what additional information is needed before a go-no-go decision can be made at screen 2. When ideas are reviewed at screen 1, they should be checked for their fit with the technology and product market strategies of the company, and their likely commitment of resources. If an idea passes this screen, it passes into the area where project bounds are detailed and required knowledge is specified. If the idea is not ready to move on, then the specific tasks needed to pass screen 1 are agreed upon and assignments and a schedule are made for completing them. A second important function of screen 1 is that it begins to identify competing concepts and ideas that might be integrated into platform development projects. *Platform projects* are development projects that establish the basic product architecture that leads to a succession of follow-on derivative products.

Screen 2 is a go-no-go review in which senior management selects the product and process options that will become product development projects. Any project that passes screen 2 will be funded and staffed with every expectation that it will be carried through to introduction in the marketplace. The time between screens 1 and 2 is usually only 1 to 2 months and is spent taking the data and information developed for Screen 1 and putting it into a form that will enable senior management to choose among a set of competing projects. This process provides much important input to the project problem definition.

2.3
IDENTIFYING CUSTOMER NEEDS

Increasing worldwide competitiveness brings greater focus on the customer's wishes. Engineers and businesspeople are seeking answers to such questions as: Who are my customers? What does the customer want? and How can I provide it?

Webster defines a customer as "one that purchases a product or service." This is the definition of the customer that most people have in mind, the *external customer.* These are the people or organizations that buy what the company sells. Another way to state this is that these are the groups that can decide whether or not to pay their money. All others are constituencies. From a total quality management viewpoint, the definition of customer can be broadened to "anyone who receives or uses what an individual or organization provides." For example, the design engineer who receives information on the properties of three potential materials for his or her design is an *internal customer* of the materials specialist. From the viewpoint of developing the product design specification for an improved product, we focus on external customers, such as end users. From the viewpoint of completing the myriad of decisions and details that make up a successful product design, we must deal with a host of internal customers. Such internal customers as corporate management, manufacturing personnel, the sales staff, and field service personnel must be considered.

2.3.1 Gathering Information from Customers

It is the customer's desires that ordinarily drive the development of the product, not the engineer's vision of what the customer should want.[1] Information on the customer's needs is obtained through a variety of channels:[2]

- *Interviews with customers:* An active sales force should be continuously meeting with present and potential customers. Some corporations have account teams whose responsibility is to visit key customer accounts to probe for problem areas and to cultivate and maintain friendly contact. They should feed back information on current product strengths and weaknesses that will be helpful in product upgrades. An even better approach is for the design team to interview single customers in the service environment where the product will be used. Key questions to ask are: What do you like or dislike about this product? What factors do you consider when purchasing this product? What improvements would you make to this product?
- *Focus groups:* A focus group is an arranged discussion with 6 to 12 customers or potential customers of a product. Usually, the meeting is led by a facilitator who uses prepared questions to guide the discussion about the merits and disadvantages of the product. Often the focus group is held in a room with a one-way window that provides for videotaping of the discussion. In both the interviews and the focus groups it is important to record the customer's response in his or her own words. Any interpretation is held until the analysis of results. The facilitator should not hold slavishly to the prepared questions but should follow up on any surprise

---

1. Of course, in some instances new technology makes possible designs and products for which the customer has no conception. These are situations that the engineer delights in, but they are the exception, not the rule.
2. K. T. Ulrich and S. D. Eppinger, "Product Design and Development," McGraw-Hill, New York, 1995, pp. 33–51.

What Is Our Real Business?

Often it takes some time for a company to realize what business it should be in. Consider the case of the Black & Decker Corp. In 1984, Black & Decker purchased the General Electric Co.'s line of small appliances, including toasters, steam irons, and coffee makers. This was a move toward diversification, at a time when the company's sales of hand power tools appeared stagnated and severely threatened by overseas competition.

But small appliances is a low profit margin business, especially when compared with its DeWalt brand of high-end power tools, launched in 1992. As a result, Black & Decker announced in early 1998 that it would sell most of its household products division and concentrate on its high-end power tool business. What had happened?

This is a clear example of market stratification and brand identification. The identification of Black & Decker with small appliances created an unfavorable image in the minds of the high-end customers of power tools, carpenters and contractors. They reasoned, if B & D makes toasters and popcorn poppers then their tools must be "wimpy." It was only when Black & Decker created the line of high-quality DeWalt tools, with their distinctive bright yellow color, that major inroads began to be made in this high-end market segment, where profit margins average 30 percent compared with 5 percent in appliances. Today the DeWalt brand enjoys 45 percent of the U.S. market for professional power tools. This shift in business strategy goes hand in hand with other market shifts, where more homeowners and other amateur crafters are trading up to the professional level of power tools.

answers in an attempt to uncover latent needs of which the customer is not consciously aware.

- *Customer surveys:* A written questionnaire is best used for gaining opinions about the redesign of existing products or new products that are well understood by the public. Innovative new products are better explored with interviews or focus groups. Other common reasons for conducting a survey are to identify or prioritize problems and to assess whether an implemented solution to a problem was successful. A survey can be administered by mail, over the telephone, or in face-to-face interviews. One type of question is to list the features of the product and ask the customer to rank order them according to their preferences. If there are more than six or eight features, this is hard to do, and it is better to ask the customer to compare each feature, one by one, i.e., pairwise comparison. There should always be several open-ended questions to allow for unanticipated responses. It is important to give the survey a pilot run to check for ambiguities and misunderstanding in the questions before the survey is distributed.
- *Customer complaints:* A sure way to learn about needs for product improvement is from customer complaints that are received either through returned product, from dealer input or input from service centers, or with a customer telephone or e-mail hot line. Statistics on warranty claims can pinpoint design defects.

2.3.2 Constructing a Survey Instrument

Regardless of the method used to gain information from customers, considerable thought needs to go into developing the survey instrument.[1] The following steps should be followed.

1. Determine the survey purpose. Write a short paragraph stating the purpose of the survey and what will be done with the results. Be clear about who will use the results and whether they want hard statistics from surveys or would prefer more anecdotal results from focus groups.
2. Determine the type of data-collection method to be used.
3. Identify what specific information is needed. Each question should have a clear goal. Write this down so you are clear about what you are trying to learn. You should have no more questions than the absolute minimum you need to learn what you need to learn.
4. Design the questions. Each question should be unbiased, unambiguous, clear, and brief. There are three categories of questions: (1) attitude questions—how the customers feel or think about something; (2) knowledge questions—questions asked to determine whether the customer knows the specifics about a product or service; and (3) behavior questions—usually contain phrases like "how often," "how much," or "when." Some general rules to follow in writing questions are:

   Do not use jargon or sophisticated vocabulary.
   Focus very precisely. Every question should focus directly on one specific topic.
   Use simple sentences. Two or more simple sentences are preferable to one compound sentence.
   Do not lead the customer toward the answer you want.
   Avoid questions with double negatives because they may create misunderstanding.
   Always include the choice of Other _____. This ensures that the list of choices is inclusive.
   Always include one open-ended question. Open-ended questions can reveal insights and nuances, and tell you things you would never think to ask.

   Questions can have the following types of answers:

   yes—no—don't know
   strongly agree—mildly agree—neutral—mildly disagree—strongly disagree. (On a 1–5 scale such as this, always set up the numerical scale so that a high number means a good answer.)
   rank order—list in descending order of preference
   unordered choices—choose (b) over (d) or (b) from a, b, c, d, e.

   The number of questions should be such that they can be answered in 30 minutes.

---

1. P. Salant and D. A. Dillman, "How to Conduct Your Own Survey," Wiley, New York, 1994; R. B. Frary, "A Brief Guide to Questionnaire Development," **http://www.ericae.net//ft/tamu/vpiques3.htm**.

Design the printed survey form so that tabulating and analyzing data will be easy. Be sure to include instructions for completing and returning it.

5. Arrange the order of questions so that they provide context to what you are trying to learn from the customer. Group the questions by topic, and start with easy ones.

6. Pretest the survey. Before distributing the survey to the customer, always pretest it on a smaller sample. This will tell you whether any of the questions are poorly worded so that they may be misunderstood, whether the rating scales are adequate, and whether the questionnaire is too long.

7. Administer the survey. Key issues in administering the survey are whether the people surveyed constitute a representative sample for fulfilling the purpose of the survey, and what size sample must be used to achieve statistically significant results. Answering these questions requires special expertise and experience. Consultants in the area of marketing should be used for really important situations.

EXAMPLE. A student design team[1] selected the familiar "jewel case" that protects a compact disc in storage as a product needing improvement. As a first step the team brainstormed (see Sec. 3.6) to develop ideas for possible improvements to the CD case (Fig. 2.2). The following ideas were generated in response to the question: What functions or attributes of a CD case need improvement?

1. Case more resistant to cracking
2. Easier to open
3. Add color
4. Better waterproofing
5. Make it lighter
6. More scratch-resistant
7. Easier extraction of CD from the circular fastener
8. Streamlined look
9. Case should fit the hand better
10. Easier to take out leaflet describing the CD
11. Use recyclable plastic
12. Make interlocking cases so they stack on top of each other without slipping
13. Better locking case
14. Hinge that doesn't come apart

Next, the ideas for improvement were grouped into common areas by using an *affinity diagram*. A good way to achieve this is to write each of the ideas on a Post-it note and place them randomly on a wall. The team then examines the ideas and arranges them into columns of logical groups. Place a header card to denote the category of the group.

---

1. The original concept for this problem was developed by a team of business and engineering students at the University of Maryland, College Park. Team members were Barry Chen, Charles Goldman, Annie Kim, Vikas Mahajan, Kathy Naftalin, Max Rubin, and Adam Waxman. The results of their study have been modified significantly by the author.

Compact Disc Case
Product Improvement Survey

A group of students in ENES 190 is attempting to improve the design and usefulness of the standard storage case for compact discs. Please take 10 minutes to fill out this customer survey and return it to the student marketer.

Please indicate the level of importance you attach to the following aspects of a CD case.
1 = low importance   5 = high importance

	1	2	3	4	5
1. A more crack-resistant case	1	2	3	4	5
2. A more scratch-resistant case	1	2	3	4	5
3. A hinge that doesn't come apart	1	2	3	4	5
4. A more colorful case	1	2	3	4	5
5. A lighter case	1	2	3	4	5
6. A streamlined look (aerodynamically sleek)	1	2	3	4	5
7. A case that fits your hand better	1	2	3	4	5
8. Easier opening CD case	1	2	3	4	5
9. Easier extraction of the CD from the circular fastener	1	2	3	4	5
10. Easier to take out leaflet describing contents of the CD	1	2	3	4	5
11. A more secure locking case	1	2	3	4	5
12. A waterproof case	1	2	3	4	5
13. Make the case from recyclable plastic	1	2	3	4	5
14. Make it so cases interlock so they stack on each other without slipping	1	2	3	4	5

Please list any other improvement features you would like to see in a CD case. _____
_____

_____

Would you be willing to pay more for a CD if the improvements you value with a 5 or 4 rating are available on the market?   yes   no

If you answered yes to the previous question, how much more would you be willing to pay? _____

How many CD's do you own (approximately)? _____

FIGURE 2.2
Customer survey for the compact disc case.

Stronger	Aesthetics	Opening and Extracting	Environment	Other
1	3	2	4	12
6	5	7	11	
14	8	10		
	9	13		

The affinity diagram was used to organize the questions on the survey that was distributed to potential customers.

2.3.3 Evaluating Customer Needs

To evaluate the customer responses, we could calculate the average score for each question, using a 1–5 scale. Those questions scoring highest would represent aspects of the product ranked highest in the mind of the customers. Alternatively, we can take the number of times a feature or attribute of a design is mentioned in the survey, and divide by the total number of customers surveyed. For the questionnaire shown above, we might use the number of responses to each question rating a feature as either a 4 or a 5. For the questions given above, this result is shown in Table 2.1.

It is worth noting that a response to a questionnaire of this type really measures the need obviousness as opposed to need importance. To get at true need importance, it is necessary to conduct face-to-face interviews or focus groups, and to record the actual words used by the persons interviewed. These responses need to be studied in depth, a tedious process. Also, it is important to realize that often respondents will omit talking about factors that are very important to them, because they seem so obvious. Safety or durability are good examples.

It is important to divide customer needs into two groups: hard constraints that absolutely must be satisfied (*musts*) and softer needs that can be traded off against other customer needs (*wants*). Customer needs can best be identified from focus group surveys or from the higher-ranking items in the written survey.

The relative frequency of responses from a survey can be displayed in a bar graph or a Pareto diagram (Fig. 2.3). In the bar graph the frequency of responses to each of the questions is plotted in order of the question number. In the Pareto diagram the frequency of responses is arranged in order of decreasing frequency, with the item of highest frequency at the left-hand side of the plot. Questions with less than 40 percent response rate have been omitted. This plot clearly identifies the most important customer requirements—the vital few. From these plots and Table 2.1 we conclude that the customer is most concerned with a more crack-resistant case (number 1) and that the convenience features of being able to stack the cases in a stable, interlocking way (number 14), and making it easier to extract the leaflet (number 10) and extract the CD (number 9) from the case appeal to the customer.

TABLE 2.1
Summary of responses from customer survey for CD case

Question number	Number of responses with 4 or 5 rating	Relative frequency
1	70	81.4
2	38	44.2
3	38	44.2
4	17	19.8
5	17	19.8
6	20	23.2
7	18	20.9
8	38	44.2
9	40	46.5
10	43	50.0
11	24	27.9
12	36	41.8
13	39	45.3
14	47	54.6

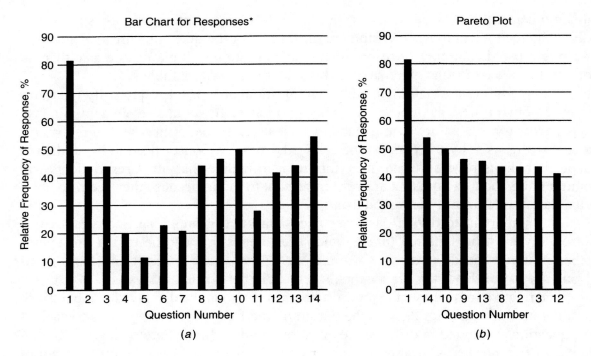

FIGURE 2.3
(*a*) Frequency of response plotted against question number in a conventional bar graph.
(*b*) Same data plotted as a Pareto diagram.
*Counts responses for each question that scored either 4 or 5.

2.4
BENCHMARKING

Benchmarking is a method for measuring a company's operations against the best companies both inside and outside of the industry.[1] It takes its name from the surveyor's benchmark or reference point from which elevations are measured. Benchmarking, as used in modern business context, is the search for industry best practices that lead to superior performance. Benchmarking can be used for product comparisons in the design and manufacturing of products, in service functions such as delivery and warranty issues, or in business areas like order entry, billing, financing, and repair.

Regardless of the focus of the benchmarking effort, it usually includes the following steps:

• Select the product, process, or functional area of the company that is to be benchmarked.

---

1. R. C. Camp, "Benchmarking," 2d ed., Quality Press, American Society for Quality, Milwaukee, 1995; M. J. Spendolini, "The Benchmarking Book," Amacom, New York, 1992; M. Zairi, "Effective Benchmarking: Learning from the Best," Chapman & Hall, New York, 1996 (many case studies).

- Identify the key performance *metrics* that will be measured and used for comparison. For example, for a product some metrics might be number of parts, estimated product cost, or material utilization for each component. For a manufacturing process the metrics might be yield of good parts, cycle time per part, or setup time. From a business viewpoint, metrics might be fraction of sales to repeat customers, percent of returns, or return on investment.
- Identify the *best-in-class companies* for each product or process to be benchmarked. A best-in-class company is one that performs the process at the lowest cost with the highest degree of customer satisfaction, or has the largest market share of a product type. This search should be broad, and in addition to including direct competitors, it can include companies in the same industry but who are not direct competitors, future or latent competitors, and companies in a totally different industry but which perform similar functions. For example, a consumer electronics company wishing to improve its direct sales to customers might benchmark a retail mail-order clothing company. If benchmarking is focused only on competitors, it may not lead to the best-in-class ranking. The number of companies chosen should be from four to six, should be as diverse a set as possible, and should exhibit good financial performance.
- Compare the best-in-class products or processes with the in-house equivalent using the performance metrics. The objective is to identify gaps in performance between the in-house product or process and the best-in-class companies.
- Specify programs and actions to meet and exceed the competition. The goal is for the in-house product or process to become the best in class. This requires a definitive action plan, with suitable resource commitment, and an agreed-upon schedule of milestones for achieving this goal.

A process similar to but more narrow than benchmarking is *reverse engineering*. This entails the dismantling of a product to determine its technology and how it is made, with the purpose of replication. The "tear-down" of a product is often a part of product benchmarking, but without the intent of copying the design. However, the collection of this type of benchmark information provides a better understanding of the solutions selected by the competition.

Collection of benchmark data is a critical issue. Much business data is available from published sources, government publications, and trade associations. Establishing an internal network of product experts within the company can often provide a pool of information about competing products and companies. Other sources of information are industry consultants and suppliers. Usually, detailed information will require the mailing of questionnaires and visits to companies. Sometimes trade or professional associations can facilitate such a visit, but arranging such visits usually comes down to having good contacts and offering information from your own company that may seem useful to the companies you wish to visit. Benchmarking operates most effectively on a quid pro quo basis.

Finally, it is important to realize that benchmarking is not a one-time effort. The competition will be working hard to improve, just as you have been doing. Benchmarking should be viewed as the first step in a process of continuous improvement.

2.5
CUSTOMER REQUIREMENTS

From a global viewpoint we should recognize that there is a hierarchy of human needs that motivate individuals in general.[1]

1. *Physiological needs* such as thirst, hunger, sex, sleep, shelter, and exercise. These constitute the basic needs of the body; and until they are satisfied, they remain the prime influence on the individual's behavior.
2. *Safety and security needs,* which include protection against danger, deprivation, and threat. When the bodily needs are satisfied, the safety and security needs become dominant.
3. *Social needs* for love and esteem by others. These needs include belonging to groups, group identity, and social acceptance.
4. *Psychological needs* for self-esteem and self-respect and for accomplishment and recognition.
5. *Self-fulfillment needs* for the realization of one's full potential through self-development, creativity, and self-expression.

As each need in this hierarchy is satisfied, the emphasis shifts to the next higher need.

Our design problem should be related to the basic human needs, some of which may be so obvious that in our modern technological society they are taken for granted. However, within each basic need there is a hierarchy of problem situations.[2] As the type I problem situations are solved, we move to the solution of higher-level problems within each category of basic need. It is characteristic of our advanced affluent society that, as we move toward the solution of type II and III problem situations, the perception of the need by society as a whole becomes less universal.

	Problem situation		
Basic need	**I**	**II**	**III**
Food	Hunger	Vitamin deficiency	Food additives
Shelter	Freezing	Cold	Comfort
Work	Availability	Right to work	Work fulfillment

Problem situation	Analysis of problem	Societal perception of need
I	None required	Complete agreement
II	Definition of problem	Some disagreement in priorities
	Calculation of cost	
	Setting of priorities	
III	Analysis of present and future costs	Strong disagreement on most issues
	Analysis of present and future risks	
	Environmental impact	

1. A. H. Maslow, *Psych. Rev.,* vol. 50, pp. 370–396, 1943.
2. Based on ideas of Prof. K. Almenas, University of Maryland.

Many current design problems deal with type III situations in which there is strong societal disagreement over needs and the accompanying goals. The result is protracted delays and increasing costs.

The customer requirements should be characterized as to performance, time, cost, and quality. *Performance* deals with what the design should do when it is completed and in operation. The *time* dimension includes all time aspects of the design. Currently, much effort is being given to reducing the cycle time to market for new products.[1] In many consumer products, the first to market with a great product captures the market. *Cost* pertains to all monetary aspects of the design. It is a paramount consideration, for everything else being roughly equal, cost determines most customers' buying decisions. *Quality* is a complex characteristic with many aspects and definitions. For now we will define quality as the totality of features and characteristics of a product or service that bear on its ability to satisfy stated or implied needs.

A more inclusive customer requirement than the four listed above is *value*. Value is the worth of a product or service. It can be expressed by the function provided divided by the cost, or the quality provided divided by the cost.

Studies of large successful companies have shown that the return on investment correlated with high market share and high quality. Garvin[2] identified the eight basic dimensions of quality for a manufactured product.

- *Performance:* The primary operating characteristics of a product. This dimension of quality can be expressed in measurable quantities, and therefore can be ranked objectively.
- *Features:* Those characteristics that supplement a product's basic functions. Features are frequently used to customize or personalize a product to the customer's taste.
- *Reliability:* The probability of a product failing or malfunctioning within a specified time period. See Chap. 11.
- *Durability:* A measure of the amount of use one gets from a product before it breaks down and replacement is preferable to continued repair. Durability is a measure of product life. Durability and reliability are closely related.
- *Serviceability:* Ease and time to repair after breakdown. Other issues are courtesy and competence of repair personnel and cost and ease of repair.
- *Conformance:* The degree to which a product's design and operating characteristics meet both customer expectations and established standards. These standards include industry standards and safety and environmental standards.
- *Aesthetics:* How a product looks, feels, sounds, tastes, and smells. The customer response in this dimension is a matter of personal judgment and individual preference. This area of design is chiefly the domain of the *industrial designer,* who is more artist than engineer. An important technical issue that affects aesthetics is *ergonomics,* how well the design fits the human user.
- *Perceived quality:* This dimension generally is associated with reputation. Advertising helps to develop this dimension of quality, but it is basically the quality of similar products previously produced by the manufacturer that influences reputation.

---

1. G. Stalk, Jr., and T. M. Hout, "Competing against Time," The Free Press, New York, 1990.
2. D. A. Garvin, *Harvard Business Review,* November–December, 1987, pp. 101–109.

The dimensions of performance, features, and conformance are interrelated. When competing products have essentially the same performance and many of the same features, customers will tend to expect that all producers of the product will have the same quality dimensions. In other words, customer expectations set the baseline for the product's conformance. Table 2.2 illustrates this by giving the performance criteria and features commonly found in three common household products.

We need to recognize that there are four levels of customer requirement:[1] (1) expecters, (2) spokens, (3) unspokens, and (4) exciters. These requirements must be satisfied at each level before addressing those at the next level.

- *Expecters:* These are the basic attributes that one would expect to see in the product, i.e., standard features. Expecters are frequently easy to measure and are used often in benchmarking.
- *Spokens:* These are the specific features that customers say they want in the product. Because the customer defines the product in terms of these attributes, the designer must be willing to provide them to satisfy the customer.
- *Unspokens:* These are product attributes the customer does not generally talk about, but are nevertheless important to him or her. They cannot be ignored. They may be attributes the customer simply forgot to mention or was unwilling to talk

TABLE 2.2
Performance criteria and features of three common products

Washing machines	Refrigerators	Self-propelled lawn mowers
Performance	*Performance*	*Performance*
Amount of water used	Efficiency	Motor horsepower
Cleanliness of clothes	Temperature	Handling
	Temperature distribution	Maneuverability
Features		Sharpness of turns
Automatic shutoff for	*Features*	Ease of use
unbalanced load	Freezer light	Starting the engine
Number of agitator speeds	Size (interior volume)	Handling of grass catcher
Number of spin-dry speeds	Automatic icemaker	Shifting gears
Number of water fill levels	Location and size of freezer	Changing cutter height
Bleach dispenser	Adjustable door shelves	Vacuum action to draw
Automatic control of water	Solid or wire shelves	cuttings into catcher
temperature	Humidity controlled crisper	Cuts evenly
Porcelain lid		Works well in tall grass
Discharge pump can lift water	*Conformance*	Mulching action uniformly
to 6 ft (2 m) above washer	Compressor noise level	disperses chips
	Chlorofluorocarbon (CFC) or	
	hydrofluorocarbon (HFC)	*Features*
		Grass catcher capacity

From E. B. Magrab, "Integrated Product and Process Design and Development," CRC Press, Boca Raton, 1997. With permission.

1. E. A. Magrab, "Integrated Product and Process Design," CRC Press, Boca Raton, 1997, pp. 91–92.

about or simply does not realize he or she wants. It takes great skill on the part of the design team to identify the unspoken requirements.

- *Exciters:* Often called *delighters,* these are product features that make the product unique and distinguish it from the competition. Note that the absence of an exciter will not make customers unhappy, since they do not know what is missing.

Customer satisfaction increases as the product fulfills requirements higher up in this hierarchy. Expecters must be satisfied first because they are the basic characteristics that a product is expected to possess. Spokens give greater satisfaction because they go beyond the basic level and respond to specific customer desires. Unspokens are an elusive category, while true exciters will serve to make a product unique. As we have seen in Sec. 2.3, not all customer requirements are equal. It is important to identify those requirements which are most important and ensure they are delivered in the product.

Customer complaints tend to be about expecter-type requirements. Therefore, a product development strategy aimed at solely eliminating complaints may not result in highly satisfied customers. To obtain this, you must adopt a strategy for actively seeking the "voice of the customer."

2.6
QUALITY FUNCTION DEPLOYMENT

Quality function deployment (QFD) is a planning and problem-solving tool that is finding growing acceptance for translating customer requirements into the engineering characteristics of a product.[1] It is a largely graphical method that systematically looks at all of the elements that go into the product definition as a group effort. As you will see below, the nature of the information that is required for the QFD diagram forces the design team to answer questions that might be glossed over in a less rigorous methodology and to learn what it does not know about the problem. Because it is a group decision-making activity, it creates a high level of buy-in and group understanding of the problem. Finally, QFD requires that the customers' requirements be expressed as measurable design targets in terms of engineering parameters. Thus, QFD is a natural precursor to establishing the product design specification (see Sec. 2.7).

QFD was developed in Japan in the early 1970s, with its first large-scale application in the Kobe Shipyard of Mitsubishi Heavy Industries. It was rapidly adopted by the Japanese automobile industry. By the mid-1980s many U.S. auto, defense, and electronic companies were using QFD. A recent survey of 150 U.S. companies showed that 71 percent of these have adopted QFD since 1990. These companies reported that 83 percent believed that using QFD had increased customer satisfaction with their products, and 76 percent felt it facilitated rational design decisions. It is important to remember these statistics because using QFD requires considerable

---

1. As will be discussed below, QFD can be rolled out all the way from the product planning stage, which is the focus here, through the detail part design to the production planning stage.

commitment of time and effort. Most, however, report that the time spent in QFD saves time later in design, especially in minimizing changes caused by poorly understanding the problem.

The layout of the QFD diagram is shown in Fig. 2.4. Because of this configuration, it is often called the *house of quality*.[1] The following is a description of what is found in each of the "rooms" of this house.

1. *Customer requirements (whats)* are gathered by the team as discussed in Sec. 2.3. To aid in understanding, group these requirements as identified by an affinity diagram.
2. *Competitive assessment* shows how the top two or three competitive products rank with respect to the customer requirements. This section starts with ranking each customer requirement on a scale of 1 to 5 and then, by considering the

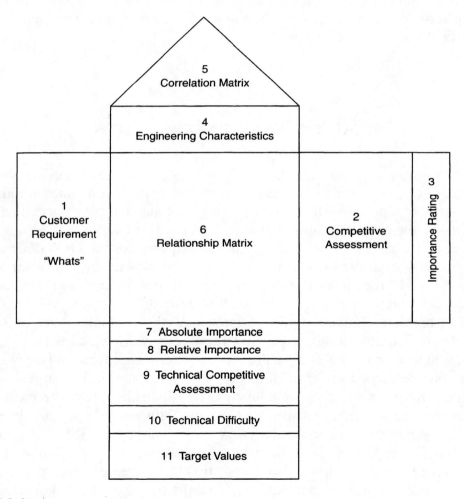

FIGURE 2.4
House of quality format for QFD. Numbers of "rooms" correlate with description in text.

1. J. R. Hauser and D. Clausing, "The House of Quality," *Harvard Business Review,* May–June 1988, pp. 63–73.

planned improvement and any requirements that are planned for special attention (sales points), it builds up to an importance rating.

3. *Importance rating:* For details on how this is arrived at, see the example that follows.

4. *Engineering characteristics (hows)* that enable satisfying the customer requirements are listed in columns. A way to arrive at the **ECs** is to ask the question: "What can I control that allows me to meet my customer's needs?" These must not be specific design details or solutions but must be characteristics that can be measured and given target values like weight, force, velocity, etc. It is desirable to label each **EC** to indicate the preferred direction of the magnitude of the characteristic. Thus a ⇑ or a + indicates that a higher value is better, and a ⇓ or a − indicates that a lower value is better.

5. *The correlation matrix* shows the degree of interdependence among the engineering characteristics in the "roof of the house." It is better to recognize these coupling relationships early in the design process so that appropriate trade-offs can be made. Usually a 9 or ● is used to signify a strong relationship and a 3 or ○ is for a medium relationship.

6. *The relationship matrix* determines the correlation between the engineering characteristics, **EC**, and the customer requirements, **CR**. To do this take each **CR**, and for each **EC**, in turn, ask whether it will significantly, moderately, slightly, or not at all impact the customer need. Generally, a nonlinear 9/3/1/0 (blank) scale[1] is used to weight disproportionately those **ECs** that strongly affect customer requirements.

7. To determine the *absolute importance,* first multiply the numerical value in each of the cells of the relationship matrix (6) by the importance rating (3). Then, sum the numbers in the cells of each column. These totals show the absolute importance of each engineering characteristic in meeting the customer requirements.

8. *Relative importance* is the absolute importance, normalized on a scale from 1 to 100. To arrive at this, total the values of absolute importance. Then, take each value of absolute importance, divide it by the total, and multiply by 100. Those **ECs** with the highest rating should be given special attention, for these are the ones that have the greatest effect upon customer satisfaction.

9. *The technical competitive assessment* benchmarks your company performance against two or three top competitors for each of the engineering characteristics. Generally a scale of 1–5 (best) is used. Often this information is obtained by getting examples of the competitor's product and testing them. Note that the data in this room compares each of the product performance characteristics with those of the closest competitors. This is different from the competitive assessment in room 2, where we compared the closest competitors with respect to each of the customer requirements.

10. *Technical difficulty* indicates the ease with which each of the engineering characteristics can be achieved. Basically, this comes down to an estimate by the design

---

1. The original Japanese workers in QFD used the symbols ●, ○, and △, taken from the racing form symbols for win, place, and show, for 9, 3, and 1.

team of the probability of doing well in attaining desired values for each **EC**. Again a 1 is a low probability and a 5 represents a high probability of success.

11. Setting *target values* is the final step in the QFD. By knowing which are the most important **ECs**, understanding the technical competition, and having a feel for the technical difficulty, the team is in a good position to set the targets for each engineering characteristic. Setting targets at the beginning of the design process provides a way for the design team to gauge the progress they are making toward satisfying the customer's requirements as the design proceeds.

You can see that the QFD summarizes a great deal of information in a single diagram. It will be one of the important reference documents during the progress of the design. Like most design documents, as more information is developed about the design the QFD should be updated. Not all design situations will call for a complete QFD as described here. However, as a minimum, rooms 1, 3, 4, 6, 8, and 11 should be used.

> **EXAMPLE.** The design of an improved case to protect and store compact discs, which was introduced in Sec. 2.3, will be continued. Based on the customer responses recorded in Fig. 2.3*a,* the "whats" are listed in room 1, grouped according to major category of customer requirements. Only those **CRs** that received a frequency of 40 percent or higher are listed here. One additional requirement, cost, is added because it is the major requirement of the recording and distribution companies, namely, that a CD case with improved features cost them no more than they are now paying. See Fig. 2.5.
>
> Next turn to room 2. The *customer importance* is established by taking the results from the customer surveys and allocating them along a 1–5 scale, where 5 is the highest. This region of the QFD is devoted chiefly to competitive assessment of the product, comparing the best of existing products with the proposed product. For the CD case little benchmarking data is available, since CD cases are a very generic product. However, we can rate the existing CD cases on the market against the new CD case that is planned to be offered for sale, again on a 1–5 scale. The ratio of planned to existing is called the *improvement ratio.* Since we plan to include some new features in the new CD case design, we expect to have some "talking points" or "sales features" that will aid in introducing the new product into the market. These *sales points* are rated, with a 1.5 given to the highest sales points and 1.3 to lower-rated features. For the CD case, we rate as high sales points the higher toughness case and easier opening case, and the ability to stack many CDs without tumbling.
>
> The *improvement ratio* (room 3) is given by the product of *customer importance* × *improvement ratio* × *sales points.* The *relative weight* is each value of importance weight divided by the sum of all values of importance weight. Note that the sum of the relative weights equals unity. Five **CRs** rank highest: 1, 3, 4, 5, and 10. The **CR** cost does not appear in this list, because we rated it low on improvement ratio and sales points; our goal is to design a CD case with improved features at the same cost as the current case. The way to look at this is that cost is a *must requirement,* while all the others are *want requirements.* Strictly speaking, the QFD should not mix needs that are musts and those that are wants. However, we included cost in the QFD so it would not be forgotten.
>
> Room 4 lists the engineering characteristics (the "hows") that enable the design team to meet the customer requirements. These are the technical requirements that the design must possess, without getting to a specific level of detail. In different words, they are the translation of the **CRs** into the internal or technical language of the organization, sometimes called the *substitute quality characteristics.*[1] They are arrived at by the team steep-

---

1. L. Cohen, "Quality Function Deployment," Addison-Wesley, Reading, MA, 1995.

Strong positive ●
Positive ○
Negative ×
Strong negative #

9 = Strong
3 = Moderate
1 = Weak

	Toughness of plastic	Recyclable plastic	New hinge design	Time to open	Force needed to open	No. times to grab	Clearance / CD-case	Improved shape	Flat side / top & bottom	Cost of manufacture	Customer importance	CD case on market	Planned CD case	Improvement ratio	Sales points	Improvement ratio	Relative weight
Strength																	
1. Crack-resistant case	9	1									5	4	5	1.3	1.5	9.8	0.14
2. Scratch-resistant case	9										4	4	4	1.0	1.0	4.0	0.06
3. Hinge doesn't come apart			9								4	3	5	1.7	1.0	6.8	0.10
Ergonomics																	
4. Easier opening				3	9						4	3	5	1.7	1.5	10.2	0.15
5. Easier to remove leaflet						9					4	2	4	2.0	1.0	8.0	0.11
6. Easier extraction of CD							9				4	3	3	1.0	1.0	4.0	0.06
7. Fits hand better								9			2	4	4	1.0	1.0	2.0	0.03
New features																	
8. More secure locking					9						3	3	4	1.3	1.0	3.9	0.06
9. Recyclable plastic		9									4	3	4	1.3	1.0	5.2	0.07
10. Stacking stability									9		4	3	5	1.7	1.5	10.2	0.15
11. Cost										9	5	5	5	1.0	1.0	5.0	0.07
Abs. importance	1.80	0.63	1.04	0.45	1.89	0.99	0.54	0.27	1.35	0.63	9.59					69.1	1.00
Rel. importance	0.19	0.07	0.11	0.05	0.20	0.10	0.05	0.03	0.14	0.06							
CD case now on market	2.0			5.0	8.0	2				0.15							
Direction of movement	↑	×	×	↓	↓	↓	↑	×	×	S							
Target value	5.0			2.0	6.0	1				0.15							
Units	J/cm			sec	oz.	Num.		mm		$							

FIGURE 2.5
QFD table for the compact disc case example.

ing itself in the relevant technologies of the problem and then using brainstorming to generate ideas about the required product functions. Often more **ECs** than are shown in Fig. 2.5 are used, but a smaller number is used here because of the simplicity of the product, and for brevity in the example. Ideally, the **ECs** are characteristics that can be measured and given target values. A few of the **ECs** in Fig. 2.5 violate that precept because of the desire to embed an idea in the QFD which is important but not readily quantified.

The correlation matrix, room 5, records possible interactions between **ECs** for future trade-off decisions. For example, increasing the toughness of the plastic from which the case is made may have a negative impact on the cost of the manufactured CD case. A new hinge design will have a positive impact on the force to open the CD case.

The relationship matrix, room 6, correlates the engineering characteristics to the customer requirements (**ECs** vs. **CRs**). In the systems used in Fig. 2.5, a strong correlation is worth 9, a medium correlation 3, and a weak correlation 1. The objective is to make sure that every customer requirement is addressed by at least one engineering characteristic. If a row of **CRs** is blank, then the team should reexamine whether this is a real customer need, and if it is, then they should identify one or more **ECs** that address this need. Similarly, if any of the columns are blank, then it indicates that the design is imposing technical requirements that satisfy no customer requirements.

The importance of the **ECs** is determined by multiplying each of the cells in the matrix by its relative weight, and summing each column to give the *absolute importance* (room 7). For the **EC** "number of times to grab the leaflet" the absolute importance is $9 \times 0.11 = 0.99$. The sum of all the importance ratings is 9.59, so the *relative importance* for this **EC** is $(0.99/9.59) = 0.10$. We note that the most important technical requirements are the toughness of the plastic and the force to open the CD case.

We now need to establish target values for those **ECs** that can be quantified. We record the units in which **EC** is expressed, and the direction which indicates improvement. This can be increase $\uparrow$ or decrease $\downarrow$, the same S, or yes Y or no N, or simply whether the characteristic will be considered in the design, X. In this example we give the values for the **ECs** of the current CD cases on the market, and the target values for the new design.[1]

The QFD method is used most often in the planning of a product, as has just been illustrated above. However, QFD can be used throughout the product design process.[2] Figure 2.6 shows how the product planning "house of quality" feeds into the design of individual parts, and this into the process planning, and finally into production planning. We note that the **ECs** of the house of quality become the input for the part design QFD, with the target values of the house of quality becoming the constraints for that matrix. Thus, as shown in Fig. 2.6, each QFD feeds critical design information to the matrix that is downstream from it.

2.7
PRODUCT DESIGN SPECIFICATION

The product design specification (PDS) is the basic control and reference document for the design and manufacture of the product.[3] The PDS is a document which contains all of the facts related to the outcome of the product development. It should avoid forcing the design and predicting the outcome, but it should also contain the realistic constraints that are imposed on the design. Creating the PDS finalizes the process of establishing the customer needs and wants, prioritizing them, and beginning to cast them into a technical framework so that design concepts can be estab-

---

1. Special software usually is used to construct the QFD diagram. Three packages are QFD/Capture, International Techne Group, 5303 DuPont Circle, Milford, OH, 45150; QFD Scope, Integrated Quality Dynamics, and QFD Designer from American Supplier Institute.
2. D. Clausing, "Total Quality Development," ASME Press, New York, 1994; J. B. ReVelle, J. W. Moran, and C. A. Cox, "The QFD Handbook," Wiley, New York, 1998.
3. S. Pugh, "Total Design," Chap. 3, Addison-Wesley, Reading, MA, 1990.

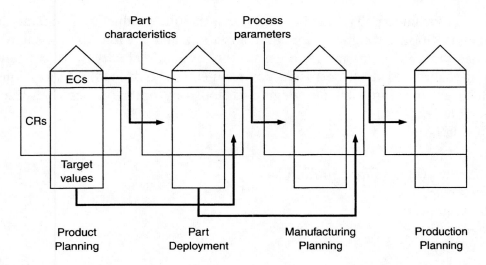

FIGURE 2.6

Example of how the results of product planning QFD feed into QFD for designing the individual parts, and this in turn feeds a QFD for manufacturing planning, which ultimately leads to a production planning sheet.

lished. The process of group thinking and prioritizing that developed the QFD diagram provides an excellent input to writing the PDS. However, it must be understood that the PDS is evolutionary and will change as the design process proceeds. But, at the end of the process the PDS will describe in writing the product that is intended to be manufactured and marketed.

Listed below are the elements that are to be found in a product design specification. Not every product will require consideration of every item in this list, but many will. The list demonstrates the complexity of product design.

In-Use Purposes and Market

- Product title
- Purpose or function the product is to perform
- Predictable unintended uses the product may be put to
- Special features of the product
- What types of products will the product compete against and who makes them?
- What is the intended market?
- Why is there a need for this product?
- Relationship of the product to other company products
- Anticipated market demand (units per year)
- Target company selling price and estimated retail price

Functional Requirements

- Functional performance—flow of energy, information, materials; operational steps; efficiency; accuracy
- Physical requirements—size, weight, shape, surface finish

- Service environment. The total environment that the product must operate in from the factory floor, through storage, transportation, and use must be considered. This includes range of temperature, pressure range, wind velocity, rain and salt spray, humidity, dirt and dust, corrosive environments, shock loading, vibration, noise level, insect and bird damage, degree of abuse by operators. Product must have acceptable shelf life.
- Life-cycle issues

  Useful life
  Reliability (mean time to failure)
  Robustness
  Maintainability
  Diagnosability
  Testability
  Repairability
  Installability
  Retirement from service and recyclability
  Cost of operation (energy costs, crew size, etc.)

- Human factors

  Aesthetics
  Man-machine interface, *ergonomics*
  User training

Corporate Constraints

- Time to market. Is there adequate time, given the resources, to design a quality product and its manufacturing process?
- Manufacturing requirements (in-house, in-country issues). Will it be required to use in-house manufacturing capabilities, and if so, will this limit available manufacturing processes and constrain cost reduction? Are there limitations on materials selection because of corporate policies?
- Suppliers. Do existing relationships with suppliers limit choices?
- Trademark, logo, brand name. What are the constraints, if any, in using these marketing tools?
- Financial performance. What are the corporate criteria on profitability and return on investment (ROI) that must be met?
- Corporate ethics. The product team should exhibit high professional ethics in dealing with suppliers, owners of intellectual property, corporate citizens, society at large, and each other.

Social, Political, and Legal Requirements

- Safety and environmental regulations. Not only must all U.S. regulations be met, but those of the European Community (EC) need to be considered for products that are expected to be exported.
- Standards. Search for, list, and use all pertinent product standards that may be applicable.

- Safety and product liability. Strong documentation of the design process, careful design of warning labels, in appropriate languages, and adherence to safety standards are the main defenses against product liability suits. Critical parts should be documented in the PDS so that the designer may give priority to ensuring these parts will be as reliable and safe as possible.
- Patents and intellectual property. All areas of useful information should be consulted prior to launching the design. Knowledge of the patent art is needed to avoid infringement. Arrange for licenses to use critical pieces of technology.

The PDS should be as complete as possible about what the design should do, but it should say as little as possible about how the requirements are to be met. Whenever possible the specification should be expressed in quantitative terms, and when appropriate it should give limits within which acceptable performance lies. For example: The power output of the engine should be 5 hp, plus or minus 0.25 hp. Remember that the PDS is a dynamic document. While it is important to make it as complete as possible at the outset of design, do not hesitate to change it as you learn more as the design evolves.

EXAMPLE. The CD jewel case given in Secs. 2.3 and 2.6 is continued here. From the information in Figs. 2.3 and 2.5 we can write the preliminary product design specification.

Product title
Compact disc jewel case.

Purpose
To provide an improved way to store and protect compact discs.

New or special features
Stronger; less susceptible to cracking on dropping.
Easier and quicker to open and extract the CD.
Easier to remove the descriptive leaflet.
More stable in stacking.

Competition
Will compete against standard hinged CD case produced by many plastics manufacturers.

Intended market
We will sell direct to largest producers of prerecorded music. Approximately 500 million CD jewel boxes are sold each year in the United States. Secondary market will be CD for computer games.

Need for product
User survey has shown customer interest in new features; 50 percent of people surveyed expressed willingness to pay a bit more for an improved product. Our business strategy is to produce a superior product at the existing cost to music producers.

Relationship to existing products line

This is a start-up venture. No other products currently exist.

Market demand

Current U.S. market is about 500 million units annually. We anticipate a 5 percent market share by year 2 (25 million units), growing to 20 percent share by year 5.

Price

We anticipate selling CD jewel cases at a unit price of $0.15 in bulk lots. The manufacturing cost should be no more than $0.12 per unit.

Functional performance

Protects the CD from dirt, scratches, spilled liquids.
Secures the CD firmly in the case.
Allows for easy opening of case.
Allows for stable stacking of many CDs.
Allows easy removal of descriptive leaflet.
Able to be dropped on floor from height of 3 ft without opening or cracking.

Physical requirements

Same size as regular CD case (5.5 × 4.87 × 0.4 in).
Approximately same weight as regular CD case.
Rectangular shape with rounded corners.
Smooth, but not slippery surface.
Transparent, so that identification material can be read on both sides.

Service environment

Case material should be stable from −20 to 120°F, 20 to 100 percent relative humidity.

Life-cycle issues

Opening/closure mechanism must not fail for 1000 cycles.
Case made from recyclable material.

Human factors

Allows display of artwork or advertisements on two large flat surfaces.
No sharp corners or edges to cause cuts or snag clothing.
Rounded edges give good "feel."
Opening of case must be simple. Closure must be positive, and give an audible click.

Corporate constraints

Must be in market within 6 months.
Manufacturing will be contracted to suppliers.
Will use the trademark CD-EASE.
Must conform to corporate code of ethics.

Legal requirements

No toxic materials to be associated with manufacture.

Use of rosette to hold CD firmly in cradle will require license to U.S. patent. See U.S. patents 4613044, 5450951, and 5425451.

2.8
SUMMARY

Problem definition is the most crucial step in the engineering design process. If the problem is not properly defined, then all subsequent effort may prove to be for naught. This is especially true in product design, where considerable time and effort must be spent in listening to and analyzing the *voice of the customer.* The steps in problem definition for product design are:

- Position the product in the corporate product line as part of a product platform.
- Identify the customer needs: use interviews, focus groups, surveys, customer complaints.
- Evaluate the customer needs: separate into musts and wants, and prioritize the wants.
- Conduct benchmarking with best-in-class companies.
- Begin to identify the customer requirements. Recognize the four levels of requirements: expecters, spokens, unspokens, exciters.
- Build a QFD diagram as a team exercise to clearly establish the relationship between the customer requirements and the engineering characteristics of the design.
- With all of the above information, write a product design specification (PDS). The PDS becomes the controlling documentation for the design.

For a detailed description of a product development, starting with the voice of the customer and ending with a QFD, see Shiba et al.[1] The product in this case is a stripping basket, a device used by saltwater fly fishermen to collect their line before they cast it out.

BIBLIOGRAPHY

Customer Needs and Product Alignment

Meyer, M. H., and A. P. Lehnerd: "The Power of Product Platforms," The Free Press, New York, 1997.

Smith P. G., and D. G. Reinertsen: "Developing Products in Half the Time: New Rules, New Tools," 2d ed., Wiley, New York, 1996.

---

1. S. Shiba, A. Graham, and D. Walden, "A New American TQM," pp. 201–239, Productivity Press, Portland, OR, 1993.

Ulrich, K. T., and S. D. Eppinger: "Product Design and Development," McGraw-Hill, New York, 1995, Chaps 2, 3, 4.
Urban, G. L., and J. R. Hauser: "Design and Marketing of New Products," 2d ed., Prentice-Hall, Englewood Cliffs, NJ, 1993.

Quality Function Deployment

Bickell, B. A., and K. D. Bickell: "The Road Map to Repeatable Success: Using QFD to Implement Change," CRC Press, Boca Raton, FL, 1995.
Clausing, D.: "Total Quality Development," ASME Press, New York, 1995.
Cohen, L.: "Quality Function Deployment," Addison-Wesley, Reading, MA, 1995.
Day, R. G.: "Quality Function Deployment," ASQC Quality Press, Milwaukee, WI, 1993.
Guinta, L. R., and N. C. Praizler: "The QFD Book," Amacom, New York, 1993.
King, B.: "Better Designs in Half the Time," 3d ed., GOAL/QPC, Methuen, MA, 1989.

Customer Requirements and PDS

McGrab, E. A.: "Integrated Product and Process Design," CRC Press, Boca Raton, FL, 1997.
Pugh S.: "Total Design," Addison-Wesley, Reading, MA, 1990.
Ullman, D. G.: "The Mechanical Design Process," 2d ed., McGraw-Hill, New York, 1997.

PROBLEMS AND EXERCISES

2.1. Select 10 products from a catalog for a supplier of household items (not clothing) and decide which needs in Maslow's hierarchy of human needs they satisfy. Then, identify the particular product features that make the products attractive to you.

2.2. The demand for most edible fish exceeds the supply. While fish can be raised in ponds on land or in ocean enclosures close to shore, there are limitations of scale. The next step is mariculture—fish farming in the open sea. Develop a new product business development plan for such a venture.

2.3. The transistor, followed by the microprocessor, is one of the most far-reaching products ever developed. Make a list of the major products and services that have been impacted by these inventions.

2.4. Write a survey to find what customers want in a washing machine.

2.5. Take 10 min and individually write down small things in your life, or aspects of products that you use, that bother you. You can just name the product, or better yet, give an attribute of the product that "bugs you." Be as specific as you can. You are really creating a needs list. Combine this with other lists prepared by members of your design team. Perhaps you have created an idea for an invention.

2.6. Suppose you are the inventor of a new device called the helicopter. By describing the functional characteristics of the machine, list some of the societal needs that it is expected to satisfy. Which of these have come to fruition, and which have not?

2.7. A focus group of housewives was convened to show them an innovative clothespin and ask what characteristics they want in a clothespin. The comments were as follows:

> It needs to grip tightly.
> I have arthritis. They shouldn't be too hard to open or close.
> I don't like pins that get tangled in my clothes basket.
> It better not stain the clothes.
> If I'm going to buy new clothespins at that price, they better last a long time.
> I don't want them to look shabby after long use.

Translate these customer requirements into engineering characteristics of the product.

2.8. Complete the relationship matrix (room 6) and the correlation matrix (room 5) for a house of quality for a heating and air-conditioning design project. The customer requirements are lower operating costs; improved cash flow; managed energy use; increased occupant comfort; and easy to maintain. The engineering characteristics are energy efficiency ratio ≥ 10; zonal controls; programmable energy management system; payback ≤ 1 year; and 2-hr spare parts delivery.

2.9. A product design team is designing an improved flip-lid trash can such as would be found in a family kitchen. The problem statement is as follows:

> Design a user-friendly, durable flip-lid trash can that opens and closes reliably. The trash can must be lightweight yet tip-resistant. It must combat odor, fit standard kitchen trash bags, and be safe for all users in a family environment.

With this information, and a little research and imagination where needed, construct a QFD for this design project.

2.10. Write a problem statement for cross-country skis that allow skiing on dirt or grass. List the "musts" and "wants" separately.

2.11. Write a product design specification for the flip-lid trash can described in Prob. 2.9.

3

TEAM BEHAVIOR AND TOOLS

3.1
INTRODUCTION

A recent column in *The Wall Street Journal* was headed "Engineering Is Re-engineered into a Team Sport." The article went on to say, "These firms want people who are comfortable operating in teams and communicating with earthlings who know nothing about circuit-board design or quantum mechanics." This is to emphasize that when industry leaders are asked what they would like to see changed in engineering curricula they invariably respond, "Teach your students to work effectively in teams." A more near term reason for devoting this chapter to team behavior is that the engineering design courses for which this text is intended are mostly focused around team-based projects. All too often we instructors thrust you students into a team situation without providing proper understanding of what it takes to achieve a smooth functioning team. Most often things work out just fine, but at a cost of extra hours of trial and error to find the best way to function as a team. Indeed, the greatest complaint that students have about project design courses is *"it takes too much time."* This chapter is designed to give you an understanding of the team building process and introduce you to some tools that people have found helpful in getting results through teams.

Why all the fuss about teams? Basically, it is because, properly handled, teams outperform individuals. Certainly, in most engineering design, because of the complexity of the problem, teams are a necessity. No one person could possess all of the knowledge and skill needed for a successful solution, and no one person working 20 hours per day could complete all of the tasks that need to be done.

A team is a small number of people with complementary skills who are committed to a common purpose, performance goals, and approach for which they hold themselves mutually accountable.[1] There are two general types of teams: teams that do real

---

1. J. R. Katzenbach and D. K. Smith, "The Wisdom of Teams," HarperCollins, New York, 1994.

TABLE 3.1
Differences between a working group and a team

Working group	Team
Strong, clearly focused leader	Individual and mutual accountability
The group's purpose is the same as the broader organizational mission	Specific team purpose that the team itself develops
Individual work products	Collective work products
Runs efficient meetings	Encourages open-ended discussion and active problem-solving meetings
Measures its effectiveness indirectly by its influence on others	Measures performance directly by assessing collective work products
Discusses, decides, and delegates	Discusses, decides, and does real work together

From J. R. Katzenbach and D. K. Smith, "The Wisdom of Teams," HarperCollins, New York, 1994.

work, like design teams, and teams that make recommendations. Both are important, but we focus here on the former. Most people have worked in groups, but a working group is not necessarily a team. Table 3.1 clearly defines the differences. We see from Table 3.1 that a team is a high order of group activity. Many groups do not reach this level, but it is a goal truly worth achieving.

3.2
WHAT IT MEANS TO BE AN EFFECTIVE TEAM MEMBER

There is a set of attitudes and work habits that you need to adopt to be a good team member. First and foremost, you need to *take responsibility for the success of the team.* Without this commitment, the team is weakened by your presence. Without this commitment, you shouldn't be on the team.

Next, you need to *be a person who delivers on commitments.* This means that you consider membership on the team as something worthwhile and that you are willing to rearrange your job and personal responsibilities to satisfy the needs of the team. On occasions when you cannot complete an assignment, always notify the team leader as soon as possible so other arrangements can be made.

Much of the team activities takes place in meetings where members share their ideas. Learn to *be a contributor to discussions.* Some of the ways that you can contribute are by asking for explanations to opinions, guiding the discussion back on track, and pulling together and summarizing ideas.

Listening is an art that not all of us have learned to practice. Learn to *give your full attention to whomever is speaking and demonstrate this by asking helpful questions.* To help focus on the speaker, take notes and never do distracting things like reading unrelated material, writing letters, walking around, or interrupting the speaker.

Develop techniques for getting your message across to the team. This means thinking things through briefly in your own mind before you speak. Always speak in a loud, clear voice. Have a positive message, and avoid "put-downs" and sarcasm. Keep focused on the point you are making. Avoid rambling discussion.

Learn to give and receive useful feedback. The point of a team meeting is to benefit from the collective knowledge and experience of the team to achieve an agreed-upon goal. Feedback is of two types. One is a natural part of the team discussion. The other involves corrective action for improper behavior by a member of the team[1] (see Sec. 3.6).

The following are characteristics of an effective team:

- Team goals are as important as individual goals.
- The team understands the goals and is committed to achieving them.
- Trust replaces fear and people feel comfortable taking risks.
- Respect, collaboration, and open-mindedness are prevalent.
- Team members communicate readily; diversity of opinions is encouraged.
- Decisions are made by consensus and have the acceptance and support of the members of the team.

I hope you will want to learn how to become an effective team member. Most of this chapter is devoted to helping you do that. Being a good team member is not a demeaning thing at all. Rather, it is a high form of group leadership. Being recognized as an effective team member is a highly marketable skill. Corporate recruiters say that the traits they are looking for in new engineers are communication skills, team skills, and problem-solving ability.

3.3
TEAM ROLES

We have just discussed the behavior that is expected of a good team member. Within a team members assume different roles in addition to being an active team member.

An important role that is external to the team but vital to its performance is the *team sponsor.* The team sponsor is the manager who has the need for the output of the team. He or she selects the team leader, negotiates the participation of team members, provides any special resources needed by the team, and formally commissions the team.

The *team leader* convenes and chairs the team meetings using effective meeting management practices (see Sec. 3.5). He or she guides and manages the day-to-day activity of the team by tracking the team's accomplishment toward stated goals, helping team members develop their skills, communicating with the sponsor about progress, trying to remove barriers toward progress, and helping to resolve conflict within the team. In general, there are three styles of team leadership: the traditional or autocratic leader, the passive leader, and the facilitative leader. Table 3.2 lists some major characteristics of these types of leaders. Clearly, the facilitative leader is the modern type of leader who we wish to be leading teams.

Many teams in industry include a *facilitator,* a person trained in group dynamics who assists the leader and the team in achieving its objectives by coaching them in

---

1. P. R. Scholtes et al., "The Team Handbook," Joiner Associates, Madison, WI, 1988; "The Team Memory Jogger," Joiner Associates, 1995.

TABLE 3.2
Characteristics of three leadership types

Traditional leader	Passive leader	Facilitative leader
Directive and controlling	Hands off	Creates open environment
No questions—just do it	Too much freedom	Encourages suggestions
Retains all decision-making authority	Lack of guidance and direction	Provides guidance
Nontrusting	Extreme empowerment	Embraces creativity
Ignores input	Uninvolved	Considers all ideas
Autocratic	A figurehead	Maintains focus; weighs goals vs. criteria

team skills and problem-solving tools, and assisting in data-collection activities. Sometimes the facilitator leads the meeting, especially if a controversial subject is being discussed. While the facilitator functions as a team member in most respects, she or he must remain neutral in team discussions and stand ready to provide interventions to attain high team productivity and improved participation by team members or, in extreme situations, to resolve team disputes. A key role of the facilitator is to keep the group focused on its task.

Sometimes teams have a *process observer.* The process observer is a member of the team appointed on a rotating basis to observe the process and progress of the meeting. He or she assists the facilitator in keeping the discussion on track, encouraging full participation of team members, and encouraging listening. Often, the facilitator also serves in the role of process observer. One task of the process observer is to look for hidden agendas that prevent an effective team process, like individuals who continually shirk work or who are overly protective of their organizational unit. When serving as process observer, the team member does not take part actively in the discussion.

3.4
TEAM DYNAMICS

Students of team behavior have observed that most teams go through five stages of development.[1]

1. *Orientation (forming):* The members are new to the team. They are probably both anxious and excited, yet unclear about what is expected of them and the task they are to accomplish. This is a period of tentative interactions and polite discourse, as the team members undergo orientation and acquire and exchange information.
2. *Dissatisfaction (storming):* Now the challenges of forming a cohesive team become real. Differences in personalities, working and learning styles, cultural

1. R. B. Lacoursiere, "The Life Cycle of Groups," Human Service Press, New York, 1980; B. Tuckman, Developmental Sequence in Small Groups, *Psychological Bulletin*, no. 63, pp. 384–399, 1965.

We Don't Want a General Patton

Many student design teams have difficulty with team leadership. Unless the instructor insists on each team selecting a leader, the natural egalitarian student spirit tends to work against selecting a team leader. Often students prefer to rotate the leadership assignment. While this procedure has the strong benefit of giving each student a leadership experience, it often leads to spotty results and is definitely a time-inefficient procedure.

One approach that works well for semester-long projects is to start out by rotating the leadership assignment for about 1 month. This gives everyone in the team a chance at leadership, and it also demonstrates which students have the strongest leadership talents. Often a natural leader emerges. The team should embrace such a person and make him or her their leader. Of course, in this enlightened era, we want nothing other than a facilitative leader.

---

backgrounds, and available resources (time to meet, access to and agreement on the meeting place, access to transportation, etc.) begin to make themselves known. Disagreement, even conflict, may break out in meetings. Meetings may be characterized by criticism, interruptions, poor attendance, or even hostility.

3. *Resolution (norming):* The dissatisfaction abates when team members establish group norms, either spoken or unspoken, to guide the process, resolve conflicts, and focus on common goals. The norms are given by rules of procedure and the establishment of comfortable roles and relationships among team members. The arrival of the resolution stage is characterized by greater consensus[1] seeking, and stronger commitment to help and support each other.

4. *Production (Performing):* This is the stage of team development we have worked for. The team is working cooperatively with few disruptions. People are excited and have pride in their accomplishments, and team activities are fun. There is high orientation toward the task, and demonstrable performance and productivity.

5. *Termination (Adjourning):* When the task is completed, the team prepares to disband. This is the time for joint reflection on how well the team accomplished its task, and reflection on the functioning of the team.

It is important for teams to realize that the dissatisfaction stage is perfectly normal and that they can look forward to its passing. Many teams experience only a brief stage 2 and pass through without any serious consequences. However, if there are serious problems with the behavior of team members, they should be addressed quickly. Also, some teams can be expected to lose a member or add a member after the team formation has begun. They must all recognize that changing even one team member makes it a new team and that they must again all go through the five stages of team development on an accelerated schedule.

One way or another, a team must address the following set of psychosociological conditions.

---

1. Consensus means general agreement or accord. Consensus does not require 100 percent agreement of the group. Neither is 51 percent agreement a consensus.

- *Safety:* Are the members of the team safe from destructive personal attacks? Can team members freely speak and act without feeling threatened?
- *Inclusion:* Team members need to be allowed equal opportunities to participate. Rank is not important inside the team. Make special efforts to include new, quiet members in the discussion.
- *Appropriate level of interdependence:* Is there an appropriate balance between the individuals' needs and the team needs? Is there a proper balance between individual self-esteem and team allegiance?
- *Cohesiveness:* Is there appropriate bonding between members of the team?
- *Trust:* Do team members trust each other and the leader?
- *Conflict resolution:* Does the team have a way to resolve conflict?
- *Influence:* Do team members or the team as a whole have influence over members? If not, there is no way to reward, punish, or work effectively.
- *Accomplishment:* Can the team perform tasks and achieve goals? If not, frustration will build up and lead to conflict.

It is important for the team to establish some guidelines for working together. Guidelines will serve to ameliorate the dissatisfaction stage and are a necessary condition for the resolution stage. The team should begin to develop these guidelines early in the orientation stage. Table 3.3 lists some suggested guidelines that the team could discuss and modify until there is consensus.

TABLE 3.3
Suggested guidelines for an effective team

- We will be as open as possible but will honor the right of privacy.
- Information discussed in the team will remain confidential.
- We will respect differences between individuals.
- We will respect the ideas of others.
- We will be supportive rather than judgmental.
- We will give feedback directly and openly, in a timely fashion. Feedback will be specific and focus on the task and process and not on personalities.
- We will all be contributors to the team.
- We will be diligent in attending team meetings. If an absence is unavoidable, we will promptly notify the team leader.
- When members miss a meeting we will share the responsibility for bringing them up to date.
- We will use our time wisely, starting on time, returning from breaks, and ending our meetings promptly.
- We will keep our focus on our goals, avoiding sidetracking, personality conflicts, and hidden agendas. We will acknowledge problems and deal with them.
- We will not make phone calls or interrupt the team during meetings.
- We will be conscientious in doing assignments between meetings and in adhering to all reasonable schedules.

TEAM SIGNATURES

_____   _____

_____   _____

_____   _____

TABLE 3.4
Different behavioral roles found in groups

Helping roles		Hindering roles
Task roles	**Maintenance roles**	
Initiating: proposing tasks; defining problem	Encouraging	Dominating: asserting authority or superiority
Information or opinion seeking	Harmonizing: attempting to reconcile disagreement	Withdrawing: not talking or contributing
Information or opinion giving	Expressing group feeling	Avoiding: changing the topic; frequently absent
Clarifying	Gate keeping: helping to keep communication channels open	Degrading: putting down others' ideas; joking in barbed way
Summarizing	Compromising	Uncooperative: Side conver-
Consensus testing	Standard setting and testing: checking whether group is satisfied with procedures	sations: whispering and private conversations across the table

People play various roles during a group activity like a team meeting. It should be helpful in your role as team leader or team member to recognize some of the behavior listed briefly in Table 3.4. It is the task of the team leader and facilitator to try to change the hindering behavior and to encourage team members in their various helping roles.

3.5
EFFECTIVE TEAM MEETINGS

Much of the work of teams is accomplished in team meetings. It is in these meetings that the collective talent of the team members is brought to bear on the problem, and in the process, all members of the team "buy in" to its solution. Students who complain about design projects taking too much time often are really expressing their inability to organize their meetings and manage their time effectively.

At the outset it is important to understand that an effective meeting requires planning. This is the responsibility of the person who will lead the meeting. Meetings should begin on time and last for about 90 min, the optimum time to retain all members' concentration. A meeting should have a written agenda, with the name of the designated person to present each topic and an allotted time for discussion of the topic. If the time allocated to a topic proves to be insufficient, it can be extended by the consent of the group, or the topic may be given to a small task group to study further and report back at the next meeting of the team. In setting the agenda, items of greatest urgency should be placed first on the agenda.

The team leader directs but does not control discussion. As each item comes up for discussion on the agenda, the person responsible for that item makes a clear statement of the issue or problem. Discussion begins only when it is clear that every participant understands what is intended to be accomplished regarding that item. One reason for keeping teams small is that every member has an opportunity to contribute to the discussion. Often it is useful to go around the table in a round robin fashion, asking each person for their ideas or solutions, while listing them on a flip chart or blackboard. No criticism or evaluation should be given here, only questions for clarification. Then the ideas are discussed by the group, and a decision is reached. It is important that this be a group process and that an idea become disassociated from the individual who first proposed it.

Decisions made by the team in this way should be consensus decisions. When there is a consensus, people don't just go along with the decision, they invest in it. Arriving at consensus requires that all participants feel that they have had their full say. Try to help team members to avoid the natural tendency to see new ideas in a negative light. However, if there is a sincere and persuasive negative objector, try to understand their real objections. Often they have important substance, but they are not expressed in a way that they can be easily understood. It is the responsibility of the leader to keep summing up for the group the areas of agreement. As discussion advances, the area of agreement should widen. Eventually you come to a point where problems and disagreement seem to melt away, and people begin to realize that they are approaching a decision that is acceptable to all.

3.5.1 Simple Rules for Meeting Success

1. Pick a regular meeting location and try not to change it.
2. Pick a meeting location that: *(a)* is agreeable and accessible to all (unless your team is trying to "get away"), *(b)* has breathing room when there is full attendance plus a guest or two, *(c)* has a pad or easel in the room, *(d)* isn't too hot, too cold, or too close to noisy distractions.
3. Regular meeting times are not as important as confirming the time of meetings. Once a meeting time has been selected, confirm it immediately in writing (e-mail or memo). Remain flexible on selecting meeting length and frequency. Shape the time that the team spends together around the needs of the work to be accomplished.
4. Send an e-mail reminder to team members just before the first of several meetings.
5. If you send materials out in advance of a meeting, bring extra copies just in case people forget to bring theirs, or it did not arrive. Do not send out agendas or reading materials in advance unless you give people at least four business days to look things over.
6. Start on time, or no later than 5 to 7 min from the stated starting time.
7. Pass out an agenda at the beginning of the meeting and get the team's concurrence to the agenda. Start every meeting with "what are we trying to accomplish today?"
8. Rotate the responsibility for writing meeting summaries of each meeting. The summaries should document: *(a)* when did the team meet, *(b)* what were the issues discussed (in outline form), *(c)* decisions, agreements, or apparent consensus on issues, *(d)* next meeting date and time, *(e)* "homework" for next meeting. In general, meeting summaries should not exceed one page, unless you are attaching results from group brainstorming, lists of issues, ideas, etc. Meeting summaries should be distributed by the assigned recorder within 48 h of the meeting.

9. Notice members who come late, leave early, or miss meetings. Ask if the meeting time is inconvenient or competing demands are keeping them from meetings. Ask if the team sponsor could help by talking with their supervisor.

10. Observe team members who are not speaking. Near the end of the discussion, ask them directly for their opinion on an issue. Consult them after the meeting to be sure that they are comfortable with the team and discussion.

11. Occasionally use meeting evaluations (perhaps every second or third meeting) to gather anonymous feedback on how the group is working together. Meeting evaluations should be turned in to the facilitator, who should summarize the results, distribute a copy of those results to everyone, and lead a brief discussion at the next meeting on reactions to the meeting evaluations and any proposed changes in the meeting format.

12. Do not bring guests or staff support or add team members without seeking the permission of the team.

13. Avoid canceling meetings. If the team leader cannot attend, an interim discussion leader should be designated.

14. End every meeting with an "action check": *(a)* what did we accomplish/agree upon today? *(b)* what will we do at the next meeting? *(c)* what is everyone's "homework," if any, before the next meeting?

15. Follow up with any person who does not attend, especially people who did not give advance notice. Call to update them about the meeting and send them any materials that were passed out at the meeting. Be sure they understand what will take place at the next meeting.

For smooth team operation, it is important to:

- Create a team roster. Ask team members to verify mailing addresses, e-mail addresses, names, and phone numbers of administrative support staff. Include information about the team sponsor. Use e-mail addresses to set up a distribution list for your team.
- Organize important material in team binders. Include the team roster, team charter, essential background information, data, critical articles, etc.

3.6
PROBLEMS WITH TEAMS

A well-functioning team achieves its objectives quickly and efficiently in an environment that induces energy and enthusiasm. However, it would be naive to think that everything will always go well with teams. Therefore, we spend a little time in discussing some of the common problems encountered with teams, and possible solutions. As a starting point, review Table 3.4, for the helping and hindering roles that people play in groups.

The characteristics of a good team member are:

- Respects other team members without question
- Listens carefully to the other team members
- Participates but does not dominate

- Self-confident but not dogmatic
- Knowledgeable in his or her discipline
- Communicates effectively
- Disagrees but with good reason and in good taste

The characteristics of a disruptive team member are:

- Shows lack of respect for others
- Tends to intimidate
- Stimulates confrontation
- Is a dominant personality type
- Talks all the time, but does not listen
- Does not communicate effectively
- Overly critical

Handling a disruptive member requires a skilled team leader or facilitator. What can we do about the team member who dominates the team discussion? Such people often are quick-thinking idea people who make important contributions. One way to deal with this is to acknowledge the important contributions from the person and then shift the discussion to another member by asking them a question. If the domination continues, talk to the member outside of the meeting.

Another disruptive type is the member who is overly critical and constantly objects to point after point. If this type of behavior is allowed to go on, it will destroy the spirit of openness and trust that is vital for a good team performance. This behavior is harder to control. The leader should continually insist that the comments be restated to be more positive, and if the offender can't or won't do this, then the leader should do it. Again, a strong talk outside of the meeting to point out the destructive nature of the behavior is called for, and if there is no improvement, then this member should be asked to leave the team.

A less disruptive type is the person who obstinately disagrees with some point. If this is based on information that the member is sharing with the team, then it is a good part of the process. However, if the disagreement becomes focused on personalities or an unwillingness to reach consensus, then it becomes disruptive behavior. To combat this, ask members to summarize the position they disagree with, to be sure they understand the group's position. Then, ask them to make positive recommendations to see whether there is an area of agreement. If these steps fail, then change the subject and move on, returning to the subject another time.

A common team problem occurs when the team strays too far from the topic. This happens when the leader is not paying strict attention and suddenly finds the team "out in left field." The team can be brought back by asking whether the current discussion is leading to the agreed-upon objective, as guided by the agenda. The leader should introduce new material into the discussion that is more closely related to the objective. The literature is replete with additional suggestions on how to handle problem situations in teams.[1]

---

1. R. Barra, "Tips and Techniques for Team Effectiveness," Barra International, New Oxford, PA, 1987, pp. 60–67; D. Harrington-Mackin, "The Team Building Tool Kit," American Management Association, New York, 1994.

3.7
PROBLEM SOLVING TOOLS

In this section we present some common problem-solving tools that are useful in any problem situation, whether as part of your overall design project or in any other business situation—as in trying to identify new sources of income for the student ASME chapter. These tools are especially well suited for problem solving by teams. They have a strong element of common sense and do not require sophisticated mathematics, so they can be learned and practiced by any group of educated people. They are easy to learn, but a bit tricky to learn to use with real expertise. These tools have been codified within the discipline called *total quality management*.[1]

Many strategies for problem solving have been proposed. The one that we have used and found effective is a simple three-phase process.[2]

- Problem definition
- Cause finding
- Solution finding and implementation

Table 3.5 lists the tools which are most applicable in each phase of the problem-solving process. Most are described below in a long exercise that illustrates their use. A few are found in other sections of this text.

Having read Chap. 2, it will come as no surprise that we view problem definition as the critical phase in any problem situation. A problem can be defined as the difference between a current state and a more desirable state. Often the problem is posed by management or the team sponsor, but until the team redefines it for itself, the problem has not been defined. The problem should be based on data, which may reside in the reports of previous studies, or in surveys that the team undertakes to define the problem. In working toward an acceptable problem definition, the team uses *brainstorming* and the *affinity diagram*. The process by which this is accomplished within a team is called the *nominal group technique*. The outcome of the problem-definition stage is a well-crafted problem statement.

The objective of the cause-finding stage is to identify all of the possible causes of the problem and to narrow them down to the most probable *root causes*. This phase starts with the gathering of data and analyzing the data with simple statistical tools. The first step in data analysis is the creation of a *check sheet* in which data is recorded by classifications. Numeric data may lend itself to the construction of a histogram, while a Pareto chart or simple bar chart may suffice for other situations. Run charts may show correlation with time, and scatter diagrams show correlation with critical parameters. Once the problem is understood with data the *cause-and-effect diagram*

---

1. J. W. Wesner, J. M. Hiatt, and D. C. Trimble, "Winning with Quality: Applying Quality Principles in Product Development," Addison-Wesley, Reading, MA, 1995; C. C. Pegels, "Total Quality Management," Boyd & Fraser, Danvers, MA, 1995; W. J. Kolarik, "Creating Quality," McGraw-Hill, New York, 1995; S. Shiba, A. Graham, and D. Walden, "A New American TQM," Productivity Press, Portland, OR, 1993.
2. Ralph Barra, "Tips and Techniques for Team Effectiveness," Barra International, PO Box 325, New Oxford, PA.

TABLE 3.5
Problem-solving tools

Problem definition	Cause finding	Solution planning and implementation
Brainstorming	*Gathering data*	Brainstorming
Affinity diagram	Interviews	How-how diagram
Nominal group technique	Focus groups (see Sec. 2.3)	Concept selection
	Surveys	method (see Sec. 5.9)
	Analyzing data	Force field analysis
	Check sheet	Implementation plan
	Histogram (see Sec. 10.4)	
	Search for root causes	
	Cause-and-effect diagram	
	Why-why diagram	
	Interrelationship digraph	

and the *why-why diagram* are effective tools for identifying possible causes of the problem. The *interrelationship digraph* is a useful tool for identifying root causes.

With the root causes identified, the objective of the solution-finding phase is to generate as many ideas as possible as to how to eliminate the root causes. Brainstorming clearly plays a role, but this is organized with a *how-how diagram*. With solutions identified, the pros and cons of a strategy for implementing them is identified with *force field analysis*. Finally, the specific steps required to implement the solution are identified and written into an *implementation plan*. Then, as a last step, the implementation plan is presented to the team sponsor.

We have outlined briefly a problem-solving strategy that utilizes a number of tools that are often associated with total quality management[1] (TQM). These tools are described below within the context of a single problem.

> **EXAMPLE.** The problem-solving methodology and tools listed in Table 3.5 are presented through a long example. First we describe the tool and then illustrate it with a continuing example.

Problem Definition

A group of engineering honors students[2] was concerned that more engineering seniors were not availing themselves of the opportunity to do a senior research project. All engineering departments listed this as a course option, but only about 5 percent of the students chose this option. To properly define the problem, the team brainstormed around the question "Why do so few senior engineering students choose to do a research project?"

---

1. M. Brassard and D. Ritter, "The Memory Jogger™II, A Pocket Guide of Tools for Continuous Improvement," GOAL/QCP, Methuen, MA, 1994; N. R. Tague, "The Quality Toolbox," ASQC Quality Press, Milwaukee, WI, 1995.
2. The team of students making this study in 1994 was Brian Gearing, Judy Goldman, Gebran Krikor, and Charnchai Pluempitiwiriyawej. The results of the team's study have been modified appreciably by the author.

Brainstorming. Brainstorming is a group technique for generating ideas in a non-threatening, uninhibiting atmosphere. It is a group activity in which the collective creativity of the group is tapped and enhanced. The objective of brainstorming is to generate the greatest number of alternative ideas from the uninhibited responses of the group. Brainstorming is most effective when it is applied to specific rather than general problems. It is frequently used in the problem-definition phase and solution-finding phase of problem solving.

There are four fundamental brainstorming principles.

1. *Criticism is not allowed.* Any attempt to analyze, reject, or evaluate ideas is postponed until after the brainstorming session. The idea is to create a supportive environment for free-flowing ideas.
2. *Ideas brought forth should be picked up by the other people present.* Individuals should focus only on the positive aspects of ideas presented by others. The group should attempt to create chains of mutual associations that result in a final idea that no one has generated alone. All output of a brainstorming session is to be considered a group result.
3. *Participants should divulge all ideas entering their minds without any constraint.* All members of the group should agree at the outset that a seemingly wild and unrealistic idea may contain an essential element of the ultimate solution.
4. *A key objective is to provide as many ideas as possible within a relatively short time.* It is not unusual for a group to generate 20 to 30 ideas in 1/2 hour of brainstorming. Obviously, to achieve that output the ideas are described only roughly and without details.

There are some generalized questions that have proved helpful. By posing them to yourself or to the group during a brainstorming session, you can stimulate the flow of ideas.

Combinations: What new ideas can arise from combining purposes or functions?
Substitution: What else? Who else? What other place? What other time?
Modification: What to add? What to subtract? Change color, material, motion, shape?
Elimination: Is it necessary?
Reverse: What would happen if we turn it backward? Turn it upside down? Inside out? Oppositely?
Other use: Is there a new way to use it?

A brainstorming session must have a facilitator to control the group and to record the ideas. Write down the ideas verbatim on a flip chart or blackboard. Large Post-it notes are good because they can be used in subsequent phases of problem solving without imposing a need for transcribing. Start with a clear, specific written statement of the problem. Allow a few minutes for members to collect their thoughts, and then begin. Go around the group, in turn, asking for ideas. Anyone may pass, but all should be encouraged to contribute. Build on (piggyback on) the ideas of others. Encourage creative, wild, or seemingly ridiculous notions. There is no questioning, discussion, or criticism of ideas. Generally the ideas build slowly, reach a point where they flow faster than they can be written down, and then fall off. When the group has exhausted all ideas, stop. After a pause for refreshment, review the list for comprehension by seeking clarification on each idea generated. Go through each idea asking, "Does this idea deserve further consideration?" If not, put a bracket around it but do not cross it off the list. This allows any member of the group to reinstate the idea later.

When the student group brainstormed, they obtained the following results.

Problem: Why do so few engineering seniors do a research project?

Students are too busy.

Professors do not talk up research opportunity.

They are thinking about getting a job.

They are thinking about getting married.

They are interviewing for jobs.

They don't know how to select a research topic.

I'm not interested in research. I want to work in manufacturing.

I don't know what research the professors are interested in.

The department does not encourage students to do research.

I am not sure what research entails.

It is hard to make contact with professors.

I have to work part-time.

Pay me and I'll do research.

I think research is boring.

Lab space is hard to find.

Faculty just use undergraduates as a pair of hands.

I don't know any students doing research.

I haven't seen any notices about research opportunities.

Will working in research help me get into grad school?

I would do it if it was required.

An alternative form of brainstorming, called *brainwriting,* is sometimes used when the topic is so controversial or emotionally charged that people will not speak out freely in a group. In brainwriting the team members sit around a table and each person writes four ideas on a sheet of paper. Then she or he places the sheet in the center of the table and selects a sheet from another participant to add four additional ideas. That sheet goes back in the center, and another sheet is chosen. The process ends when no one is generating more ideas. Then the sheets are collected, and the ideas collated and discussed.

Affinity diagram. The affinity diagram identifies the inherent similarity between items. It is used to organize ideas, facts, and opinions into natural groupings. In Sec. 2.3 we used the affinity diagram to organize the questions in the customer requirement survey. There we pointed out that a way to do this was to record the ideas on Post-it notes or file cards. Next, each idea is "scrubbed," i.e., each person explains what they wrote on each card so that each team member understands it the same. This often identifies more than one card with the same thought, or reveals cards that have more than one idea on them. If this happens, additional cards are made up. Then the notes or cards are sorted into loosely related groupings. If an idea keeps being moved between two groups because of disagreement as to where it belongs, make a duplicate and put it in both groups. Also, create a group called "Other" for ideas that do not seem to fall in any of the other categories.

As the team becomes more comfortable with the organization, create a header card that broadly describes the content of the group. This often shows that an idea has been put in the incorrect group. This is a time when discussion is allowed, and people may be called upon to defend their idea or where it is placed. When we do this for the brainstorming exercise, we get:

Time constraints
　　Students are too busy.
　　They are interviewing for jobs.
　　I have to work part-time.
Faculty issues
　　Professors don't talk up research opportunities.
　　The department does not encourage students to do research.
　　It is hard to make contact with professors.
　　Faculty just use undergraduates as a pair of hands.
　　I would do it if it was required.
Lack of interest
　　They are thinking about getting a job.
　　[They are thinking about getting married.]
　　I'm not interested in research. I want to work in manufacturing.
　　[Pay me and I'll do research.]
　　I think research is boring.
　　I would do it if it was required.
Lack of information
　　They don't know how to select a research topic.
　　I don't know what research the professors are interested in.
　　I'm not sure what research entails.
　　I don't know any students doing research.
　　I haven't seen any notices about research opportunities.
　　Will working in research help me get into graduate school?
Other
　　Lab space is hard to find.

Note that in the discussion a few of the ideas have been bracketed and removed from active consideration.

Nominal group technique (NGT). The nominal group technique (NGT) is a method of group idea generation and decision making. Often it starts with silent brainstorming (brainwriting) to generate the ideas. The use of the term "nominal" in this method comes from the fact that it often starts out with a nominal, i.e., silent and independent idea generation, group activity, and as we shall see, independent evaluation by each team member.

If the number of choices generated by brainstorming is large, it may be useful to employ some *list reduction* methods. Start with the entire list of ideas displayed so that everyone can see them. For each item ask the question, "Should this item continue to be considered?" A simple majority vote keeps the item on the list; otherwise it is marked with brackets. At the end of voting, any item marked with brackets can be put back on the list by a single team member. Next, each idea is compared with all others, in a pairwise fashion, to decide whether they are different ideas. If all team members feel they are essentially the same, then the ideas are combined with a new wording.

The last step of the NGT involves decision making, with the members of the team acting independently and anonymously. If the number of choices is relatively small, then each person can *rank order* the choices. For example, if there are five choices, A, B, C, D, E, each person would associate a value of 1 to 5 to each choice, where 5 is best. The ranking for all members of the team would be combined, and the choice with the highest score would be the team's first choice. When the number of choices is large, e.g., 20, it becomes difficult to rank order so many items. Here, the "one-half plus one" approach is often used. The team is asked to pick the top 11 items $(20/2)+1$ in rank order. Again, the ranking of each team member is combined to arrive at the overall team decision.

A variation on decision making by ranking is rating by *multivoting*. Each team member receives a number of votes, usually about one-third of the total number of choices. You can distribute these votes among as many or as few choices as you wish. Often the voting is done by giving each team member the appropriate number of colored sticky dots, and the voting is done by going to the flip chart and pasting them beside your choice(s). Multivoting usually proceeds in stages. In the first round those choices with only a few votes are eliminated. The number of votes per member is adjusted, and a second round of voting is held. The process is repeated until a clear favorite emerges. If the list is reduced to only a few choices with no clear favorite, then the multivoting process should stop, and the team should discuss their options and make a decision by ranking.

The advantage of the NGT is that team members with differing styles of providing input are treated equally because the process imposes the same format requirement on each member. Strong personalities do not unduly influence the outcome. The volume of the loudmouth is turned down while the soft-spoken voice is more clearly heard.

The student team clarified their understanding of the problem by using the NGT to eliminate some extraneous ideas about the low student participation in research projects. Using the affinity diagram as a guide, they carried out silent brainstorming to arrive at the ideas in the following table.

Ideas	Brian	Judy	Gebran	Charn	Total
A. Lack of readily available information about research topics	2	3	1	4	10
B. Lack of understanding of what it means to do research	4	4		1	9
C. Time constraints			4		4
D. No strong tradition of undergraduate research					0
E. Lack of mandatory research course	1				1
F. Lack of student interest		1	2	3	6
G. Lack of incentives	3	2	3	2	10

Using ranking by "half plus one" the students concluded that ideas A, B, and G were very close in terms of contributing to the low participation in research projects. (Note that straight ranking of seven ideas would have been perfectly feasible.) They carried out a second round of ranking with the results given in the table below.

Ideas	Brian	Judy	Gebran	Charn	Total
A. Lack of readily available information about research topics	2	1	1	2	6
B. Lack of understanding of what it means to do research	3	3	3	3	12
C. Lack of incentives	1	2	2	1	6

As a result of a second round of ranking, the team of four students formed the tentative impression that a lack of understanding on the part of undergraduates about what it means to do research is a strong contributor to the low participation by students in research projects. However, they realized that they were but four honors students, whose ideas might be at variance with a wider group of engineering students. They realized that a larger database was needed as they went into the cause-finding stage of problem solving.

Cause finding

Pareto chart. As a first step in data collection the students prepared a survey of what undergraduate students thought about research. They asked whether they were interested in doing research, whether they were currently doing research, and asked them to give an importance ranking for the seven possible causes shown in the above table, with idea D omitted. A very similar survey was given to faculty.

The results of the survey are best displayed by a *Pareto chart.* This is a bar chart used to prioritize causes or issues, in which the cause with the highest frequency of occurrence is placed at the left, followed by the cause with the next frequency of occurrence, and so on. It is based on the Pareto principle, which states that a few causes account for most of the problems, while many other causes are relatively unimportant. This is often stated as the *80/20 rule,* that roughly 80 percent of the problem is caused by only 20 percent of the causes—or 80 percent of the sales—come from 20 percent of the customers—or 80 percent of the tax income comes from 20 percent of the taxpayers, etc. A Pareto chart is a way of analyzing the data that *identifies the vital few in contrast to the trivial many.*

Of the 75 surveys received from undergraduate students, a surprising 93 percent said they were interested in doing a research project, while 79 percent felt there was a lack of undergraduate involvement in research. The Pareto chart for the student ranking of the causes why they do not do research is shown in Fig. 3.1. Lack of understanding of what it means to do research has moved to second place, to be replaced in first place by "lack of information about research topics." However, if one thinks about these results they would conclude that "no mandatory research course" is really a subset of "lack of understanding about research," so that this remains the number one cause of the problem. It is interesting that the Pareto chart for the faculty surveys showed lack of facilities and funding, and lack of incentives, in the one/two position.

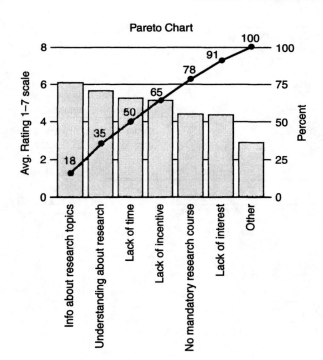

FIGURE 3.1
Pareto chart for average rating of reasons why undergraduate students do not do research projects. Based on survey of students with 75 responses.

Otherwise the order of causes of the problem was about the same. Referring again to Fig. 3.1, note that this contains another piece of information in addition to relative importance. Plotted along the right axis is the cumulative percent of responses. We note that the first five categories (first four when the above correction is made) contain 80 percent of the responses.

Cause-and-effect diagram. The cause-and-effect diagram, also called the fishbone diagram (after its appearance), or the Ishikawa diagram (after its originator), is a powerful graphical way of identifying the factors that cause a problem. It is used after the team has collected data about possible causes of the problem. It is often used in conjunction with brainstorming to collect and organize all possible causes and converge on the most probable root causes of the problem.

Constructing a cause-and-effect diagram starts with writing a clear statement of the problem (effect) and placing it in a box to the right of the diagram. Then the backbone of the "fish" is drawn horizontally out from this box. The main categories of causes, "ribs of the fish," are drawn at an angle to the backbone, and labeled at the ends. These may be categories specific to the problem, or more generic categories such as *methods, machines* (equipment), *materials,* and *people* for a problem dealing with a production process, and *policies, procedures, plant,* and *people* for a service-related process. Ask the team, "What causes this?" and record the cause, not the symptom, along one of the ribs. Dig deeper, and ask what causes the cause you just recorded, so the branches develop subbranches and the whole chart begins to look like the bones of a fish. In recording ideas from the brainstorming session, be succinct but use problem-oriented statements to convey the sense of the problem. As the diagram builds up, look for root causes. One way to identify root causes is to look for causes

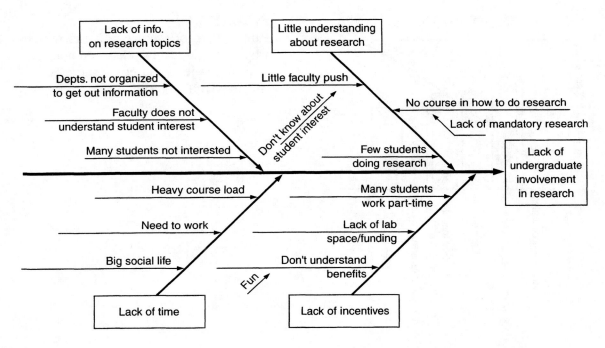

FIGURE 3.2
Cause-and-effect diagram for lack of undergraduate student involvement in research.

that appear frequently within or across categories. Possible root causes are circled on the chart, and the team discusses them and may vote on them. Every attempt is made to use data to verify root causes.

Figure 3.2 shows the cause-and-effect diagram generated by the students to understand the causes for the low student involvement in research. We note that time pressures caused by heavy course loads and necessity to work part-time are one possible root cause, while others center around the lack of understanding of students about what it means to do research and the lack of appreciation by faculty of student interest in doing research.

Why-why diagram. To delve deeper into root causes, we turn to the why-why diagram. This is a tree diagram, which starts with the basic problem and asks "Why does this problem exist?" in order to develop a tree with a few main branches and several smaller branches. The team continues to grow the tree by repeatedly asking "why" until patterns begin to show up. Root causes are identified by causes that begin to repeat themselves on several branches of the why-why tree.

The Pareto chart, when reinterpreted, shows that student lack of understanding about research was the most important cause of low student participation in research. The cause-and-effect diagram also shows this as a possible root cause. To dig deeper we build the why-why diagram shown in Figure 3.3. This begins with the clear statement of the problem. The lack of understanding about research on the part of the undergraduates is two-sided: the faculty don't communicate with the students about opportunities, and the students don't show initiative to find out about it. The team, in asking why, came up with three substantial reasons. Again, they asked why, about

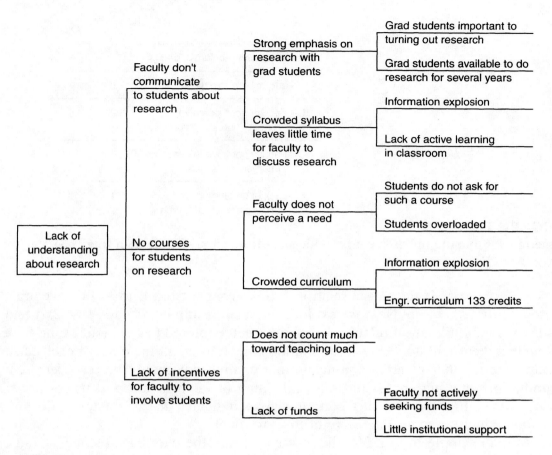

FIGURE 3.3
Why-why diagram for lack of student understanding about research.

each of these three causes, and asking why yet a third time builds up a tree of causes. At this stage we begin to see patterns of causes appearing in different branches of the tree—a sign that these are possible root causes. These are:

- Students and curriculum are overloaded.
- The information explosion is a major cause of the above.
- The faculty don't perceive a need to provide information about research.
- The faculty perceive a low student interest in doing research.
- A lack of resources funding and space limits faculty involvement in undergraduate research.

Narrowing down this set of causes to find the root cause is the job of the next tool.

Interrelationship digraph This is a tool that explores the cause-and-effect relationships among issues and identifies the root causes. The major causes (from 4 to 10) identified by the cause-and-effect diagram are laid out in a large circular pattern (Fig. 3.4). The cause and influence relationships are identified by the team between each cause or factor in turn. Starting with A (chosen at random) we ask whether a causal relationship exists between A and B, and if so, whether the direction is stronger from

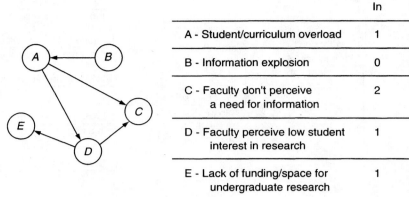

	In	Out
A - Student/curriculum overload	1	2
B - Information explosion	0	1
C - Faculty don't perceive a need for information	2	0
D - Faculty perceive low student interest in research	1	2
E - Lack of funding/space for undergraduate research	1	0

FIGURE 3.4
Interrelationship digraph to identify root causes from why-why diagram (Fig. 3.3).

A to B or B to A. If the causal relationship is stronger from B to A, then we draw an arrow in that direction. Next we explore the relationship between A and C, A and D, etc., in turn, until causal relationships have been explored between all of the factors. Note that there will not be a causal relationship between all factors. For each cause or factor, the number of arrows going in and coming out should be recorded. A high number of outgoing arrows indicates the cause or factor is a root cause or driver. A factor with a high number of incoming arrows indicates that it is a key indicator and should be monitored as a measure of improvement.

In the example in Fig. 3.4, the root causes are the overloaded students and curriculum, and the fact that the faculty perceive that there is a low undergraduate student interest in doing research. The key input is that the faculty do not perceive a need to supply information on research to the undergraduates. Solutions to the problem should then focus on ways of reducing student overload and developing a better understanding of the student interest in doing research.

Solution planning and implementation

While this is the third of three phases, it does not consume one-third of the time in the problem-solving process. This is because, having identified the true problem and the root causes, we are most of the way home to a solution. The objective of solution finding is to generate as many ideas as possible on "how" to eliminate the root causes and to converge on the best solution. To do this we first employ brainstorming and then use multivoting or other evaluation methods to arrive at the best solution. The concept-selection method and other evaluation methods are discussed in Sec. 5.9.

How-how diagram. A technique that is useful for exposing gaps in the causal chain of action is the how-how diagram.[1] Like the why-why diagram, the how-how diagram is a tree diagram, but it starts with a proposed solution and asks the question "How do we do that?" The how-how diagram is best used after brainstorming has generated a set of solutions and an evaluation method has narrowed them to a small set.

---

1. R. Barra, op. cit.

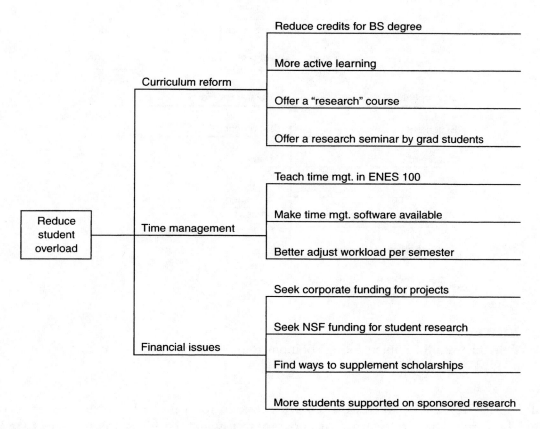

FIGURE 3.5
How-how diagram for problem of reducing student overload, so more students will be able to engage in research projects.

A how-how diagram is constructed for the question "How can we reduce the overload on students?" Brainstorming and multivoting had shown the main issues to be:

- Curriculum reform
- Student time management
- Student and faculty financial issues

Specific solutions that would lead to improvements in each of these areas are recorded in Fig. 3.5.

Force field analysis. Force field analysis is a technique that identifies those forces that both help (drive) and hinder (restrain) the implementation of the solution of a problem. In effect, it is a chart of the pros and cons of a solution, and as such, it helps in developing strategies for implementation of the solution. This forces team members to think together about all the aspects of making the desired change a permanent change, and it encourages honest reflection on the root causes of the problem and its solution. The first step in constructing the force field diagram (Fig. 3.6) is to draw a large T on a flip chart. At the top of the T, write a description of the problem that is being addressed. To the far right of the T, write a description of the ideal solution that we would like to achieve. Participants then list forces (internal and external)

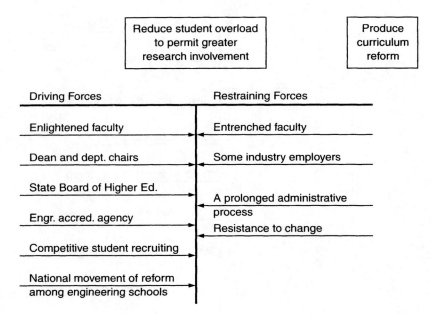

FIGURE 3.6
Force field diagram for implementing solutions to reducing student overload.

that are driving the organization toward the solution on the left side of the vertical line. The forces that are restraining movement toward the ideal solution are listed on the right side of the vertical line. Using a consensus voting method, prioritize the driving forces that should be strengthened to achieve the most movement toward the ideal solution state. Also, identify the restraining forces that would allow the most movement toward the goal if they were removed. This last step is important, because change is more often achieved by removing barriers than by simply pushing the positive factors for change.

Figure 3.6 shows that the key to achieving the needed curriculum reform is to bring aboard some recalcitrant faculty, with help from the dean and departmental chairs. The change process should be expected to be administratively protracted, but doable.

Implementation plan. The problem-solving process should end with the development of specific actions to implement the solution. In doing this, think hard about maximizing the driving forces and minimizing the restraining forces listed in Fig. 3.6. The implementation plan takes the specific actions listed on the how-how diagram and lists the specific steps, in order, that must be taken. It also assigns responsibility to each task, and gives a required completion date. The implementation plan also gives an estimate of the resources (money, people, facilities, material) required to carry out the solution. In addition, it prescribes what level of review and frequency of review of the problem implementation will be followed. A final, but a very important part of the plan, is to list the metrics that will measure a successful completion of the plan.

The team working to increase undergraduate student participation in research evaluated the three major issues for "reduction of student overload" in the how-how

IMPLEMENTATION PLAN

Date: 8/10/00

PROBLEM STATEMENT: Increase the undergraduate student participation in research.

PROPOSED SOLUTION: Create an action team of faculty and students within the college to produce major curriculum reform, to include reduction of credits for the BS degree from 133 to 123 credits, more teaching by active learning, and more opportunity for undergraduate students to do research.

SPECIFIC STEPS:

	Responsibility	Completion date
1. Create curriculum reform action team	Dean	9/30/00
2. Discuss issues with Faculty Council/Dept. Chairs	Dean	10/30/00
3. Hold discussion with dept. faculty	Team	11/15/00
4. Discuss with College Industrial Advisory Council	Dean/Team	11/26/00
5. Discuss with Student Council	Team	11/30/00
6. Day of learning about active learning	Team	1/15/01
7. Dept. curriculum committees begin work	Dept. Chairs	1/30/01
8. Teach "research course" as honors seminar	Team	5/15/01
9. Organize "research seminar," taught by grad students	Team	5/15/01
10. Preliminary reports by dept. curriculum committees	Dean/Team	6/2/01
11. Fine-tuning of curriculum changes	Curric. Com.	9/15/01
12. Faculty votes on curriculum	Dept. Chairs	10/15/01
13. Submittal of curriculum to Univ. Senate	Dean	11/15/01
14. Vote on curriculum by Univ. Senate		2/20/02
15. Implementation of new curriculum	Dean/Chairs	9/1/02

RESOURCES REQUIRED

Budget: $15,000. Speakers for Day of Learning

People: None additional; redirection of priorities is needed.

Facilities: Reserve Dean's Conference Room, each month, 1st and 3rd Wed, 3-5 pm.

Materials: covered in budget above.

REVIEWS REQUIRED

Monthly meeting between team leader and Dean.

MEASURES OF SUCCESSFUL PROJECT ACHIEVEMENT

Reduction in credits for BS degree from 133 to 123 credits.

Increase in number of undergraduates doing research project from 8% to 20%.

Increase in number of engineering students graduating in 4 years.

Increase in number of undergraduates going to graduate school.

FIGURE 3.7

Implementation plan for creating curriculum reform.

diagram (Fig. 3.5). They decided that curriculum reform and financial issues were of equal importance, with time management of lesser importance. The implementation plan for the issue of curriculum reform is shown in Fig. 3.7. A similar plan dealing with financial issues would also be developed. It is important to realize that close communication with the team sponsor, or the manager responsible for the problem solution, is needed to avoid overstepping the limits of authority.

Epilogue. This was not just an isolated student exercise. Over the next 3 years the number of credits for a BS degree was reduced from 133 to 122 credits in all engineering programs. Most of them adopted active learning modes of instruction. A major corporate grant was received to support undergraduate student projects and many faculty included undergraduates in their research proposals. The level of student participation in research projects doubled.

Plan-do-check-act. The plan-do-check-act (PDCA) cycle is a basic concept of TQM. Its origin goes back to Walter Shewhart, an early pioneer of statistical quality control. The idea behind PDCA is that once a solution is arrived at we try it out in a small way to see how it works. This is the *do* stage. Everything that preceded it in problem solving is the *plan* stage. In the *do* stage we collect data to compare with the preexisting situation. In the *check* stage we compare the results with the new solution with the old conditions (baseline data) to determine whether the change has produced the intended improvement. This is an important yet subtle point. Much problem solving neglects this check and assumes that because considerable thought and effort has gone into finding a solution, it will produce the intended improvement. If, indeed, the change is positive, then we *act* to standardize the change in appropriate policies and procedures. If the change is not positive or if it is not as great as we need, then we return to the *plan* stage. The PDCA cycle is a continuous process. In cases where the change "checked out" and we act to implement the change, we are never satisfied with the result. Depending upon priorities and time we revisit the problem topic to search for even better performance in the spirit of continuous improvement.

3.8
TIME MANAGEMENT

Time is an invaluable and irreplaceable commodity. You will never recover the hour you squandered last Tuesday. All surveys of young engineers making an adjustment to the world of work point to personal time management as an area that requires increased attention. The chief difference between time management in college and as a practicing engineer is that time management in the world of work is less repetitive and predictable than when you are in college. For instance, you are not always doing the same thing at the same time of the day, as you do when you are taking classes as a college student. If you have not done so, you need to develop a personal time management system that is compatible with the more erratic time dimension of professional practice. Remember, effectiveness is doing the right things, but efficiency is doing those things the right way, in the shortest possible time.

An effective time management system is vital to help you focus on your long-term and short-term goals. It helps you decipher urgent tasks from important tasks. It is the only means of gaining free time for yourself. Each of you will have to work out a time management system for yourself. The following are some time-tested points to achieve it:

- Start with written goals of what you want to accomplish for the year and for the month.
- Next find out where you spend your time. Start by keeping a log of how you spend your time for a period of at least 1 week, divided into 30-min increments. Classify each activity into one of four categories: (1) important and urgent; (2) important but

not urgent; (3) urgent but not important; and (4) not important and not urgent. From this study you should identify things you are spending time on that you should not be doing. Also, this study should get you in the habit of prioritizing the tasks you have to do, and focusing on the important and urgent items.

- Make a written plan for each day, with the tasks you want to accomplish in priority order. Do this on an 8 1/2 by 11 sheet of paper, not on a lot of little notes to yourself. You may decide to invest in a paper-based or computer-based personal planning system, but ordinary sheets of paper will get the job done. Be cognizant of the 80/20 rule, that 80 percent of your positive results will come from the vital 20 percent of your activities, the urgent and important.
- Set personal deadlines, in addition to business-imposed deadlines, to inspire action and avoid procrastination.
- Learn to act immediately and constructively. After reading a memo, hanging up from a phone conversation, or talking with a visitor in your office, take a specific action like responding to the memo, scheduling a meeting, or digging out a follow-up correspondence file. When doing paperwork, try to handle each paper no more than once.
- Avoid a cluttered desk and office. This requires a good filing system and perseverance.
- Schedule an entire block of time for a major project. Make sure there are no distractions at this time.
- Identify your best time of day, in terms of energy level and creative activity, and try to schedule your most challenging tasks for that time period.
- Group like tasks, e.g., returning phone calls or writing memos, into periods of common activity for more efficient performance.
- Occasionally make appointments with yourself to reflect on your work habits, and think creatively about the future.

3.9
PLANNING AND SCHEDULING

It is an old business axiom that time is money. Therefore, planning future events and scheduling them so they are accomplished with a minimum of time delay is an important part of the engineering design process. For large construction and production projects, detailed planning and scheduling is a must. Computer-based methods for handling the large volume of information have become commonplace. However, engineering design projects of all magnitudes of scale can profit greatly by applying the simple planning and scheduling techniques discussed in this chapter.

One of the most common criticisms leveled at the young graduate engineer is an overemphasis on technical perfection of the design and not enough concern for completing the design on time and below the estimated cost. Therefore, the planning and scheduling tools presented in this chapter can profitably be applied at the personal level as well as to the more complex engineering project.

In the context of engineering design, *planning* consists of identifying the key activities in a project and ordering them in the sequence in which they should be performed. *Scheduling* consists of putting the plan into the time frame of the calendar.

The major decisions that are made over the life cycle of a project fall into four areas: performance, time, cost, and risk.

Performance: The design must possess an acceptable level of operational capability or the resources expended on it will be wasted. The design process must generate satisfactory specifications to test the performance of prototypes and production units.

Time: In the early phases of a project the emphasis is on accurately estimating the length of time required to accomplish the various tasks and scheduling to ensure that sufficient time is available to complete those tasks. In the production phase the time parameter becomes focused on setting and meeting production rates, and in the operational phase it focuses on reliability, maintenance, and resupply.

Cost: The importance of cost in determining what is feasible in an engineering design has been emphasized in earlier chapters. Keeping costs and resources within approved limits is one of the chief functions of the project manager.

Risk: Risks are inherent in anything new. Acceptable levels of risk must be established for the parameters of performance, time, and cost, and they must be monitored throughout the project. The subject of risk is considered in detail in Chap. 11.

The first step in developing a plan is to identify the activities that need to be controlled. The usual way to do that is to start with the entire system and identify the 10 or 20 activities that are critical. Then the larger activities are broken down into subactivities, and these in turn are subdivided until you get to tasks performed by single persons. Generally the work breakdown proceeds in a hierarchical fashion from the system to the subassembly to the component to the individual part.

3.9.1 Bar chart

The simplest scheduling tool is the bar, or Gantt, chart (Fig. 3.8). The activities are listed in the vertical direction, and elapsed time is recorded horizontally. This shows clearly the date by which each activity should start and finish, but it does not make clear how the ability to start one activity depends upon the successful completion of other activities.

The dependence of one activity on another can be shown by a network logic diagram like Fig. 3.9. This diagram clearly shows the precedence relations, but it loses the strong relation with time that the bar chart displays.

Note that a *critical path* through the network can be determined. In this case it is the 20 weeks required to traverse the path *a–b–c–d–e–f–g,* and it is shown on the

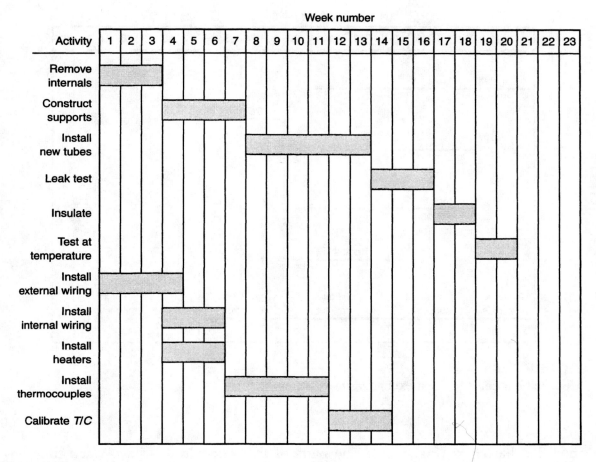

FIGURE 3.8
Bar chart for prototype testing a heat exchanger.

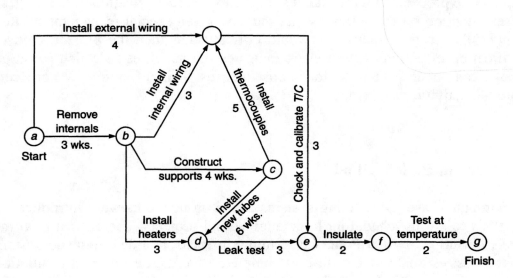

FIGURE 3.9
Network logic diagram for heat exchanger.

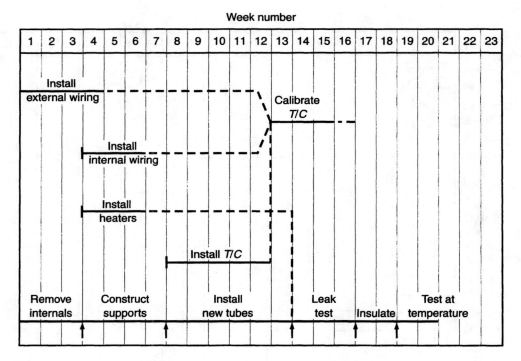

FIGURE 3.10
Modified bar chart for heat exchanger tests.

modified bar chart (Fig. 3.10). The parts of the schedule that have slack time are shown dashed. *Slack* is the time by which an activity can exceed its estimated duration before failure to complete the activity becomes critical. For example, for the activities of installing heaters, there is a 7-week slack before the activities must be completed to proceed with the leak testing. Thus, the identification of the longest path focuses attention on the activities that must be given special management attention, for any delay in those activities would critically lengthen the project. Conversely, identification of activities with slack indicates the activities in which some natural slippage can occur without serious consequences. This, of course, is not license to ignore the activities with slack.

3.9.2 Critical-Path Method

Two computer-based scheduling systems based on networks were introduced in the late 1950s to aid in scheduling large engineering projects. The critical-path method (CPM), developed by Du Pont and Remington Rand, is a deterministic system that uses the best estimate of the time to complete a task. The program evaluation and review technique (PERT), developed for the U.S. Navy, uses probabilistic time estimates. The techniques have much in common. We shall start by considering CPM.

The basic tool of CPM is an arrow network diagram similar to Fig. 3.9. The chief elements of this diagram are:

1. An *activity*—time-consuming effort that is required to perform part of a project. An activity is shown on an arrow diagram by a line with an arrowhead pointing in the direction of progress in completion of the project.
2. An *event*—the end of one activity and the beginning of another. An event is a point of accomplishment and/or decision. A circle is used to designate an event.

There are several logic restrictions to constructing the network diagram.

1. An activity cannot be started until its tail event is reached. Thus, if $\overset{A}{\longrightarrow}\bigcirc\overset{B}{\longrightarrow}$

   activity B cannot begin until activity A has been completed. Similarly, if $\overset{C}{\longrightarrow}\bigcirc\begin{smallmatrix}D\\E\end{smallmatrix}$ activities D and E cannot begin until activity C has been completed.

2. An event cannot be reached until all activities leading to it are complete. If $\begin{smallmatrix}F\\G\end{smallmatrix}\bigcirc\overset{H}{\longrightarrow}$ activities F and G must precede H.

3. Sometimes an event is dependent on another event preceding it, even though the two events are not linked together by an activity. In CPM we record that situation by introducing a dummy activity, denoted $----\blacktriangleright$. A *dummy activity* requires zero time and has zero cost. Consider two examples:

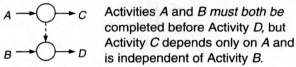 Activities *A* and *B must both be* completed before Activity *D*, but Activity *C* depends only on *A* and is independent of Activity *B*.

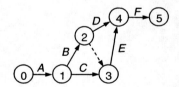 Activity *A* must precede both *B* and *C*. *B* must precede *D* and *E*. *C* must precede *E*. *D* and *E* must precede *F*.

The longest time through the network (the critical path) may be determined by inspection for a relatively simple network like the one in Fig. 3.10, but a methodology for the much more complex problems found in engineering project management must be established. To do so we establish the following parameters.

Earliest start time (ES): The earliest time an activity can begin when all preceding activities are completed as rapidly as possible.

Latest start time (LS): The latest time an activity can be initiated without delaying the minimum completion time for the project.

Earliest finish time (EF): EF = ES+D, where *D* is the duration of each activity.

Latest finish time (LF): LF = LS+D

Total float (TF): The slack between the earliest and latest start times. TF = LS−ES. An activity on the critical path has zero total float.

In CPM the estimate of each activity duration is based on the most likely estimate of time to complete the activity. All durations should be expressed in the same time units, such as days or weeks. The sources of time estimates are records of similar projects, calculations involving the manpower needs, legal restrictions, and technical considerations.

The network diagram in Fig. 3.10 has been redrawn as a CPM network in Fig. 3.11. To facilitate solution with computer methods, the events that occur at the nodes have been numbered serially. The node number at the tail of each activity must be less than that at the head. The ES times are determined by starting at the first node and making a forward pass through the network while adding each activity duration in turn to the ES of the preceding activity. The details are shown in Table 3.6

The LS times are calculated by a reverse procedure. Starting with the last event, a backward pass is made through the network while subtracting the activity duration from the limiting LS at each event. The calculations are detailed in Table 3.7. We note that, for calculating LS, each activity starting from a common event can have a different late start time, whereas all activities starting from the same event had the same early start time.

The chief work is in establishing ES and LS times. Once that is accomplished, the remaining boundary time parameters can be determined by routine operations; see Table 3.8. The critical path is identified by the activities with zero total float.

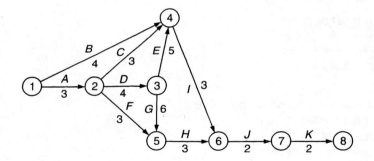

FIGURE 3.11
CPM diagram for heat exchanger project.

TABLE 3.6
Calculation of early start time based on Fig. 3.11

Event	Activity	ES	Comment
1	A, B	0	Conventional to use ES = 0 for the initial event
2	C, D, F	3	$ES_2 = ES_1 + D = 0 + 3 = 3$
3	E, G	7	$ES_3 = ES_2 + D = 7$
4	I	12	At a merge like 4 the largest ES+D of the merging activities is used
5	H	13	$ES_5 = ES_3 + 6 = 13$
6	J	16	$ES_6 = ES_5 + 3 = 16$
7	K	18	
8	—	20	

TABLE 3.7
Calculation of late start times based on Fig. 3.11

Event	Activity	LS	Event	Activity	LS
8	—	20	5-2	F	10
8-7	K	18	4-3	E	8
7-6	J	16	4-2	C	10
6-5	H	13	4-1	B	9
6-4	I	13	3-2	D	3
5-3	G	7	2-1	A	0

TABLE 3.8
Summary of boundary timetable

Activity	Description	D, weeks	ES	LS	EF	LF	TF
A	Remove internals	3	0	0	3	3	0
B	Install external wiring	4	0	9	4	13	9
C	Install internal wiring	3	3	10	6	13	7
D	Construct supports	4	3	3	7	7	0
E	Install thermocouples	5	7	8	12	13	1
F	Install heaters	3	3	10	6	13	7
G	Install new tubes	6	7	7	13	13	0
H	Leak test	3	13	13	16	16	0
I	Check thermocouples	3	12	13	15	16	1
J	Insulate	2	16	16	18	18	0
K	Test prototype at temperature	2	18	18	20	20	0

ES is determined by forward pass through network.
LS is determined by backward pass through network.
EF = ES+D.
LF = LS+D.
TF = LS−ES.

Generally in a CPM problem we are interested in two classes of solutions:

1. The least-cost solution using costs associated with the normal time to complete the activities.
2. The least-time solution in which crash costs are incurred to reduce the time, e.g., by employing overtime, extra workers, or bringing in extra production equipment.

3.9.3 PERT

The program evaluation and review technique (PERT) uses the same ideas as CPM; but instead of using the most likely time estimate, it uses a probabilistic estimate of time for completion of an activity. The designer is asked to make an optimistic time estimate o if everything goes smoothly and a pessimistic time estimate p if everything goes badly. The most likely time m is bracketed between those values. The time estimates are assumed to follow a beta frequency distribution that gives the expected time as

$$t_e = \frac{o + 4m + p}{6} \tag{3.1}$$

The expected time is a mean value that divides the area under the frequency distribution into two equal parts. In PERT the expected time is computed for each activity, and the expected times are used to determine the critical path and the boundary times as illustrated for the CPM technique.

The expected time for each activity also has a standard deviation (see Sec. 10.5), which describes its scatter, given by

$$\sigma \frac{p - o}{6} \tag{3.2}$$

The standard deviation along a path in the PERT network is the square root of the sum of the individual variances for the separate activities along that path.

$$\sigma_{\text{path}} = \sqrt{\Sigma \sigma^2} \tag{3.3}$$

Knowing the variance for each activity permits the calculation of the probability that a certain scheduled event will be completed on schedule. If SS is the scheduled start of a particular event, called a milestone, and ES is the earliest start time for the event, then

$$z = \frac{SS - ES}{\sigma_{\text{path}}} \tag{3.4}$$

where z is the standard normal deviate and represents the area under the standardized normal frequency distribution (see Sec. 10.5). If, for example, $z = 0$, there is a 50 percent probability of completing the event on the scheduled date. If $z = -0.5$, there is a 30 percent probability.

PERT/COST is an attempt to include cost data in the CPM-PERT type of network scheduling program. The original concept involved costs at a very high level of detail, but that has proved very cumbersome because of the need for continual updating, re-estimating, and cost changes due to design changes. In most cases, PERT/COST is operated with costs aggregated to a considerable degree.

Project management software is common for the personal computer and workstation. The three scheduling techniques discussed in this chapter can be found in many software versions in a range of complexity and price. They are often reviewed in computer magazines.

3.10
SUMMARY

This chapter considered methods for making you a more productive engineer. Some of the ideas, time management and scheduling, are aimed at the individual, but most of this chapter deals with helping you work more effectively in teams. Most of what is covered here falls into two categories: attitudes and techniques.

Under attitudes we stress:

- The importance of delivering on your commitments, and of being on time
- The importance of preparation, for a meeting, for a field test, etc.

- The importance of giving and learning from feedback
- The importance of using a structured problem-solving methodology
- The importance of managing your time

With regard to techniques, we have presented information on the following:

Team processes:
- Team guidelines (rules of the road for teams)
- Rules for successful meetings
  Problem-solving tools (TQM):
- Brainstorming
- Affinity diagram
- Nominal group technique
- Multivoting
- Pareto chart
- Cause-and-effect diagram
- Why-why diagram
- Interrelationship digraph
- How-how diagram
- Force field analysis
- Implementation plan
  Scheduling tools:
- Bar chart (Gantt chart)
- Critical path method (CPM)
- Program evaluation and review technique (PERT)

Further information on these tools can be found in the references listed in the Bibliography. Also given there are software packages for applying some of these tools.

BIBLIOGRAPHY

Team Methods

Cleland, D. I.:"Strategic Management of Teams," Wiley, New York, 1996.
Harrington-Mackin, D.: "The Team Building Tool Kit," American Management Association, New York, 1994.
Katzenbach, J. R., and D. K. Smith: "The Wisdom of Teams," HarperBusiness, New York, 1993.
Quick, T. L.: "Successful Team Building," American Management Association, New York, 1992.
Scholtes, P. R., et al.: "The Team Handbook," Joiner Associates, Madison, WI, 1988.

Problem-Solving Tools

Barra, R.: "Tips and Techniques for Team Effectiveness," Barra International, New Oxford, PA, 1987.
Brassard, M., and D. Ritter: "The Memory Jogger™ II," Goal/QPC, Methuen, MA, 1994.
Folger, H. S., and S. E. LeBlanc: "Strategies for Creative Problem Solving," Prentice-Hall, Englewood Cliffs, NJ, 1995.

Ozeki, K., and T. Asaka: "Handbook of Quality Tools: The Japanese Approach," Productivity Press, Inc., Cambridge, MA, 1990.

Tague, N. R.: "The Quality Toolbox," ASQC, Quality Press, Milwaukee, WI, 1995.

Planning and Scheduling

Cleland, D. I., and W. R. King: "Systems Analysis and Project Management," 2d ed., McGraw-Hill, New York, 1975.

Lewis, J. P.: "Mastering Project Management," McGraw-Hill, New York, 1988.

Martin, P., and K. Tate, "Project Management Memory Jogger™," Goal/QPC, Methuen, MA, 1997.

Meredith, D. D., K. W. Wong, P. W. Woodhead, and R. H. Wortman: "Design and Planning of Engineering Systems," 2d ed., Prentice-Hall, Englewood Cliffs, NJ, 1985.

Rosenau, M. D.: "Successful Project Management," 3d ed., Wiley, New York, 1998.

Project Management Software

LOWER-END SOFTWARE PACKAGES

Can schedule tasks in Gantt, update schedules over time. More like an advanced personal planner.

Milestones, Etc. 5.0, KIDAS Software, Austin, TX.
Schedule+, Microsoft Corp., Redmond, WA.

MIDRANGE PACKAGES

Can schedule tasks and manage resources within a fairly large project.

Microsoft Project 98, Microsoft Corp., Redmond, WA.
Project Scheduler 7, Scitor Corp., Menlo Park, CA.
SureTrak Project Manager 2.0, Primavera Systems, Bala Cynwyd, PA.
TurboProject Professional, IMSI, San Rafael, CA.

HIGH-END PACKAGES

Handle larger projects and include resource assignment and leveling, people scheduling and time sheets, interface with financial data.

Primavera Project Planner, Primavera Systems, Bala Cynwyd, PA.
SuperProject 4.0, Computer Associates International, Islandia, NY.

PROBLEMS AND EXERCISES

3.1. For your first meeting as a team do some team building activities to help you get acquainted.

   (a) Ask a series of questions, with each person giving an answer in turn. Start with the first question and go completely around the team, then the next, etc. Typical questions might be: (1) What is your name? (2) What is your major and class?

(3) Where did you grow up or go to school? (4) What do you like best about school? (5) What do you like least about school? (6) What is your hobby? (7) What special skills do you feel you bring to the team? (8) What do you want to get out of the course? (9) What do you want to do upon graduation?

(b) Do a brainstorming exercise to come up with a team name and a team logo.

3.2. Early in the process of forming a team, have a serious discussion to draw up team ground rules. These are rules of agreement about behavior at team meetings and agreement on how team members will give and receive feedback. These are distinct from the rules for an effective meeting discussed in Sec 3.5.

3.3. Teams often find it helpful to create a team charter between the team sponsor and the team. What topics should be covered in the team charter?

3.4. To learn to use the TQM tools described in Sec. 3.7, spend about 4 h total of team time to arrive at a solution for some small problem that is familiar to the students and they feel needs improvement. Look at some aspect of an administrative process in the department or campus. Be alert to use the TQM tools in your design project.

3.5. After about 2 weeks of team meetings, invite a disinterested and knowledgeable person to attend a team meeting as an observer. Ask them to give a critique of what they found. Then invite them back in 2 weeks to see if you have improved your team performance.

3.6. Develop a rating system for effectiveness of team meetings.

3.7. Keep a log of how you spend your time over the next week. Break it down by 30-min intervals.

3.8. The following restrictions exist in a scheduling network. Determine whether the network is correct; and if it is not, draw the correct network.

(a) A precedes C
B precedes E
C precedes D and E

(b) A precedes D and E
B precedes E and F
C precedes F

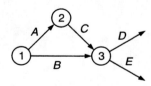

3.9. The development of an electronic widget is expected to follow the following steps.

Activity	Description	Time est., weeks	Preceded by
A	Define customer needs	4	
B	Evaluate competitor's product	3	
C	Define the market	3	
D	Prepare product specs	2	B
E	Produce sales forecast	2	B
F	Survey competitor's marketing methods	1	B
G	Evaluate product vs. customer needs	3	A, D
H	Design and test the product	5	A, B, D
I	Plan marketing activity	4	C, F
J	Gather information on competitor's pricing	2	B, E, G
K	Conduct advertising campaign	2	I
L	Send sales literature to distributors	4	E, G
M	Establish product pricing	3	H, J

Establish the arrow network diagram for this project and determine the critical path by using the CPM technique.

4

GATHERING INFORMATION

4.1
THE INFORMATION PROBLEM

We have already seen in Chap. 2 that the need for information about potential markets can be crucial in a design project. There are many, many other pieces of information that you will need to find and validate quickly. For example, we might need to find the suppliers and costs of fractional-horsepower motors with a certain torque and speed. At a lower level of detail, we would need to know the geometry of the mounting brackets for the motor we select for the design. At a totally different level, we might need to know whether the totally new trade name we created for a new product line infringes on any existing trade names, and further, whether it will cause any cultural problems when pronounced in Spanish, Japanese, and Mandarin Chinese. Clearly, the information needed for an engineering design is more diverse and less readily available than that needed for conducting a research project, for which the published technical literature is the main source of information. We choose to emphasize the importance of the information-gathering step in design by placing this chapter early in this text and in the sequence of design steps (Fig. 4.1).

This chapter gives some suggestions for coping with your information needs. It is not intended to be encyclopedic or contain all the information on how and where to look. The first step you should take is to become familiar with your local information sources. Visit your university or company library and make friends with the librarian. Find out what is available and what your organization is prepared to do to help you with your information needs.

The next thing you should do is develop a personal plan for coping with information. The world technical literature is doubling every 10 to 15 years. That amounts to about 2 million technical papers a year, or a daily output that would fill seven sets of the Encyclopaedia Britannica. This tremendous flood of information aids greatly in the development of new knowledge, but in the process it makes obsolete part of what you already know. To develop a personal plan for information processing is one of the

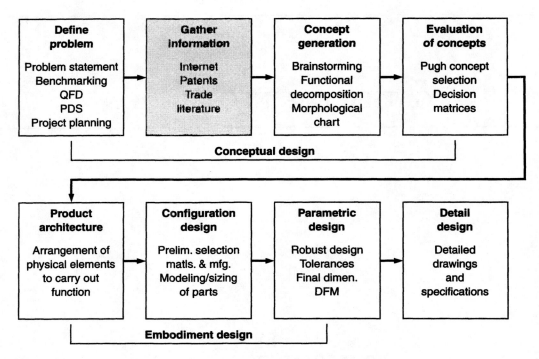

FIGURE 4.1
Steps in design process, showing early placement of the gathering information step.

most effective things you can do to combat your own technological obsolescence. Such a plan begins with the recognition that you cannot leave it entirely to your employer to finance your needs in this area. As a professional, you should be willing to allocate a small portion of your resources, e.g., 1 percent of your net annual salary, for adding to your technical library and your professional growth. This includes the purchase of new textbooks in fields of current or potential interest, specialized monographs, software, membership in professional societies, and subscriptions to technical journals and magazines. In one way or another, you should attend conference and technical meetings where new ideas on subjects related to your interest are discussed.

You should develop your own working files of technical and business information that is important to your work. A good way to do so is to put articles and information you want to have as ready reference into large three-ring binders with page dividers marking off different areas of interest. Material of less current interest may be stored in folders in filing cabinets. A common difficulty, once you start this activity, is compulsive saving. In order that your files will not grow without bound, be selective. Adopt the policy of discarding outdated material when you replace it with newer information. If you are concerned with losing track of possibly useful articles by discarding older material, you might compromise by keeping only the title page, which contains the abstract, and also possibly the last page, which contains the conclusions and references.

To have current awareness of your technical field, you should take a three-pronged approach:[1] (1) read the core journals in your chief area of interest, (2) utilize current awareness services, (3) participate in selective dissemination programs.

---

1. B. E. Holm, "How to Manage Your Information," Reinhold Book Corp., New York, 1968.

Every professional must read enough journals and technical magazines to keep up with the technology in the field and be able to apply the new concepts that have been developed. These journals, which should be read on a monthly basis, should come from three categories:

1. General scientific, technical, and economic (business) news. The monthly magazine of your main professional society would fit here.
2. Trade magazines in your area of interest or business responsibility.
3. Research-oriented journals in your area of interest.

Reading regularly in the above three categories is a major aspect of keeping current in your field. However, for many people this will not cover as wide a spectrum of the published literature as is required. Therefore, secondary current awareness services have been developed. Some of them provide abstracts of articles, others just the titles of articles. The abstract services available in each discipline, e.g., *Engineering Index* and *Metals Abstracts,* are scanned by some serious professionals each month to see what new information has been published. This usually requires spending several hours in the library. *Current Contents: Engineering and Technology* is a weekly publication of the Institute for Scientific Information, Philadelphia, which reproduces the title pages of a large number of engineering publications. A computerized index provides the addresses of authors if you want to write for reprints. The advantage of *Current Contents* is that it is less expensive than a full abstract service, so you can have an individual or shared subscription. Your technical library should have a copy.

Selective dissemination is concerned with sending specific information to the individual who has a need for and interest in it. Many company librarians provide such a service. Researchers in a common field will often develop a "community of interest" and keep each other informed by sharing their papers and ideas. As more and more technical information is put into computer database, it becomes easier to provide selective dissemination.

There is general recognition that engineers as professionals make much less use of the published technical literature than do scientists and other technical professionals. Some of this difference may be due to differences in education, but mostly it is due to a basic difference in how technical information is organized and stored.[1] Almost all major indexing systems index by subjects, i.e., the names of things. This is ideal for the expert concerned with research or analysis, who is very familiar with the vocabulary in a narrow technical field. However, indexing by name is a severe handicap for the design engineer, who is involved in synthesis. The designer, concerned with finding the best way to solve a problem, wants to start the search with the function of what is needed. There is a vast array of devices for attaining those functions, but there is no organized way to help the designer identify the functions by name so they can be uncovered in a literature search. Also, the synthesis-oriented design engineer is concerned with attributes, e.g., higher energy efficiency and lower material cost. Although they frequently are described in technical articles, the attributes very seldom are included in indexing terms.

1. E. J. Breton, *Mech. Eng.,* pp. 54–57, March 1981.

Thus, it is not surprising that a recent study revealed that engineers collect most of their advanced technical information from discussions with vendors, salespeople, consultants, and other engineers. Partly that is because information on new products, the buildings blocks of technology, is poorly handled in the technical literature. A 12-month study[1] of news releases on new products in trade magazines showed that over 65 percent were actually old products or were old products with cosmetic alterations.

4.2
COPYRIGHT AND COPYING

A copyright is the exclusive legal right to publish a tangible expression of literary or artistic work, and it is therefore the right to prevent the unauthorized copying by another of that work. In the United States a copyright is awarded for a period of the life of the copyright holder plus 50 years. It is not necessary to publish a copyright notice for a work to be copyrighted. A copyright comes into existence when one fixes the work in "any tangible medium of expression." Unlike for a patent, with a copyright there is no extensive search to ensure the degree of originality of the work.

A major revision of the copyright law of 1909 went into effect on January 1, 1978. The present copyright law covers original works of authorship that are literary works as well as pictorial, graphic, and sculptural works. Important for engineering design is the fact that the new law is broad enough to cover for the first time written engineering specifications, sketches, drawings, and models.[2] However, there are two important limitations to this coverage. Although plans, drawings, and models are covered under the copyright law, their mechanical or utilitarian aspects are expressly excluded. Thus, the graphic portrayal of a useful object may be copyrighted, but the copyright would not prevent the construction from the portrayal of the useful article that is illustrated.

The other limitation pertains to the fundamental concept of copyright law that one can copyright not an idea, but only its tangible expression. The protection offered the engineer under the new law lies in the ability to restrict the distribution of plans and specifications by restricting physical copying. An engineer who retains ownership of plans and specifications through copyrighting can prevent a client from using them for other than the original, intended use and can require that they be returned after the job is finished.

A major impetus for revising the copyright law was to make the law compatible with the technology of fast, inexpensive copying machines. The new law retains the principle of *fair use* in which an individual has the right to make a single copy of copyrighted material for personal use for the purpose of criticism, comment, news reporting, teaching, scholarship, or research. Copying which does not constitute fair use must pay a royalty fee to the Copyright Clearance Center. While the U.S. Copyright Act does not directly define fair use, it does base it on four factors:[3]

---

1. Ibid.
2. H. K. Schwentz and C. J. Hardy, *Professional Engineer,* pp. 32–33, July 1977.
3. D. V. Radack, *JOM,* February 1996, p. 74.

- The purpose and character of the use—is it of a commercial nature or for nonprofit educational purposes?
- The nature of the copyrighted work—is it a highly creative work or a more routine document?
- The amount of the work used in relation to the copyrighted work as a whole.
- The effect of the use on the potential market value of the copyrighted work. Usually this is the most important of the factors.

4.3
HOW AND WHERE TO FIND IT

The search for information can be performed more efficiently if a little thought and planning are used at the outset. First, be sure you understand the purposes for which the information is being sought. If you are looking for a specific piece of information, e.g., the yield strength of a new alloy or the cost of a miniature ball bearing, you should pursue one set of information sources. However, if your purpose is to become familiar with the state of the art in an area that is new to you, you should follow a different course. Table 4.1, based on a listing by Woodson,[1] shows the many sources of information that are open to you.

TABLE 4.1
Sources of information for engineering design

I. Public sources
   A. Federal departments and agencies (Defense, Commerce, Energy, NASA, etc.)
   B. State and local government (highway department, departments dealing with land use, consumer safety, building codes, etc.)
   C. Libraries—community, university, special
   D. Universities, research institutions, museums
   E. Foreign governments—embassies, commercial attaches
   F. Internet—Much information is free. Some requires fees.

II. Private sources
   A. Nonprofit organizations and services
      1. Professional societies
      2. Trade and labor associations
      3. Membership organizations (motorists, consumers, veterans, etc.)
   B. Profit-oriented organizations
      1. Vendors (include manufacturers, suppliers, financiers). Catalogs, samples, test data, cost data and information on operation, maintenance, servicing and delivery
      2. Other business contacts with manufacturers and competitors
      3. Consultants
   C. Individuals
      1. Direct conversation or correspondence
      2. Personal friends, associates, "friends of friends"
      3. Faculty

1. T. T. Woodson, "Introduction to Engineering Design," chap. 5, McGraw-Hill, New York, 1966.

In reviewing this list, you can divide the sources of information, into (1) people who are paid to assist you, e.g., the company librarian or consultant, (2) people who have a financial interest in helping you, e.g., a potential supplier of equipment for your project, and (3) people who help you out of professional responsibility or friendship.

All suppliers of materials and equipment provide sales brochures, catalogs, technical manuals, etc., that describe features and operation of their products. Usually this information can be obtained at no cost by checking the reader service card that is enclosed in most technical magazines. Much of this information is now available on the Internet. Practicing engineers commonly build up a file of such information. Generally a supplier who has reason to expect a significant order based on your design will most likely provide any technical information about the product that is needed for you to complete your design.

It is only natural to concentrate on searching the published technical literature for the information you need, but don't overlook the resources available among your colleagues. The professional files or notebooks of engineers more experienced than you can be a gold mine of information if you take the trouble to communicate your problem in a proper way. Remember, however, that the flow of information should be a two-way street. Be willing to share what you know, and above all, return the information promptly to the person who lent it to you. The surest way to get shut off is to gain a reputation as a moocher.

In seeking information from sources other than libraries (see Sec. 4.4), a direct approach is best. Whenever possible, use a phone call rather than a letter. A direct dialogue is vastly superior to the written word. However, you may want to follow up your conversation with a letter. Open your conversation by identifying yourself, your organization, the nature of your project, and what it is you need to know. Preplan your questions as much as possible, and stick to the subject of your inquiry. Don't worry about whether the information you seek is confidential information. If it really is confidential, you won't get an answer, but you may get peripheral information that is helpful. Above all, be courteous in your manner and be considerate of the time you are taking from the other person. Some companies employ an outside service that networks technical experts to supply pieces of information.[1]

It may take some detective work to find the person to call for the information. You may find the name of a source in the published literature or in the program from a recent conference you attended. The Yellow Pages in the telephone directory or an Internet search engine are good places to start. For product information, you can start with the general information number that is listed for almost every major corporation or check their homepage on the worldwide web. To locate federal officials, it is helpful to use one of the directory services that maintain up-to-date listings and phone numbers.

It is important to remember that information costs time and money. It is actually possible to acquire too much information in a particular area, far more than is needed to make an intelligent decision. One can consider that each decision in the design process is a balance between the risk of proceeding with what you have versus the cost of gaining more information to minimize the risk.

However, do not underestimate the importance of information gathering or the effort required in searching for information. Many engineers feel that this isn't real

---

1. B. Boardman, *Research Technology Management*, July-August 1995, pp. 12–13.

engineering, but surveys of how design engineers use their time show that they spend about 15 to 20 percent of their time searching for information, a like percent in meetings, and a similar percent writing reports and engaging in other forms of communication. The time spent actually designing is often less than 50 percent of the total effort.

4.4
LIBRARY SOURCES OF INFORMATION

In the preceding section we considered the broad spectrum of information sources and focused mostly on the information that can be obtained in the business world. In this section we shall deal with the type of information that can be obtained from library sources. The library is the most important resource for students and young engineers who wish to develop professional expertise quickly.

A library is a repository of information that is published in the open or unclassified literature. Although the scope of the collection will vary with the size and nature of the library,[1] all technical libraries will have the capability of borrowing books and journals for you or providing, for a fee, copies of needed pages from journals and books. Many technical libraries also carry selected government publications and patents, and company libraries will undoubtedly contain a collection of company technical reports (which ordinarily are not available outside the company).

When you are looking for information in the library you will find a hierarchy of information sources, as shown in Table 4.2. These sources are arranged in increasing order of specificity. Where you enter the hierarchy depends on your own state of knowledge about the subject and the nature of the information you want to obtain. If

TABLE 4.2
Hierarchy of library
information sources

Technical dictionaries

Encyclopedias

Handbooks

Textbooks and monographs

Bibliographies

Indexing and abstract services

Technical and professional journals

Translations

Technical reports

Patents

Catalogs and manufacturers' brochures

---

1. If you do not have a good technical library at your disposal, you can avail yourself via mail of the fine collection of the Engineering Societies Library, now located at the Linda Hall Library, 5109 Cherry Street, Kansas City, MO 64110-2498; (800)-662-1545; e-mail: requests@lhl.lib.mo.us; Internet web page: http://www.lhl.lib.mo.us/.

you are a complete neophyte, it may be necessary to use a technical dictionary and read an encyclopedia article to get a good overview of the subject. If you are quite familiar with the subject, then you may simply want to use an index or abstract service to find pertinent technical articles. Most sources of information will be found in the reference section of the library.

The search for information can be visualized along the paths shown in Fig. 4.2. Starting with a limited information base, you should consult technical encyclopedias and library's public access catalog, today automated in most libraries, to search out broad introductory texts. As you become expert in the subject, you should move to more detailed monographs and/or use abstracts and indexes to find pertinent articles in the technical literature. Reading these articles will suggest other articles (cross references) that should be consulted. Another route to important design information is the patent literature (Sec. 4.7).

The task of translating your own search needs into the terminology that appears in the library catalog is often difficult. As mentioned previously, library catalogs,

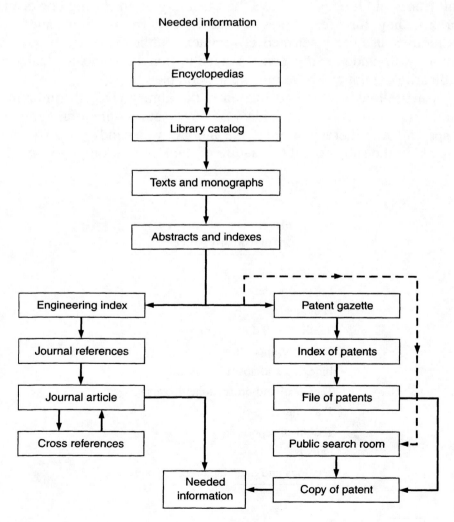

FIGURE 4.2
Flow diagram for an information search.

whether in card form or on-line, are developed for more traditional scholarly and research activities. The kinds of questions raised in the context of engineering design may cut through the card catalog at an "oblique section." When trying to convey the needs and objectives of your search to the librarian, the best tactic is to tell the librarian *what it is you do not know* rather than describe what you already know. Two parameters that describe the efficiency of your information search are:

$$\text{Precision} = \frac{\text{number of relevant documents retrieved}}{\text{total number retrieved}}$$

$$\text{Recall} = \frac{\text{number of relevant documents retrieved}}{\text{number of relevant documents in the collection}}$$

4.4.1 Dictionaries and Encyclopedias

At the outset of a project dealing with a new technical area there may be a need to acquire a broad overview of the subject. English language technical dictionaries usually give very detailed definitions. Also, they often are very well illustrated. Some useful references are:

Davis, J. R. (ed.): "ASM Materials Engineering Dictionary," ASM International, Materials Park, OH, 1992.

Nayler, G. H. F.: "Dictionary of Mechanical Engineering," 4th ed., Butterworth-Heinemann, Boston, 1996.

Parker, S. P. (ed.): "McGraw-Hill Dictionary of Engineering," McGraw-Hill, New York, 1997.

Parker, S. P. (ed.): "McGraw-Hill Dictionary of Scientific and Technical Terms," 5th ed., McGraw-Hill, New York, 1994.

Technical encyclopedias are written for the technically trained person who is just beginning to learn about a new subject. Thus, encyclopedias are a good place to start out if you are only slightly familiar with a subject because they give a broad overview rather quickly. In using an encyclopedia, spend some time checking the index for the entire set of volumes to discover subjects you would not have looked up by instinct. Some useful technical encyclopedias are:

Bever, M. B. (ed.): "Encyclopedia of Materials Sciences and Engineering," 8 vols., The MIT Press, Cambridge, MA, 1986.

"McGraw-Hill Encyclopedia of Environmental Science and Engineering," 3d ed., McGraw-Hill, New York, 1993.

"McGraw-Hill Encyclopedia of Physics," 2d ed., McGraw-Hill, New York, 1993.

"McGraw-Hill Encyclopedia of Science and Engineering," 8th ed., 20 vols., McGraw-Hill, New York, 1997. Also available on CD-ROM.

4.4.2 Handbooks

Undoubtedly, some place in your engineering education a professor has admonished you to reason out a problem from "first principles" and not be a "handbook engineer." That is sound advice, but it may put handbooks in a poor perspective that is undeserved.

Handbooks are compendia of useful technical data. Many handbooks also provide ample technical description of theory and its application, so they are good refreshers of material once studied in greater detail. You will find that an appropriately selected collection of handbooks will be a vital part of your professional library.

An extensive list of handbooks dealing with the material properties of metals, ceramics, and polymers is given in Sec. 8.4. A compendium of handbooks and reference books concerned with various manufacturing processes is given in Sec. 9.2. We list below some basic engineering handbooks that cover most of the other engineering disciplines. Many handbooks are becoming available on CD-ROM so that keyword searches and searches for specific concepts or terms can be made. This greatly increases the usefulness of a large handbook.

Baumeister, T. (ed.): "Marks' Standard Handbook for Mechanical Engineering," 10th ed., McGraw-Hill, New York, 1996.

Christiansen, D. (ed.): "Electronics Engineers' Handbook," 4th ed., McGraw-Hill, New York, 1996.

Fink, D. G., and H. Beaty: "Standard Handbook for Electrical Engineers," 13th ed., McGraw-Hill, New York, 1993.

Karassik, I. J., et al.: "Pump Handbook," 2d ed., McGraw-Hill, New York, 1986.

Kobayashi, A. S. (ed.): "Handbook of Experimental Mechanics," 2d ed., Wiley, New York, 1993.

Kreith, F. (ed.): "The Mechanical Engineering Handbook," CRC Press, Boca Raton, FL, 1997.

Kutz, M. (ed.): "Mechanical Engineers' Handbook," 2d ed., Wiley, New York, 1998.

Loftin, M. K. (ed.): "Standard Handbook for Civil Engineers," 4th ed., McGraw-Hill, New York, 1995.

Maynard, H. B. (ed.): "Industrial Engineering Handbook," 3d ed., McGraw-Hill, New York, 1971.

Parmley, R. O.: "Standard Handbook of Fastening and Joining," 3d ed., McGraw-Hill, New York, 1997.

Perry, R. H., (ed.): "Perry's Chemical Engineers' Handbook," 7th ed., McGraw-Hill, New York, 1997.

Salvendy, G. (ed.): "Handbook of Industrial Engineering," 2d ed., Wiley, New York, 1992.

Smith, E. H. (ed.): "Mechanical Engineer's Reference Book," 12th ed., Butterworth-Heinemann, London, 1994.

Tapley, B. D. "Eshbach's Handbook of Engineering Fundamentals," 4th ed., Wiley, New York, 1990.

Tucker, A. B. (ed.): "The Computer Science and Engineering Handbook," CRC Press, Boca Raton, FL, 1996.

Walsh, R. A.: "Electromechanical Design Handbook," 2d ed., McGraw-Hill, New York, 1994.

Woodson, W. E. (ed.): "Human Factors Design Handbook," 2d ed., McGraw-Hill, New York, 1991.

Handbooks are often highly specialized. For example, there is the "Metering Pump Handbook," "Dudley's Gear Handbook," and the long-running favorite "Roark's Formulas for Stress and Strain."

4.4.3 Textbooks and Monographs

New technical books are continually being published. A good way to keep up to date is to scan the books-in-print column of your professional society's monthly magazine, or to belong to a technical book club. If you want to find out what books are available in a particular field consult "Books in Print," available in nearly every library, or use an Internet book selling service such as amazon.com.

4.4.4 Indexing and Abstracting Services

Indexing and abstracting services provide current information on periodical literature, and they also provide a way to retrieve published literature. An *indexing service* cites the article by title, author, and bibliographic data. An *abstracting service* also provides a summary of the contents of the article. Although indexing and abstracting services primarily are concerned with articles from periodicals, many often include books and conference proceedings, and some list technical reports and patents. The following is a list of indexes and abstracts that cover most of the engineering disciplines.

> *Applied Mechanics Reviews*
> *Applied Science and Technology Index* (formerly *Industrial Arts Index*)
> *Ceramic Abstracts*
> *Chemical Abstracts*
> *Computing Reviews*
> *Corrosion Abstracts*
> *Engineered Materials Abstracts*
> *Engineering Index*
> *Environment Index*
> *Fuels and Energy Abstracts*
> *Highway Research Abstracts*
> *International Aerospace Abstracts*
> *Mechanical Engineering Abstracts*
> *Metals Abstracts* [combines ASM *Review of Metals Literature* (U.S.) and *Metallurgical Abstracts* (British)]
> *Science Abstracts A: Physics Abstracts*
> *Science Abstracts B: Electrical and Electronics Abstracts*
> *Science Abstracts C: Computer and Control Abstracts*
> *Solid State and Superconductivity Abstracts*

A useful source to much detailed information is *Dissertation Abstracts,* which gives abstracts of most doctoral dissertations completed in the United States and Canada. A copy of the dissertation can be ordered at nominal cost.

The reader should know that the situation with respect to indexes and abstracts is in a state of flux at the present time. Many abstracting services have made their products available on CD-ROM, or more recently directly on the Internet (see Sec. 4.6). Others are going direct from print to the Internet, while others are dropping print copies altogether. The advantage of using CD-ROM or the Internet is speed of searching, but also it gives the ability to do "pinpoint searching" at the intersection of several databases.

Conducting a search of the published literature is like putting together a complex puzzle. One has to select a starting place, but some starts are better than others. A good strategy[1] is to start with the most recent subject indexes and abstracts and try to find a current review article or general technical paper. The references cited in it will be helpful in searching back along the "ancestor references" to find the research that led to the current state of knowledge. However, this search path will miss any references that were overlooked or ignored by the original researchers. Therefore, the next step should involve citation searching to find the "descendant references" using *Science Citation Index.*[2] Once you have a reference of interest, you can use *Citation Index* to find all other references published in a given year that cited the key reference. Because they are on CD-ROM or on-line, such searches can be done quickly and precisely. These two search strategies will uncover as many references as possible about the topic. The next step is to identify the key documents. One way to do this is to identify the references with the greatest number of citations, or those that other experts in the field cite as particularly important. You must remember that it takes 6 to 12 months for a reference to be included in an index or abstract service, so current research will not be picked up using this strategy. Current awareness can be achieved by searching *Current Contents* on a regular basis using keywords, subject headings, journal titles, and authors already identified from your literature search. One must also be aware that much information needed in engineering design cannot be accessed through this strategy because it is never listed in scientific and technical abstract services. For this information, the Internet is becoming a vital resource (see Sec. 4.6).

The scientific and technical literature is increasing exponentially. A natural response to this explosion of knowledge is the division into subfields, and this brings with it the development of new journals. The resulting cost from this proliferation means that not every library can afford to carry every journal. If your library does not have a journal or book that you need, ask the librarian to obtain it for you by the Interlibrary Loan (ILL) service. A detailed directory to periodicals and indexing services is *Ulrich's International Periodicals Directory,* published annually in five volumes.

4.4.5 Translations

Although English is the predominant world language for scientific literature, about one-third of the world's scientific and technical literature is produced in the Soviet Union, China, and Japan in languages that are unfamiliar to over 95 percent of scientists and engineers in the United States. Therefore, to avail yourself of information published in those languages, as well as in more common scientific languages like German and French, you should be familiar with sources of translations.

Unfortunately, machine translation by computer, while improving steadily, has not yet reached the point where a finished translation can be done routinely. Therefore, most technical translation must be performed by an experienced translator. Working unaided, a translator typically can complete 5 pages a day. Starting with a machine translation as a first draft, this can be increased to about 15 pages. Because technical

---

1. L. G. Ackerson, *RQ,* vol. 36, pp. 248–260, 1996.
2. Note that there are different version of *Citation Index* for biological, chemical, physical, and engineering and technology publications.

translation is expensive, it is important to make the existence of translations widely available. The best source of this information is the National Translations Center, Library of Congress, Washington, DC. Phone (202)-707-0100.

4.4.6 Catalogs, Brochures, and Business Information

An important kind of design information is catalogs, brochures, and manuals giving information on materials and components that can be purchased from outside suppliers. Most engineers build up quite a collection of this trade literature, often using the reply cards in trade magazines as a way of obtaining new information. Visits to trade shows are an excellent way to become acquainted quickly with the products offered by many vendors. When faced with the problem of where to turn to find information about an unfamiliar new component or material, start with the *Thomas Register of American Manufacturers*. This large multivolume annual publication gives the names and addresses of manufacturers by product and service, as well as company profiles and an extensive catalog file. Many trade publications also publish annual product locators. Rather than worry about keeping a large collection of supplier catalogs, many companies subscribe to a "package library" that provides this information on microfilm, CD-ROM, or via the Internet.

Most technical libraries also contain certain types of business or commercial information that is important in design. Information on the consumption or sales of commodities and manufactured goods by year and state is collected by the federal government and is available in the U.S. Department of Commerce *Census of Manufacturers* and the Bureau of the Census *Statistical Abstract of the United States*. This type of statistical information, important for marketing studies, is also sold by commercial vendors. In using this data it is arranged by industry according to the *Standard Industrial Classification* codes (SIC code). For example, products in the primary metals industries start with 33, those in transportation equipment 37, etc.

4.5
GOVERNMENT SOURCES OF INFORMATION

The federal government either conducts or pays for about 35 percent of the research and development in this country. That generates an enormous amount of information, mostly in the form of technical reports. This R&D enterprise is concentrated in defense, space, environmental, medical, and energy-related areas. It is an important source of information, but all surveys indicate that it is not utilized nearly as much as it ought to be.[1]

The Government Printing Office (GPO) is the federal agency with the responsibility for reproducing and distributing federal documents. Although it is not the sole source of government publications, it is the place to start. It publishes the *Monthly*

---

1. J. S. Robinson, "Tapping the Government Grapevine," 2d ed., The Oryx Press, Phoenix, AZ, 1993.

Catalog of United States Government Publications, the most comprehensive bibliography of unclassified federal publications. The *Publications Reference File,* published bimonthly on microfiche, lists the publications for sale by the GPO.

Reports prepared under contract by industrial and university R & D organizations ordinarily are not available from the GPO. These reports may be obtained from the National Technical Information Service (NTIS), a branch of the Department of Commerce. NTIS, a self-supporting agency through sale of information, is the nation's central clearinghouse for U.S. and foreign technical reports, federal databases, and software. Searches for technical reports should begin with *Government Reports Announcements and Index* (GRA & I) or its computerized counterpart, NTIS Bibliographic Database. This database is searchable by titles, authors, accession number, contract number, or subject.

About one-quarter of the NTIS collection is foreign reports and translations. The Japanese Technical Literature Act of 1986 requires NTIS to monitor Japanese technical activity and collect and translate Japanese technical reports. These and other translations are listed in the weekly *NTIS Foreign Abstract Newsletter.*

In searching for government sources of information, the GPO will give a broader spectrum of information, while NTIS will focus you on the technical report literature. However, even with the vast collection at NTIS it does not have all federally sponsored technical reports. Because agency submissions are voluntary rather than legally mandated, about one-third of the federal technical reports do not reach NTIS. Its collection is chiefly based on NASA and the Departments of Defense and Energy. Another large collection of technical reports, mostly on microfiche, is in the Science and Technology Division of the Library of Congress. This contains reports from 60 countries. Information on how to access these sources is given in Table 4.3.

TABLE 4.3
Sources of government technical information

Source	Addresses
Government Printing Office	Superintendent of Documents, Government Printing Office, Washington, DC 20402
www.gpo.gov/su_docs/locate.html	(202)-783-3238
	Mail orders go to: Box 371594, Pittsburgh, PA 15250-7954
National Technical Information Service	5285 Port Royal Road Springfield, VA 22161
www.ntis.gov	(703)-487-4650
Library of Congress Science Reference Section www.loc.gov	10 First Street, S.E. Washington, DC 20540 (202)-707-5580
National Institute for Standards and Technology National Center for Standards and Certification Information www.nist.gov	Administration Building, Room A629 Gaithersburg, MD 20899 (301)-975-4040

4.6
INFORMATION FROM THE INTERNET

The fastest-growing communication medium is the Internet. Not only is this becoming the preferred form of personal and business communication via e-mail, but it is rapidly becoming a major source for data retrieval and a channel of commerce. The Internet is a computer network interconnecting numerous computers or local computer networks. Worldwide, the number of host computers on the Internet has increased from less than 100,000 in 1992 to over 18 million 5 years later. These computer networks are linked by a set of common technical protocols so that users in a Macintosh network can communicate with or use the services located, for example, in a Unix network. These protocols are known as the *transmission control protocol/Internet protocol,* or the TCP/IP protocol suite. The Internet functions with a communications technology called *packet-switching,* which breaks the data into small fragments. Each fragment is packed, coded for its source and designation, and sent onto the transmission line. Thus, packets of digital data from various sources pour into the Internet and find each destination. Upon arriving at the destination, the packets are unpacked and reassembled to recover the original data. This data can be text, graphics, pictures, sound, video, or computer code.[1]

The Internet consists of many pathways. A frequently used service is e-mail, a worldwide electronic mail system. You can send and receive e-mail from almost any part of the Internet with almost any on-line software. Many of the public access files, databases, and software on the Internet are available in its FTP archives using the File Transfer Protocol. Another Internet service is Telnet, which allows your computer to enter the files of another computer. Remote access of your library's public access catalog system is most likely through Telnet. Usenet is the part of the Internet devoted to on-line discussion groups, or "newsgroups." The most recent and most rapidly growing component of the Internet is the World Wide Web, an enormous, far-flung collection of colorful onscreen documents that are linked to each other by highlighted words called hypertext.

The World Wide Web (WWW) was initially developed to build a distributed hypermedia system.[2] A hypermedia system is written in a *hypertext language* such as HTML (hypertext markup language), such that "point and click" connections allow the user to jump from one information source to another on the Internet. The system aims at giving global access to a universe of documents. As one hypertext link in a document leads to another and yet another, the links form a web of information, i.e., a worldwide web. The World Wide Web is a subset, although a very important subset, of the Internet. Its popularity comes from the fact that it makes distributing and accessing digital information simple and inexpensive. Its weakness is that it is just a

---

1. For a history of the Internet see http://www.isoc.org/internet-history. A comprehensive site at the Library of Congress gives information on Internet search tools, collections of Internet resources, U.S. government resources, and tutorials on the Internet. http://lcweb.loc.gov/global/.
2. For a history of the WWW see http://www.w3.org/pub/WWW/History.html. For an introduction to the web see http://www.robelle.com/www-paper/intro.html.

huge collection of documents arranged in no defined order. Using the web therefore requires a search engine.

When people say they are "surfing the web" they mean they are randomly seeking and reading Internet addresses to see what is there. While this can be exhilarating for a first-time user of the Web, it is akin to a person attempting to find a book in a 2 million volume library without first consulting the catalog. Locations on the Internet are identified by *universal resource locators* (URL). For example, a URL that gives a brief history of the Internet is http://www.isoc.org/internet-history. The prefix http://www indicates we are trying to access an HTTP server on the World Wide Web at a computer with the domain name "isoc.org" (the nonprofit organization known as The Internet Society). The document in question is stored in that computer in a file called "internet-history."

Before the advent of the World Wide Web there were tools that allowed users to search the Internet.[1] Archie is software designed to find computer files from Internet servers using FTP. Gopher is a menu-driven interface that allows users to access a huge electronic library of documents on the Internet, especially on FTP, Telnet, and Usenet servers. The search engine for Gopher is called Veronica. These search tools are still used, but they have been replaced in popularity by a number of user-friendly, highly graphical search tools—often called *web browsers.* The most commonly used web browsers today are the Netscape Communicator and the Microsoft Internet Explorer. Most browsers allow access to FTP, Telnet, and Usenet servers.

To search the World Wide Web requires a *search engine.* Most of these search engines work by preindexing and regularly updating pointers to a huge number of URLs on the Web. As a result, when you enter your search criteria you are searching a powerful database of the search engine, but not the Web itself, which would be impossibly slow. Each search engine works differently in combing through the Web. Some scan for information in the title or header of the document, while others look at the bold headings on the page. In addition the way the information is sorted, indexed, and categorized differs between search engines. Therefore, all search engines will not produce the same result for a specific inquiry.

Fortunately, most search engines are supported by advertisements, and so they are free to users. The most commonly used general-purpose search engines are listed below.

Web search engines

Name	Web address	Description
AltaVista	http://www.altavista.digital.com	Huge database. Updated daily. Most eclectic of search engines
Excite	http://www.excite.com	A search query on Excite searches the entire Web for documents containing related concepts, not just the keywords
HotBot	http://www.hotbot.com	A new addition among search engines. Offers many advanced search features

---

1. J. He, Search Engines on the Internet, *Experimental Techniques,* January/February 1998, pp. 34–38.

InfoSeek	http://infoseek.com	One of largest databases. Covers www, Gopher, and FTP. One of largest followings among science/engineering web sites
Lycos	http://lycos.com	One of largest Web indexes. Database updated frequently
Yahoo	http://www.yahoo.com	Attracts largest number of users. Strong topical index of Web sites. Provides jump points to other large search engines

It is important to understand how search engines obtain and maintain their databases. One method is registration, in which you must register your web site using an on-line form. In your submittal you suggest keywords by which the site is indexed. This method has the advantage of providing some kind of review or screen to what will be found by the search engine. This increases the relevance of what is found by the search engine, but it also limits the scope of the web that is covered. Yahoo is the chief user of this method. The other extreme is a search engine that acquires its database with a robot crawler (or spider). This is sophisticated software that crawls over all portions of the Web, far and wide, to collect and index its contents. AltaVista is the best example of this type of data acquisition. Most search engines are combinations of these two methods, actively soliciting site registrations but also sending out robot crawlers.

There are two general types of search methodologies.[1] One, exemplified by Yahoo, acts as a *search tree*. Its contents are manually updated lists of Web resources structured in a hierarchical fashion. Any resource on the Web can be found only if a reference to it has been entered actively into the search tree. Suppose we are interested in finding vendors of centrifugal pumps, and design characteristics of these pumps. The home page of Yahoo opens to a list of 14 major categories. We select the entry for Science (it is unfortunate that most search engines list Engineering as a subcategory under science). The sequence going lower into the classification system is: Science → Engineering → Mechanical Engineering → Indices → Mechanical Engineering-World Wide Web Virtual Library. At this site we have multiple branches. Selecting Mechanical Engineering Vendor Pages, we find a limited set of vendors, about a total of 60, but no vendors of centrifugal pumps. As an alternate choice we find a category University ME Departments, and check on MIT. Drilling down to Lectures, we click on Sketch Modeling and find a nicely illustrated tutorial on how to make product models from cardboard and foam board (http://me.mit.edu/lectures/sketch-modelling). Thus we have illustrated the joy of occasional net surfing but we have not satisfied our utilitarian objective of finding detailed information on centrifugal pumps.

Next we turn to automatic searching on Yahoo. Entering "centrifugal pump(s)" as the search topic returned 32 Web sites. Most of these were the names and hyperlink connections to pump manufacturers, but it did turn up a forum about ideas for pump sizing and total head calculation in centrifugal pumps.

---

1. L. Perrochon, *IEEE Communications Magazine,* June 1996, pp.142–145.

The second strategy for building a search engine is to build a Web *search index.* As the robot crawlers traverse the Web they build a huge index of the words in the pages covered. The search engine permits the search of this index. Obviously, the search engine can only find what has been indexed. However, since the indexing of pages is performed automatically, more pages are indexed by indexes than by trees. Also, because any page is added by the crawler without any human judgment, the number of documents returned for a query can be very large. For example, we continued our search for information on vendors of centrifugal pumps on the search engine HotBot. Entering Centrifugal pumps in the search box, and telling the engine to look for "all the words" in the "last two years" in "North America(.com)" returned 7154 matches. Selecting "all the words" tells HotBot to search for pages that contain "centrifugal" and "pumps" at least once on every page, but not necessarily in the order "centrifugal pumps." This is similar to a Boolean AND or + search. Searching for "any of the words" will return pages that contain one or more of the words. This is similar to a Boolean OR or − search. For this example it returned 202,134 pages. Selecting "the exact phrase" tells HotBot to find documents that contain Centrifugal pumps in the exact order shown here. This gave 2543 responses.

It is important to realize that much of the information retrieved from the Internet is "raw data" in the sense that it has not been reviewed for correctness by peers or an editor. There is a tendency to think that everything on the Web is current material, but that may not be so. Much material gets posted and is never updated. Another problem is the volatility of Web pages. Web pages disappear when their webmaster changes job or loses interest. With increasing use of advertisement on the Internet there is a growing concern about the objectivity of the information that is posted there. All of these are points that the intelligent reader must consider when enjoying and utilizing this fast-growing information resource.

Another important point is the degree to which a search engine covers all of the material out on the web. A recent study[1] estimated that even the best search engine (HotBot) covered about one-third of the 320 million Web pages. Therefore, the best strategy for maximizing the retrieval of information from the Internet is to pick two or three search engines. Take the time to learn the details of search strategies with each one, and then get practice at using them.

4.6.1 Engineering URLs

There are many URLs devoted to engineering topics.[2] The table on p. 137 lists some URLs that might be most useful for a student starting a design project.

---

1. Science, Apr. 1, 1998, *Wall Street Journal,* Apr. 3, 1998.
2. B. J. Thomas, "The World Wide Web for Scientists and Engineers," American Society of Mechanical Engineers, Fairfield, NJ, 1998.

Internet Starter Kit on Mechanical Design

Name and organization	URL	Description
Technical information:		
WWW Virtual Library: Mechanical Engineering at Stanford University	http://CDR.stanford.edu/ html/WWW-ME/home.html	A good place to start. Provides access to University ME departments, ME vendor pages, and a variety of on-line services
Mechanical Engr. Electronic Design Library at U. Mass	http://www.ecs.umass.edu/mie/ labs/mda/dlib/dlib.html	Everything to support many student projects. Materials data/design of std. machine components/design for manufacturing/fits and tolerances/standards and codes/vendor catalogs/ergonomics
National Technical Information Service	http://ntis.gov	3 million reports on file. Abstract of 370,000 reports received since 1990 can be searched
NASA Technical Reports Server	http://techreports.larc.nasa.gov/ cgi-bin/NTRS	Covers all NASA centers. Abstracts only. Reports must be ordered
Mechanical Engineering magazine	http://www.memagazin	Back issues of ME magazine to August 1996
Journal of Mechanical Design—ASME	http://www-jmd.engr.ucdavis .edu/jmd/	Can search back issues of JMD by subject
Machine Design magazine on-line	http://www.penton.com/md/	On-line version of *Machine Design*
Patents (see Sec 4.7)		
Commercial and marketing information:		
Switch Board	http://www.switchboard.com	Will find telephone number of persons without knowing city and state. Must know street and city for a company phone number
Thomas Register	http://thomasregister.com	Allows search of 155,000 companies, 60,000 product and service categories, and 124,000 brand names. Requires registration
Machine Design Product Locator	http://www.pdem.net	Product and manufacturers' directory. Web address directory
Industry Net	http://www.industry.net	Information on new products
Government Printing Office	http://access.gpo.gov	Information on products available from GPO
Commerce Business Daily	http://cbd.cos.com	Daily publication of U.S. Department of Commerce giving procurement opportunities, contract awards, and surplus property for sale
STAT-USA	http://stat-usa.gov	One-stop site for U.S. business, economic, and trade statistics and information. Cost is modest
Gale Business Resources	http://galenet.gale.com	Database containing information on 450,000 U.S. and international companies. Statistical data and info. on market share. May be cost for service, but available in many college libraries

Given the complexity and heterogeneity of the Web,[1] it is not surprising that various information-processing companies have created specialized subscription information packages from the Web and other on-line databases. The Engineering Information Village, created by Engineering Information Inc., is a good example. From its Web site (http://www.ei.org) one can connect to nearly 30 databases, including Ei Compendex, Ei Manufacturing, and Ei MechDisc. Access to financial and business statistics is also provided.

Information Handling Services Group (IHS Group) is a major international publisher of electronic information databases for the technical and business markets. The IHS Engineering Resource Center provides a single source via the World Wide Web of vendor catalogs, specifications, and standards (http://www.ihs.com/erc). The IHS Group's British affiliate ESDU provides electronically more than 200 volumes of validated engineering design data containing more than 1200 design guides with supporting software (http://www.esdu.com). These cover some 20 subject areas in structural, mechanical, aeronautical, and chemical engineering.

It also is clear that as Web-based commerce increases engineers will utilize the Web in design to a greater degree. Computer-based design catalogs available on the Internet are beginning to play a big role.[2] These will provide ready access to what is available, its technical characteristics and cost. Technical calculations for strength, capacity, etc., will be done in the Web page. The graphics will allow checking the component for its interface with other components in the system that is being designed. Finally, the graphics will be capable of being imported into the CAD model of the design. Parts of this component design system already exist on the Internet, but the integrated system is yet to come.

4.7
PATENT LITERATURE

The U.S. patent system is the largest body of information on technology in the world. At present there are over 5 million U.S. patents, and the number is increasing at a rate close to 100,000 each year. Old patents can be very useful for tracing the development of ideas in an engineering field, while new patents describe what is happening at the frontiers of the field. Only about 20 percent of the technology that is contained in U.S. patents can be found elsewhere in the published literature.[3] Therefore, the engineer who ignores the patent literature is aware of only the tip of the iceberg of information.

---

1. For a guide to finding business statistics on the web see P. Bernstein, "Finding Statistics Online," Information Today, Inc., Medford, NJ, 1998.
2. The DesignSuite from InPart (www.inpart.com) contains over 150,000 models of standard components and their performance data. The database can be searched by a hierarchical file structure (bearing/radial bearing/double-pillow block bearing) or with a graphical file that gives thumbnail pictures of the components. Once the component has been selected, its geometric model can be downloaded into the user's computer-aided design program. This database not only aids the component selection process but eliminates the need to draw the part in the design drawings.
3. P. J. Terrago, *IEEE Trans. Prof. Comm.,* vol. PC-22, no. 2, pp. 101–104, 1979.

4.7.1 Intellectual Property

The term *intellectual property* refers to the protection of ideas with patents, copyrights, trademarks, and trade secrets. These entities fall within the broad area of property law and, as such, can be sold or leased just like other forms of property. Also, just as property can be stolen or trespassed upon, so intellectual property can be infringed. We have already learned something about copyrights (Sec. 4.2). A *trademark* is any name, word, symbol, or device that is used by a company to identify their goods or services and distinguish them from those made or sold by others. The right to use trademarks is obtained by registration and extends indefinitely so long as the trademark continues to be used. A *trade secret* is any formula, pattern, device, or compilation of information which is used in a business to create an opportunity over competitors who do not have this information. Sometimes trade secrets are information which could be patented but for which the corporation chooses not to obtain a patent because it expects that defense against infringement will be difficult. Since a trade secret has no legal protection, it is essential to maintain the information in secret.

4.7.2 Patents

Article 1, Section 8 of the Constitution of the United States states that Congress shall have the power to promote progress in science and the useful arts by securing for limited times to inventors the exclusive right to their discoveries. A patent granted by the U.S. government gives the patentee the right to prevent others from making, using, or selling the patented invention. Any patent application filed since 1995 has a term of protection that begins on the date of the grant of the patent and ends on a date 20 years after the filing date of the application. The 20-year term from the date of filing brings the United States into harmony with most other countries in the world in this respect. The most common type of patent, the *utility patent,* may be issued for a new and useful machine, process, article of manufacture, or composition of matter. In addition *design patents* are issued for new ornamental designs and *plant patents* are granted on new varieties of plants. Computer software generally is protected by copyright, but there is a growing tendency for patenting where the software is embedded in the computer hardware or where the computational circuitry is identifiable from other portions of the circuitry.

In patent law a process is defined as an operation performed by rule to produce a certain result. In addition, patent law defines a patentable process to include *a new use* of a known process, machine, manufacture, or composition of matter. Thus, a new use for a known compound which is not analogous to a known use may be a patentable process. However, not all processes are patentable. Methods of doing business or natural laws or phenomena, as well as mathematical equations and methods of solving them are not patentable subject matter.

There are three general criteria for awarding a patent.

1. The invention must be *new* or *novel.*
2. The invention must be *useful.*
3. It must be nonobvious to a person skilled in the art covered by the patent.

A key requirement is novelty. Thus, if you are not the first person to propose the idea your cannot expect to obtain a patent. If the invention was made in another country but it was known or used in the United States before the date of the invention in the United States it would not meet the test of novelty. Finally, if the invention was published anywhere in the world before the date of invention but was not known to the inventor it would violate the requirement of novelty. The requirement for usefulness is rather straightforward. For example, the discovery of a new chemical compound (composition of matter) which has no useful application is not eligible for a patent. The final requirement, that the invention be unobvious, can be subject to considerable debate. A determination must be made as to whether the invention would have been the next logical step based on the state of the art at the time the discovery was made. If it was, then there is no patentable discovery.

The requirement for novelty places a major restriction on publication prior to filing a patent application. In the United States the printed publication of the description of the invention anywhere in the world more than one year before the filing of a patent application results in automatic rejection by the Patent Office. It should be noted that to be grounds for rejection the publication must give a description detailed enough so that a person with ordinary skill in the subject area could understand and make the invention. Also, public use of the invention or its sale in the United States one year or more before patent application results in automatic rejection. The patent law also requires diligence in *reduction to practice*. If development work is suspended for a significant period of time, even though the invention may have been complete at that time, the invention may be considered to be abandoned. Therefore, a patent application should be filled as soon as it is practical to do so.

In the case of competition for awarding a patent for a particular invention, the patent is awarded to the inventor who can prove the earliest date of conception of the idea and can demonstrate reasonable diligence in reducing the idea to practice.[1] The date of invention can best be proved in a court of law if the invention has been recorded in a bound laboratory notebook with prenumbered pages and if the invention has been witnessed by a person competent to understand the idea. For legal purposes, corroboration of an invention must be proved by people who can testify to what the inventor did and the date when it occurred. Therefore, having the invention disclosure notarized is of little value since a notary public usually is not in a position to understand a highly technical disclosure. Similarly, sending a registered letter to oneself is of little value. For details about how to apply, draw up, and pursue a patent application the reader is referred to the literature on this subject.[2]

---

1. A major difference between U.S. patent law and almost every other country's laws is that in the United States a patent is awarded to the first person to invent the subject matter, while in other countries the patent is awarded to the first inventor to file a patent application. Another difference is that in any country but the United States public disclosure of the invention before filing the applications results in loss of patent rights on grounds of lack of novelty.

2. W. G. Konold, "What Every Engineer Should Know about Patents," 2d ed., Marcel Dekker, New York, 1989; D. S. Goldstein, "Intellectual Property Protection," Professional Publishers, Belmont, CA, 1992; M. A. Lechter (ed.), "Successful Patents and Patenting for Engineers and Scientists," IEEE Press, New York, 1995.

4.7.3 Technology Licensing

The right to exclusive use of technology that is granted by a patent may be transferred to another party through a licensing agreement. A license may be either an exclusive license, in which it is agreed not to grant any further licenses, or a nonexclusive license. The licensing agreement may also contain details as to geographic scope, e.g., one party gets rights in Europe, another gets rights in South America. Sometimes the license will involve less than the full scope of the technology. Frequently consulting services are provided by the licensor for an agreed-upon period.

Several forms of financial payment are common. One form is a paid up license which involves a lump sum payment. Frequently the licensee will agree to pay the licensor a percentage of the sales of the products that utilize the new technology, or a fee based on the extent of use of the licensed process. Before entering into an agreement to license technology it is important to make sure that the arrangement is consistent with U.S. antitrust laws or that permission has been obtained from appropriate government agencies in the foreign country.

4.7.4 The Patent Literature

The *Gazette of the U.S. Patent Office* is issued each Tuesday with the weekly issuance of patents. It contains an abstract and selected figures from each patent that is issued that week. The *Gazette* is very helpful for keeping current on the patent literature and for getting a quick overview of a patent. It is widely disseminated in the United States.

The "Annual Index" of patents is published each year in two volumes, one an alphabetical index of patentees and the other an index of inventions by subject matter. These can be used to obtain the patent number, and then the *Gazette* can be used to learn about the patent. All U.S. patents may be examined in the public search room in Crystal City, VA (near Washington, DC). The main advantage of visiting the search room is that patents are grouped according to classes and subclasses. However, 58 libraries nationwide are designated as Patent Depository Libraries and contain most U.S. patents. In these libraries, the patents are arranged according to number.

Patents have been arranged into about 400 classes, and each class is subdivided into many subclasses.[1] The "Index to Classification" is a loose-leaf volume that lists the major subject headings into which patents have been divided. Once the Index identifies the appropriate class numbers, the searcher should go to the "Manual of Classification." This loose-leaf volume lists each class, with its subclasses, in numerical order. By searching the "Manual of Classification," you can identify the classes and subclasses that are likely to be of interest. It is important to realize that subjects will often be found in more than one patent class.

An on-line computerized classification system called CASSIS (Classification and Search Support Information System) is available at all of the Patent Depository

---

1. K. J. Dodd, *IEEE Trans. Prof. Comm.*, vol. PC-22, no. 2, pp. 95–100, 1971.

Libraries around the nation. For a given patent number CASSIS will display all its locations in the Patent Classification System (PCS). For a given technology as described by a PCS classification, CASSIS will display the numbers of all patents assigned to that classification. Also, CASSIS will identify all classifications whose full titles contain designated key words. Finally, CASSIS will search the alphabetical list of subject headings in the index to the PCS to identify the classifications containing subject matter of interest.

A *patentability search* is a search of the patent literature to determine whether an invention can be patented and what the scope of the patent protection would be. This search draws on the information assembled in the search, especially the prior art and background of the invention. By carefully studying the claims in the prior art, the patent attorney can construct claims that are neither too broad (so as to be precluded by prior patents) or too narrow (so as to limit the usefulness of the patent).

An *infringement search* is an exhaustive search of the patent literature to determine whether an idea is likely to infringe on patents held by others. Often it is undertaken when making a new product is contemplated.

If you find your patent or idea in possible infringement with an existing patent, you may fight back by challenging the validity of the patent in the courts. To do so requires a *validity search*. More than half of all patents challenged are ruled invalid by the courts. A patent is really not good until it is tried and held valid by the courts, although it is presumed valid when issued by the Patent Office.

The homepage for the U.S. Patent and Trademark Office is http://www.uspto.gov. The full text of the patents from the present to 1976 is available. Other sites are http://patents.ibm.com/ and http://sunsite.unc.edu/patents/. All of these sites provide patent information without charge. They also allow access to the "Manual of Classification" and will suggest strategies for patent searching.[1] Patent searching can be found on the Internet for a fee where there are special search requirements.

4.7.5 Reading a Patent

Because a patent is a legal document, it is organized and written in a style much different from the style of the usual technical paper. Patents must stand on their own and contain sufficient disclosure to permit the public to practice the invention after the patent expires. Therefore, each patent is a complete exposition on the problem, the solution to the problem, and the applications for the invention in practical use.

Figure 4.3 shows the first page of a patent for a compact disc case. This page carries bibliographic information, information about the examination process, an abstract, and a general drawing of the invention. At the very top we find the inventor, the patent number, and the date of issuance. Below the line on the left we find the title of the invention, the inventor(s) and address(es), the date the patent application was filed, and the application number. Next are listed the class and subclass for both the

---

1. A tutorial on the basics of patent searching is available from the University of Texas at Austin via the Internet at http://www.lib.utexas.edu/Libs/ENG/PTUT/ptut.html. This tutorial focuses on the use of the CASSIS system of classification.

United States Patent [19]

Blase

[11] **Patent Number:** **5,425,451**

[45] **Date of Patent:** **Jun. 20, 1995**

[54] **COMPACT DISC CASE**

[76] Inventor: **William F. Blase,** 1409 Golden Leaf Way, Stockton, Calif. 95209

[21] Appl. No.: **238,695**

[22] Filed: **May 5, 1994**

[51] Int. Cl.⁶ **B65D 85/57**
[52] U.S. Cl. **206/313;** 206/309
[58] Field of Search 206/307–313, 206/387, 444

[56] **References Cited**

U.S. PATENT DOCUMENTS

3,042,469	7/1962	Lowther	206/311
3,265,453	8/1966	Seide	206/311
4,613,044	9/1986	Saito et al.	
4,694,957	9/1987	Ackeret	206/309
4,736,840	4/1988	Deiglmeier	
4,875,743	10/1989	Gelardi et al.	206/309
4,998,618	3/1991	Borgions	206/307
5,099,995	3/1992	Karakane et al.	206/309
5,168,991	12/1992	Whitehead et al.	
5,176,250	1/1993	Cheng	206/313
5,205,405	4/1993	O'Brien et al.	
5,244,084	9/1993	Chan	206/309
5,332,086	7/1994	Chuang	206/444

FOREIGN PATENT DOCUMENTS

3440479	5/1986	Germany	206/309

Primary Examiner—Jimmy G. Foster

[57] **ABSTRACT**

A new and improved compact disc case apparatus includes a lower case assembly and an upper case assembly which are placed in registration with each other to form an enclosure assembly. The enclosure assembly includes a side which contains a slot. A pivot assembly is connected between the lower case assembly and the upper case assembly adjacent to a first lower corner and a first upper corner. A disc retention tray is positioned between the lower case assembly and the upper case assembly such that the disc retention tray can be selectively moved to an open position or a closed position. In the closed position, the disc retention tray is housed completely in the enclosure assembly. In the open position, the disc retention tray is substantially outside the enclosure assembly such that a disc can be selectively taken off of and placed on the disc retention tray. The disc retention tray includes a handle portion. The enclosure assembly includes a truncated corner which is distal to the first lower corner and the first upper corner and which is adjacent to the slotted side. The handle portion of the disc retention tray projects from the truncated corner of the enclosure assembly when the disc retention tray is in a closed position. The disc retention tray includes a recessed edge portion. The recessed edge portion of the disc retention tray is located adjacent to the handle portion of the disc retention tray

3 Claims, 4 Drawing Sheets

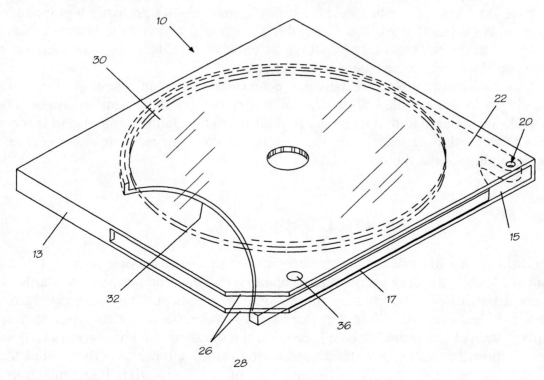

FIGURE 4.3
The first page of a United States patent for a compact disc case.

U.S. patent system and the international classification system and the U.S. classes in which the examiner searched for prior art. The references are the patents that the examiner cited as showing the most prior art at the time of the invention. The rest of the page is taken up with a detailed abstract and a key drawing of the invention. Additional pages of drawings follow, each keyed to the description of the invention.

The body of the patent starts with a section on the Background of the Invention, followed by the Summary of the Invention and a Brief Description of the Drawings. Most of the patent is taken up by the description of the Preferred Embodiment. This comprises a detailed description and explanation of the invention, often in legal terms and phrases that are strange-sounding to the engineer. The examples cited show as broadly as possible how to practice the invention, how to use the products, and how the invention is superior to prior art. Not all examples describe experiments that were actually run, but they do provide the inventor's teaching of how they should best be run. The last part of the patent comprises the *claims* of the invention. These are the legal description of the rights of invention. The broadest claims are usually placed first, with more specific claims toward the end of the list. The strategy in writing a patent is to aim at getting the broadest possible claims. The broadest claims are often disallowed first, so it is necessary to write narrower and narrower claims so that not all claims are disallowed.

There is a very important difference between a patent disclosure and a technical paper. In writing a patent, inventors and their attorneys purposely broaden the scope to include all materials, conditions, and procedures that are believed to be equally likely to be operative as the conditions that were actually tested and observed. The purpose is to develop the broadest possible claims. This is a perfectly legitimate legal practice, but it has the risk that some of the ways of practicing the invention that are described in the embodiments might not actually work. If that happens, then the way is left open to declare the patent to be invalid.

Another major difference between patents and technical papers is that patents usually avoid any detailed discussion of theory or why the invention works. Those subjects are avoided to minimize any limitations to the claims of the patent that could arise through the argument that the discovery would have been obvious from an understanding of the theory.

4.8
CODES AND STANDARDS

The importance of codes and standards in design was discussed in Sec. 1.12. The United States is the only industrialized country in which the national standards body is not a part of or supported by the national government. The American National Standards Institute (ANSI) is the coordinating organization for the voluntary standards system of the United States. It certifies the standards-making processes of other organizations,[1] initiates new standards-making projects, represents the United States on the International Standards Committees of the International Organization for Standardization (ISO), and examines the standards prepared by other organizations to

---

1. For an extensive list of standards sponsoring organizations see T. A. Hunter, Designing to Codes and Standards, "ASM Handbook," vol. 20, ASM International, Materials Park, OH.

determine whether they meet the requirements for consensus so as to be included as an ANSI standard.

The American Society for Testing and Materials (ASTM) is the major organization that prepares standards in the field of materials and product systems. It is the source of more than half of the existing ANSI standards.

The Standards Development Services (SDSS) of the National Institute of Standards and Technology (NIST) manages the voluntary product standards program established by Part 10, Title 15 of the Code of Federal Regulations.

Trade associations produce or review voluntary standards. Those that have produced a substantial number of standards include:

- American Petroleum Institute
- Association of American Railroads
- Electronics Industries Association
- Manufacturing Chemists Association
- National Electrical Manufacturers Association

A number of professional and technical societies have made important contributions through standards activities. The most active are:

- American Association of State Highway and Transportation Officials
- American Concrete Institute
- American Society of Agricultural Engineers
- American Society of Mechanical Engineers
- Institute of Electrical and Electronics Engineers
- Society of Automotive Engineers

The ASME prepares the well-known Boiler and Pressure Vessel Code that is incorporated into the laws of most states. The ASME Codes and Standards Division also published performance test codes for turbines, combustion engines, and other large mechanical equipment.

Several other important standards-making organizations are:

- National Fire Protection Association (NFPA)
- Underwriters Laboratories, Inc. (UL)
- Factory Mutual Engineering Corp. (FMEC)

The Department of Defense (DOD) is the most active federal agency in developing specifications and standards. The General Services Agency (GSA) is charged with preparing standards for common items such as light bulbs and hand tools.

The following are key reference sources for information about specifications and standards.

- "Annual Catalog"
  American National Standards Institute
  10 East 40th Street
  New York, NY 10016
- "Annual Book of ASTM Standards"
  ASTM
  1916 Race Street
  Philadelphia, PA 19107

The Book of Standards is in 48 volumes and contains over 8500 standards.

- "Index of Specifications and Standards"
  U.S. Department of Defense
  Washington, DC
- "Index of Federal Specifications and Standards"
  U.S. General Services Administration
  GPO, Washington, DC
- "Index and Directory of U.S. Industry Standards," 2d ed., 1984
  Information Handling Services
  Englewood, CO 80150

  References to over 400 U.S. standards organizations and more than 26,000 individual standards

- "World Industrial Standards Speedy Finder," 1983
  ASTM
  Philadelphia, PA 19107

  Can locate a specific standard by either number or product name for U.S., U.K., W. Germany, France, or Japan.

- R. B. Toth (ed.): "Standards Management," ANSI, New York, 1989

The following specialized volumes dealing with metals are available.

- "Unified Numbering System for Metals and Alloys," 5th ed., ASTM, 1989.
- "Worldwide Guide to Equivalent Irons and Steels," ASM, 3d ed., 1993.
- "Worldwide Guide to Equivalent Nonferrous Metals and Alloys," ASM, 3d ed., 1996.

The National Source for Global Standards is a Web-based information service sponsored by ANSI. It provides free bibliographic access to more than 250,000 standards at http://www.nssn.org. This includes reference to ASTM, SAE, and MIL standards, as well as British and German (V.D.I.) standards. Information on where to order the standard is provided.

4.9
EXPERT SYSTEMS

A very different source of information is the new field of *expert systems*[1] or *knowledge-based systems*. These computer-based systems simulate the role of an expert in solving some problem using an information database provided by the expert and decision rules for interpreting the data. Expert systems is an active area of the field of *artificial intelligence*.[2] Other areas of artificial intelligence are automated reasoning,

1. J. Liebowitz (ed.), "The Handbook of Applied Expert Systems," CRC Press, Boca Raton, FL, 1997; J. N. Siddall, "Expert Systems for Engineers," Marcel Dekker, New York, 1990; M. Green, "Knowledge Aided Design," Academic Press, New York, 1992.
2. P. H. Winston, "Artificial Intelligence," Addison-Wesley, Reading, MA, 1977.

intelligent databases, knowledge acquisition, knowledge bases and knowledge representation, machine learning, natural languages, and vision and sensing.

An expert system acquires knowledge through knowledge-acquisition software tools from a trained specialist called a knowledge engineer. The knowledge engineer obtains his or her knowledge from one or more experts in the technical area, called domain experts. Once the expert system has been constructed this relationship need no longer exist. A prime advantage of expert systems is that they capture the knowledge of experts that may otherwise be lost through death or retirement. Moreover, they can contain the cumulative knowledge of several experts, they are available any time of day or night, and they can be distributed widely throughout an organization. However, it should be quickly added that expert systems are not a substitute for a human expert. Unless a problem is fully understood, which can come only from humans, the expert system project will fail.

The user of an expert system works through a keyboard interface. The input consists of system facts and suppositions of varying degrees of validity. The user interface tends to be highly interactive, following the format of a question and answer session. The expert system returns answers, recommendations, or diagnoses. In a design expert system a graphics interface may be required in order to visualize the object being designed. At present most expert systems utilize a specialized database, but they are moving rapidly to be able to draw upon generalized databases.

The elements of an expert system are shown in Fig. 4.4. The two major divisions are the knowledge base and the inference engine. The knowledge base is unique to a particular domain but the inference engine may be common to many domains of knowledge. The *knowledge acquisition facility* is the component responsible for entering the knowledge into the database. At its simplest level this facility acts as an editor and knowledge is entered directly in a form acceptable by the language in which the expert system is written. On a more sophisticated level this facility can translate an input in natural language into the representation that the knowledge base can understand. This is an important feature in design, for unless the user is willing to learn the programming language in which the expert system is written it would be impossible to customize the knowledge base.

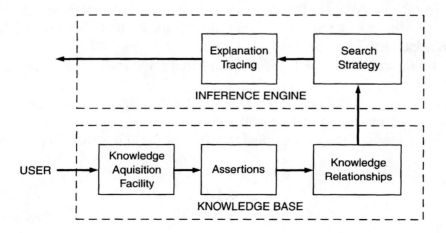

FIGURE 4.4
General structure of an expert system.

The *assertions* component, also called the working memory or temporary data store, contains the knowledge about the particular problem being solved. Data are represented by predicate logic, by frames, or by semantic networks. The *knowledge relationships* component contains formulas showing the relationship among several pieces of information. The "if-then" production rule is the most common relationship. This rule has the form:

IF condition THEN action

For example: IF stress level exceeds 85 ksi THEN part will fail. In any knowledge base there is a balance between the assertion of facts (declarative knowledge) and the rules for manipulating those facts (procedural knowledge). Generally, the less knowledge declared the greater the procedural knowledge required, and vice versa.

The inference engine contains the control mechanisms for the expert system. In a production rules expert system the AI reasoning is responsible for choosing which rule to perform next. This constitutes the *search strategy*. Since the probability of one rule following another is less than 100 percent in most cases, it has been necessary to incorporate uncertainty into the rules. With a small number of rules it is practical to search in random order, but if the number of rules is large it is necessary to partition into sublists on some logical basis. *Explanation tracing* is provided to retrace the chain of production rules that led to the development of the system. This greatly enhances the credibility of the expert system.

Note that an expert system goes well beyond the usual bibliographic source of information in that it contains information, but in addition, it contains decision rules that allow that information to be applied to some specific problem. They are finding use in applications like assisting manufacturing personnel in operating equipment and in preliminary designs of fairly standard problems where the expert system substitutes for the experience of the designer. The benefits to be expected from growth in the use of expert systems in design include:

- The ability to capture valuable expertise and then to put it comfortably into the hands of a novice.
- The ability to improve the consistency of designs within an organization.
- The ability to eliminate errors in problem solving.
- The ability to interface the expert system with advanced software for engineering analysis. By further increasing the analytical capacity the amount of detail the system can cope with is expanded.
- The ability to search large databases for optimal selection of concepts, components, and materials.
- The ability to search design libraries for similar designs, so that engineers can learn from past experience and avoid duplication.
- The ability to reduce the cost of design while at the same time improving quality.

4.10
SUMMARY

The gathering of design information and data is not a trivial task. It requires knowledge of a wide spectrum of information sources. These sources are, in increasing order of specificity:

- The World Wide Web, and its access to digital databases
- Business catalogs and other trade literature
- Government technical reports and business data
- Published technical literature, including trade magazines
- Network of professional friends, aided by e-mail
- Network of professional colleagues at work
- Corporate consultants

At the outset it is a smart move to make friends with a knowledgeable librarian or information specialist in your company or at a local library who will help you become familiar with the information sources and their availability. Also, devise a plan to develop your own information resources of handbooks, texts, tearsheets from magazines, computer software, Web sites, etc., that will help you grow as a true professional.

BIBLIOGRAPHY

Anthony, L. J.: "Information Sources in Engineering," Butterworth, Boston, 1985.
"Guide to Materials Engineering Data and Information," ASM International, Materials Park, OH, 1986.
Mildren, K. W., and P. J. Hicks: "Information Sources in Engineering," 3d ed., Bowker Saur, London, 1996.
Wall, R. A. (ed.): "Finding and Using Product Information," Gower, London, 1986.

PROBLEMS AND EXERCISES

4.1. Prepare in writing a personal plan for combating technological obsolescence. Be specific about the things you intend to do and read.

4.2. Select a technical topic of interest to you.
  (a) Compare the information that is available on this subject in a general encyclopedia and a technical encyclopedia.
  (b) Look for more specific information on the topic in a handbook.
  (c) Find five current texts or monographs on the subject.

4.3. Use the indexing and abstracting services to obtain at least 20 current references on a technical topic of interest to you. Use appropriate indexes to find 10 government reports related to your topic.

4.4. Where would you find the following information?
  (a) The services of a taxidermist.
  (b) A consultant on carbon-fiber-reinforced composite materials.
  (c) The price of an X3427 semiconductor chip.
  (d) The melting point of osmium.
  (e) The proper hardening treatment for AISI 4320 steel.

4.5. Discuss how priority is established in a patent litigation.

4.6. How would you obtain information about a U.S. patent given the following conditions:
- (*a*) you know the patent number?
- (*b*) you know only the patentee's name?
- (*c*) you know the patent number and want to know prior development in the field?
- (*d*) no patent numbers or names are given?

4.7. What is the distinction between copyright and patent protection for software?

5

CONCEPT GENERATION AND EVALUATION

5.1
INTRODUCTION

With a clear product design specification developed in Chap. 2 we have arrived at the point where we are ready to generate design concepts, evaluate them, and decide which one will be carried forward to a final product. Figure 5.1 shows where we are in the eight-step design process. The principle that guides this work is that put forth

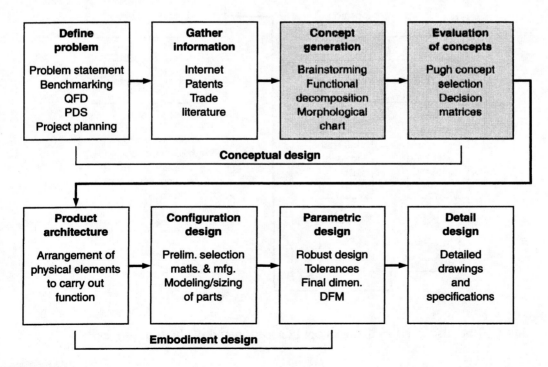

FIGURE 5.1
Steps in the design process, showing concept generation and evaluation as the essential and completing steps in conceptual design.

by the noted American architect-engineer Louis Henri Sullivan, "form follows function." By this we mean, if the functions of the design are clearly understood, then its appropriate form or structure will be easier to determine.

At the outset it is important to understand what is meant by concept generation. A design concept is an idea that is sufficiently developed that it can be evaluated in terms of physical realizability; i.e., the means of performing each major function has been determined. This may take the form of simple calculations, sketches, circuit diagrams, proof-of-concept models, or a detailed written description of the concept. Concept generation does not mean seizing upon the first feasible concept and beginning to refine it into a product design. This might be appropriate for a simple redesign, but in general this procedure will lead to a poor design. The process that we will employ in this chapter will result in the generation of multiple design concepts. Then, with a set of design concepts we will subject them to an evaluation scheme to determine the best concept or small subset of best concepts. Finally, a decision process will be used to decide on the best concept to develop into the final design.

Everyone would like to enhance their creativity and feel more secure in their ability to generate creative design concepts. For this reason Sec. 5.2 deals with some of the rapidly growing knowledge about creativity, and Sec. 5.3 discusses methods for enhancing creativity. The process for concept generation that we shall use follows closely that suggested by Ulrich and Eppinger[1] while the evaluation process is similar to that used by Ullman.[2] These are shown in Fig. 5.2.

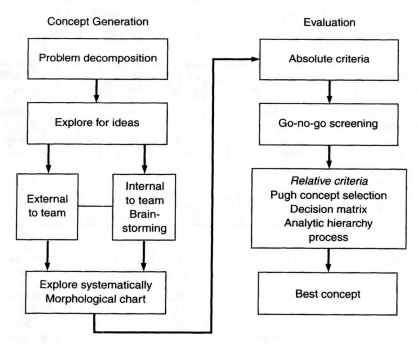

FIGURE 5.2
Steps that will be discussed in the concept generation and evaluation process.

1. K. T. Ulrich and S. D. Eppinger, "Product Design and Development," McGraw-Hill, New York, 1995.
2. D. G. Ullman, "The Mechanical Design Process," 2d ed., McGraw-Hill, New York, 1997.

5.2
CREATIVITY AND PROBLEM SOLVING

Creative thinkers are distinguished by their ability to synthesize new combinations of ideas and concepts into meaningful and useful forms. Engineering creativity is more akin to inventiveness than research. We would all like to be called "creative," yet most of us, in our ignorance of the subject, feel that creativity is reserved for only the chosen few. There is the popular myth that creative ideas arrive with flashlike spontaneity—the flash of lightning and clap of thunder routine. However, students of the creative process[1] assure us that most creative ideas occur by a slow, deliberate process that can be cultivated and enhanced with study and practice. We are all born with an inherent measure of creativity, but the process of maturation takes a toll on our native capacity.

A characteristic of the creative process is that initially the idea is only imperfectly understood. Usually the creative individual senses the total structure of the idea but initially perceives only a limited number of the details. There ensues a slow process of clarification and exploration as the entire idea takes shape. The creative process can be viewed as moving from an amorphous idea to a well-structured idea, from the chaotic to the organized, from the implicit to the explicit. Engineers, by nature and training, usually value order and explicit detail and abhor chaos and vague generality. Thus, we need to train ourselves to be sensitive and sympathetic to those aspects of the creative process. We need, also, to understand that the flow of creative ideas cannot be turned on upon command. Therefore, we need to recognize the conditions and situations that are most conducive to creative thought. We must also recognize that creative ideas are elusive, and we need to be alert to capture and record our creative thoughts.

Listed below are some positive steps you can take to enhance your creative thinking. A considerable literature has been written on creativity,[2] but the steps given here[3] encompass most of what has been suggested:

1. *Develop a creative attitude:* To be creative it is essential to develop confidence that you can provide a creative solution to a problem. Although you may not visualize the complete path through to the final solution at the time you first tackle a problem, *you must have self-confidence*; you must believe that a solution will develop before you are finished. Of course, confidence comes with success, so start small and build your confidence up with small successes.
2. *Unlock your imagination:* You must rekindle the vivid imagination you had as a child. One way to do so is to begin to question again. Ask "why" and "what if,"

---

1. E. Raudsepp, *Chem. Eng.,* pp. 101–104, Aug. 2, 1976; pp. 95–102, Aug. 16, 1976.
2. J. R. M. Alger and C. V. Hays, "Creative Synthesis in Design," Prentice-Hall, Englewood Cliffs, NJ, 1964; E. Van Frange, "Professional Creativity," Prentice-Hall, Englewood Cliffs, NJ, 1959; A. F. Osborne, "Applied Imagination," 3d ed., Charles Scribner's Sons, New York, 1965; E. Lumsdaine and M. Lumsdaine, "Creative Problem Solving," McGraw-Hill, New York, 1995; E. DeBono, "Serious Creativity," HarperCollins, New York, 1992.
3. R. J. Bronikowski, *Chem. Eng.,* July 31, 1978, pp. 103–108.

even at the risk of displaying a bit of naïveté. Scholars of the creative process have developed thought games that are designed to provide practice in unlocking your imagination and sharpening your power of observation.[1]

3. *Be persistent:* We already have dispelled the myth that creativity occurs with a lightning strike. On the contrary, it often requires hard work. Most problems will not succumb to the first attack. They must be pursued with persistence. After all, Edison tested over 6000 materials before he discovered the species of bamboo that acted as a successful filament for the incandescent light bulb. It was also Edison who made the famous comment, "Invention is 95 percent perspiration and 5 percent inspiration."

4. *Develop an open mind:* Having an open mind means being receptive to ideas from any and all sources. The solutions to problems are not the property of a particular discipline, nor is there any rule that solutions can come only from persons with college degrees. Ideally, problem solutions should not be concerned with company politics. Because of the NIH factor (not invented here) many creative ideas are not picked up and followed through.

5. *Suspend your judgment:* We have seen that creative ideas develop slowly, but nothing inhibits the creative process more than critical judgment of an emerging idea. Engineers, by nature, tend toward critical attitudes, so special forbearance is required to avoid judgment at an early stage.

6. *Set problem boundaries:* We place great emphasis on proper problem definition as a step toward problem solution. Establishing the boundaries of the problem is an essential part of problem definition. Experience shows that this does not limit creativity, but rather focuses it.

A creative experience often occurs when the individual is not expecting it and after a period when they have been thinking about something else. The secret to creativity is to fill the mind and imagination with the context of the problem and then relax and think of something else. As you read or play a game there is a release of mental energy which your preconscious can use to work on the problem. Frequently there will be a creative "Ah-ha" experience in which the preconscious will hand up into your conscious mind a picture of what the solution might be. Since the preconscious has no vocabulary, the communication between the conscious and preconscious will be by pictures or symbols. This is why it is important for engineers to be able to communicate effectively through three-dimensional sketches.

To achieve a truly creative solution to a problem a person must utilize two thinking styles: *vertical* or *convergent thinking* and *lateral* or *divergent thinking*. Vertical thinking is the type of analytical thought process reinforced by most engineering courses where one moves forward in sequential steps after a positive decision has been made about the idea. If a negative decision is made at any point in the process, you must retrace your steps along the analysis trail until the original concept statement is reached. In lateral thinking your mind moves in many different directions, combining different pieces of information into new patterns (synthesis) until several solution concepts appear. Table 5.1 compares the characteristics of vertical and lateral thinking.

---

1. E. Raudsepp, "Creative Growth Games," 2d ed., Jove Publications, New York, 1982.

TABLE 5.1
Characteristics of vertical and lateral thinking

Vertical or convergent thinking	Lateral or divergent thinking
Only one correct solution (selective)	Many possible solutions (generative)
Analytical process (judgmental)	Nonjudgmental
Movement is made in a sequential, rule-based manner	Movement is made in a more random pattern
If a positive decision cannot be made at a step, progress stops	If a positive decision cannot be made at a step, thinking jumps
Follows only most likely decision path	Follows all paths
Deals only with reality as science knows it today	Can create its own reality (fantasy)
Classifications and labels are rigid	Reclassifies objects to generate ideas

Source: B. Lee Tuttle, Creative Concept Development, "ASM Handbook," vol. 20, 1997.

Cognitive studies have shown that the left hemisphere of the brain concentrates in processing information that is analytical, logical, or sequential in nature. The right hemisphere functions by recognizing relationships, integrating and synthesizing information, and arriving at intuitive insights. Engineers often are characterized as being left-brained, but there is no reason that you cannot become a whole-brain individual.

5.2.1 Invention

An invention is something novel and useful. As such, we generally can consider it to be the result of creative thought. A study of a large number of inventions[1] showed that inventions can be classified into seven categories:[2]

1. *The simple or multiple combination:* The most elementary form of invention is a simple combination of two existing inventions to produce a new or improved result.
2. *Labor-saving concept:* This is a higher level of invention sophistication in which an existing process or mechanism is changed in order to save effort, produce more with the same effort, or dispense with a human operator.
3. *Direct solution to a problem:* This category of invention is more typical of what we can consider to be engineering problem solving. The inventor is confronted with a need and sets out deliberately to design a system that will satisfy the need.
4. *Adaptation of an old principle to an old problem to achieve a new result:* This is a variation of category 3. The problem (need) has been in existence for some time, and the principle of science or engineering that is key to its solution also has been known. The creative step consists in bringing the proper scientific principle to bear on the particular problem so as to achieve the useful result.

---

1. G. Kivenson, "The Art and Science of Inventing," 2d ed., pp. 14–20, Van Nostrand Reinhold, New York, 1982.
2. For a Web Site that provides information on evaluation of inventions, tips on finding financial support for inventions and patenting inventions, see html://www.inventorsdigest.com.

5. *Application of a new principle to an old problem:* A problem is rarely solved for all time; instead, its solution is based on the then current limitations of knowledge. As knowledge (new principles) becomes available, its application to old problems may achieve startling results. As an example, the miniaturization of electronic and computer components is creating a revolution in many areas of technology.

6. *Application of a new principle to a new use:* People who are broadly knowledge-able about new scientific and engineering discoveries often are able to apply new principles in completely different disciplinary areas or areas of technology.

7. *Serendipity:* The mythology of invention is full of stories about accidental discoveries that led to great inventions. Lucky breaks do occur, but they are rare. Also, they hardly ever happen to someone who is not already actively pursuing the solution of a problem. Strokes of good fortune seem to be of two types. The first occurs when the inventor is actively engaged in solving a problem but is stymied until a freak occurrence or chance observation provides the needed answer. The second occurs when inventors suddenly gain a valuable insight or discover a new principle that is not related to the problem they are pursuing. They then apply the discovery to a new problem, and the result is highly successful.

5.2.2 A Psychological View of Problem Solving

Some psychologists describe the creative problem-solving process in terms of a simple four-stage model.

Preparation (*stage* 1): The elements of the problem are examined and their inter-relations are studied.

Incubation (*stage* 2): You "sleep on the problem."

Inspiration (*stage* 3): A solution or a path toward the solution suddenly emerges.

Verification (*stage* 4): The inspired solution is checked against the desired result.

This is obviously a simplified model, since we know that many problems are solved more by perspiration than by inspiration. Nevertheless, there is great value in letting a problem lie fallow so as to give the preconscious mind a chance to operate.

It is useful to understand something about how the mind stores and processes information. We can visualize the mind as a three-element computer.

1. The *preconscious mind* is a vast storehouse of information, ideas, and relations based on past education and experience.

2. The *conscious mind* compares the information and ideas stored in the preconscious mind with external reality.

3. The *unconscious mind* acts on the other two elements. It may distort the relation of the conscious and preconscious through its control of symbols and the generation of bias.

The exact details of how the human mind processes information are still the subject of much active research, but it is known that the mind is very inferior to modern computers in its data-processing capacity. It can picture or grasp only about seven or eight things at any instant. Thus, the mind can be characterized as a device with extremely low information-processing capacity combined with a vast subliminal store of information. Those characteristics of the mind have dominated the development of problem-solving methods.

Our attempts at problem solving often are stymied by the mind's low data-processing rate, so that it is impossible to connect with the information stored in the preconscious mind. Thus, an important step in problem solving is to study the problem from all angles and in as many ways as possible to understand it completely. Most problems studied in that way contain more than the seven or eight elements that the mind can visualize at one time. Thus, the elements of the problem must be "chunked together" until the chunks are small enough in number to be conceptualized simultaneously. Obviously, each chunk must be easily decomposed into its relevant parts.

Another important step in problem solving is the generation of divergent ideas and relations. The brainstorming technique described in Sec. 3.6 is one of the generation methods. The objective of this step is to stir up the facts in the preconscious mind so that unusual and creative relationships will be revealed.

5.3
CREATIVITY METHODS

Improving creativity is a popular endeavor. Over two dozen techniques for developing creative thinking have been proposed.[1] A check on the Internet at amazon.com revealed several hundred books on the subject. There are four factors that help improve a person's creativity, and creativity methods aim at strengthening these characteristics.

- *Sensitivity:* The ability to recognize that a problem exists
- *Fluency:* The ability to produce a large number of alternative solutions to a problem
- *Flexibility:* The ability to develop a wide range of approaches to a problem
- *Originality:* The ability to produce original solutions to a problem

5.3.1 Mental Blocks

Before looking at ways of enhancing creativity it is important to understand how mental blocks interfere with creative problem solving.[2] A *mental block* is a mental wall that prevents the problem solver from correctly perceiving a problem or conceiving its solution. There are many different types of mental blocks.

Perceptual blocks

The most frequently occurring perceptual blocks are:

- *Stereotyping:* Thinking conventionally or in a formulaic way about an event, person, or way of doing something. Not thinking "out of the box."

---

1. See the Web site http://www.ozemail.com.au/~caveman/Creative/Techniques/index.
2. J. L. Adams, "Conceptual Blockbusting," 3d ed., Addison-Wesley, Reading, MA, 1986.

Space Capsule Heat Shield

In the early days of the NASA space program a critical unsolved problem was how to protect the space capsule from burning up due to the frictional heating from reentry into the earth's atmosphere. Initially the problem was stated as "Find a metal capable of withstanding the heat of reentry."

After months of frustrating failure the problem was stated more broadly as "How can we keep the space capsule from burning up in the earth's atmosphere?" This broader problem formulation led to solutions based on

- High melting point, low thermal conductivity nonmetallic materials
- Ablative materials, that burn slowly and fall away
- Solutions that do not use a heat shield

- *Information overload:* You become so overloaded with minute details that you are unable to sort out the critical aspects of the problem.
- *Limiting the problem unnecessarily:* Broad statements of the problem help keep the mind open to a wider range of ideas.

Emotional blocks

These are obstacles that reduce the freedom with which you can explore and manipulate ideas. They also interfere with your ability to conceptualize readily.

- *Fear of risk taking:* This is inbred in us by the educational process.
- *Unease with chaos:* People, and many engineers in particular, are uncomfortable with highly unstructured situations.
- *Adopting a judgmental attitude:* We often approach problem solving with a negative attitude and jump too quickly to judgment.
- *Unable or unwilling to incubate:* In our busy lives, we don't take the time to let ideas lie dormant so they can incubate properly.

Cultural blocks

People acquire a set of thought patterns from living in a culture. For example, the U.S. culture currently is one which avoids problem solving around issues that are termed "politically incorrect."

Environmental blocks

The environment in which we work can have a strong influence on creativity. If the workplace is noisy, hot, or subject to frequent distractions, creativity will suffer. The attitude in your organization also contributes to this environment. Some organizations place a higher importance on being creative than others, and this affects the level of creativity.

Intellectual blocks

Lacking the necessary information base or the necessary intellectual skills can be a barrier to creativity.

5.3.2 Brainstorming

The most common method for creating ideas is brainstorming. The brainstorming process was described in Sec. 3.6. Two additional pointers for effective brainstorming are:

- Carefully define the problem at the start. Time spent here can avoid wasting time generating solutions to the wrong problem.
- Allow 5 min for each individual to think through the problem on their own before starting the group process. This avoids a follow-the-leader type of thought process.

One way to help brainstorming participants is to enlarge their search space by using a checklist to help them develop a budding idea. The originator of brainstorming proposed such a list,[1] which has been modified by Eberle[2] into the acrostic SCAMPER. See Table 5.2. The questions in the SCAMPER checklist are applied to the problem in the following way:[3]

- Read aloud the first SCAMPER question.
- Write down ideas or sketch ideas that are stimulated by the question.
- Rephrase the question and apply it to the other aspects of the problem.
- Continue applying the questions until the ideas cease to flow.

Because the SCAMPER questions are very generalized, they sometimes will not apply to a specific technical problem. Therefore, if a question fails to evoke ideas, move on quickly to the next question. A group that will be doing product development

TABLE 5.2
SCAMPER checklist to aid in brainstorming

Proposed change	Description
Substitute	What if used in a different material, process, person, power source, place, or approach?
Combine	Could I combine units, purposes, or ideas?
Adapt	What else is like this? What other idea does it suggest? Does the past offer a parallel? What can I copy?
Modify, magnify, minify	Could I add a new twist? Could I change the meaning, color, motion, form, or shape? Could I add something? Make stronger, higher, longer, thicker? Could I subtract something?
Put to other uses	Are there new ways to use this as is? If I modify it, does it have other uses?
Eliminate	Can I remove a part, function, person without affecting outcome?
Rearrange, reverse	Could I interchange components? Could I use a different layout or sequence? What if I transpose cause and effect? Could I transpose positive and negative? What if I turn it backward, upside down, or inside out?

1. A. Osborne, "Applied Imagination," Charles Scribner & Sons, New York, 1953.
2. R. Eberle, "SCAMPER: Games for Imagination Development," D.O.K. Press, Buffalo, NY, 1990.
3. B. L. Tuttle, Creative Concept Development, "ASM Handbook," vol. 20, pp. 39–48, ASM International, Materials Park, OH 1997.

over time in a particular area should attempt to develop their own questions tailored to the situation.

Another way to stimulate ideas is with a random input. The random input can come from opening the dictionary, or any book, and randomly selecting a word. The word is used to act as a trigger to change the pattern of thought that has resulted in a mental block. Creativity pioneer Edward de Bono breaks blocks by requiring the participants to find a connection between the problem and some object, like a clock or a vase.

5.3.3 Synectics

Synectics[1] is a technique for creative thinking which draws on analogical thinking, i.e., on the ability to see parallels or connections between apparently dissimilar topics. Four types of analogies are used.

1. *Direct analogies:* Most of these are found in biological systems.[2]
2. *Personal analogies:* The designer imagines what it would be like to use one's body to produce the effect that is being sought, e.g., what it would feel like to be a helicopter rotor?
3. *Symbolic analogies:* These are poetic metaphors and similes in which one thing is identified with aspects of another, e.g., the *mouth* of a river, a *tree* of decisions.
4. *Fantasy analogies:* Here we let our imagination run wild and wish for things that don't exist in the real world.

5.3.4 Force-Fitting Methods

There are a large number of techniques that encourage new ideas by forcing the mind to make creative leaps. They are most often used when a team becomes stuck and can't come forth with many ideas. The SCAMPER checklist shown in Table 5.2 is one of the most widely used methods.

Another trigger to break mind blocks and open the search space is use the analogy and fantasy concepts from synectics to ask participants to explore possibilities that otherwise seem impossible, by asking what would happen if they were possible. For example, "What if gravity didn't exist?" One approach is to first define the problem's constraints, and then ask "what if" as these are removed in turn. Once free from constraints, novel ideas often flow. Then the real world constraints are reintroduced and the solution is modified to work within the constraints.

---

1. W. J. J. Gordon, "Synectics," Harper & Row, New York, 1961.
2. T. W. D'Arcy, "Of Growth and Form," Cambridge Univ. Press, 1961; S. A. Wainwright *et al.*, "Mechanical Design in Organisms," Arnold, London, 1976; M. J. French, "Invention and Evolution: Design in Nature and Engineering," 2d ed., Cambridge University Press, New York, 1994; S. Vogel, "Cat's Paws and Catapults: Mechanical Worlds of Nature and People," W. W. Norton & Co., New York, 1998.

Note that the inventor of the Velcro fastener, George de Mestral, conceived the idea after wondering why cockleburrs stuck to his wool socks. Under the microscope he found that hook-shaped projections on the burrs grasped loops in the wool sock. After a long search he found that a nylon material could be formed into hooks that would retain their shape.

Attribute listing creates a checklist by listing the important attributes, parts, or functions of a problem. The group focuses on each attribute, in turn, and answers questions such as "Why does it have to be this way?"

5.3.5 Mind Map

A very useful technique for note taking and the generation of ideas by association is the mind map[1] and its close relation, the *concept map*.[2] A mind map is created on a large sheet of paper. The problem is drawn at the center. Think about what factors, ideas, or concepts are directly related to the problem. Write them down surrounding the central problem. Underline or circle them and connect them to the central problem. Figure 5.3 shows a mind map or concept map created for a project on the recy-, cling of steel and aluminum scrap.[3] Note that this is a good method to use before you start to write a report or major written document to ensure that all necessary topics will be covered in the document.

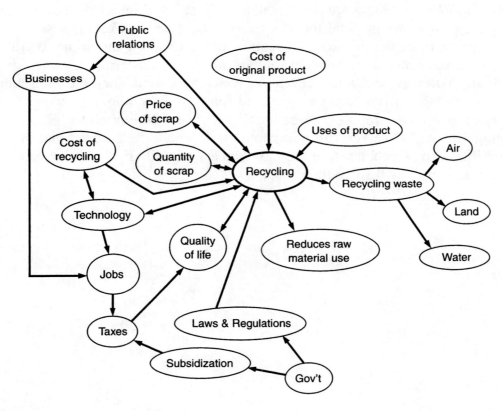

FIGURE 5.3
Concept map for the recycling of a metal like steel or aluminum.

1. Tony Buzan, "Use Both Sides of Your Brain," Dutton, New York, 1983.
2. J. D. Novak and D. B. Gowan, "Learning How to Learn," Cambridge Press, New York, 1984.
3. I. Nair, Decision Making in the Engineering Classroom, *J. Engr. Education,* vol. 86, no. 4, pp. 349–356, 1997.

5.4
CREATIVE IDEA EVALUATION

As we saw in Sec. 3.7, the objective in brainstorming is to generate as many ideas as possible. Quantity counts above quality, and wild ideas are encouraged. Now we need to look at these ideas more critically, with the objective of shaping them into a smaller subset of ideas that can be practically implemented as solutions.[1] The objective of creative idea evaluation is not to come up with a single or very small number of solutions. This is achieved by the evaluation methods considered in Sec. 5.9. The purpose of this step in concept generation is synthesis of creative yet practical ideas.

The first step is to sort the ideas into categories. See discussion on the affinity diagram in Sec. 3.7. Now a second round of brainstorming takes place. The team works with one category at a time, or if the team is large it breaks into subgroups and each works on a category. The objective is to reduce the category to fewer ideas that are more fully developed and of high quality. During this round of brainstorming discussion is encouraged as the team elaborates, adds detail, and hitchhikes on ideas. Some of the force-fitting methods discussed in the previous section are employed. This is a period of *synthesis* as ideas are combined, force-fitted, and integrated into new, better-quality ideas. It is not unusual for new ideas to be generated in this session, and for these to prove to be the best ideas. Creative idea evaluation should not be rushed. It can easily take two or three times as long as the first brainstorming.

Finally, with new and better-developed ideas in each category, the team should try to take a good idea from each category and force-fit them into yet another small set of ideas. These ideas are likely to be highly creative solutions to the problem, since the categories will have very little in common. It should be realized that this step is not possible with all problems. In this case you are left with lists of valuable ideas that when implemented will solve the problem.

5.6
CONCEPTUAL DECOMPOSITION

In solving any complex problem, a common tactic is to decompose the problem into smaller parts that are easier to manage. In breaking the system into subsystems, it is important to do it in such a way that the connections of elements in terms of structure and function within the "chunks" are stronger than those between the chunks. In prod-

---

1. The average engineer knows 50 to 100 physical and chemical laws, principles, and effects which can be used in the solution of design problems, but there are over 6000 such effects described in the scientific literature. Altshuller and his coworkers cataloged these with respect to function. They are available as part of the Invention Machine software.

uct design we typically start with a product or major subassembly and break this into subsidiary subassemblies and components. For example, an automobile would be decomposed into the major subassemblies of engine, drive train, suspension system, steering system, and body.

There are two chief approaches to conceptual decomposition. In *decomposition in the physical domain* the product or subassembly is decomposed directly into its subsidiary subassemblies and components. The second method is *functional decomposition*. Here the emphasis is on identifying *only* the subfunctions required to achieve the overall function. Then as a second step the embodiments (shape, force, motion, etc.) to achieve each subfunction are identified.

Most engineers instinctively follow the direct approach of physical decomposition by sketching a subassembly or part and by decomposing a design without thinking explicitly about the functions each component is created to perform. However, the approach of functional decomposition is inherently more basic. It builds on the principle that form follows function, but more importantly, because it does not initially impose a design, it allows more leeway for creativity and generates a wide variety of alternative solutions. The great advantage of functional decomposition is that the method facilitates the examination of options that most likely would not have been considered if the designer moved quickly to selecting specific physical principles or, even worse, selecting specific hardware.

5.6.1 Decomposition in the Physical Domain

Product conceptual design by physical decomposition starts with the product design specification (PDS), and possibly an industrial designer's preliminary concept of the size and shape. The first step is to decompose the product into those subassemblies and components that are essential for the overall functioning of the product. We need to be able to describe in qualitative physical terms how these design elements will work together to accomplish the required functions of the product. Thus, function is not ignored totally in physical decomposition. We need to be able to describe the principal functions of each subsidiary subassembly and component. We also need to understand the interactions or connections that each of these design elements has with each other, i.e., the *couplings*. Coupling among subsidiary subassemblies and components can be physical, as when they are physically connected, or can be energy or force connection. Another important requirement may be the allocation of some scarce resource like space, weight, or cost among the subsystems.

An important design consideration which is beginning to emerge at this point is *product architecture* (see Sec. 6.2). Product architecture is the scheme by which the functional elements of the product are arranged into physical building blocks (*chunks*). While product architecture is completely established in the phase of design called embodiment design, its origins start here.

Generally there is more than a single stage of conceptual decomposition for a product. Each of the subassemblies created at the first level of decomposition will be decomposed into its subassemblies and components, and each of these subassemblies will be decomposed into its subassemblies and components, until, ultimately, only components remain. For example, the automobile engine subassembly is decomposed into, among other things, an engine block and an ignition system, which is

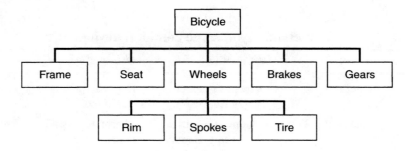

FIGURE 5.7
Direct decomposition of a bicycle into subassemblies and components.

decomposed into spark plugs, a wiring harness, and a fuel injection subassembly. Figure 5.7 shows the decomposition in the physical domain of a bicycle.

As the decomposition proceeds to lower and lower levels, the situation regarding design information changes. The information that is available about a subassembly that is created at the first level of decomposition is only slightly different from the state of information for the product as a whole. For a subassembly created two levels down, we not only have that information but additional specific information about the functions and couplings of the subassembly with the product. Note that the functions of subassemblies or components "down in the pile" are very different from the functions of the product. The functions of a spark plug are very specific and not even mentioned in the PDS of the product. The functions of subassemblies tend to be more specific and more technical than are the functions of a product, which are more closely aligned with the needs of the customer. These are the types of narrowly defined problems you have addressed in most of your design courses.

Another fact that should be clear by now is that large or complex products have a very large number of coupled subassemblies and components. The Boeing 777 air transport has one million parts, not counting rivets. Thus, information management in product development can be a very major and challenging problem.

5.6.2 Functional Decomposition

In functional decomposition the system's functions are described as a transformation between an initial state and a desired final state. We consider *function* to be in the nature of a *physical behavior* or *action*. Function tells us *what* the product must do, while its form or structure tells *how* it will accomplish it. Table 5.5 illustrates the functionality of several common devices.

The approach to concept generation by functional decomposition originated with the German school of design methodology.[1] From Table 5.5 we can see that the inputs and outputs to the functional devices are described in terms of either energy flow, material flow, or information flow (signals). Functions associated with a flow of energy are classified both by the type of energy and by its action on the system.

---

1. G. Pahl and W. Beitz, "Engineering Design," 2d ed., edited by Ken Wallace, Springer-Verlag, London, 1996; R. Koller, "Konstruktionslehre fuer den Maschinenbau," Springer-Verlag, Berlin, 1985.

TABLE 5.5
Functionality of some common devices

Device	Input	Function	Other effects	Output
Nozzle	Fluid flow	Increase velocity of fluid	Decrease pressure of fluid	Fluid flow
Motor	Electrical energy	Convert electrical energy to rotating mechanical energy	Thermal energy generated	Rotating mechanical energy
Pump	Fluid flow and mechanical energy	Increase pressure of fluid	Change direction of flow? Thermal energy	Fluid flow
Gear	Rotating mechanical energy	Change speed of rotation	Change direction of rotation	Rotating mechanical energy
Electric resistance element	Electrical energy	Convert to thermal energy	Element increases in temperature	Thermal energy
Pencil	Mechanical energy	Transfer graphite from pencil to paper		Graphite deposit on paper
Expansion valve in refrigeration system	Liquid refrigerant	Reduce temperature of refrigerant	Reduce pressure of refrigerant	Refrigerant (two-phase mixture)
Lever or wrench	Energy (force or torque in motion)	Increase magnitude of force or torque		Energy
Switch	Mechanical energy (force in motion)	Separate or join contacts	Flow of electricity enabled or stopped	Position of contacts moved
Room thermostat	Flow of room air	Separate or join contacts	Flow of electricity enabled or stopped	Position of contacts moved

J. R. Dixon and C. Poli, "Engineering Design and Design for Manufacturing," Field Stone Publishers, Conway, MA, 1995. Used with permission.

Normal energy types are mechanical, electrical, chemical, fluid, and thermal. The actions of a function are described by action verbs. A small initial set would be change, change back, enlarge, reduce, change in direction, conduct, insulate, connect, separate, join, divide, store, and destore. A much larger set of mechanical design action verbs is given in Table 5.6.

Material flow is divided into three main classes: (1) through-flow or material-conserving processes, in which material is manipulated to change its position or shape, (2) diverging flow, in which the material is divided into two or more parts, and (3) converging flow, in which material is joined or assembled.

Functions associated with information flow will be found in the form of mechanical or electrical signals, or software instructions. Usually, information flows are part of an automatic control system or the interface with a human being. For example, if you attached a bracket with screws, after you tighten the screws you would wiggle the bracket to see if it was securely attached. The observation of the system's response to wiggling is an information flow that confirms that the bracket is properly attached.

TABLE 5.6
Action verbs to be used with mechanical design

Absorb/remove	Drive	Rectify
Actuate	Grasp	Release
Amplify	Guide	Rotate
Assemble/disassemble	Hold or fasten	Secure
Attach	Increase/decrease	Separate
Change	Interrupt	Shield
Channel or guide	Join/separate	Start/stop
Clear or avoid	Lift	Steer
Collect	Limit	Store
Conduct	Locate	Supply
Control	Mix	Support
Convert	Move	Transform
Couple/interrupt	Orient	Translate
Direct	Position, relative to	Verify
Dissipate	Protect	

Source: D. G. Ullman, "The Mechanical Design Process," 2d ed., McGraw-Hill, New York, 1997.

The process of functional decomposition describes the design problem in terms of a flow of energy, material, and information. This creates a detailed understanding at the beginning of the process about *what* the product is expected to do. Some of this information is already contained in the QFD (see Sec 2.6). With the overall function defined by these flows, we decompose it into subfunctions expressed by a verb-noun combination. For example, in the function structure of a potato harvester we might use "separate leaves" (verb) (noun). The verb indicates what is being done by the product, and the noun indicates who or what is receiving the action. Next the subfunctions are reordered to give a logical order to achieve the overall objective of the design. Finally, each subfunction is examined to see whether it is decomposed as finely as possible. If not, then sub-subfunctions, and maybe even sub-sub-subfunctions, are created.

> **EXAMPLE.** The design of a compact disc "jewel" case that was initiated in Chap. 2 is continued here. Turn to the QFD diagram (Fig. 2.5) to refresh your memory about the requirements of such a product.

1. *State the overall function that needs to be accomplished.* Put this one most important function inside of the system box (Fig. 5.8). Now the flows in and flows out need to be identified. Remember that energy and material must be conserved; i.e., whatever goes into the system must come out or be stored in the system. Information flow often is related to knowing whether the system is performing as expected. Also, shown at the top of the diagram are objects that interact or interface with the system. This "black box" model of the product shows the input and output flows for the primary high-level function of the design task.

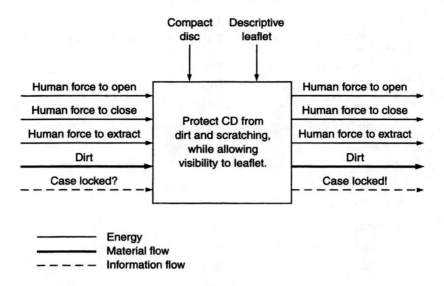

FIGURE 5.8
Overall system diagram for the CD jewel case.

2. *Create descriptions of subfunctions.* The objective of this step is to decompose the overall function in the black box into subfunctions described by verb-noun-modifier combinations. For example, *release disc from rosette.* (The rosette is the prickly plastic centerpiece that secures the CD in the case.) The customer needs (*whats*) in the QFD provide guidance about what functions the product should contain. Any structure-oriented *how* suggestions should be suppressed because they add detail too soon. It may be hard, at first, to think only in terms of function, since we conventionally think about functions through their physical embodiments.

Start with the overall function and break it down into separate subfunctions. Each subfunction represents a change or transformation in the flow of energy, material, or information. A useful way to do this is to trace the flow as it is transformed from its initial state to its final state when it leaves the product system boundary. Brainstorming or personal analogy to imagine you are actually in the flow or are in the role of the product may be useful in this process. Write the subfunctions in Post-It notes so they can be rearranged in step 3. Figure 5.9 shows several subfunctions generated for the CD case.

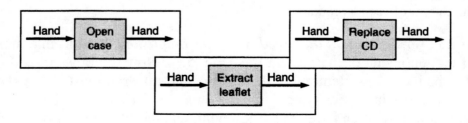

FIGURE 5.9
Several subfunctions generated from the overall function involving movement of the human hand.

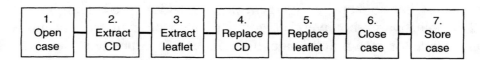

FIGURE 5.10
Subfunctions required to open and close the CD case.

For the situation of a redesign problem, or where you are benchmarking a competitor's product, it is often possible to disassemble the product, one component at a time, to identify the subfunctions. Note what objects—features, components, assemblies, people—it interfaces with, and record the flow of energy, materials, and information between them.

3. *Arrange the subfunctions in logical order.* For some problems this is a trivial step, but for other design problems it can be major. The object is to order the functions and subfunctions found in step 2 to achieve the overall function in step 1. The QFD shows that one of the major customer needs is easier opening of the case and removing of the CD and the leaflet. Figure 5.10 shows the sequence of subfunctions to remove the CD and the leaflet.

4. *Refine the subfunctions.* The objective is to refine the subfunctions as finely as possible. Refinement stops when a subfunction can be fulfilled by a single solution that is an object or action, and the level of detail is sufficient to address the customer needs. For example, the subfunction 1.0 Open Case can be decomposed into 1.1 Hold and Grip Case, 1.2 Disengage Locking Mechanism, and 1.3 Expose CD.

Having now identified the functions and subfunctions, we are ready to generate design concepts. This is the subject of the next section.

Functional decomposition is not easy to implement in all situations. Dixon[1] suggests the compromise approach of starting with a physical decomposition and then identifying the functions that each subassembly and component fulfills. Then you can focus on ways of fulfilling the identified functions, and look for ways to separate and combine functions. Although this approach is not as general as functional decomposition, it is less abstract and therefore may be easier to implement.

5.7
GENERATING DESIGN CONCEPTS

Design concepts are the means for providing function. They are the *hows*. The exploration for ideas for concepts can take two general paths. First, as many as possible of the resources external to the design team that were described in Chap. 4 should be employed. Examples include reading patents, benchmarking related products, talking with consultants, and exploring the Web. The more information that is gathered about the problem the better will be the ideas leading to design concepts. Second, it is within the design team that the hard work of concept generation finally takes place. This

---

1. J. R. Dixon and C. Poli, "Engineering Design and Design for Manufacture," Field Stone Publishers, Conway, MA , pp. 6–8.

process occurs in two steps, a divergent process and a convergent process (see Fig. 5.14). The objective in the divergent step is to uncover as many concepts as possible that can provide for each function identified in the decomposition (Sec. 5.5). The convergent step combines these individual concepts into overall design concepts that satisfy all of the functional requirements.

5.7.1 Concept Development

Ultimately it is the storehouse of personal and team knowledge and creativity that generates design concepts. Studies of problem solving suggest that a group of people working as individuals for a period of time will generate more and better concepts than the same people working together for the same period.[1] This does not denigrate the importance of teams. Teams are vital for refining concepts, communication, and building consensus. The best procedure is for each team member to spend several hours working as an individual on some subset of the problem, such as how to satisfy some subfunction. The aids to creativity discussed in Sec. 5.3 should be employed. Then the team assembles to discuss and improve the concepts developed individually.[2]

As a result of the exploration for ideas, the team will have collected tens of fragments of design concepts.[3] These are solutions that provide *hows* for the various subfunctions.

5.7.2 Morphological Chart

The morphological chart arranges the functions and subfunctions in logical order, and for each subfunction lists the possible *hows*. The method was first proposed by Zwicky.[4] The word morphology means the study of shape or form; so morphological analysis is a way of creating new forms, i.e., design concepts. The purpose of the method is to uncover combinations of ideas that comprise design concepts that might not ordinarily be generated.

> **EXAMPLE.** We return to our now familiar problem of the design of the CD case. Table 5.7 shows the morphological chart built upon the earlier functional decomposition. We note that many ways of accomplishing the subfunctions are listed. No details of the possible embodiments are given except descriptive words or a very simple sketch. Note that for a few subfunctions only a single conceptual idea is given. This means that the designer has made a fundamental assumption. In this instance it is that the CD case will be opened by a human hand, and not by some other feasible but impractical method as with a robot

---

1. J. E. McGrath, "Groups: Interaction and Performance," Prentice-Hall, Englewood Cliffs, NJ, 1984.
2. K. T. Ulrich and S. D. Eppinger, op. cit., p. 90.
3. For many examples of how to apply the ideas in Table 5.2 to mechanical design see E. B. Magrab, "Integrated Product and Process Design and Development," CRC Press, Boca Raton, FL, 1997, pp. 114–126. Also see N. P. Chironis, "Mechanisms and Mechanical Devices Source Book," 2d ed., McGraw-Hill, New York, 1996.
4. F. Zwicky, "The Morphological Method of Analysis and Construction," Courant Anniversary Volume, pp. 461–470, Interscience Publishers, New York, 1948.

TABLE 5.7
Morphological chart for the design of a CD case

Subfunction	Concepts				
	(1)	(2)	(3)	(4)	(5)
1.0 Open case					
1.1 Hold and grip case	Flat box	Grooved box	Curved box	Case with handle	Rubber grab strips
1.2 Disengage lock	Friction lock	Inclined plane lock	Magnetic lock	Clamp lock	Clicking hinge lock
1.3 Expose CD	Conventional hinge	One-piece flex plastic hinge	Slide-out, like matchbox	Tilt like shampoo bottle top	
2.0 Extract CD					
2.1 Disengage from securing system	Conventional "rosetta"	Lift/lock device	Padded cradle		
2.2 Grasp CD and remove	Hand				
3.0 Extract leaflet					
3.1 Disengage from securing system	Tabs	Holding slot	Velcro straps	Tab that swivels	No securing system
3.2 Remove leaflet	Hand				
4.0 Replace CD					
4.1 Place CD in securing system	Hand				
4.2 Engage securing system	2-finger push	Whole hand			
5.0 Replace leaflet					
5.1 Place leaflet in securing system	Slide into position	Lay in position			
5.2 Engage securing system	Slide under tabs or in slot	Swivel tabs	Attach Velcro		
6.0 Close case					
6.1 Engage lock	Friction surfaces	Put magnets together	Slide platen into position		
7.0 Store case					
7.1 Place case in desired location	Put on table	Put on another CD	Put in special CD holder		

or your mouth. Another reason that only a single idea would be given could be that a physical embodiment was being given, or it could be that the design team is weak on ideas. We call this limited *domain knowledge*.

5.7.3 Combining Concepts

The next step is to combine concepts to arrive at a set of definitive design concepts. We note that the number of possible combinations is quite large. For the example given above there are $5 \times 5 \times 4 \times 3 \times 5 \times 2 \times 2 \times 3 \times 3 \times 3 = 162,000$ combinations, clearly too many to follow up in detail. We need to select one fragmentary concept for each subfunction. Some may be clearly infeasible or impractical and are not selected. However, care should be taken not to make this judgment too hurriedly. If in doubt, save an idea for the evaluation step (Sec. 5.9). Also, realize that some concepts will satisfy more than one subfunction. Likewise, not all subfunctions are independent, but rather they are coupled. This means that their solutions can be evaluated only in conjunction with the solutions for other subfunctions.

Do not rush into evaluation of design concepts. Outstanding designs often evolve out of several iterations of combining concept fragments from the morphological chart and working them into an integrated solution. This is a place where a smoothly functioning team pays off.

Although design concepts are quite abstract at this stage, it often is very helpful to utilize rough sketches. Sketches help us associate function with form, and they aid with our short-term memory as we work to assemble the pieces of a design. Moreover, sketches in a design notebook are an excellent way of documenting the development of a product for patent purposes.[1]

> **EXAMPLE.** Five design concepts for the CD case were evolved from the morphological chart in Table 5.7. The numbers after each feature ( ) represent the column in Table 5.7 where it is found.
>
> Concept 1. Conventional square box (1), with an inclined plane lock (2), and a slide-out matchbox for a hinge. The CD is secured with a conventional "rosetta" (1), while the leaflet is secured with tabs (1).
>
> Concept 2. A streamlined curved box to fit the hand (3), with a friction lock (2) and a conventional hinge (3). The CD is secured in padded elastomer cradle (3) and the CD cases are designed to stack flat (2).
>
> Concept 3. The box is grooved to the shape of the fingers (2), with a magnetic lock (3) and conventional hinges (1). A new lift/lock secures the CD (2). The leaflet fits in a slot in the top of the case (2).
>
> Concept 4. A standard square box (1) with magnetic lock (3) and conventional hinges (1). The CD is secured with a padded cradle (3), while the leaflet is secured with Velcro straps (3).
>
> Concept 5. A curved box (3) with inclined plane lock (2), with a slide-out match box (3). The CD is held by a rosetta (1) and the leaflet fits into a slot (2). The cases are designed to stack (2).

---

1. The notebook of the creative genius Leonardo da Vinci is available on CD-ROM from Corbis Corporation, 1996.

5.9
EVALUATION METHODS

We have reached the point where we must choose which concept or small set of concepts to develop into finished designs. Unfortunately, we are forced to make this choice at a stage in the design process where we still have very little detailed information. Thus, we need initial evaluation methods that can be applied during the relatively unstructured process of concept development. Other evaluation methods will be useful later on in design when we must make choices based on more detailed technical information. To aid in learning about a full spectrum of evaluation methods, we shall temporarily abandon our practice of presenting new ideas in a sequence tied to the design process, and rather present a full spectrum of evaluation methods in this section.

Evaluation involves *comparison*, followed by *decision making*. To make a valid comparison the concepts must exist at the same level of abstraction. In an *absolute comparison* the concept is directly compared with some set of requirements. In a *relative comparison* the concepts are compared with each other.

1. N. P. Suh, op. cit.
2. E. B. Magrab, "Integrated Product and Process Design and Development," chap. 4, CRC Press, Boca Raton, FL, 1997.

5.9.1 Comparison Based on Absolute Criteria

As we saw in Fig. 5.2, our scheme begins by comparing the concepts to a series of *absolute filters*.[1]

1. *Evaluation based on judgment of feasibility of the design:* The initial screen is based on the overall evaluation of the design team as to the feasibility of each concept. Concepts should be placed into one of three categories:

    (a) It is not feasible (it will never work)? Before discarding an idea, ask "why is it not feasible?" If judged not feasible, will it provide new insight into the problem?

    (b) It is conditional—it might work if something else happens? The something else could be the development of a critical element of technology or the appearance in the market of a new microchip that enhances some function of the product.

    (c) Looks as if it will work! This is a concept that seems worth developing further. Obviously, the reliability of these judgments is strongly dependent on the expertise of the design team. When making this judgment, err on the side of accepting a concept unless there is strong evidence that it will not work.

2. *Evaluation based on assessment of technology readiness:* Except in unusual circumstances, the technology used in a design must be mature enough that it can be used in the product design without additional research effort. *Product design is not the appropriate place to do R & D.* Some indicators of technology maturity are:

    (a) Can the technology be manufactured with known processes?

    (b) Are the critical parameters that control the function identified?

    (c) Are the safe operating latitude and sensitivity of the parameters known?

    (d) Have the failure modes been identified?

    (e) Does hardware exist that demonstrates positive answers to the above four questions?

3. *Evaluation based on go-no-go screening of the customer requirements:* After a design concept has passed filters 1 and 2, the emphasis shifts to establishing whether it meets the customer requirements framed in the QFD. Each customer requirement must be transformed into a question to be addressed to each concept. The questions should be answerable as either yes (go), maybe (go), or no (no-go). The emphasis is not on a detailed examination (that comes below) but on eliminating any design concepts that clearly are not able to meet an important customer requirement.

    EXAMPLE.

    Question: In concept 5 (Sec. 5.7), is the CD case easy to open?

    Answer: Maybe (go).

    Question: Will the locking of the case be secure in concept 5?

    Answer: Yes (go).

---

1. D. G. Ullman, op. cit., pp. 155–160.

Proceed in this way through all of the customer requirements. Note that if a design concept shows mostly goes, but it has a few no-go responses, it should not be summarily discarded. The weak areas in the concept may be able to be fixed by borrowing ideas from another concept. Or the process of doing this go-no-go analysis may trigger a new idea.

5.9.3 Measurement Scales

Rating a design characteristic among several alternative designs is a measurement. Therefore, we need to have some idea of the various scales that can be used in such ranking.[1] A *nominal scale* is a named category or identifier like "thin" or "shiny." This is not a very quantitative scale of measurement, although data of this type can be counted and the mode determined. The next measurement scale is an *ordinal scale,* in

1. K. N. Otto, Measurement Methods for Product Evaluation, *Research in Engineering Design,* vol. 7, pp. 86–101, 1995.

which items are ranked. Each item in the set is deemed better than or worse than its counterparts, and is placed in order. This is called an ordinal scale because the elements are only ordered. This measurement scale says nothing about how far apart the elements are from each other. Both the mode and the median can be determined for data measured on this scale. Note that the Pugh concept selection method uses an ordinal scale.

A method of ranking alternatives on an ordinal scale is to use *pairwise comparison*. Each design objective or criterion is listed and is compared to every other objective, two at a time. In making the comparison the objective that is considered the more important of the two is given a 1 and the less important objective is given as a 0. The total number of possible comparisons is $N = n(n - 1)/2$, where n is the number of objectives under consideration.

Consider the case where there are five design objectives, A, B, C, D, and E. In comparing A vs. B we consider A to be more important, and give it a 1. In comparing A vs. C we feel C ranks higher and a 0 is recorded. Thus, the table is completed. The rank order established is B, D, A, E, C.

Design objectives	A	B	C	D	E	Row total
A	—	1	0	0	1	2
B	0	—	1	1	1	3
C	1	0	—	0	0	1
D	1	0	1	—	1	3
E	0	0	1	0	—	1
						10

If we need information on how much worse A is relative to B, then an *interval scale* is needed. It is used when a quantitative scale is desired, but the objectives have no identifiable units of measure. An interval measurement scale has values with an arbitrary endpoint. The scale has no zero value. For example, we could distribute the results from the above example along a 1–10 scale to create an interval scale.

D							E		
B			A				C		
10	9	8	7	6	5	4	3	2	1

The most important objectives have been given a value of 10, and the others have been given values relative to this.

A *ratio scale* is an interval scale in which a zero value is used to anchor the scale. In an interval scale some arbitrary value is assigned to the base point. A ratio scale is needed to establish meaningful weighting factors.

5.9.4 Weighted Decision Matrix

A decision matrix is a method of evaluating competing concepts by ranking the design criteria with weighting factors and scoring the degree to which each design concept

TABLE 5.8
Evaluation scheme for design objectives

11-point scale	Description	5-point scale	Description
0	Totally useless solution	0	Inadequate
1	Very inadequate solution		
2	Weak solution	1	Weak
3	Poor solution		
4	Tolerable solution	2	Satisfactory
5	Satisfactory solution		
6	Good solution with a few drawbacks		
7	Good solution	3	Good
8	Very good solution		
9	Excellent (exceeds the requirement)	4	Excellent
10	Ideal solution		

meets the criterion. In doing this it is necessary to convert the values obtained for different design criteria into a consistent set of values. The simplest way of dealing with design criteria expressed in a variety of ways is to use a point scale. A 5-point scale is used when the knowledge about the criteria is not very detailed. An 11-point scale (0–10) is used when the information is more complete (Table 5.8). It is best if several knowledgeable people participate in this evaluation.

EXAMPLE. A heavy steel crane hook, for use in supporting ladles filled with molten steel as they are transported through the steel mill, is being designed. Three concepts have been proposed: (1) built-up from steel plates, welded together; (2) built-up from steel plates, riveted together; (3) a monolithic cast-steel hook.

The first step is to identify the design criteria by which the concepts will be evaluated. The product design specification is a prime source of this information. The design criteria are identified as (1) material cost, (2) manufacturing cost, (3) time to produce another if one fails, (4) durability, (5) reliability, (6) reparability.

The next step is to determine the weighting factor for each of the design criteria. A good way to proceed is to construct a hierarchical objective tree (Fig. 5.15). The weights of the individual categories at each level of the tree must add to 1.0. We should note that this is a simplified problem. Many problems could have two or more additional levels of hierarchy. To get the weight of a factor on a lower level, multiply the weights as you go up the chain. Thus, the weighting factor for material cost, $O_{111} = 0.3 \times 0.6 \times 1.0 = 0.18$.

The decision matrix is given in Table 5.9. The weighting factors are calculated from Fig. 5.15. The score for each concept for each criterion is derived from Table 5.8. The rating for each concept at each design criterion is obtained by multiplying the score by the weighting factor. The overall rating for each concept is the sum of these ratings.

The weighted decision matrix indicates that the best overall design concept would be a crane hook made from elements cut from steel plate and fastened together with rivets.

The simplest procedure in comparing design alternatives is to add up the ratings for each concept and declare the concept with the highest score the winner. A better

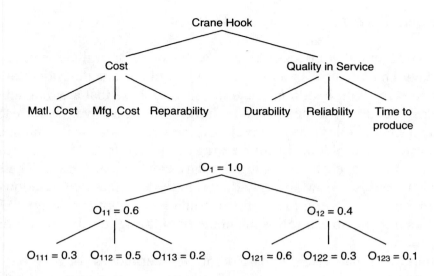

FIGURE 5.15
Objective tree for the design of a crane hook.

TABLE 5.9
Weighted decision matrix for a steel crane hook

Design criterion	Weight factor	Units	Built-up plates welded			Built-up plates riveted			Cast steel hook		
			Magnitude	Score	Rating	Magnitude	Score	Rating	Magnitude	Score	Rating
Material cost	0.18	¢/lb	60	8	1.44	60	8	1.44	50	9	1.62
Manufacturing cost	0.30	$	2500	7	2.10	2200	9	2.70	3000	4	1.20
Reparability	0.12	Experience	Good	7	0.84	Excellent	9	1.08	Fair	5	0.60
Durability	0.24	Experience	High	8	1.92	High	8	1.92	Good	6	1.44
Reliability	0.12	Experience	Good	7	0.84	Excellent	9	1.08	Fair	5	0.60
Time to produce	0.04	Hours	40	7	0.28	25	9	0.36	60	5	0.20
					7.42			8.58			5.66

way to use the decision matrix is to examine carefully the components that make up the rating to see what design factors influenced the result. This may suggest areas for further study or raise questions about the validity of the data or the quality of the individual decisions that went into the analysis. Pugh points out[1] that the outcome of a decision matrix depends heavily on the selection of the criteria. He worries that the method may instill an unfounded confidence in the user and that the designer will tend to treat the total ratings as being absolute.

---

1. S. Pugh, op. cit., pp. 92–99.

5.9.5 Analytic Hierarchy Process (AHP)

Saaty's analytic hierarchy process (AHP) is well suited for evaluation problems whose objectives have a hierarchical structure.[1] AHP is a multicriteria decision-making process that allows working with both numerical factors and those that are intangible and subjective. It provides a way to determine both the weights and values for each criterion in a consistent, methodologically correct, and intuitively acceptable manner.

Many evaluation problems in engineering design are framed in a hierarchy or system of stratified levels, each consisting of many elements or factors. The basic question to be answered is: "How strongly do the individual factors at the lowest level of the hierarchy influence its top factor, the overall objective of the design?" Figure 5.16 shows the hierarchical structure for the crane hook design problem introduced in the previous section.

AHP starts with pairwise comparison of the alternatives for each of the decision criteria to convert the verbal impression of importance into a numerical value. The criteria are arranged as the rows and columns of a matrix. Start with the first criterion in the first row and ask the question "How much more strongly does this criterion influence the outcome than the other criterion?" In answering this question, use Saaty's 9-point scale given in Table 5.10. This 9-point scale has been validated by statistical tests to give reproducibly accurate results. Moreover, it is a scale that people use instinctively.

> **EXAMPLE.** We shall use the AHP method to determine which design concept is best for the design of a crane hook (see previous example). The first task is to determine the weighting factors for each of the design criteria. This is done with a square matrix (Table 5.11). Start with the first row. Material cost is just as important as material cost in ranking the design criteria, so we put a 1.0 in the first cell. A value of 1.0 is put in each cell along the matrix diagonal because these cells compare one criterion with itself. Now we compare material cost with manufacturing cost and ask how much more important material cost is

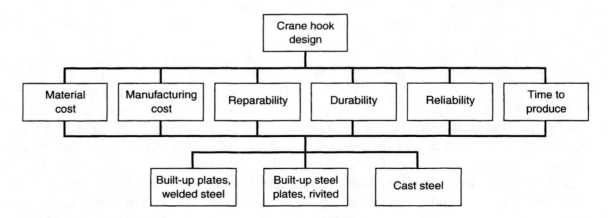

FIGURE 5.16
Hierarchical structure of the crane hook design.

---

1. T. L. Saaty, "The Analytic Hierarchy Process," McGraw-Hill, New York, 1980; T. L. Saaty, "Decision Making for Leaders," 3d ed., RWS Publications, Pittsburgh, PA, 1995.

TABLE 5.10
Saaty's fundamental scale for pairwise comparison

Intensity of importance	Definition	Description
1	Equal importance	Two activities contribute equally to the objective
3	Moderate importance	Judgment and experience slightly favor one activity over another
5	Strong importance	Judgment and experience strongly favor one activity over another
7	Very strong or demonstrated importance	An activity is favored very strongly over another; its dominance demonstrated in practice
9	Extreme importance	The evidence favoring one activity over another is of the highest possible
2, 4, 6, 8	These ratings are used to compromise between the above values	

TABLE 5.11
Square matrix to determine weighting factors

	Material cost	Manufacturing cost	Reparability	Durability	Reliability	Time to produce
Material cost	1	1/5 = 0.20	3	1/5 = 0.20	3	7
Manufacturing cost	5	1	7	3	3	7
Reparability	1/3 = 0.33	1/7 = 0.14	1	1/5 = 0.20	1/3 = 0.33	5
Durability	5	1/3 = 0.33	5	1	3	7
Reliability	1/3 = 0.33	1/3 = 0.33	3	1/3 = 0.33	1	7
Time to produce	1/7 = 0.14	1/7 = 0.14	1/5 = 0.20	1/7 = 0.14	1/7 = 0.14	1
Total	11.8	2.14	19.2	4.87	10.47	34.0

than manufacturing cost. Since we decide that manufacturing cost really is more important than material cost, we leave this cell blank for the moment and pass on. We ask how important is material cost compared with reparability, and decide from Table 5.10 that it is of moderate importance. Score a 3. We pass on along the first row in the manner just described. Now we are in the second row. We ask whether manufacturing cost is more important than material cost, and decide that it scores a 5 because it is of strong importance. Since manufacturing cost is considered strongly more important (5) than material cost, the importance of materials cost relative to manufacturing cost must be 1/5, or 0.20, and we enter this value in the second cell of row 1. Proceeding through the matrix of pairwise comparisons in this manner results in Table 5.11.

TABLE 5.12
Normalized values of Table 5.11, giving weighting factors

	Material cost	Manufacturing cost	Reparability	Durability	Reliability	Time to produce	Total	Weighting factor (AVG)
Material cost	0.085	0.093	0.156	0.041	0.286	0.206	0.867	0.144
Manufacturing cost	0.424	0.467	0.364	0.616	0.286	0.206	2.363	0.394
Reparability	0.028	0.065	0.052	0.041	0.031	0.147	0.364	0.061
Durability	0.424	0.154	0.260	0.205	0.286	0.206	1.535	0.256
Reliability	0.028	0.154	0.156	0.068	0.095	0.206	0.707	0.118
Time to produce	0.012	0.065	0.010	0.029	0.013	0.029	0.158	0.026
	1.000	1.000	1.000	1.000	1.000	1.000	6.000	1.000

Next we normalize the entries in each cell by dividing by the total for each column in Table 5.11. The average of the rows gives the weighting factor for each design criterion (Table 5.12). This is strictly true only if the pairwise comparisons are completely consistent. This is measured by the inconsistency ratio (IR). IR = 0 denotes complete consistency. IR $\leq$ 0.1 is considered to be acceptable. Consistency implies the transitivity relationship that if i is more important than j, and j is more important than k, then i is more important than k. Determining IR involves calculating the eigenvector of the matrix represented by Table 5.11. A much quicker way is to use the software developed for AHP.[1] Note that the values of the weighting factor have changed somewhat, compared with Table 5.9, because of the different evaluation approach used in the AHP method.

Now we will construct a decision matrix similar to Table 5.9. The magnitudes of the criterion factors for the three design concepts are given in that table. Let us convert the magnitudes for the manufacturing cost into ratings that can be used with AHP. Because a smaller number for cost is a "better number," we shall first convert the cost data by taking their reciprocals. Thus, a low cost will rate higher on this scale. The rating for each alternative is its fraction of the total.

	Built-up welded plates	Built-up riveted plates	Cast	
Manufacturing cost	2500	2200	3000	$ per crane hook
	400	454	333	reciprocal $\times 10^{-6}$
	0.34	0.38	0.28	fraction of total

Suppose we decide that the reparability of the crane hooks would be as given below. This ranking is based on expert judgment. It says that a crane hook built up by riveting cut steel plate is much easier to repair than a monolithic cast steel hook. The rating would be determined as follows.

---

1. Expert Choice®, version 9.0, available from Decision Support Software, Pittsburgh, PA.

	Built-up welded plates	Built-up riveted plates	Cast	
Reparability	6	10	1	Ranking
	0.35	0.59	0.06	Fraction of total

We can use AHP to create a ranking of the three design concepts with respect to the criterion durability. This is based on the judgment of the team applying Table 5.10 in the way illustrated above. Here we use a format that combines Tables 5.11 and 5.12 (see Table 5.13). It is important to realize rating values developed with the AHP are numbers on a ratio scale. Thus, we can multiply and divide these numbers without being concerned whether these operations are meaningful.

Now we are ready to combine the pieces of information into a decision matrix (Table 5.14). The rating values for the three design concepts come from the above small tables,

TABLE 5.13
AHP pairwise comparison to rank the design concepts with respect to durability

	Welded plate		Riveted plate		Cast		Total		Rating (average)
Welded plate	1.00	0.23	1/3 = 0.33	0.22	3.00	0.33		0.78	0.26
Riveted plate	3.00	0.69	1.00	0.65	5.00	0.56		1.90	0.63
Cast	1/3 = 0.33	0.08	1/5 = 0.20	0.13	1.00	0.11		0.32	0.11
Total	4.33	1.00	1.53	1.00	9.00	1.00		3.00	1.00

TABLE 5.14
Decision matrix for the crane hook problem

Design criterion	Weight factor	Welded plate	Riveted plate	Cast		Welded plate	Riveted plate	Cast
Material cost	0.14	0.31	0.31	0.38		0.043	0.043	0.053
Manufacturing cost	0.39	0.34	0.38	0.28		0.133	0.148	0.109
Reparability	0.06	0.35	0.59	0.06		0.021	0.035	0.004
Durability	0.25	0.26	0.63	0.11		0.065	0.157	0.027
Reliability	0.12	0.33	0.43	0.24		0.040	0.052	0.029
Time to produce	0.03	0.31	0.49	0.20		0.008	0.013	0.005
Total	1.00					0.31	0.45	0.23

plus others constructed in a similar way. In the same way as for the weighted decision matrix, each rating value for each concept is multiplied by the appropriate weighting factor for the design criterion. This gives the three columns to the right. The sum of each column is the relative importance of the design concept. Once again the riveted plate design is rated superior. Table 5.14 also shows how different design concepts rate with respect to various design criteria. For example, the cast hook rates rather low in ease of repair and durability.

We have carried out the AHP analysis step by step to give you a feel for what is involved. Using the Expert Choice® software would be a much quicker and better way of arriving at the results because it would allow the weighting factors to be adjusted readily to achieve an IR ≤ 0.1. The outcome comparable to Table 5.14, when the software is used, is shown in the table below.

**Decision matrix for the selection
of crane hook design**

Welded plate	Riveted plate	Cast
0.32	0.50	0.17
IR = 0.08		

Analysis made with Expert Choice®

5.10
DECISION MAKING

In the previous section we presented a number of ways of evaluating alternative design concepts or problem solutions so as to establish the "best solution." These were analysis techniques that helped us establish a logical decision process. Another way to approach the problem is through the field of decision analysis, which is an important area of study in the larger field of *operations research*. The use of decision analysis methods to make decisions in engineering design is an active area of research.

5.10.1 Behavioral Aspects of Decision Making

Making a decision is a stressful situation for most people. This psychological stress arises from at least two sources.[1] First, decision makers are concerned about the material and social losses that will result from either course of action that is chosen. Second, they recognize that their reputations and self-esteem as a competent decision maker are at stake. Severe psychological stress brought on by decisional conflict can be a major cause of errors in decision making. There are five basic patterns by which people cope with the challenge of decision making.

1. I. L. Janis and L. Mann, *Am. Scientist,* November–December, 1976, pp. 657–667.

1. *Unconflicted adherence:* Decide to continue with current action and ignore information about risk of losses.
2. *Unconflicted change:* Uncritically adopt whichever course of action is most strongly recommended.
3. *Defensive avoidance:* Evade conflict by procrastinating, shifting responsibility to someone else, and remaining inattentive to corrective information.
4. *Hypervigilance:* Search frantically for an immediate problem solution.
5. *Vigilance:* Search painstakingly for relevant information that is assimilated in an unbiased manner and appraised carefully before a decision is made.

All of these patterns of decision making, except the last one, are defective.

The quality of a decision does not depend on the particulars of the situation as much as it does on the manner in which the decision-making process is carried out. We will attempt to discuss the basic ingredients in a decision and the contribution made by each.[1] The basic ingredients in every decision are listed in the accompanying table. That a substitution is made for one of them does not necessarily mean that a bad decision will be reached, but it does mean that the foundation for the decision is weakened.

Basic ingredients	Substitute for basics
Facts	Information
Knowledge	Advice
Experience	Experimentation
Analysis	Intuition
Judgment	None

A decision is made on the basis of available facts. Great effort should be given to evaluating possible bias and relevance of the facts. Emphasis should be on preventing arrival at the right answer to the wrong question. It is important to ask the right questions to pinpoint the problem. When you are getting facts from subordinates, it is important to guard against selectivity—the screening out of unfavorable results. The status barrier between a superior and a subordinate can limit communication and transmission of facts. The subordinate fears disapproval, and the superior is worried about loss of prestige. Remember that the same set of facts may be open to more than one interpretation. Of course, the interpretation of qualified experts should be respected, but blind faith in expert opinion can lead to trouble.

Facts must be carefully weighed in an attempt to extract the real meaning: knowledge. In the absence of real knowledge, we must seek advice. It is good practice to check your opinions against the counsel of experienced associates. That should not be interpreted as a sign of weakness. Remember, however, that even though you do make wise use of associates, you cannot escape accountability for the results of your decisions. You cannot blame failures on bad advice; for the right to seek advice includes the right to accept or reject it. Many people may contribute to a decision, but the decision maker bears the ultimate responsibility for its outcome. Also, advice must be

---

1. D. Fuller, *Machine Design,* July 22, 1976, pp. 64–68.

sought properly if it is to be good advice. Avoid putting the adviser on the spot; make it clear that you accept full responsibility for the final decision.

There is an old adage that there is no substitute for experience, but the experience does not have to be your own. You should try to benefit from the successes and failures of others. Unfortunately, failures rarely are recorded and reported widely. There is also a reluctance to properly record and document the experience base of people in a group. Some insecure people seek to make themselves indispensable by hoarding information that should be generally available. Disputes between departments in an organization often lead to restriction of the experience base. In a well-run organization someone in every department should have total access to the records and experience of every other department.

Before a decision can be made, the facts, the knowledge, and the experience must be brought together and evaluated in the context of the problem. Previous experience will suggest how the present situation differs from other situations that required decisions, and thus precedent will provide guidance. If time does not permit an adequate analysis, then the decision will be made on the basis of intuition, an instinctive feeling as to what is probably right (an educated guess). An important help in the evaluation process is discussion of the problem with peers and associates.

The last and most important ingredient in the decision process is judgment. Good judgment cannot be described, but it is an integration of a person's basic mental processes. Judgment is a highly desirable quality, as evidenced by the fact that it is one of the factors usually included in personal evaluation ratings. Judgment is particularly important because most decisional situations are shades of gray rather than either black or white. An important aspect of good judgment is to understand clearly the realities of the situation.

A decision usually leads to an *action*. A situation requiring action can be thought of as having four aspects:[1] should, actual, must, and want.

The *should aspect* identifies what ought to be done if there are no obstacles to the action. A should is the expected standard of performance if organizational objectives are to be obtained. The should is compared with the *actual*, the performance that is occurring at the present point in time. The *must* action draws the line between the acceptable and the unacceptable action. A must is a requirement that cannot be compromised. A *want* action is not a firm requirement but is subject to bargaining and negotiation. Want actions are usually ranked and weighted to give an order of priority. They do not set absolute limits but instead express relative desirability.

To summarize this discussion of the behavioral aspects of decision making, we list the sequence of steps that are taken in making a good decision.[2]

1. The objectives of a decision must be established first.
2. The objectives are classified as to importance. (Sort out the musts and the wants.)
3. Alternative actions are developed.
4. The alternatives are evaluated against the objectives.

---

1. C. H. Kepner and B. B. Tregoe, "The Rational Manager: A Systematic Approach to Problem Solving and Decision Making," Princeton Research Press, Princeton, NJ, 1976.
2. Ibid.

5. The choice of the alternative that holds the best promise of achieving all of the objectives represents the tentative decision.
6. The tentative decision is explored for future possible adverse consequences.
7. The effects of the final decision are controlled by taking other actions to prevent possible adverse consequences from becoming problems and by making sure that the actions decided on are carried out.

5.10.4 Decision Trees

The construction of a decision tree is a useful technique when decisions must be made in succession into the future. Figure 5.19 shows the decision tree concerned with deciding whether an electronics firm should carry out R&D in order to develop a new product. The firm is a large conglomerate that has had extensive experience in electronics manufacture but no direct experience with the product in question. With the preliminary research done so far, the director of research estimates that a $4 million ($4M) R&D program conducted over 2 years would provide the knowledge to introduce the product to the marketplace.

A decision point in the decision tree is indicated by a square, and circles designate chance events (states of nature) that are outside the control of the decision maker. The length of line between nodes in the decision tree is not scaled with time, although the tree does depict precedence relations.

The first decision point is whether to proceed with the $4M research program or abandon it before it starts. We assume that the project will be carried out. At the end of the 2-year research effort the research director estimates there is a 50-50 chance of

1. J. Von Neumann and O. Morgenstern, "Theory of Games and Economic Behavior," 2d ed., Princeton University Press, Princeton, NJ, 1947; R. L. Keeney and H. Raiffa, "Decisions with Multiple Objectives: Preferences and Value Tradeoffs," Wiley, New York, 1976.
2. D. L. Thurston, "Research in Engineering Design," vol. 3, pp. 105–122, 1991.

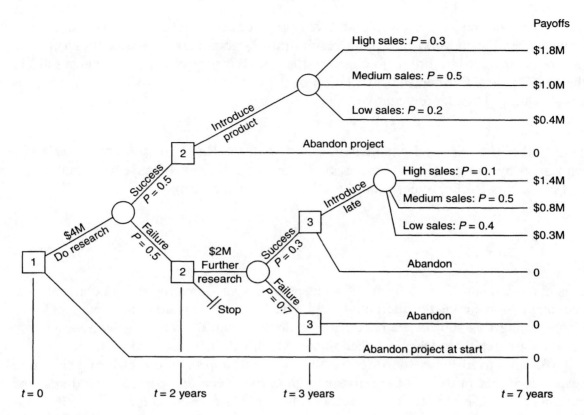

Payoffs

High sales: $P = 0.3$ $1.8M

Medium sales: $P = 0.5$ $1.0M

Low sales: $P = 0.2$ $0.4M

Abandon project   0

Introduce product

High sales: $P = 0.1$ $1.4M

Medium sales: $P = 0.5$ $0.8M

Low sales: $P = 0.4$ $0.3M

Introduce late

Abandon   0

Success $P = 0.5$

Failure $P = 0.5$

$4M Do research

$2M Further research

Success $P = 0.3$

Failure $P = 0.7$

Stop

Abandon   0

Abandon project at start   0

$t = 0$ $t = 2$ years $t = 3$ years $t = 7$ years

FIGURE 5.19
Decision tree for an R&D project.

being ready to introduce the product. If the product is introduced to the market, it is estimated to have a life of 5 years. If the research is a failure, it is estimated that an investment of an additional $2M would permit the R&D team to complete the work in an additional year. The chances of successfully completing the R&D in a further year are assessed at 3 in 10. Management feels that the project should be abandoned if a successful product is not developed in 3 years because there will be too much competition. On the other hand, if the product is ready for the marketplace after 3 years, it is given only a 1 in 10 chance of producing high sales.

The payoffs expected at the end are given to the far right at the end of each branch. The dollar amounts should be discounted back to the present time by using techniques of the time value of money (Chap. 13). Alternatively, the payoff could be expressed in terms of utility. As a decision rule we shall use the largest expected value of the payoff. Other decision rules, such as *maximin,* could be used.

The best place to start in this problem is at the end of the branches and work backward. The expected values for the chance events are:

$$E = 0.3(1.8) + 0.5(1.0) + 0.2(0.4) = 1.12 \text{ for the on-time project}$$

$$E = 0.1(1.4) + 0.5(0.8) + 0.4(0.3) = 0.66 \text{ for the delayed project at decision point 3}$$

$$E = 0.3(0.66) + 0.7(0) - 2 = -\$1.8M \text{ for the delayed project at decision point 2}$$

Thus, carrying the analysis for the delayed project backward to $\boxed{2}$ shows that to continue the project beyond that point results in a large negative expected payoff. The proper decision, therefore, is to abandon the research project if it is not successful in the first 2 years. Further, the calculation of the expected payoff for the on-time project at point $\boxed{1}$ is a large negative value.

$$E = 0.5(1.12) + 0.5(0) - 4.0 = -\$3.44$$

Thus, either the expected payoff is too modest or the R&D costs are too great to be warranted by the payoff. Therefore, based on the estimates of payoff, probabilities, and costs, this R&D project should not have been undertaken.

5.11
SUMMARY

This chapter deals with the heart of conceptual design—creating design concepts and deciding which among the alternatives is the best to carry forward in the design process. In presenting this subject we have tried to discuss both the attitudes with which you should approach these tasks and techniques which will help you find solutions.

We have tried to set the stage so that you will approach the task of generating design concepts in the most creative way possible. Keep an open mind and suspend judgment at the early stages of idea development. Learn to think with both hemispheres of your brain. Learn to brainstorm effectively, and to apply at least one other creativity tool such as the SCAMPER checklist, force fitting, or the mind map. Pay attention to and learn more about the theory of inventive problem solving (TRIZ). But above all, be persistent and realize that everyone has a degree of creativity, and the prize often goes to the person who works at the problem the hardest.

Concept development begins with decomposition of the problem. There are two majors ways to do this:

1. Physical decomposition breaks the design down into subassemblies and components. It continues down in the hierarchy until a level is reached where everything that has been decomposed is a component.
2. Functional decomposition is more basic, in that it breaks the design down in terms of the functions it must accomplish in terms of energy, material, and information flow. Functions are expressed by a verb-noun combination.

Generating concepts should start with individual effort using creativity aids and the information you have gathered using the sources discussed in Chap. 4. The functional decomposition serves as the roadmap, as the individuals work to generate concepts, not embodiments, to provide each function. Then, as a team they assemble these ideas into a morphological chart. Finally, the design team picks and chooses from the possible alternatives to develop a set of design concepts that look as if they meet the functional requirements.

Now the emphasis shifts to the evaluation of the design concepts to select the one, or few, which are carried forward to a final design. The first step in evaluation is comparing the concepts against a set of absolute criteria.

- Feasibility (will it work?)
- Assessment of technology readiness

Next, in an approximate way each concept is tested against a set of go-no-go questions based on the customer requirements framed in the QFD. The intent is to screen out obvious "losers." Be generous with awarding the "benefit of the doubt."

Those concepts deemed "possible winners" are passed to the next step. The evaluation tool most applicable to the level of detail usually available in conceptual design is Pugh's concept selection method. This method compares each concept relative to a reference concept and for each design criterion determines whether the concept is better than, poorer than, or about the same as the reference concept. This is an intensive team exercise, from which improved concepts often result.

For evaluation of designs for which more detail is available, typically at the subassembly or component level, a weighted decision matrix or a decision matrix based on the analytic hierarchy process are useful tools. Alternatively, the evaluation may be formulated in terms of the methods of decision analysis.

BIBLIOGRAPHY

Creativity

Bailey, R. L.: "Disciplined Creativity for Engineers," Ann Arbor Science Publishers, Ann Arbor, MI, 1978.
De Bono, E.: "Serious Creativity," HarperCollins, New York, 1992.
Lumsdaine, E., and M. Lumsdaine: "Creative Problem Solving," McGraw-Hill, New York, 1995.
Weisberg, R. W.: "Creativity: Beyond the Myth of Genius," W. H. Freeman, New York, 1993.

Conceptual Design Methods

Clausing, D.: "Total Quality Development," ASME Press, New York, 1994.
Cross, N.: "Engineering Design Methods," 2d ed., Wiley, New York, 1994.
French, M. J.: "Conceptual Design for Engineers," Springer-Verlag, New York, 1985.
Otto, K. P., and K. L. Wood: Conceptual and Configuration Design of Products and Assemblies, "ASM Handbook," vol. 20, pp. 15–32, ASM International, Materials Park, OH, 1997.
Pugh, S.: "Total Design," Addison-Wesley, Reading, MA, 1990.
Starkey, C. V.: "Engineering Design Decisions," Edward Arnold, London, 1992.
Ullman, D. G.: "The Mechanical Design Process," 2d ed., McGraw-Hill, New York, 1997.
Ulrich, K. T., and S. D. Eppinger: "Product Design and Development," McGraw-Hill, New York, 1995.

PROBLEMS AND EXERCISES

5.1. Select two pages at random from a large mail-order catalog. Select one item from each page and try to combine the two items into a useful innovation.

5.2. A technique for removing a blockage in the creative process is to apply transformation rules to an existing unsatisfactory solution. Some common transformation operators are

(1) put to other uses, (2) modify, (3) magnify, (4) diminish, (5) substitute, (6) rearrange, (7) reverse, (8) combine. A related technique is to use Roget's *Thesaurus* to suggest leads for alternative solutions. A key word from the existing solution is looked up in the thesaurus, and it provides a number of related and opposite words that stimulate new approaches.

Apply these techniques to the following problem. As a city engineer you are asked to suggest ways to eliminate puddles from pedestrian walkways after a rainstorm. Start with the obviously inadequate solution of waiting for the puddles to evaporate.

5.3. This problem will test your skills at lateral thinking. Join the pattern of dots with four straight lines. You cannot remove the pencil from the paper once you have started, so that the line is continuous.

$$
\begin{matrix}
\bullet & \bullet & \bullet \\
\bullet & \bullet & \bullet \\
\bullet & \bullet & \bullet
\end{matrix}
$$

5.4. As central station power plant operators consider reconverting from oil or gas to coal as the energy source, they sometimes find that there is not a suitable large land area near the plant that can be used for on-the-ground coal storage. Conduct a brainstorming session to propose alternative solutions to a conventional coal pile.

5.5. What are the questions that need to be asked and answered in order to prepare a problem statement? Develop a problem statement for the situation described in Prob. 5.4. Include the following elements in the problem statement: (1) need statement, (2) goals, (3) constraints and trade-offs, and (4) criteria for evaluating the design.

5.6. Use the idea of a morphological box (a three-dimensional morphological chart) to develop a new concept for personal transportation. Use as the three main factors (the axes of the cube) power source, media in which the vehicle operates, and method of passenger support.

5.7. Disassemble a small appliance or hand tool. Create a chart showing how the product is decomposed in the physical domain.

5.8. For the product used in Prob. 5.7, create a functional decomposition diagram.

5.9. Create a functional decomposition of an overhead projector.

5.10. Create a functional decomposition of the flip-lid trash can described in Prob. 2.9.

5.11. Using the results of Prob. 5.10, generate a number of design concepts for an improved flip-lid trash can. Evaluate the concepts using Pugh's concept selection method.

5.12. In the search for more environmentally friendly design, paper cups have replaced Styrofoam cups in some fast-food restaurants. These cups are not as good insulators, and the paper cups often get too hot for the hand. A design team is in search of a better disposable coffee cup. The designs to be evaluated are: (*a*) the current paper cup, (*b*) a standard Styrofoam cup, (c) a rigid injection-molded cup with a handle, (d) a double-wall disposable plastic cup, (e) a paper cup with a pull-out handle, and (f) a paper cup with a cellular wall. These design concepts are to be evaluated with the current paper cup as the datum.

The engineering characteristics on which the cups are evaluated are:

1. Temperature in the hand
2. Temperature of the outside of the cup
3. Material environmental impact
4. Indenting force of cup wall
5. Porosity of cup wall
6. Manufacturing complexity
7. Ease of stacking the cups
8. Ease of use by customer
9. Temperature loss of coffee over time

Using your knowledge of fast-food coffee cups, use the Pugh concept selection method to select the most promising design.

5.13. The following factors may be useful in deciding which brand of automobile to purchase: interior trim, exterior design, workmanship, initial cost, fuel economy, handling and steering, braking, ride, and comfort. To assist in developing the weighting factor for each of those attributes, group the attributes into four categories of body, cost, reliability, and performance and use a relevance tree to establish the individual weighting factors.

5.14. Four preliminary designs for sport-utility vehicles had the characteristics listed in the table below. First, see if you can get the same weighting factors as listed in the table. Using the weighted decision matrix, which design looks to be the most promising?

Characteristics	Parameter	Weight factor	Design A	Design B	Design C	Design D
Gas mileage	Miles per gal	0.175	20	16	15	20
Range	Miles	0.075	300	240	260	400
Ride comfort	Rating	0.40	Poor	Very good	Good	Fair
Ease to convert to 4-wheel drive	Rating	0.07	Very good	Good	Good	Poor
Load capacity	lb.	0.105	1000	700	1000	600
Cost of repair	Avg. of 5 parts	0.175	$700	$625	$600	$500

5.15. Repeat Prob. 5.14 using the AHP method.

5.16. Construct a simple personal decision tree over whether to take an umbrella when you go to work on a cloudy day.

5.17. This decision concerns whether to develop a microprocessor-controlled machine tool. The high-technology microprocessor-equipped machine costs $4 million to develop, and the low-technology machine costs $1.5 million to develop. The low-technology machine is less likely to receive wide customer acclaim ($P = 0.3$) vs. $P = 0.8$ for the microprocessor-equipped machine. The expected payoffs (present worth of all future profits) are as follows:

	Strong market acceptance	Minor market acceptance
High technology	$P = 0.8$	$P = 0.2$
	PW = \$16 M	PW = \$10M
Low technology	$P = 0.3$	$P = 0.7$
	PW = \$12M	PW = 0

If the low-technology machine does not meet with strong market acceptance (there is a chance its low cost will be more attractive than its capability), it can be upgraded with microprocessor control at a cost of \$3.2 million. It will then have an 80 percent chance of strong market acceptance and will bring in a total return of \$10 million. The nonupgraded machine will have a net return of \$3 million. Draw the decision tree and decide what you would do on the basis of various decision criteria.

6.8
DESIGN FOR THE ENVIRONMENT

Protection of the earth's environment is high on the value scale of most citizens of the world's developed countries. Accordingly, most corporations realize that it is in their best interest to take a strong proenvironment attitude and approach to their business.

---

1. J. G. Bralla, op. cit., Chap. 16; M. A. Moss, "Designing for Minimum Maintenance Expense," Marcel Dekker, New York, 1985.

Moreover, there is near universal recognition that the most cost-effective way to improve the long-term environmental condition of our planet is through early and high-priority concern for the environment in product design—so-called green design.[1] A large proportion of our environmental problems are linked to the selection and use of particular technologies without previous adequate regard for the environmental consequences. Currently, and even more in the future, environmental impact will be considered in design along with function, appearance, cost, quality, and more traditional design factors.

Greater concern for the environment in product design places emphasis on *life-cycle design* through:

- Minimizing emissions and waste in the manufacturing process.
- Looking at all the ways that the product negatively impacts the environment. A polluting product is a defective product.
- Looking at ways to increase the useful life of the product, thereby prolonging the time when new material and energy resources need to be committed to a replacement product.

The useful life may be limited by degraded performance due to wear and corrosion, damage (either accidental or because of improper use), or environmental degradation. Other reasons to terminate the useful life not related to life-cycle issues are technological obsolescence (something better has come along) or styling obsolescence.

There are a variety of design strategies to extend a product's useful life.[2]

- *Design for durability:* Durability is the amount of use one gets from a product before it breaks down and replacement is preferable to repair.
- *Design for reliability:* Reliability is the ability of a product to neither malfunction nor fail within a specified time period.
- *Create an adaptable design:* A modular design allows for continuous improvement of the various functions.
- *Repair:* Feasibility of replacing nonfunctioning components to attain specified performance.
- *Remanufacture:* Worn parts are restored to like-new condition to attain specified performance.
- *Reuse:* Find additional use for the product or its components after the product has been retired from its original service.
- *Recyclability:* Reprocessing of the product to recover some or all of the materials from which it is made. This requires that the product can be disassembled cost-effectively, that the materials can be identified and have an economic value in excess of the cost (see Sec. 8.14).
- *Disposability:* All materials that are not recycled can be legally and safely disposed of.

---

1. U.S. Congress, Office of Technology Assessment, "Green Products by Design: Choices for a Cleaner Environment," OTA-E-541, Government Printing Office, Washington, DC, October 1992; S. B. Billatos and N. A. Basaly, "Green Technology and Design for the Environment," Taylor & Francis, Washington, DC, 1997.
2. E. B. Magrab, "Integrated Product and Process Design and Development," CRC Press, Boca Raton, FL, 1997, p. 251.

The accepted way of assessing the effects that products and processes have on the environment is with *life-cycle assessment* (LCA).[1] Figure 1.15 shows the life cycle for materials, and Fig. 6.12 shows a more general framework that is used for LCA. Life-cycle assessment proceeds in three stages:

- *Inventory analysis:* The flows of energy and materials to and from the product during its life are determined quantitatively.
- *Impact analysis:* Consideration of all potential environmental consequences of the flows cataloged above.
- *Improvement analysis:* Results of the above two steps are translated into specific actions that reduce the impact of the product or the process on the environment.

Detailed life-cycle assessments are often time-consuming and expensive to carry out in engineering systems, so other less rigorous scoring methods are used,[2] as described in Sec. 6.8.2.

It is generally believed that improvement of the environment is the joint responsibility of all citizens, joined by business and government. Government plays a crucial role, usually through regulation, to ensure that all businesses share equitably in the cost of an improved environment. Since these increased product costs often are passed on to the customer, it is the responsibility of government to use the tool of regulation prudently and wisely. Here the technical community can play an important role by providing fair and timely technical input to government. Finally, many vision-

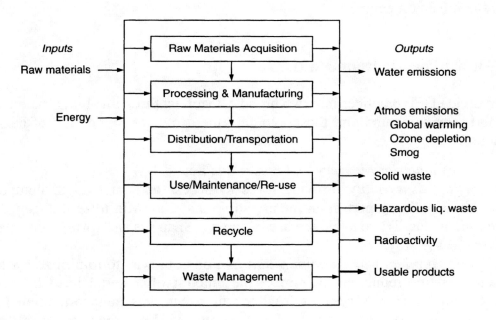

FIGURE 6.12
Framework for developing a life-cycle analysis.

1. T. E. Graedel and B. R. Allenby, "Design for Environment," Prentice-Hall, Upper Saddle River, NJ, 1996.
2. T. E. Graedel, "Streamlined Life-Cycle Assessment," Prentice-Hall, Upper Saddle River, NJ, 1998.

Diesel Engine Stages a Comeback?

The environmental pressure to reduce greenhouse gases is leading automotive engineers to take another look at small diesel engines. The diesel uses no spark plugs and burns fuel more efficiently than the gasoline engine. Because it gets greater fuel mileage the output of emission gases is less. Historical problems with diesel engines have been high noise and dirty exhaust.

Computerized fuel-control systems have quieted the engine and eliminated the "diesel bark." New catalytic converters have significantly improved NO_x emissions. The new diesel engines no longer belch clouds of black soot. The remaining environmental problem is microscopic particles of soot in the emissions, which can be removed with filters.

Another advantage of the diesel engine is its ability to run on a wider variety of fuels than the gasoline engine. Experimental engines have been run on nonfossil fuels and on a fuel made from natural gas.

---

aries see a future world based on *sustainable development* in which the world resources will no longer be depleted because the rate of resource consumption will be balanced by the rate of resource regeneration. Industry will operate with renewable energy and material resources and massive recycling. Designs will be based on many technologies different from those used today, e.g., the electric car vs. the gasoline internal-combustion engine.[1]

6.8.1 Design for Environment (DFE)[2]

We can divide DFE practices into two broad categories: those involving material recycling and remanufacture, and those avoiding the use of or production of hazardous substances.

1. *Design for material recovery and reuse:* See Sec. 8.14.
2. *Design for disassembly:* Provide for easy access and removal of components. Avoid embedding a part in an incompatible material. Minimize the use of adhesives and welds. Try to avoid the use of screws. Snap fits and spring clips make for easier disassembly.
3. *Design for product waste minimization:* An obvious way to minimize waste is to practice source reduction. Minimize the amount of material used by avoiding overdesign. This also saves cost. Realize which materials are incompatible in recycling and will have to be separated and segregated. Keep the number of different materials used in the design to a minimum to reduce recycling costs. Understand

---

1. Two design for environment web sites are: http://dfe.stanford.edu and http://www.flash.net/~rcade/dfe/index.html.
2. J. Fiksel (ed.), "Design for Environment," Chap. 8, McGraw-Hill, New York, 1996.

that certain adhesives, paints, inks, and labels can cause contamination in recycling, and avoid these materials. Integral labels are preferred to discrete labels that have to be removed at great cost before recycling.

4. *Design for waste recovery and reuse in processing:* The waste associated with a product can be a small fraction of the waste generated by the processes that produced the product. Since the selection of a material for a part is intimately associated with how it will be manufactured (see Chap. 8), consider as part of this decision process the environmental implications for manufacturing. Be alert to ways of reducing process waste.[1]

5. *Design for packaging recovery:* Be alert to changes in industrial packaging that are allowing for the recovery, recycling, and reuse of packaging. Look for ways to redesign shipping containers so that they can be reused.

6. *Avoid the use of hazardous or undesirable materials:* Keep up on changes on government regulations and lists of hazardous materials. Avoid these if at all possible. If they must be used, be knowledgeable about safety precautions for their use. For example, avoid the use of CFC refrigerants, use aqueous solvents for cleaning instead of chlorinated solvents, and use biodegradable materials whenever possible.

7. *Consider the environmental hazards of production workers:* The overall design should consider the people who work on the production line to make the product. They should not be put at risk by environmental hazards. This includes such harmful effects as exhaust gases from machines, smoke, exposure to very high or very low temperatures, noise, or radiation. Allowable workplace conditions are spelled out by government regulations like OSHA.

8. *Design for noise reduction:* Excessive noise is often overlooked as an environmental hazard. Many production environments are quite noisy, exceeding the generally accepted limit of 80 decibels. The two approaches to noise reduction are (1) design the system so that the noise does not exceed a preset threshold, and (2) insulate the source of the noise by enclosing it or by designing the foundation so that the noise does not escape to the environment.[2]

6.8.2 DFE Scoring Methods

Environmental concerns can be entered into the QFD diagram as a separate category of customer wants. This ensures that environmental issues get important attention at the concept design stage.

A decision matrix can be used as an assessment matrix to serve as a substitute for the life-cycle assessment. The stages in the life cycle of a product would be listed as the rows and the environmental concerns such as material choice, energy use, solid waste, liquid waste, and gaseous emissions are listed as the columns. Graedel and Allenby[3] give a checklist and guidelines for using this matrix for products (Appendix F) and for processes (Appendix G).

---

1. H. Freeman (ed.), "Standard Handbook of Hazardous Waste Treatment and Disposal," 2d ed., McGraw-Hill, New York, 1998.
2. D. A. Bies and C. H. Hansen, "Engineering Noise Control: Theory and Practice," 2d ed., E & Fn Spon, Chapman & Hall, Inc., London, 1996.
3. T. E. Graedel and B. R. Allenby, op. cit.

Software for evaluating the environmental impact of designs is available. These tools take input from LCA and regulations and use it in a more pragmatic way to assess the environmental impact of alternative designs by a scoring system. One tool is oriented more toward electronic products[1] and the other builds on a well-established design for assembly methodology applicable to a wide range of products.[2]

11

RISK, RELIABILITY, AND SAFETY

11.1
INTRODUCTION

We start this chapter by defining terms which are often confused in the public mind but which actually have precise technical meanings. A *hazard* is the potential for human, property, or environmental damage. A cracked steering linkage, a leaking fuel line, or a loose step all represent hazards. Another term for a hazard is an *unsafe condition,* a condition which if not corrected can reasonably be expected to result in failure and/or injury. A hazard is not a function of probability. It is a function of the consequence of the causal factors.

A *risk* is the likelihood, expressed either as a probability or as a frequency, of a hazard's materializing. Risk is part of our individual existence and that of society as a whole. As young children we were taught about risks. "Don't touch the stove." "Don't chase the ball into the street." As adults we are made aware of the risks of society in our everyday newspaper and newscast. Thus, depending upon the particular week, the news makes us concerned about the risk of all-out nuclear war, a terrorist attack, or an airplane crash. The list of risks in our highly complex technological society is endless.

Table 11.1 lists the six classes of hazards to which society is subject. We can see that categories 3 and 4 are directly within the realm of responsibility of the engineer and categories 2, 5, and possibly 6 provide design constraints in many situations. Risk exists only when a hazard exists and something of value is exposed to the hazard.

Risk assessment has become increasingly important in engineering design as the complexity of engineering systems has increased. The risks associated with engineering systems do not arise because risk avoidance procedures were ignored in the design. One category of risks arises from external factors that were considered acceptable at the time of design but which subsequent research has revealed to be a health or safety hazard. A good example is the extensive use of sprayed asbestos coating as an insulation and sound barrier before the toxicity of asbestos fibers was known. A

TABLE 11.1
Classification of societal hazards

Category of hazard	Examples
1. Infections and degenerative diseases	Influenza, heart disease, AIDS
2. Natural disasters	Earthquakes, floods, hurricanes
3. Failure of large technological systems	Failure of dams, power plants, aircraft, ships, buildings
4. Discrete small-scale accidents	Automotive accidents, power tools, consumer and sport goods
5. Low-level, delayed-effect hazards	Asbestos, PCB, microwave radiation, noise
6. Sociopolitical disruption	Terrorism, nuclear weapons proliferation, oil embargo

From W. W. Lowrance, in R. C. Schwing and W. A. Albus (eds.), "Social Risk Assessment," Plenum Press, New York, 1980.

second category of risks comes from abnormal conditions that are not a part of the basic design concept in its normal mode of operation. Usually these abnormal events stop the operation of the system without harming the general public, although there may be danger to the operators. Other systems, such as passenger aircraft or Three-Mile Island, pose a potential risk and cost to the larger public. Risks in engineering systems are often associated with operator error. Although these should be designed for, it is a difficult task to anticipate all possible future events. This topic is discussed in Secs. 11.4 and 11.5. Finally, there are the risks associated with design errors and accidents. Clearly, these should be eliminated, but since design is a human activity, errors and accidents will occur.

Most reasonable people will agree that society is not risk-free and cannot be made so.[1] However, an individual's reaction to risk depends upon three main factors: (1) whether the person feels in control of the risk or whether the risk is imposed by some outside group, (2) whether the risk involves one big event (like an airplane crash) or many small, separate occurrences, and (3) whether the hazard is familiar or is some strange, puzzling risk like a nuclear reactor. Through the medium of mass communications the general public has become better informed about the existence of risks in society, but they have not been educated concerning the need to accept some level of risk and to balance risk avoidance against cost. It is inevitable that there will be conflict between various special-interest groups when trying to decide on what constitutes an acceptable risk.

Reliability is a measure of the capability of a part or a system to operate without failure in the service environment. It is always expressed as a probability; e.g., a reliability of 0.999 implies that there is probability of failure of 1 part in every 1000. The mathematics of reliability is introduced in Sec. 11.3.

Safety is relative protection from exposure to hazards. A thing is safe if its risks are judged to be acceptable.[2] Therefore, two different activities are involved in deter-

---

1. E. Wenk, "Tradeoffs: Imperatives of Choice in a High-Tech World," Johns Hopkins University Press, Baltimore, 1986.
2. W. W. Lowrance, "Of Acceptable Risk," William Kaufman, Inc., Los Altos, CA, 1976.

mining how safe a design is: (1) a risk assessment, which is a probabilistic activity, and (2) a judgment of the acceptability of that risk, which is a societal value judgment.

11.1.1 Regulation as a Result of Risk

In a democracy when the public perception of a risk reaches sufficient intensity, legislation is enacted to control the risk. That usually means the formation of a regulatory commission that is charged with overseeing the regulatory act. In the United States the first regulatory commission was the Interstate Commerce Commission (ICC). The following federal organizations have a major role to play in some aspects of technical risk.

Consumer Product Safety Commission (CPSC)
Environmental Protection Agency (EPA)
Federal Aviation Agency (FAA)
Federal Highway Administration (FHA)
Federal Railway Administration (FRA)
Nuclear Regulatory Commission (NRC)
Occupational Safety and Health Administration (OSHA)

Some of the federal laws concerning product safety are listed in Table 11.2. The rapid acceleration of interest in consumer safety legislation is shown by the dates of enactment of these regulatory laws. However, there are many who say that regulation has gone too far. For example, the Fastener Quality Act was passed in response to failures in defense equipment from companies selling substandard fasteners with phony inspection certificates. The resulting regulation is 200 pages long, and is reported to be costing the automotive industry $300 million per year for compliance. In the

TABLE 11.2
A sample of federal laws concerning product safety

Year	Legislation
1893	Railroad Appliance Safety Act
1938	Food, Drug, and Cosmetic Act
1953	Flammable Fabrics Act
1960	Federal Hazardous Substance Act
1966	National Traffic and Motor Vehicle Safety Act
1968	Fire Research and Safety Act
1969	Child Protection and Toy Safety Act
1970	Poison Prevention Packaging Act
1970	Lead-Based Paint Poison Prevention Act
1970	Occupational Safety and Health Act
1971	Federal Boat Safety Act
1972	Consumer Product Safety Act
1988	Fastener Quality Act

United States some 60 federal agencies issue more than 1800 regulations a year; the Code of Federal regulations contains more than 130,000 pages.[1]

Legislation has the important result that it charges all producers of a product with the cost of complying with the product safety regulations. Thus, we are not faced with the situation in which the majority of producers spend money to make their product safe but an unscrupulous minority cuts corners on safety to save on cost. However, in complex engineering systems it may be very difficult to write regulations that do not conflict with each other and work at cross purposes. The automobile is a good example.[2] Here, separate agencies have promulgated regulations to influence fuel economy, exhaust emissions, and crash safety. The law to control emissions also reduces fuel efficiency by 7.5 percent, but the fuel efficiency law has forced the building of smaller cars that have increased crash fatalities by an additional 1400 per year. The need for a strong technical input into the regulatory process should be apparent from this example.

A common criticism of the regulatory approach is that decisions are often made arbitrarily. That is understandable when we consider that a regulatory agency often has a congressional mandate to protect the public from "unreasonable risk." Since there usually are no widely agreed-on definitions of unreasonable risk, the regulators are accused of being hostile to or soft on the regulated industry, depending upon the individual's point of view. Sometimes the regulating agency specifies the technology for meeting the target level of risk. This removes the incentive for innovation in developing more effective methods of controlling the risk.

11.1.2 Standards

Standards are one of the most important ways in which the engineering profession makes sure that society receives a minimum level of safety and performance. They are a set of rules that tell what must be done in particular situations. For example, EPA Standard AP-50 sets the maximum annual average concentration of sulfur dioxide at 80 μg/m^3 and the maximum 24-h average at 365 μg/m^3. Standards may be voluntary or mandatory. Mandatory standards are issued by governmental agencies, and violations are treated like criminal acts for which fines and/or imprisonment may be imposed. Voluntary standards are prepared by a committee of interested parties (industry suppliers and users, government, and the general public), usually under the sponsorship of a technical society or a trade association. Approval of a new standard generally requires agreement by nearly all participants in the committee. Therefore, voluntary standards are consensus standards. They usually specify only the lowest performance level acceptable to all members of the standards committee. Thus, a voluntary standard indicates the lowest safety level that an industry intends to provide in the product it manufactures, whereas a mandatory standard indicates the lowest safety level the government will accept. Because mandatory standards frequently set more stringent requirements than voluntary standards do, they force manufacturers to inno-

1. *The Economist,* Aug. 2, 1997, p. 2.
2. L. B. Lave, *Science,* vol. 212, pp. 893–899, May 22, 1981.

vate and advance the state of the art, but often at increased cost to the consumer. That, of course, requires that the mandatory standards be based on realistically obtainable levels.

Another classification of standards is design (specification) standards versus performance standards.[1] Design standards specify the acceptable levels of technical details, such as minimum flow rate and minimum yield strength. Performance standards specify the minimum performance characteristics without specifying the individual technical details. Thus, the supplier has more freedom to innovate and arrive at the same end point. Performance standards can include design specifications as examples of current state-of-the-art methods of meeting the performance criteria.

Although the concept of performance standards has gained considerable attention recently, the vast majority of standards are design standards. It is much more difficult and expensive to write a good performance standard because it must be more general and all-encompassing. Performance standards do not eliminate the problems of determining proper quality levels, and reliable laboratory tests of actual product performance may not be available. Therefore, one often is forced to fall back on specifying a series of well-known and accepted test standards, which are related in some not too well defined way to the product performance.

11.1.3 Risk Assessment

The assessment of risk is an imprecise process involving judgment and intuition. However, triggered by the consumer safety movement and the public concern over nuclear energy, a growing literature has evolved.[2] The level of risk, as perceived by an individual or the public, can be classified as tolerable, acceptable, or unacceptable.[3]

Tolerable risk: We are prepared to live with the level of risk but we want to continue to review its causes and seek ways of reducing the risk.

Acceptable risk: We accept the level of risk as reasonable and would not seek to expend much resources to reducing it further.

Unacceptable risk: We do not accept this level of risk and would not participate in the activity or permit others to participate.

Many regulations are based on the principle of making the risk "as low as reasonably practicable" (ALARP). This means that all reasonable measures will be taken to reduce risks that lie in the tolerable region until the cost to achieve further risk reduction becomes greatly disproportionate to the benefit.

Data on risk are subject to considerable uncertainty and variability. In general, three classes of statistics are available: (1) financial losses (chiefly from the insurance

1. D. Hemenway, "Performance vs. Design Standards," NBS GCR-80-287, October 1980 (PB81-120362).
2. C. Starr, *Science,* vol. 165, pp. 1232–1238, Sept. 19, 1969; N. Rasmussen, et al., *Reactor Safety Study,* WASH-1400, U.S. Nuclear Regulatory Commission, 1975; W. D. Rowe, "An Anatomy of Risk," Wiley, New York, 1977; R. Wilson, *Technology Review,* vol. 81, no. 4, pp. 41–46, 1979; J. D. Graham, L. C. Green, and M. J. Roberts, *In Search of Safety,* Harvard University Press, Cambridge, 1988.
3. D. J. Smith, "Reliability, Maintainability, and Risk," 5th ed., Butterworth-Heinemann, Oxford, 1997.

TABLE 11.3
Fatality rate

Cause of fatality	Fatality per person per year
Smoking (20 per day)	5×10^{-3}
Cancer, in general	3×10^{-3}
Race car driving	1×10^{-3}
Motor vehicle driving	3×10^{-4}
Fires	4×10^{-5}
Poison	2×10^{-5}
Industrial machinery	1×10^{-5}
Air travel	9×10^{-6}
Railway travel	4×10^{-6}
California earthquake	2×10^{-6}
Lightning	5×10^{-7}

industry), (2) health information, and (3) accident statistics. Usually the data are differentiated between fatalities and injuries. Risk is usually expressed as the probability of the risk of a fatality per person per year. A risk that exceeds 10^{-3} fatalities per person per year is generally considered unacceptable while a rate that is less than 10^{-5} is not of concern to the average person.[1] The range 10^{-3} to 10^{-5} is the tolerable range. However, an individual's perception of risk depends upon the circumstances. If the risk is voluntarily assumed, like smoking or driving a car, then there is a greater acceptance of the risk than if the risk was assumed involuntarily, as with traveling in a train or breathing secondhand smoke. There is a large difference between individual risk and societal risk. While 10^{-3} is the boundary where unacceptable risk begins for a single voluntary death, the acceptable fatality rate shifts to about 10^{-5} if 100 deaths are involved. Table 11.3 gives some generally accepted fatality rates for a variety of risks.

The most common approach in risk assessment is a benefit-cost analysis (Sec. 13.11). One difficulty with this approach is that benefits are counted in lives saved while costs are in monetary terms. This requires the often distasteful task of placing a value on a human life. One way to do this is the human capital approach, which estimates the lost earnings potential of the victim, with allowance for the pain and suffering of the victim's loved ones. This is about $2.6 million for a life lost in a highway accident.[2] Another approach is the "willingness to pay" method, in which people are asked directly what they would be willing to pay to avoid danger or harm.

11.4
DESIGN FOR RELIABILITY

The design strategy used to ensure reliability can fall between two broad extremes. The *fail-safe approach* is to identify the weak spot in the system or component and provide some way to monitor that weakness. When the weak link fails, it is replaced, just as the fuse in a household electrical system is replaced. At the other extreme is what can be termed "the one-horse shay" approach. The objective is to design all components to have equal life so the system will fall apart at the end of its useful lifetime just as the legendary one-horse shay did. Frequently an *absolute worst-case approach* is used; in it the worst combination of parameters is identified and the design is based on the premise that all can go wrong at the same time. This is a very conservative approach, and it often leads to overdesign.

Two major areas of engineering activity determine the reliability of an engineering system. First, provision for reliability must be established during the earliest design concept stage, carried through the detailed design development, and maintained during the many steps in manufacture. Once the system becomes operational, it is imperative that provision be made for its continued maintenance during its service.[1]

The steps in building reliability into a design are shown in Fig. 11.8. The process starts at the beginning of conceptual design by clearly laying out the criteria for success of the design, estimating the required reliability, the duty cycle, and carefully considering all of the factors that make up the service environment. In the configuration step of embodiment design the physical arrangement of components can critically affect reliability. In laying out functional block diagrams, consider those areas which strongly influence reliability, and prepare a list of parts in each block. This is the place to consider various redundancies and to be sure that physical arrangement allows good access for maintenance. In the parametric step of embodiment design select components with high reliability. Build and test both computer and physical prototypes. These should be subjected to the widest range of environmental conditions. Establish failure modes and estimate the system and subsystem MTBF. Detail design is the place for the final revision of specifications, for building and testing the preproduction prototype, and the preparation of the final production drawings. Once the design is released to the production organization the design organization is not finished with it. Production models are given further environmental tests, and these help establish the quality assurance program (see Sec. 12.2) and the maintenance schedules. When the product is put into service with customers there is a steady feedback concerning field failures and MTBFs that helps in redesign efforts and follow-on products.

---

1. H. P. Bloch and F. K. Gleitner, "An Introduction to Machinery Reliability Assessment," 2d ed., Gulf Publishing Co., Houston, TX, 1994; H. P. Bloch, "Improving Machinery Reliability," 3d ed., Gulf Publishing Co., 1998; H. P. Bloch, "Machinery Failure Analysis and Troubleshooting," Gulf Publishing Co., Houston, TX, 1998.

Design Stage	Design Activity
	Problem definition:
Conceptual design	Estimate reliability requirement
	Determine likely service environment
	Configuration design:
	Investigate redundancy
Embodiment design	Provide accessibility for maintenance
	Parametric design:
	Select highly reliable components
	Build and test physical and computer prototypes
	Full environmental tests
	Establish failure modes/FMEA
	Estimate MTBF
	User trials/modification
Detail Design	Produce & test preproduction prototype
	Final estimate of reliability
	Production models:
Production	Further environmental tests
	Establish quality assurance program
	Deliver to customer:
Service	Feedback field failures and MTBFs to designers
	Repair and replace
	Retirement from service

FIGURE 11.8
Reliability activities throughout design, production, and service.

11.4.1 Causes of Unreliability

The malfunctions that an engineering system can experience can be classified into five general categories.[1]

1. *Design mistakes:* Among the common design errors are failure to include all important operating factors, incomplete information on loads and environmental conditions, erroneous calculations, and poor selection of materials.

2. *Manufacturing defects:* Although the design may be free from error, defects introduced at some stage in manufacturing may degrade it. Some common examples are (1) poor surface finish or sharp edges (burrs) that lead to fatigue cracks and (2) decarburization or quench cracks in heat-treated steel. Elimination of defects in manufacturing is a key responsibility of the manufacturing engineering staff,

1. W. Hammer, "Product Safety Management and Engineering." chap. 8, Prentice-Hall, Englewood Cliffs, NJ, 1980.

but a strong relationship with the R&D function may be required to achieve it. Manufacturing errors produced by the production work force are due to such factors as lack of proper instructions or specifications, insufficient supervision, poor working environment, unrealistic production quota, inadequate training, and poor motivation.

3. *Maintenance:* Most engineering systems are designed on the assumption they will receive adequate maintenance at specified periods. When maintenance is neglected or is improperly performed, service life will suffer. Since many consumer products do not receive proper maintenance by their owners, a good design strategy is to make the products maintenance-free.

4. *Exceeding design limits:* If the operator exceeds the limits of temperature, speed, etc., for which it was designed, the equipment is likely to fail.

5. *Environmental factors:* Subjecting equipment to environmental conditions for which it was not designed, e.g., rain, high humidity, and ice, usually greatly shortens its service life.

11.4.2 Minimizing Failure

A variety of methods are used in engineering design practice to improve reliability. We generally aim at a probability of failure of $P_f < 10^{-6}$ for structural applications and $10^{-4} < P_f < 10^{-3}$ for unstressed applications.

Margin of safety

We saw in Sec. 11.2 that variability in the strength properties of materials and in loading conditions (stress) leads to a situation in which the overlapping statistical distributions can result in failures. In Fig. 11.5 we saw that the variability in strength has a major impact on the probability of failure, so that failure can be reduced with no change in the mean value if the variability of the strength can be reduced.

Derating

The analogy to using a factor of safety in structural design is derating electrical, electronic, and mechanical equipment. The reliability of such equipment is increased if the maximum operating conditions (power, temperature, etc.) are derated below their nameplate values. As the load factor of equipment is reduced, so is the failure rate. Conversely, when equipment is operated in excess of rated conditions, failure will ensue rapidly.

Redundancy

One of the most effective ways to increase reliability is with redundancy (see Sec. 11.3). In parallel redundant designs the same system functions are performed at the same time by two or more components even though the combined outputs are not required. The existence of parallel paths may result in load sharing so that each component is derated and has its life increased by a longer than normal time.

Another method of increasing redundancy is to have inoperative or idling standby units that cut in and take over when an operating unit fails. The standby unit wears out much more slowly than the operating unit does. Therefore, the operating strategy often is to alternate units between full-load and standby service. The standby unit must be provided with sensors to detect the failure and switching gear to place it in service. The sensor and/or switching units frequently are the weak link in a standby redundant system.

Durability

The material selection and design details should be performed with the objective of producing a system that is resistant to degradation from such factors as corrosion, erosion, foreign object damage, fatigue, and wear.[1] This usually requires the decision to spend more money on high-performance materials so as to increase service life and reduce maintenance costs. Life cycle costing is the technique used to justify this type of decision.

Damage tolerance

Crack detection and propagation have taken on great importance since the development of the fracture mechanics approach to design (Sec. 8.16). A damage-tolerant material or structure is one in which a crack, when it occurs, will be detected soon enough after its occurrence so that the probability of encountering loads in excess of the residual strength is very remote. Figure 11.9 illustrates some of the concepts of damage tolerance. The initial population of very small flaws inherent in the material is shown at the far left. These are small cracks, inclusions, porosity, surface pits, and scratches. If they are less than a_1, they will not grow appreciably in service. Additional defects will be introduced by manufacturing processes. Those larger than a_2 will be detected by inspection and eliminated as scrapped parts. However, some cracks will be present in the components put into service, and they will grow to a size a_3 that can be detected by the nondestructive evaluation (NDE) techniques that can be used in service. The allowable design stresses must be so selected that the number of

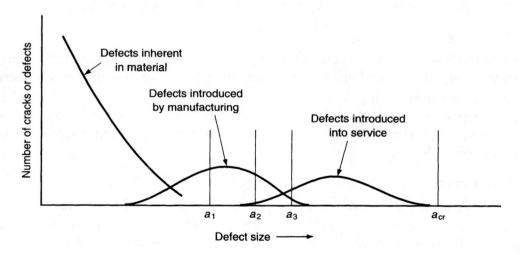

FIGURE 11.9
Distribution of defects in engineering components.

---

1. A. L. Smith (ed.), "Reliability of Engineering Materials," Butterworth, London, 1984.

flaws of size a_3 or greater will be small. Moreover, the material should be damage-tolerant so that propagation to the critical crack size a_{cr} is slow (see Sec. 8.17).

In conventional fracture mechanics analysis (Sec. 8.16) the critical crack size is set at the largest crack size that might be undetected by the NDE technique used in service. The value of fracture toughness of the material is taken as the minimum reasonable value. This is a safe but overly conservative approach. These worst-case assumptions can be relaxed and the analysis based on more realistic conditions by using probabilistic fracture mechanics[1] (PFM).

Ease of inspection

The importance of detecting cracks should be apparent from Fig. 11.9. Ideally it should be possible to employ visual methods of crack detection, but special design features may have to be provided in order to do so. In critically stressed structures special features to permit reliable NDE by ultrasonics or eddy current techniques may be required. If the structure is not capable of ready inspection, then the stress level must be lowered until the initial crack cannot grow to a critical size during the life of the structure. For that situation the inspection costs will be low but the structure will carry a weight penalty because of the low stress level.

Simplicity

Simplification of components and assemblies reduces the chance for error and increases the reliability. The components that can be adjusted by operation or maintenance personnel should be restricted to the absolute minimum. The simpler the equipment needed to meet the performance requirements the better the design.

Specificity

The greater the degree of specificity the greater the inherent reliability of design. Whenever possible, be specific with regard to material characteristics, sources of supply, tolerances and characteristics of the manufacturing process, tests required for qualification of materials and components, procedures for installation, maintenance, and use. Specifying standard items increases reliability. It usually means that the materials and components have a history of use so that their reliability is known. Also, replacement items will be readily available. When it is necessary to use a component with a high failure rate, the design should especially provide for the easy replacement of that component.

11.4.3 Sources of Reliability Data

Data on the reliability of a product clearly is highly proprietary to its manufacturer. However, the U.S. defense and space programs have created a strong interest in reliability, and this has resulted in the compilation of a large amount of data on failure rates

---

1. C. A. Rau and P. M. Besuner, *Trans. ASME*, ser. H, *J. Eng. Materials Tech.,* vol. 102, pp. 56–63, 1980; C. A. Rau, P. M. Besuner, and K. G. Sorenson, *Metal Science*, vol. 14, pp. 463–472, 1980.

and failure modes. The Reliability Analysis Center at the Rome Air Development Center (RADC), Griffiss Air Force Base, NY, is a chief repository for this data.[1] Two important publications from RADC are:

> MIL Handbook 217 gives failure rate data for electronic components.
> Nonelectronic Parts Reliability Databook gives failure rate data on a wide range of electromechanical, mechanical, hydraulic, and pneumatic parts.

Similar data has been collected and published by European governments and consultants.[2]

11.4.4 Cost of Reliability

Reliability costs money, but the cost nearly always is less than the cost of unreliability. The cost of reliability comes from the extra costs associated with designing and producing more reliable components, testing for reliability, and training and maintaining a reliability organization. Figure 11.10 shows the cost to a manufacturer of increasing the reliability of a product. The costs of design and manufacture increase with product reliability. Moreover, the slope of the curve increases, and each incremental increase in reliability becomes harder to achieve. The costs of the product after delivery to the customer, chiefly warranty or replacement costs, reputation of the supplier, etc., decrease with increasing reliability. The summation of these two curves produces the total cost curve, which has a minimum at an optimum level of reliability.[3] Other types of analyses establish the optimum schedule for part replacement to minimize cost.[4]

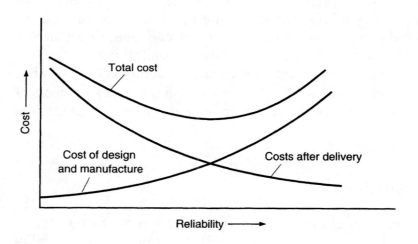

FIGURE 11.10
Influence of reliability on cost.

1. The web site for the Reliability Analysis Center is http://rac.iitri.org.
2. D. J. Smith, "Reliability, Maintainability, and Risk," 5th ed., Chap. 4, Butterworth-Heinemann, Oxford, 1997.
3. R. G. Fenton, *Trans. ASME,* Ser. B, *J. Eng. Ind.,* vol. 98, pp. 1066–1068, 1976.
4. N. W. Nelson and K. Hayashi, ibid., vol. 96, pp. 311–316, 1974.

11.9
DESIGN FOR SAFETY

Safety may well be the paramount issue in product design.[1] Norm
for granted, but the recall of an unsafe product can be very costly
liability suits, replaced product, or tarnished reputation. The prod
manufacture, to use, and to dispose of after use.[2]

A safe product is one that does not cause injury or property I
under safety is injury to the environment. Achieving safety is no
from a conscious focus on safety during design, and in knowing a
basic rules. There are three aspects to design for safety.

1. Make the product safe, i.e., design all hazards out of the produ
2. If it is not possible to make the product inherently safe, then d
   devices like guards, automatic cutoff switches, pressure-relief
   the hazard.
3. If step 2 cannot remove all hazards, then warn the user of the p
   priate warnings like labels, flashing lights, and loud sounds.

A *fail-safe design* seeks to ensure that a failure will either not
or change it to a state in which no injury or damage will occur. Tl
ants of fail-safe designs.

- Fail-passive design. When a failure occurs, the system is redt
  energy state and the product will not operate until corrective act
  cuit breaker is an example of a fail-passive device.
- Fail-active design. When failure occurs, the system remains enei
  operating mode. A redundant system kept on standby is an exar
- Fail-operational design. The design is such that the device conti
  critical function even though a part has failed. A valve that is
  will remain in the open position if it fails is an example.

---

1 C. O. Smith, Safety in Design, "ASM Handbook," vol. 20, pp. 139–145, ASM I
Park, OH, 1997.
2. For a comprehensive safety web site see http://www.safetyline.net.

11.9.1 Potential Dangers

We list below some of the general categories of safety hazards that need to be considered in design.

Acceleration/deceleration—falling objects, whiplash, impact damage
Chemical contamination—human exposure or material degradation
Electrical—shock, burns, surges, electromagnetic radiation, power outage
Environment—fog, humidity, lightning, sleet, temperature extremes, wind
Ergonomic—fatigue, faulty labeling, inaccessibility, inadequate controls
Explosions—dust, explosive liquids, gases, vapors, finely powdered materials
Fire—combustible material, fuel and oxidizer under pressure, ignition source
Human factors—failure to follow instructions, operator error
Leaks or spills
Life cycle factors—frequent startup and shutdown, poor maintenance
Materials—corrosion, weathering, breakdown of lubrication
Mechanical—fracture, misalignment, sharp edges, stability, vibrations
Physiological—carcinogens, human fatigue, irritants, noise, pathogens
Pressure/vacuum—dynamic loading, implosion, vessel rupture, pipe whip
Radiation—ionizing (alpha, beta, gamma, x-ray), laser, microwave, thermal
Structural—aerodynamic or acoustic loads, cracks, stress concentrations
Temperature—changes in material properties, burns, flammability, volatility

Product hazards are often controlled by government regulation. The U.S. Consumer Products Safety Commission is charged with this responsibility.[1] Products designed for use by children are held to much higher safety standards than products intended to be used by adults. The designer must also be cognizant that in addition to providing a safe product for the customer, it must be safe to manufacture, sell, install, and service.

In our society, products that cause harm invariably result in court suits for damages under the product liability laws. Design engineers must understand the consequences of these laws and how they must practice to minimize safety issues and the threat of litigation. This topic is covered in Chap. 15.

11.9.2 Guidelines for Design for Safety[2]

1. Recognize and identify the actual or potential hazards, and then design the product so they will not affect its functioning.
2. Thoroughly test prototypes of the product to reveal any hazards overlooked in the initial design.

---

1. See the CPSC web site, gopher://cpsc.gov.
2. C. O. Smith, op. cit.; J. G. Bralla, "Design for Excellence," McGraw-Hill, New York, chap. 17.

3. Design the product so it is easier to use safely than unsafely.
4. If field experience turns up a safety problem, determine the root cause and redesign to eliminate the hazard.
5. Realize that humans will do foolish things, and allow for it in your design. More product safety problems arise from improper product use than from product defects. A user-friendly product is usually a safe product.
6. There is a close correspondence between good ergonomic design and a safe design. For example:
   - Arrange the controls so that the operator does not have to move to manipulate them.
   - Make sure that fingers cannot be pinched by levers, etc.
   - Avoid sharp edges and corners.
   - Point-of-operation guards should not interfere with the operator's movement.
   - Products that require heavy or prolonged use should be designed to avoid cumulative trauma disorders like carpal tunnel syndrome. This means avoiding awkward positions of the hand, wrist, and arm and avoiding repetitive motions and vibration.
7. Minimize the use of flammable materials, including packaging materials.
8. Paint and other surface finishing materials should be chosen to comply with EPA and OSHA regulations for toxicity to the user and when they are burned, recycled, or discarded.
9. Think about the need for repair, service, or maintenance. Provide adequate access without pinch or puncture hazards to the repairer.
10. Electrical products should be properly grounded to prevent shock. Provide electrical interlocks so that high-voltage circuits will not be energized unless a guard is in the proper position.

11.9.3 Warning Labels

With rapidly escalating costs of product liability manufacturers have responded by plastering their products with warning labels. Warnings should supplement the safety-related design features by indicating how to avoid injury or damage from the hazards which could not be feasibly designed out of the product without seriously compromising its utility. The purpose of the warning label is to alert the user to a hazard and tell how to avoid injury from it.

For a warning label to be effective the user must receive the message, understand it, and act on it. The engineer must properly design the label with respect to the first two issues to achieve the third. The label must be prominently located on the product. Most warning labels are printed in two colors on a tough wear-resistant material, and fastened to the product with an adhesive. Attention is achieved by printing *Danger, Warning,* or *Caution* depending on the degree of the hazard. The message to be communicated by the warning must be carefully composed to convey the nature of the hazard and the action to be taken. It should be written at the sixth-grade level, with no long words and technical terms. For products that will be used in different countries the warning label must be in the local language.

13

ECONOMIC DECISION MAKING

13.1
INTRODUCTION

Throughout this book we have repeatedly emphasized that the engineer is a decision maker and that engineering design basically consists of making a series of decisions over time. We also have emphasized from the beginning that engineering involves the application of science to real problems of society. In this real-world context, one cannot escape the fact that economics (or costs) may play a role as big as, or bigger than, that of technical considerations in the decision making of design. In fact, it sometimes is said, although a bit facetiously, that an engineer is a person who can do for $1.00 what any fool can do for $2.00.

The major engineering infrastructure that built this nation—the railroads, major dams, and waterways—required a methodology for predicting costs and balancing them against alternative courses of action. In an engineering project, costs and revenues will occur at various points of time in the future. The methodology for handling this class of problems is known as engineering economy or engineering economic analysis. Familiarity with the concepts and approach of engineering economy generally is considered to be part of the standard engineering toolkit. Indeed, an examination on the fundamentals of engineering economy is required for professional engineering registration in all disciplines in all states.

The chief concept in engineering economy is that *money has a time value*. Paying out $1.00 today is more costly than paying out $1.00 a year from now. A $1.00 invested today is worth $1.00 plus interest a year from now. Engineering economy recognizes the fact that *use of money* is a valuable asset. Money can be rented in the same way one can rent an apartment, but the charge for using it is called interest rather than rent. This time value of money makes it more profitable to push expenses into the future and bring revenues into the present as much as possible.

Before proceeding into the mathematics of engineering economy, it is important to understand where engineering economy sits with regard to related disciplines like economics and accounting. Economics generally deals with broader and more global issues than engineering economy, such as the forces that control the money supply and trade between nations. Engineering economy uses the interest rate established by the economic forces to solve a more specific and detailed problem. However, it usually is a problem concerning alternative costs in the future. The accountant is more concerned with determining exactly, and often in great detail, what costs have been in the past. One might say that the economist is an oracle, the engineering economist is a fortune teller, and the accountant is an historian.

13.4
DEPRECIATION

Capital equipment suffers a loss in value with time. This may occur by wear, deterioration, or obsolescence, which is a loss of economic efficiency because of technolog-

ical advances. Therefore, a company must lay aside enough money each year t
mulate a fund to replace the obsolete or worn-out equipment. This allowance fo
of value is called depreciation. Another important aspect of depreciation is tha
federal government permits depreciation to be deducted from gross profits as a c
of doing business. In a capital-intensive business, depreciation can have a strong infl
ence on the amount of taxes that must be paid.

$$\text{Taxable income} = \text{total income} - \text{allowable expenses} - \text{depreciation}$$

The basic questions to be answered about depreciation are: (1) what is the time period over which depreciation can be taken and (2) how should the total depreciation charge be spread over the life of the asset? Obviously, the depreciation charge in any given year will be greater if the depreciation period is short (a rapid write-off).

The Economic Recovery Act of 1981 introduced the *accelerated cost recovery system* (ACRS) as the prime capital-recovery method in the United States. This was modified in the 1986 Tax Reform Act to MACRS. The statute sets depreciation recovery periods based on the expected useful life. Some examples are:

- Special manufacturing devices; some motor vehicles 3 years
- Computers; trucks; semiconductor manufacturing equipment 5 years
- Office furniture; railroad track; agricultural buildings 7 years
- Durable-goods manufacturing equipment; petroleum refining 10 years
- Sewage treatment plants; telephone systems 15 years,

Residential rental property is recovered in 27.5 years and nonresidential rental property in 31.5 years. Land is a nondepreciable asset, since it is never used up.

We shall consider four methods of spreading the depreciation over the recovery period n: (1) straight-line depreciation, (2) declining balance, (3) sum-of-the-years digits, and (4) the MACRS procedure. Only MACRS and the straight-line method currently are acceptable under the U.S. tax laws but the other methods are useful in classical engineering economic analyses.

13.4.1 Straight-Line Depreciation

In straight-line depreciation an equal amount of money is set aside yearly. The annual depreciation charge D is

$$D = \frac{\text{initial cost} - \text{salvage value}}{n} = \frac{C_i - C_s}{n} \tag{13.20}$$

The *book value* is the initial cost minus the sum of the depreciation charges that have been made. For straight-line depreciation, the book value B at the end of the jth year is

$$B = C_i - \frac{j}{n}(C_i - C_s) \tag{13.21}$$

ng-Balance Depreciation

g-balance method provides an accelerated write-off in the early years.
ation charge for the jth year D_j is a fixed fraction F_{DB} of the book value at
ing of the jth year (or the end of year $j - 1$). For the book value to equal
ge value after n years,

$$F_{DB} = 1 - \sqrt[n]{\frac{C_s}{C_i}} \tag{13.22}$$

id the book value at the beginning of the jth year is

$$B_{j-1} = C_i(1 - F_{DB})^{j-1} \tag{13.23}$$

Therefore, the depreciation in the jth year is

$$D_j = B_{j-1}F_{DB} = C_i(1 - F_{DB})^{j-1}F_{DB} \tag{13.24}$$

The most rapid write-off occurs for double declining-balance depreciation. In this
case $F_{DDB} = 2/n$ and $B_{j-1} = C_i(1 - 2/n)^{j-1}$. Then

$$D_j = C_i\left(1 - \frac{2}{n}\right)^{j-1}\frac{2}{n}$$

Since the DDB depreciation may not reduce the book value to the salvage value at
year n, it may be necessary to switch to straight-line depreciation in later years.

13.4.3 Sum-of-Years Digits Depreciation

The sum-of-years digits (SOYD) depreciation is an accelerated method. The annual
depreciation charge is computed by adding up all of the integers from 1 to n and then
taking a fraction of that each year, $F_{SOYD,j}$.

For example, if $n = 5$, then the sum of the years is $(1 + 2 + 3 + 4 + 5 = 15)$
and $F_{SOYD,2} = 4/15$, while $F_{SOYD,4} = 2/15$. The denominator is the sum of the digits;
the numerator is the digit corresponding to the jth year when the digits are arranged
in *reverse order.*

13.4.4 Modified Accelerated Cost Recovery System (MACRS)

In MACRS the annual depreciation is computed using the relation

$$D = qC_i \tag{13.25}$$

where q is the recovery rate obtained from Table 13.3 and C_i is the initial cost. In
MACRS the value of the asset is completely depreciated even though there may be a

TABLE 13.3
Recovery rates q used in MACRS method

Year	Recovery rate, q, %				
	$n = 3$	$n = 5$	$n = 7$	$n = 10$	$n = 15$
1	33.3	20.0	14.3	10.0	5.0
2	44.5	32.0	24.5	18.0	9.5
3	14.8	19.2	17.5	14.4	8.6
4	7.4	11.5	12.5	11.5	7.7
5		11.5	8.9	9.2	6.9
6		5.8	8.9	7.4	6.2
7			8.9	6.6	5.9
8			4.5	6.6	5.9
9				6.5	5.9
10				6.5	5.9
11				3.3	5.9
12–15					5.9
16					3.0

n = recovery period, years.

true salvage value. The recovery rates are based on starting out with a declining-balance method and switching to the straight-line method when it offers a faster write-off. MACRS uses a half-year convention which assumes that all property is placed in service at the midpoint of the initial year. Thus, only 50 percent of the first year depreciation applies for tax purposes and requires that a half year of depreciation be taken in year $n + 1$.

Table 13.4 compares the annual depreciation charges for these four methods of calculation.

TABLE 13.4
Comparison of depreciation methods

Year	C_i = \$6000, C_s = \$1000, n = 5			
	Straight line	Declining balance	Sum-of-years digits	MACRS
1	1000	1807	1667	1200
2	1000	1263	1333	1920
3	1000	882	1000	1152
4	1000	616	667	690
5	1000	431	333	690
6	—	—	—	348

14

COST EVALUATION

14.1
INTRODUCTION

An engineering design is not complete until we have a good idea of the cost required to build the design or manufacture the product. Generally the lowest-cost design will be successful in a free marketplace. The fact that we have placed this chapter on cost evaluation toward the end of the text does not reflect the importance of the subject. For most products and designs, cost is next to performance in importance.

An understanding of the elements that make up cost is vital, because competition between companies and between nations is fiercer than ever before. The world is becoming a single gigantic marketplace in which newly developing countries with very low labor costs are acquiring technology and competing successfully with the well-established industrialized nations. To maintain markets requires a detailed knowledge of costs and an understanding of how new technology can impact to lower costs.

We have seen that the design process makes commitments which determine 70 to 80 percent of the cost of a product. It is in the conceptual and embodiment design stages that a majority of the costs are locked into the product. Thus, in this chapter emphasis is on how cost estimates can be made early in the design process.

Some of the uses to which cost estimates are put are the following:

1. To provide information to be used in establishing the selling price of a product or a quotation for a good or service.
2. To determine the most economical method, process, or material for manufacturing a product.
3. To be used as a basis for a cost-reduction program.
4. To determine standards of production performance that may be used to control costs.
5. To provide input concerning the profitability of a new product.

It can be appreciated that cost evaluation inevitably becomes a very detailed and "nitty-gritty" activity. This type of information rarely is published in the technical literature, partly because it does not make interesting reading but more important, because costs are highly proprietary information. Therefore, the emphasis in this chapter will be on the identification of the elements of costs and on some of the more generally accepted cost evaluation methods. It should be realized that cost estimation within a particular industrial or governmental organization will follow highly specialized and standardized procedures particular to the organization. However, the general concepts of cost evaluation described here will still be valid.

14.2
CATEGORIES OF COSTS

There are two broad categories of costs:

1. *Nonrecurring costs:* These are one-time costs, which we usually call capital costs. They are divided further into capital costs, which include depreciable facilities, such as plant building or manufacturing equipment and tools, and nondepreciated capital costs, such as land.
2. *Recurring costs:* These costs are direct functions of the manufacturing operation and occur over and over again. They usually are called operating costs or manufacturing costs.

Another classification division is into fixed and variable costs. *Fixed costs* are independent of the rate of production of goods; *variable costs* change with the production rate. A cost often is called a *direct cost* when it can be directly assigned to a particular cost center, product line, or part. *Indirect costs* cannot be directly assigned to a product but must be "spread" over an entire factory. The general categories of fixed and variable costs are given below.

14.2.1 Fixed Costs

1. Indirect plant cost
   (*a*) Investment costs
   > Depreciation on capital investment
   > Interest on capital investment and inventory
   > Property taxes
   > Insurance
   (*b*) Overhead costs (burden)
   > Technical services (engineering)
   > Product design and development
   > Nontechnical services (office personnel, security, etc.)
   > General supplies
   > Rental of equipment

2. Management and administrative expenses
   (*a*) Share of corporate executive staff
   (*b*) Legal staff

(c) Share of corporate research and development staff
(d) Marketing staff

3. Selling expenses
   (a) Sales force
   (b) Delivery and warehouse costs
   (c) Technical service staff

14.2.2 Variable Costs

1. Materials

2. Direct labor (including fringe benefits)

3. Direct production supervision

4. Maintenance costs

5. Power and utilities

6. Quality-control staff

7. Royalty payments

8. Packaging and storage costs

9. Scrap losses and spoilage

Fixed costs such as marketing and sales costs, legal expense, security costs, financial expense, and administrative costs are often lumped into an overall category known as general and administrative expenses (G&A expenses). The above list of fixed and variable costs is meant to be illustrative of the chief categories of costs, but it is not exhaustive.[1]

The way the elements of cost build up to establish a selling price is shown in Fig. 14.1 The chief cost elements of direct material and direct labor determine the *prime cost.* To it must be added indirect manufacturing costs such as light, power, maintenance, supplies, and factory indirect labor. The manufacturing cost is made up of the factory cost plus general fixed expenses such as depreciation, engineering, taxes, office staff, and purchasing. The total cost is the manufacturing cost plus the sales expense. Finally, the selling price is established by adding a profit to the total cost.

Another important cost category is *working capital,* the funds that must be provided in addition to fixed capital and land investment to get a project started and provide for subsequent obligations as they come due. It consists of raw material on hand, semi-finished product in the process of manufacture, finished product in inventory, accounts receivable, and cash needed for day-to-day operation. The working capital is tied up during the life of the plant, but it is considered to be fully recoverable at the end of the life of the project.

---

1. For an expanded list of fixed and variable costs see R. H. Perry and C. H. Chilton, "Chemical Engineers' Handbook," 5th ed., pp. 25-13 and 25-27, McGraw-Hill, New York, 1973.

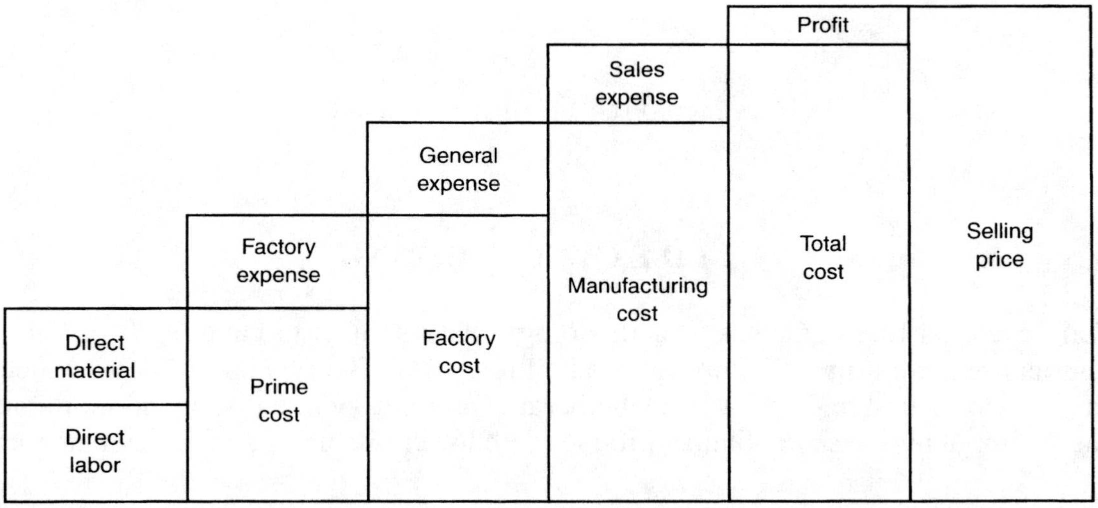

FIGURE 14.1
Elements of cost that establish the selling price.

A concept that provides a rough estimate of the investment cost for a new product is the turnover ratio:

$$\text{Turnover} = \frac{\text{annual sales}}{\text{total investment}} \qquad (14.1)$$

In the chemical industry the turnover ratio for many products is near 1.0; in the steel industry it is around 0.6. Suppose we wanted a quick estimate of the investment for a plant producing 20,000 tons/year of a chemical product that sells for 30¢/lb. Since the total annual sales are

$$0.30 \text{ \$/lb} \times 2000 \text{ lb/ton} \times 2 \times 10^4 \text{ ton/year} = 12 \times 10^6 \text{ \$/year}$$

the total plant investment is of the same magnitude for a turnover ratio of 1.0.

The fact that the variable costs depend on the rate or volume of production and fixed costs do not, leads to the idea of a break-even point (Fig. 14.2). The determination of the production lot size to exceed the break-even point and produce a profit is an important consideration. There are many things to be considered, but a common decision associated with economic lot size is how to allocate production among different machines, plants, or processes of various efficiencies or cost structure to make a product at minimum cost.

14.15
LIFE CYCLE COSTING

Life cycle costing (LCC) is a methodology that attempts to capture all of the costs associated with a product throughout its life cycle.[1] The typical problem, which we have encountered in Chap. 13, is whether it is more economical to spend more money in the initial purchase to obtain a product with lower operating and maintenance costs,

---

1. R. J. Brown and R. R. Yanuck, "Introduction of Life Cycle Costing," Prentice-Hall, Englewood Cliffs, NJ, 1985; W. J. Fabrycky and B. S. Blanchard, "Life-Cycle Cost and Economic Analysis," Prentice-Hall, 1991.

or whether it is less costly to purchase a product with lower first costs but higher operating costs. However, life cycle costing goes into the analysis in much greater detail in an attempt to evaluate all relevant costs, both present and future.

Life cycle costing, also known as "whole life costing," first found strong advocates in the area of military procurement, where it is used for comparison of competing weapons systems.[1] For a typical piece of military hardware, with a service life of 20 years, the operation and maintenance costs can be 60 to 80 percent of the life cycle cost.[2] More recently, life cycle costing has been combined with life cycle assessment (see Sec. 6.8) to consider the costs of energy consumption and pollution during manufacture and service, and the costs of retiring the product when it reaches its useful life. Expansion of the cost models beyond the traditional bounds to include pollution and disposal is an active area of research that will place the design engineer in a better position to make critical trade-offs.

The elements in the life cycle of a product are shown in Fig. 14.10. This figure emphasizes the *overlooked impact on society costs* (OISC) that are rarely quantified and incorporated into a product life cycle analysis.[3] We start with design. The actual costs incurred here are a small part of the LCC but the costs committed here comprise about 75 percent of the avoidable costs within the life cycle of the product. Moreover,

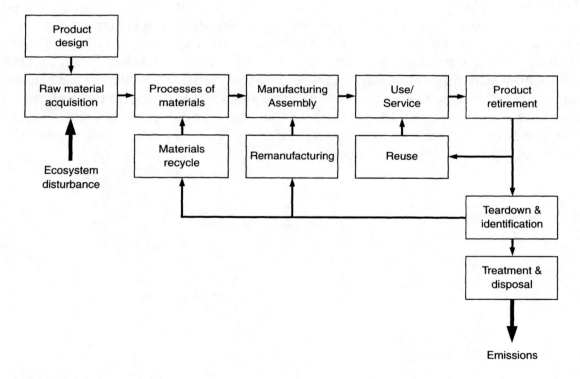

FIGURE 14.10
Total life cycle of a product.

1. MIL-HDBK 259, Life Cycle Costs in Navy Acquisitions.
2. J. J. Griffin, "Engineering Costs and Production Economics," vol. 14, 1988.
3. N. Nasr and E. A. Varel, Total Product Life-Cycle Analysis and Costing, *Proceedings of the 1997 Total Life Cycle Conference,* P-310, pp. 9–15, Society of Automotive Engineers, Warrendale, PA, 1997.

it is about 10 times less costly to make a change or correct an error in design than it is in manufacturing. The costs of acquiring the raw materials, usually by mining or oil extraction, and of processing the materials, can incur large environmental costs. These areas also often have considerable costs of carrying an inventory, and for transportation. We have concentrated in previous sections on the costs in manufacturing and assembly of products.

The cost of ownership of a product is the traditional aspect of LCC. Useful life is commonly measured by cycles of operation, length of operation, or shelf life. In design we attempt to extend life for use and service by using durable and reliable materials and components. Product obsolescence is dealt with through modular products.

Maintenance costs, especially maintenance labor costs, usually dominate other use costs. Most analyses divide maintenance costs into scheduled or preventive maintenance and unscheduled or corrective maintenance. The *mean time between failure* and *the mean time to repair* are important parameters from reliability theory (see Sec. 11.3) that impact LCC. Other costs that must be projected for the operations and support phase are: maintenance of support equipment; maintenance facility costs; pay and fringe benefits for support personnel; warranty costs and service contracts.

Once the product has reached its useful life it enters the retirement stage of the life cycle. We saw in Sec. 6.8 that other options than disposal should be considered. High-value-added products may be candidates for remanufacturing. By *value added* we mean the cost of materials, labor, energy, and manufacturing operations that have gone into creating the product. Products that lend themselves to recycling are those with an attractive *reclamation value,* which is determined by market forces and the ease with which different materials can be separated from the product. Reuse components are subsystems from a product that have not spent their useful life and can be reused in another product. Materials that cannot be reused, remanufactured, or recycled are discarded in an environmentally safe way. This may require labor and tooling for disassembly or treatment before disposal.

15

LEGAL AND ETHICAL ISSUES IN ENGINEERING DESIGN

15.1
INTRODUCTION

Engineering is not just applying scientific laws and principles to technical problems. It is basically concerned with improving the lot of society, and as such, it brings engineers into the mainstream of business and industry. Almost all entry-level engineers become involved, at least tangentially, with situations that call for some understanding of the law and situations that call for ethical judgments. Therefore, this chapter presents a brief overview of some legal and ethical issues in engineering. With topics as broad as law and ethics we can only scratch the surface, so we have chosen to focus on those issues that are most pertinent to engineering design.

The following are examples of where a design engineer might be concerned with legal and ethical issues:

- Preparing a contract to secure the services of a specialized software firm.
- Reviewing a contract to determine whether a contractor who built an automated production facility should be paid.
- Deciding whether it is legal and ethical to reverse engineer a product design.
- Managing a design project to avoid the possibility of a product liability suit.
- Protecting the intellectual property created as part of a new product development activity.
- Deciding whether to report a colleague who is taking kickbacks from a subcontractor.

The law is a formalized code of conduct describing what society feels is the proper way to behave. In other words, laws reflect what society values. As society evolves, its attitude toward behavior changes, and the laws change as well. Ethics is the study of human conduct that lays out the moral ground rules. It is intimately related to the values of society. Thus, laws and ethics, while distinct, are not independent. Ethical conduct is the behavior desired by society which is separate from the minimum standards of the law. For example, making a defective product despite taking all due care may subject you to product liability law, but it is not generally considered unethical.

This chapter comes with a warning label. *A little knowledge can be a dangerous thing.* Just as we would not expect a lawyer to practice engineering, so an engineer should not practice law. One objective of this chapter is to give you enough knowledge about the legal aspects of engineering practice to recognize when you need to take certain actions or to know when to seek legal counsel. A second objective is to help you realize that the engineering profession has expectations for your conduct and that a true professional recognizes responsibilities to the employer, the profession, and society, not just those to himself or herself.

15.2
THE ORIGIN OF LAWS

The code of American law has its origin in English *common law.* These laws derived from agreed-upon tradition and custom and were given the authority of law by decisions in the courts. Since each court decision is based on the study of previous court cases, it is often called *case law.*

Statutory law is law that is created by a legislative body, either state or federal. These laws, known as *statutes,* are often codified, as opposed to common law, and prescribe particular actions that apply to specific situations. Statutes may modify, reverse, or abolish common law doctrines. They are subject to both change and extinction by legislative action.

While the two basic types of law are common law and statutory law, many political entities contribute to the body of law. *Constitutional law,* which is based on the Constitution of the United States, defines governmental powers, especially with respect to the states, and secures the rights of the individual citizen. Municipal law is a subdivision of statutory law that is produced by towns and cities. These *municipal ordinances* deal with issues like traffic laws, zoning, and disturbance of the peace. A large body of *administrative law* has been created by rulings and regulations of federal and state agencies, other than the courts. Examples are OSHA and the EPA. Although cases involving administrative law are usually handled within the agency, disputes are finally resolved through the regular court system.

The purpose of the legal system is to protect and make life easier for each member of society. The rule of law is important not only in criminal matters, but it affects other aspects of society like politics, the economy, etc. The slow process of transformation of some former communist countries has demonstrated that an economy cannot grow and flourish without an accepted rule of law.

15.3
CONTRACTS

A contract is a promise by one person to another to do or not to do something. Only promises that the law will enforce are contracts. The three elements of a contract are:

$$\text{Contract} = \text{offer} + \text{acceptance} + \text{consideration}$$

An *offer* is an expression made by one person that leads another person to reasonably expect that the promisor wishes to create an agreement. The offer must be clear, definite, and specific, with no room for serious misunderstanding. An *acceptance* of the offer is necessary to make a contract legally binding. Both the offer and the acceptance must be voluntary acts. A contract cannot be forced on anyone. A contract is not enforceable by law unless it contains an agreement to exchange promises with value, the consideration. For example, if A and B enter into a contract in which A promises to pay B $1000 for modifying a CAD software package, both the money and the service are considerations.

15.3.1 Types of Contracts

Contracts can take many forms. They may be classified as express or implied, bilateral or unilateral. Also, a contract may be either written or verbal. Examples of contracts are purchase contracts, leases, a contract to perform a service, or an employment contract.

- An *express contract* is a contract in which all of the terms are agreed upon and expressed in words, either written or oral. An oral contract, once made, can be just as legal as a written contract, but it is much more difficult to prove and enforce. However, many states have statutes of frauds that require writing for certain contracts to be enforceable.
- An *implied contract* is a contract in which the agreement between parties is inferred by the legal system wholly or in part by their actions. For example, Jim goes to the local convenience store, where he has an account. He picks up a Sunday *New York Times* and holds it up so the clerk sees him take it and the clerk nods in return as he leaves the store with the paper. Jim has made an implied contract to pay $2 for the newspaper.
- A *bilateral contract* is a contract in which two parties have both made a promise to each other. A promise is made in return for a promise. Each party is both a promisor and a promisee.
- A *unilateral contract* is one in which the promisor does not receive a promise as consideration for her promise but instead agrees to pay if she receives an act or service. For example, Mrs. Jones says to Johnny Smith, "I promise to pay you $100 tomorrow if you will clean out my basement and garage today." Johnny immediately goes to work. This constitutes acceptance of the offer and creates a unilateral contract.

If more than one promisor or promisee is involved, the contract can take different forms (Table 15.1). The chief implication is with respect to the liabilities incurred by the different parties.

An engineer will have to deal with contracts in a number of different situations. Contracts for the purchase or sale of property are common. On taking a job you may be asked to sign a contract stating that all technical ideas that you develop belong to the company, even those conceived while not on the job. These contracts are often

TABLE 15.1
Types of contracts when there is more than one promisor or promisee

Type of contract	Number of parties	Liability
Joint	Two or more persons promise the same performance as a single party	All promisors are liable for the complete fulfillment of the contract
Several	Separate promises made by more than one promisor	Each promisor is liable for his or her individual promise
Joint and several	Two or more parties make a joint contract but also state that they are individually liable for completion of contract	All promisors face cumulative liability

negotiable at the time of employment and are something to consider when you are looking for employment. In technical dealings between companies, one of the parties may be asked to sign a *confidentiality agreement.* This is a contract in which one of the parties agrees to not disclose, make use of, or copy a design or product that the other party is about to disclose.

15.3.2 General Form of a Contract

In general, every business contract should contain the following information:

1. Introduction to the agreement. Include title and date.
2. Name and address of all parties. If one of the parties is a corporation, it should be so stated.
3. Complete details of the agreement. State all promises to be performed. Include such details as specifications, expected outcomes, etc. Give details on promises of payments, including amounts, timing of payments, interest, etc.
4. Include supporting documents such as technical information, drawings, specifications, and statements of any conditions on which the agreement depends.
5. Time and date of the start of the work and of the expected completion.
6. Terms of payment.
7. Damages to be assessed in case of nonperformance. Statement of how disputes are to be arbitrated.
8. Other general provisions of the agreement.
9. Final legal wording. Signatures of parties, witnesses, and notary public.

In addition, it is important to determine whether the contract contains an *integration clause* that establishes that it is an integrated contract and that other unwritten or oral terms are not implied.

15.3.3 Discharge and Breach of Contract

A contract is said to be *discharged* when the agreement has been performed to the satisfaction of both parties. The contracting parties can agree at any time that the con-

Gary Smith is district salesman for Zip-R Engineering Corp., manufacturers of automation equipment. He has submitted a proposal to ABC Mfg. Co. for 20 specialized robots, in response to their request for bids. The next day, Gary was talking with Joe Clark, purchasing agent for ABC. In the course of the phone conversation Joe told Gary, "Congratulations, you are a lucky guy." Gary took this as a signal that he had won the contract, and that a written agreement would be entered into later. Because it was close to the end of the quarter, and he needed this job to make his sales quota, Gary booked the job. Because Zip-R's backlog was low, they started work on the order immediately.

One week later, ABC's VP of Manufacturing decided to buy the robots from another company because of their reputation for requiring low maintenance. Can Zip-R recover damages for breach of contract?

The words "you are a lucky guy" spoken over the phone are too vague to constitute acceptance of an agreement. Without acceptance there is no legal contract. Gary had no justification for interpreting Joe's vague statement as an acceptance.

tract has been discharged. It can be discharged if it becomes impossible to perform due to circumstances outside the control of the contracting parties, e.g., *force majeure.* However, extreme difficulty in executing the contract does not discharge it even if it becomes more costly to carry out than originally anticipated.

A *breach of contract* occurs when one party fails to perform his or her part of the contract. A legal injury is said to have occurred, and the injured party can sue in court for damages.[1] General or compensatory damages are awarded to make up for the damage that occurred. Special damages are awarded for the direct financial loss due to the breach.

Often the terms of the contract contain *liquidated damages* that are agreed to beforehand in case the contract comes into dispute. If during trial these are found to be unreasonable, they will not come into force. The damages awarded at the trial will prevail. Note that the plaintiff has the obligation to act in such a way as to minimize the damages. If the court determines the damages could have been lessened through prudent action, this will be taken into consideration in setting the compensatory damages.

15.4
LIABILITY

Liability means being bound or obligated to pay damages or restitution. Two ways to incur liability are (1) breaking a contract or (2) committing a tort, e.g., fraud or negligence.

---

1. Another way to settle legal disputes is through arbitration. The United States has become a highly litigious society. In 1995 Americans filed more than 14.8M civil lawsuits and paid $121.7B in legal fees (National Center for State Courts, Research Department).

A *breach* of contract refers to violating a contract's promise. Failure to deliver detail drawings of a new machine by the date specified in the contract is a breach of contract. It makes no difference whether this was done intentionally or not.

Fraud is intentional deceitful action aimed at depriving another party of his or her rights or causing injury in some respect. Examples would be double billing or falsely certifying that a component had passed the ASME pressure vessel code.

Negligence is failing to exercise proper care and provide expertise in accordance with the standards of the profession that results in damage to property or injury to persons. This is the most common way for an engineer to incur liability to the public. For example, an engineer fails to include a major source of loading in design calculations of a public project so that the design fails. Note that being honest and well-intentioned does not absolve the engineer from a legal charge of negligence.

To be liable for negligence it must be proved that the defendant did not take reasonable and prudent action. This is determined by a jury. One way to show reasonable care is to show that you acted at the current level of technological development, i.e., the state of the art. A defense allowed in some states is to prove *contributory negligence,* that the plaintiff was negligent or could have prevented the accident had due care been taken. Sometimes it can be shown that the plaintiff willingly took an unnecessary risk that he or she was aware of, as when a person dives into a pool where the depth is clearly marked at 3 ft.

One way to limit business liability is by creating an appropriate business organization. A *corporation* is a legal entity that possesses many of the legal powers of individuals but one that exists independently of the people who own and manage it. A corporation can buy and sell property, enter into agreements, and sue and be sued. The corporation is in marked distinction from the *sole proprietorship,* in which the owner and the business are one and the same. In this case, a distinction is not made between the property of the business and the owner. The same holds for the finances of the business and the owner. A *partnership* is closer to a proprietorship but with many co-owners. All general partners are responsible for the acts and financial dealings of each other.

The corporation will be held liable for the acts of an employee who commits a civil wrong while engaged in corporate business. For example, the corporation can be fined by the EPA for the act of an employee who discharges liquid waste into a stream. Generally speaking, the corporation will incur the penalties of its employees, and the employee, in turn, may face the wrath of the corporation. Thus, working in a corporate structure provides some degree of protection from liability, but it is not absolute protection. Employees of corporations have been sued in the courts for negligence. Moreover, the trend in the courts is toward greater accountability of corporate employees. A corporate form cannot protect a professional from professional negligence.

15.5
TORT LAW

A *tort* is a *civil wrong* that involves damage committed against a person or his or her property, business, or reputation. It is a breach of the rights of an individual to be

Bill Garrison was hired by ABC Mfg. Co. as a consultant in plastic processing, with a chemical engineering degree and 10 years of experience. He was asked to recommend the equipment needed to convert a certain product line from metal to plastic parts. In particular, it was required that the production rate be at least equal to that when made with metal parts. When over $10M of new equipment was installed it was found that because of longer cycle time due to curing the plastic, the plastic line produced only 70 percent of the number of parts as made by the metal line in a given time. Can ABC hold Garrison personally responsible for this development?

Garrison can be held personally responsible to ABC for damages. As a consultant he acted as ABC's agent in designing the production line. By failing to take proper account of the plastic curing time he showed that he had not acted with due care and skill. He could be liable to ABC for negligence in tort, or for breach of contract. In addition, it was found that his 10 years of experience was in the area of polymer formulation, not plastics molding and manufacturing. If it could be shown that he misrepresented his background in order to secure the consulting contract, he could be liable for fraud.

secure in his or her person and property and be free from undue harassment.[1] Tort law is chiefly case law of the state courts, rather than statutory law. A decision in a case based on tort law hinges on three questions:

- Has a person's rights been infringed upon?
- Did the act occur as a result of negligence or actual intent on the part of the defendant?
- Did the plaintiff suffer damages as a result of the act?

Tort law deals with civil cases for which the penalty usually is monetary compensation rather than confinement. The difference between a tort and a *crime* is that a tort is a civil wrong while a crime is a wrong against society that threatens the peace and safety of the community. The victim of a crime may also bring a tort suit against the defendant to recover damages.

Tort suits involving engineers usually are concerned with one of four types of actions: (1) misrepresentation, (2) nuisance, (3) negligence, and (4) product liability. *Misrepresentation* is a false statement by a person of a fact that is known to be false, with the intent to deceive another person. When done under oath, it is called perjury. Misrepresentation is often claimed in a breach of contract suit. *Nuisance* concerns the annoyance or disturbance of a person such that the use of property becomes physically uncomfortable. Nuisances that affect the community, such as a blaring boom box at an open window, become a public nuisance. *Negligence* was defined in Sec. 15.4. *Product liability* is the action whereby an injured party seeks to recover damages for injury to person or property from a manufacturer or seller when the plaintiff alleges that a defective product or design caused the injury. This rapidly growing type of tort suit is discussed in Sec. 15.6.

---

1. "Engineering Law, Design Liability, and Professional Ethics," Professional Publications, Belmont, CA, 1983.

15.6
PRODUCT LIABILITY

Product liability refers to the legal action by which an injured party seeks to recover damages for personal injury or property loss from the producer or seller of a product. Product liability suits are pursued under the laws of tort. In no area of U.S. law has activity increased as dramatically as in personal injury product-liability civil lawsuits,[1] where suits in federal court increased 116 percent from 1995 to 1996, accounting for 14 percent of all federal civil suits filed. These span the gamut from individual suits by a single plaintiff against a single company to industrywide class action suits with thousands of plaintiffs filed against all asbestos manufacturers. Clearly the cost of preventing and defending against product liability has become a major concern for business and industry. An example of the extreme impact of product liability laws is on the manufacture of general aviation aircraft in the United States. In the 1970s the annual production of piston-engine powered light planes was from 10,000 to 15,000 per year, and accounted for more than 100,000 jobs. In the early 1990s production was barely 500 planes per year. This decrease has been blamed by many on the high costs of dealing with product liability litigation in the industry.[2]

15.6.1 Evolution of Product Liability Law

Before the industrial revolution, product liability laws did not exist. The purchaser had the responsibility to buy carefully and to use the product prudently. If the product broke or caused damage, the manufacturer was not required by law to stand behind it, although the better manufacturers gave warranties with their products. Around the mid-1800s the concept of *privity* came into use. Privity means that liability could occur only between those who entered into a contract or a direct transaction. The courts held that the injured party could sue only the party in privity. Thus, if a consumer was blinded by a broken hammer, he or she could sue only the retailer who sold him the tool; the retailer, in turn, could sue only the wholesaler, who in turn could sue the manufacturer.

A significant change occurred in 1916, when a court allowed an automobile owner to sue the manufacturer for negligence. This established the concept that manufacturers are directly liable to consumers. Clearly, from the viewpoint of recovering monetary damages it is an advantage to be able to directly sue the manufacturer, whose resources are likely to be much greater than those of a local retailer. When the Uniform Commercial Code was made law in the 1960s, it stated that there is an *implied warranty* of the fitness of products for their purposes and intended uses.

Also in the early 1960s the case law evolved to what is now called *strict product liability*. Previously manufacturers or sellers were liable only when they could be proved negligent or unreasonably careless in what they made or how they made it. It

---

1. A. S. Weintein, *Machine Design,* May 8, 1997, pp. 95–98.
2. B. E. Peterman, "Product Liability and Innovation," National Academy Press, Washington, DC, 1994, pp. 62–67.

had to be proved that a reasonable manufacturer using prudence would have exercised a higher standard of care. However, today in most states a standard of strict liability is applied. Under this theory of law the plaintiff must prove that: (1) the product was defective and unreasonably dangerous, (2) the defect existed at the time the product left the defendant's control, (3) the defect caused the harm, and (4) the harm is appropriately assignable to the identified defect. Thus, the emphasis on responsibility for product safety has shifted from the consumer to the manufacturer of products.

A related issue is the use for which the product is intended. A product intended to be used by children will be held to a stricter standard than one intended to be operated by a trained professional. Under strict liability a manufacturer may be held liable even if a well-designed and well-manufactured product injured a consumer who misused or outright abused it.

15.6.2 Goals of Product Liability Law

Only 100 years ago it was the practice in American and British law to not respond to accidental losses. It was generally held that the accident victim, not the manufacturer, should bear the economic burdens of injury. Starting in the mid-twentieth century, the law began to assume a more active role. Product liability law evolved to serve four basic societal goals: loss spreading, punishment, deterrence, and symbolic affirmation of social values.[1] Loss spreading seeks to shift the accidental loss from the victim to other parties better able to absorb or distribute it. In a product liability suit the loss is typically shifted to the manufacturer, who theoretically passes this cost on to the consumer in the form of higher prices. Often the manufacturer has liability insurance, so the cost is spread further, but at the price of greatly increased insurance rates.

Another goal of product liability law is to punish persons or organizations responsible for causing needless loss. It is important to recognize that under liability law the designer, not just the company, may be held responsible for a design defect. In extreme cases, the punishment may take the form of criminal penalties, although this is rare. More common is the assessment of punitive damages for malicious or willful acts. A third function is to prevent similar accidents from happening in the future, i.e., deterrence. Substantial damage awards against manufacturers constitute strong incentives to produce safer products. Finally, product liability laws act as a kind of symbolic reaffirmation that society values human safety and quality in products.

15.6.3 Negligence

A high percentage of product litigation alleges engineering negligence. Negligence is the failure to do something that a reasonable person, guided by the considerations that ordinarily regulate human affairs, would do. In product liability law, the seller is liable for negligence in the manufacture or sale of any product that may *reasonably be*

---

1. D. G. Owen, The Bridge, Summer, 1987, pp. 8–12.

expected to be capable of inflicting substantial harm if it is defective. Negligence in design is usually based on one of three factors:

1. That the manufacturer's design has created a concealed danger.
2. That the manufacturer has failed to provide needed safety devices as part of the design of the product.
3. That the design called for materials of inadequate strength or failed to comply with accepted standards.

Another common area of negligence is failure to warn the user of the product concerning possible dangers involved in the product use. This should take the form of warning labels firmly affixed to the product and more detailed warnings of restrictions of use and maintenance procedures in the brochure that comes with the product.

15.6.4 Strict Liability

Under the theory of strict liability, it is not necessary to prove negligence on the part of the manufacturer of the product nor is it necessary to prove breach of warranty or privity of contract. The defect itself regardless of how it got there, is sufficient to create liability under the tort laws. The fact that the injured party acted carelessly or in bad faith is not a defense under strict liability standards. The courts have acted so as to require the manufacturer to design its products in a way as to anticipate foreseeable use and abuse by the user.

Under most court decisions, defects divide into manufacturing defects and design defects.[1] Failure to conform with stated specifications is an obvious manufacturing defect. A manufacturing defect also exists when the product does not satisfy user requirements. Finally, a manufacturing defect exists when a product leaves the assembly line in a substandard condition, differs from the manufacturers intended result, or differs from other, ostensibly identical units of the same product line.

A design defect exists if the product fails to perform as safely as an ordinary consumer would expect. The criteria by which a defective and unreasonably dangerous nature of any product[2] may be tested in litigation are:

1. The usefulness and desirability of the product
2. The availability of other and safer products to meet the same need
3. The likelihood of injury and its probable seriousness
4. The obviousness of the danger
5. Common knowledge and normal public expectation of the danger
6. The avoidability of injury by care in use of the warnings
7. The ability to eliminate the danger without seriously impairing the usefulness of the product or making the product unduly expensive

---

1. C. O. Smith, Product Liability and Design, "ASM Handbook," vol. 20, pp. 146–151.
2. H. R. Piehler, A. D. Twerski, A. S. Weinstein, and W. A. Donaher, *Science,* vol. 186, p. 1093, 1974.

15.6.5 Design Aspect of Product Liability

Court decisions on product liability coupled with consumer safety legislation have placed greater responsibility on the designer for product safety. The following aspects of the design process should be emphasized to minimize potential problems from product liability.

1. Take every precaution that there is strict adherence to industry and government standards. Conformance to standards does not relieve or protect the manufacturer from liability, but it certainly lessens the possibility of product defects.
2. All products should be thoroughly tested before being released for sale. An attempt should be made to identify the possible ways a product can become unsafe (see Sec. 11.5), and tests should be devised to evaluate those aspects of the design. When failure modes are discovered, the design should be modified to remove the potential cause of failure.
3. The finest quality-control techniques available will not absolve the manufacturer of a product liability if, in fact, the product being marketed is defective. However, the strong emphasis on product liability has placed renewed emphasis on quality engineering as a way to limit the incidence of product liability.
4. Make a careful study of the system relations between your product and upstream and downstream components. You are required to know how malfunctions upstream and downstream of your product may cause failure to your product. You should warn users of any hazards of foreseeable misuses based on these system relationships.
5. Documentation of the design, testing, and quality activities can be very important. If there is a product recall, it is necessary to be able to pinpoint products by serial or lot number. If there is a product liability suit, the existence of good, complete records will help establish an atmosphere of competent behavior. Documentation is the single most important factor in winning or losing a product liability lawsuit.
6. The design of warning labels and user instruction manuals should be an integral part of the design process. The appropriate symbols, color, and size and the precise wording of the label must be developed after joint meetings of the engineering, legal, marketing, and manufacturing staffs. Use international warning symbols. (See Sec. 11.9.)
7. Create a means of incorporating legal developments in product liability into the design decision process. It is particularly important to get legal advice from the product liability angle on new innovative and unfamiliar designs.
8. There should be a formal design review before the product is released for production. (See Sec. 16.6.)

15.6.6 Business Procedures to Minimize Risk

In addition to careful consideration of the above design factors, a number of business procedures can minimize product liability risk.

1. There should be an active product liability and safety committee charged with seeing to it that the corporation has an effective product liability loss control and product safety program. This committee should have representatives from the advertising, engineering, insurance, legal, manufacturing, marketing, materials, purchasing, and quality-control departments of the corporation.
2. Insurance protection for product liability suits and product recall expenses should be obtained.
3. Develop a product usage and incident-reporting system just as soon as a new product moves into the marketplace. It will enable the manufacturer to establish whether the product has good customer acceptance and detect early signs of previously unsuspected product hazards or other quality deficiencies.

15.6.7 Problems with Product Liability Law

As product liability has grown so rapidly certain problems have developed in the implementation of the law.[1] There has been a dramatic shift in the doctrine of product liability law from negligence to strict liability but the law has proved incapable of defining the meaning of strict liability in a useful fashion. The rules of law are vague, which gives juries little guidance, and as a result verdicts appear capricious and without any definitive pattern. Another problem concerns the computation of damages once liability is established. There is great uncertainty and diversity in awarding damages for pain and suffering. Our adversarial legal system and the unfamiliarity of juries with even the rudiments of technical knowledge lead to high costs and much frustration.

The great increases in the number of product liability claims and the dollars awarded by the courts to consumers, other companies, and government have brought a clamor to bring some restraint to the situation before we become a no-fault economy in which producers and sellers will be held for all product-related injuries. Advocates of reform point to product liability insurance costs and damage awards as a significant factor in reducing American competitiveness. National product liability legislation has been introduced in the U.S. Congress to ease the situation. It aims at making tort law on product liability uniform in all the states and on speeding up product liability disputes. It proposes a limit on joint and several liability, a doctrine by which a defendant responsible for only a small portion of harm may be liable for an entire judgment award. It also calls for a limit on a product seller's liability to cases in which the harm was proximately caused by the buyer's own lack of reasonable care or a breach of the seller's warranty.

15.7
PROTECTING INTELLECTUAL PROPERTY

The protection of intellectual property by legal means has become a topic of general interest and international diplomatic negotiations. There are two conflicting motiva-

---

1. D. G. Owen, op. cit.

A small child threw an aerosol can into a blazing fireplace. The can exploded, injured the child, and the child's father sued the manufacturer of the cleaner in the spray can. The manufacturer defended itself by stating that the can contained a label warning the user not to incinerate. The child's father argued that the manufacturer should have anticipated that some cans would accidentally be incinerated and that some sort of fail-safe design should have been provided to prevent explosion.

The manufacturer of the spray can won the case by arguing that the presence of a warning label against incineration should excuse liability for the injury. This is a situation where the present state of technology does not provide for a safe means of preventing an explosion upon rapid rise in temperature. The manufacturer should not be held in liability so long as the users of the product have been clearly warned of potential dangers. In fact, the parents of the child were really negligent for allowing their child to play with an aerosol can near an open fire.

tions for this: (1) creations of the mind are becoming more valuable in the information age, and (2) modern information technology makes it easy to transfer and copy such information. We saw in Sec. 4.7 that intellectual property is protected by patents, copyrights, trademarks, and trade secrets. These entities fall within the area of property law, and as such they can be sold or leased just like other forms of property.[1]

The functional features of a design can be protected with *utility patents*. A utility patent protects not only the specific embodiments of the idea shown in the patent application but functional equivalents as well. A well-written patent is the best protection for a valuable idea. For the criteria of patentability refer to Sec. 4.7. If an idea is worth patenting, it is worth hiring an experienced patent attorney to do the job well.

A different type of patent, the *design patent,* covers the ornamental aspects of a product such as its shape, configuration, or surface decoration. Design patents are easier to obtain than utility patents, and they are easier to enforce in court. If a competitive design has essentially the same overall appearance, then it is in violation of your patent. A design patent can have only one claim, which is a serious disadvantage, because it means that every unique aspect of a product's design requires a separate patent. This can be expensive.

A copyright has only limited usefulness in protecting product designs. This form of intellectual property is primarily intended to protect writing; however, it has become the dominant method of protecting software.

Trademarks are used to protect the names or symbols (logo) of products. A related form of protection is known as *trade dress*. This consists of distinctive features of a product like its color, texture, size, or configuration. Trademark and trade dress are intended to protect the public about the source of a product, i.e., to protect against cheap "knock-offs." Trademark protection is achieved by registration with the U.S. Patent and Trademark Office, or by actual use of the trademark in the marketplace such that it achieves market recognition. Obviously, it is easier to defend against a

---

1. D. A. Gregory, C. W. Saber, and J. D. Grossman, "Introduction to Intellectual Property Law," The Bureau of National Affairs, Inc., Washington, DC, 1994.

competing trademark if it is registered. A registered trademark is issued for 20 years and can be renewed every 20 years as long as the product remains in the marketplace.

An innovation becomes a *trade secret* when a company prefers to forgo legal protection for the intellectual property. The reason for doing this is often a feeling that patents are difficult or costly to defend in the particular area of technology, or an unwillingness to let the public know what the company is doing. If the company takes active steps to protect the trade secret, then the courts will protect it as a form of intellectual property. Process innovations are more often protected by trade secrets than product innovations. Companies sometimes require nondisclosure agreements of their employees and may attempt to legally prevent an employee who leaves their employ with sensitive trade knowledge from working for a competitor in order to protect a trade secret.

15.8
THE LEGAL AND ETHICAL DOMAINS

We move now from considerations of the law to a discussion of ethics, and how ethical issues affect the practice of engineering design. Ethics is the principles of conduct that govern the behavior of an individual or a profession. It provides the framework of the rules of behavior that are moral, fair, and proper for a true professional. Ethical conduct is behavior desired by society and is above and beyond the minimum standards of the law.

The connection between legal and ethical action is illustrated by Fig. 15.1. In this model[1] the solid vertical line presents a clear distinction between what is legal and illegal, as set forth by statute and case law. The location of the dashed horizontal line between ethical and unethical behavior is much less well defined. The actions considered ethical depend on values, some of which are important to society, some to the profession, some to the employer, and some to the individual. The task of the ethical professional is to balance these value responsibilities. These values are clarified for the professional and business world by various codes of ethics (see Sec. 15.9). While

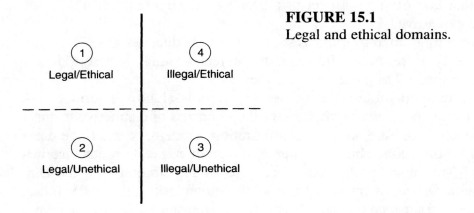

FIGURE 15.1
Legal and ethical domains.

1. S. G. Walesh, "Engineering Your Future," Chap. 11, Prentice-Hall, Englewood Cliffs, NJ, 1995; R. H. McCuen and J. M. Wallace, eds., "Social Responsibility in Engineering and Science," Prentice-Hall, Englewood Cliffs, NJ, 1987.

you would find close agreement among engineers as to whether an action is legal or illegal, you would find much greater disagreement as to whether some act is ethical or unethical.

Quadrant 1, legal and ethical behavior, is where you should strive to operate at all times. Most design and manufacturing activities fall within this quadrant. Indeed, a good case can be made that quality is dependent on ethical behavior.[1] "Doing what is right in the first place and doing what is best for all involved, when done at every level of the organization and in every work process, has proven to be the most efficient way of conducting a business."

Quadrant 2, legal and unethical, is the concern of the rest of this chapter. The goal is to explain how to identify unethical behavior and to learn what to do about it when it occurs. There is a feeling that unethical behavior in the workplace is increasing because of increasing workplace pressures and changing societal standards. Most corporations have adopted codes of ethics. Many have established an ethics office and are offering ethics training to their personnel. It is interesting that the prevailing view about ethics instruction has changed substantially. Throughout most of the twentieth century the common view about ethics was that you either learned ethics in the home when you were growing up, or it was too late. This is changing today to a view that ethics is a teachable subject that can be learned by just about everyone.

Quadrant 3, illegal and unethical, is the "go-to-jail" card. In general, most illegal acts also are unethical.

Quadrant 4, illegal and ethical, is a relatively rare event. An example could be an engineer who had signed a secrecy agreement with an employer, but then found that the employer had been engaged in producing a product that was very hazardous to the general public. Unable to get attention focused on the problem within the company, the engineer goes to the press to warn the public. The engineer has breached a contract, but in what is believed to be a highly ethical cause.

15.9
CODES OF ETHICS

We start by making a distinction between *morality* and *professional ethics*. Morality refers to those standards of conduct that apply to all individuals within society rather than only to members of a special group. These are the standards that every rational person wants every other person to follow and include standards such as the following:

- *Respect* the rights of others.
- Show *fairness* in your dealings with others.
- Be *honest* in all actions.
- *Keep promises* and contracts.
- Consider the *welfare* of others.
- Show *compassion* to others.

Note that each of these standards is based on the italicized values.

---

1. L. Bottorff, *Quality Progress*, February 1997, pp. 57–60.

By professional ethics we mean those standards of conduct that every member of a profession expects every other member to follow. These ethical standards apply to members of that group simply because they are members of that professional group. Like morality, standards of ethical conduct are value-based. Some values that are pertinent to professional ethics include[1]:

- *Honesty* and *truth*
- *Honor*—showing respect, *integrity,* and *reputation* for achievement
- *Knowledge*—gained through education and experience
- *Efficiency*—producing effectively with minimum of unnecessary effort
- *Diligence*—persistent effort
- *Loyalty*—allegiance to employer's goals
- *Confidentiality*—dependable in safeguarding information
- Protecting *public safety* and *health*

Note that some of these values are directed toward the employer (e.g., diligence), some toward the customer (e.g., confidentiality), some toward the profession (e.g., honor), and some toward society (e.g., public health and safety). These values reflect the professional's value obligations.

15.9.1 Profession of Engineering

The members of a profession are involved in an intellectual effort that requires special training that benefits society. Collectively, a group of people form a true profession only as long as they command the respect of the public and inspire confidence in their integrity and a belief that they are serving the general welfare.

The nature of professional service varies widely. The physician, lawyer, and clergyman have direct, individual relations with their clients, but an engineer usually is salaried in someone else's employ. About 95 percent of engineers work for either industry or government, and only a small, but important, percentage is in direct contact with the public as consulting engineers. Thus, the service aspect of engineering may be less obvious to the general public than in other professions.

The peculiarities of the engineering profession as compared with the professions of law and medicine carry over into the area of ethics. Because engineering lacks the homogeneous character of such professions as law and medicine, it is not surprising to find that there is no widely accepted code of engineering ethics. Most professional societies have adopted their own codes, and ABET and NSPE have adopted broader-based ethical codes. Again, because engineers who are employees of either business or government are in the great majority, they face ethical problems that self-employed professionals avoid. These arise from the conflict between the engineer's desire to gain a maximum profit for the employer (and thus achieve recognition and promotion) and the desire to adhere to a standard of ethics that places the public welfare ahead of

1. R. H. McCuen, *Ethics Education Program of the Institute for Professional Practice,* Verona, NJ, 1998.

corporate profit. For example, what can an employed engineer[1] do to expose and correct the corrupt practices of an employer? What should an engineer do if employed in a business atmosphere in which kickbacks and bribes are an accepted practice?

15.9.2 Codes of Ethics

Strong parallels exist between problem solving in design and in ethical decision making.[2] In both instances, a uniquely correct solution or response is rarely possible. However, some solutions are better than others, and some solutions are clearly unacceptable.

To provide guidance on how to behave in situations with ethical implications each engineering professional society has published a code of ethics.[3] The Code of Ethics for the American Society of Mechanical Engineers is given in Fig. 15.2. Note that the code is rather brief and quite general in its statements and that it is heavily oriented toward values. It is not a list of do's and don'ts. The three fundamental principles identify goals for the ethical behavior of engineers. Use your knowledge as an engineer for the good of humanity. Do it in an honest and impartial way. Work to increase the competence of the profession of engineering. The seven fundamental canons get a bit more specific, but they still emphasize value statements and leave many things unsaid. This generality is intentional in well-conceived codes of ethics.

The canons[4] present the general duties of an ethical engineer. They start by reinforcing the point that the safety, health, and welfare of the public is the first responsibility of the engineer. Next the canons charge engineers to work only in areas of their competence. The greater our competence, the better we will be able to protect public safety. Recognition of your real competencies is an important attribute. One should work to improve and expand their competence (canon 3), but also know when it is important to bring in other expertise to work on a design. After all, that is why we have design teams. While it is not specifically stated in canon 3, the wording implies that maintaining professional competency applies not just to technical competency but it also applies to competency in knowledge of ethics and values.

Canon 4 charges the engineer to act professionally with respect to the employer or client as faithful agents or trustees. This implies that the engineer places high importance on the values of loyalty, confidentiality, efficiency, and diligence. The second part of this canon talks about avoiding *conflicts of interest,* or the *appearance* of such conflict. A person is in a position of conflict of interest when he or she is in a position to personally benefit from actions under his or her influence, especially when the employer is unaware of this benefit. For example, a design engineer who owns considerable stock in a startup company would be in conflict of interest if he specified that company's product in his new design. Often a conflict of interest is impossible or

---

1. T. S. Perry, *IEEE Spectrum,* pp. 56–61, September 1981.
2. C. Whitbeck, "Ethics in Engineering Practice and Research," Cambridge University Press, New York, 1998, pp. 55–66.
3. A collection of the code of ethics for many professional societies can be found at http://ethics.cwru.edu.
4. A canon is an ecclesiastical or secular rule or law.

AMERICAN SOCIETY of MECHANICAL ENGINEERS
Founded 1880
CODE OF ETHICS OF ENGINEERS

THE FUNDAMENTAL PRINCIPLES

Engineers uphold and advance the integrity, honor, and dignity of the Engineering profession by:

I. using their knowledge and skill for the enhancement of human welfare;

II. being honest and impartial, and serving with fidelity the public, their employers and clients, and

III. striving to increase the competence and prestige of the engineering profession.

THE FUNDAMENTAL CANONS

1. Engineers shall hold paramount the safety, health and welfare of the public in the performance of their professional duties.

2. Engineers shall perform services only in the areas of their competence.

3. Engineers shall continue their professional development throughout their careers and shall provide opportunities for the professional and ethical development of those engineers under their supervision.

4. Engineers shall act in professional matters for each employer or client as faithful agents or trustees, and shall avoid conflicts of interest or the appearance of conflicts of interest.

5. Engineers shall build their professional reputation on the merit of their services and shall not compete unfairly with others.

6. Engineers shall associate only with reputable persons or organizations.

7. Engineers shall issue public statements only in an objective and truthful manner.

BOARD ON PROFESSIONAL PRACTICE AND ETHICS

FIGURE 15.2
The Code of Ethics of ASME International. (*Reprinted with permission.*)

impractical to avoid. In this case, the best practice is to make it known to everyone involved. For example, persons serving on study committees of the National Research Council are asked to disclose any potential conflicts of interest. You might have large stock holdings in your company, yet your expertise is vital to the study that is to be undertaken. Your conflict would be made part of the public record, and you would need to excuse yourself from deliberations if they ever come close to your area of conflict.

Avoiding the appearance of conflict of interest is as important as avoiding the conflict itself. Some areas that could get you in trouble are hiring relatives or close friends, accepting expensive gifts from vendors or customers, accepting a paid trip to a conference, or owning large blocks of stock in a competitor of your company.

In another example of conflict of interest, a law firm is forbidden by the code of ethics for lawyers to represent both parties in a dispute, even if the lawyer is asked to represent the second party in a case unrelated to the first dispute.[1] This part of the code arises from the adversarial nature of the legal system and the role that lawyers play therein. It is interesting to note that none of the engineering ethics codes would prevent a company from designing plastics plants for two directly competing companies as long as confidentiality was upheld. This points out that codes of ethics can differ significantly between different professions since professional practice can be quite different.

The fifth canon deals with how engineers treat each other in professional practice. One should not misrepresent or exaggerate their academic or professional credentials. For example, you should be able to provide documentation for all items on your résumé. Be fair in your dealings with other engineers. A good practice that will win you many friends is to be generous in giving credit for accomplishments when credit is due.

Canon 6 is self-evident. Nothing is more important over the long term than your reputation for following high ethical standards. The old adage, *we are known by the company we keep* applies here.

The last canon has many implications. It charges the engineer to be objective and truthful in professional reports, statements, and public testimony. Engineers may express publicly a professional opinion on technical subjects only when that opinion is founded upon adequate knowledge and competence in the subject matter. When making public statements, any payments you may have received by interested parties to make that statement must be disclosed.

The fundamental principles and canons are by necessity very general. This enables them to be applied to the broad gamut of situations with which engineers are involved. Some codes of ethics provide detailed *rules of practice*. The following are examples from the code of ethics of the National Society of Professional Engineers (NSPE):

- "Engineers shall not solicit or accept financial or other valuable consideration, directly or indirectly from contractors, their agents, or other parties in connection with work for employers or clients for which they are responsible."
- "Engineers shall not solicit or accept a professional contract from a governmental body on which a principal or officer of their organization serves as a member."
- "Engineers shall not reveal facts, data, or information obtained in a professional capacity without the prior consent of the client or employer except as authorized by law or this Code."

Four reasons why engineers should support their profession's code of ethics can be presented.[2] First, supporting the code helps protect engineers from being harmed by what other engineers do. Second, the code helps ensure to each engineer a work environment in which refusing to perform an unethical directive becomes easier to do. One can point to the code in support of your position. Third, supporting the code helps to make engineering a profession about which you need feel no morally justified embarrassment. Finally, supporting the code is the professional thing to do.

---

1. C. Whitbeck, op. cit.
2. M. Davis, "Thinking Like an Engineer," Oxford University Press, New York, 1998, pp. 59–60.

A young engineer on active duty with the Air Force discovers that a component used in three aircraft is overdesigned. A special adapter, costing several hundred dollars, is required for every component. The original purpose of the adapter was to permit the component to be used with a certain aircraft, but that aircraft now has been phased out of service. Thus, the adapter is redundant. The engineer tries to get the specification changed to eliminate the adapter, but she is told that the "system" will not permit this.

The resourceful engineer then submits the proposal through the suggestion system of the maintenance depot where she is assigned. She receives a phone call from a staff member informing her that as a military officer she cannot receive a monetary award for suggestions. The advice is given that she add a civil service engineer to the suggestion, and that they agree to split the award.

The potential for monetary reward through the suggestion system is rather great, but to do as suggested would be unethical. It would be dishonest and not show integrity. She submits the suggestion as originally formulated, forgoing an award that could exceed $100,000. Her reward, as a military officer, was dinner for two at the officer's club, and the start of a career with a reputation for high ethical behavior.

15.9.3 Extremes of Ethical Behavior

Ethical theory considers two extreme types of behavior. *Altruism* is a form of moral behavior in which individuals act for the sake of other people's interests. Ethical altruism is the view that individuals ought to act with each others' interests in mind. This is the viewpoint best summarized by the Golden Rule: Do unto others as you would have others do unto you. *Egoism* is a form of moral behavior in which individuals act for their own advantage. Ethical egoism is the view that individuals ought always to act to satisfy their own interests.[1] Most day-to-day practice of engineering is done in the individual's self-interest and is not in conflict with the codes of ethics. However, the codes of ethics are meant to alert the practicing professional that he or she has altruistic obligations that must be properly balanced with self-interest.

15.10
SOLVING ETHICAL CONFLICTS

It is probably safe to say that every engineer must resolve at least one ethical dilemma over the duration of his or her career. If the engineer mishandles the situation, his or her career can be damaged even in cases where he or she is trying to do the right thing. Therefore, it is important to know how to handle ethical conflicts and to have thought about conflict resolution before being confronted by a problem. A difficult problem

1. R. H. McCuen, *Issues in Engineering—Jnl. of Prof. Activities*, ASCE, vol. 107, no. E12, pp. 111–120, April 1981.

for engineers arises from their dual obligation to serve diligently and with loyalty both their employer and society. The vast majority of businesses aim to be honest and responsible corporate citizens, but the conflict between profit and societal good is potentially always present. What should you do when confronted by an ethical conflict where it is obvious that you have competing value responsibilities?

Ethical decision making is not easy. However, the chances for successfully resolving an ethical conflict can be greatly increased by following a systematic procedure. Table 15.2 presents one set of guidelines that will help ensure meeting one's professional responsibilities. Except under the unusual circumstances of imminent danger to the public, it is important that all internal steps should be explored before seeking options outside of the organization. The process of seeking resolution to an ethical conflict within the organization is usually handled through an appeals process within management or by the complaint process through the office of the ombudsman or the ethics officer. Seeking resolution outside of the organization is usually called *whistleblowing*. Table 15.2 gives a step-by-step procedure for resolving an ethical conflict or any conflict for that matter, through an internal appeals process and external to your company.

The steps that the individual should take in preparation for disclosure of unethical behavior are straightforward. Once you have studied and documented the facts and

TABLE 15.2
Procedure for Solving Ethical Conflicts*

I. Internal appeal option
A. Individual preparation
1. Maintain a record of the event and details
2. Examine the company's internal appeals process
3. Be familiar with the state and federal laws that could protect you
4. Identify alternative courses of action
5. Decide on the outcome that you want the appeal to accomplish
B. Communicate with your immediate supervisor
1. Initiate informal discussion
2. Make a formal written appeal
3. Indicate that you intend to begin the company's internal process of appeal
C. Initiate appeal through the internal chain of command
1. Maintain formal contacts as to where the appeal stands
2. Formally inform the company that you intend to pursue an external solution
II. External appeal option
A. Individual actions
1. Engage legal counsel
2. Contact your professional society
B. Contact with your client (if applicable)
C. Contact the media

R. H. McCuen, "Hydrologic Analysis and Design," 2d ed., Prentice-Hall, Englewood Cliffs, NJ, 1998.

formulated a plan for appeal, you should discuss the matter with your immediate supervisor. Failure to fully communicate your concerns to your immediate supervisor or secretly going over his or her head to higher levels is viewed as disloyalty and will be viewed negatively by all involved, even your supervisor's superior. It will also decrease the likelihood of a favorable resolution of the conflict. Often the value difference will be resolved by communicating with the immediate supervisor. However, if after fully discussing the issue with your supervisor, you feel that your supervisor is not willing or able to take appropriate action, then inform your supervisor in writing of your intention to appeal beyond that level.

The process of appealing an ethical conflict within the company is usually similar to the process of interacting with your immediate supervisor on the issue. You should have the facts and a plan of how you would like to see the issue resolved. Formal steps should follow informal discussions, and steps within the appeal chain should not be bypassed. If the internal appeal does not resolve the ethical conflict, then you should notify the company that you intend to continue with an external review of the problem.

Before expressing any public concern legal advice should be obtained. A lawyer can identify courses of action and legal pitfalls in your external appeal. While lawyers understand the legal issues, they may not have the technical background to evaluate the technical adequacy of your arguments. For this reason it might be helpful to involve an engineering professional society as an impartial judge of your arguments. Engineering societies vary widely in their willingness to become involved in these kind of activities.

If your company worked for a client in the issue about which you are concerned, then the client should be approached before going public. The client may pressure your company to resolve the issue internally, or the client may provide the resources to obtain an unbiased review of the issue.

The last resort is public disclosure by contacting the press and news TV. This is often called whistleblowing.

15.10.1 Whistleblowing

Whistleblowing is the act of reporting on unethical conduct within an organization to someone outside of the organization in an effort to discourage the organization from continuing the activity. In the usual case the charges are made by an employee or former employee who has been unable to obtain the attention of the organization's management to the problem. Sometimes whistleblowing is confined to within the organization where the whistleblower's supervision is bypassed in an appeal to higher management. An important issue is to determine the conditions under which engineers are justified in blowing the whistle. DeGeorge[1] suggests that it is morally permissible for engineers to engage in whistleblowing when the following conditions are met.

---

1. R. T. DeGeorge, *Business and Prof. Ethics Jnl.,* vol. 1, pp. 1–14, 1981.

1. The harm that will be done by the product to the public is considerable and serious.
2. Concerns have been made known to their superiors, and getting no satisfaction from their immediate superiors, all channels have been exhausted within the corporation, including the board of directors.
3. The whistleblower must have documented evidence that would convince a reasonable impartial observer that his or her view of the situation is correct and the company position is wrong.
4. There must be strong evidence that releasing the information to the public would prevent the projected serious harm.

Clearly a person engaging in whistleblowing runs considerable risk of being labeled a malcontent or of being charged with disloyalty, and possibly being dismissed. The decision to blow the whistle requires great moral courage. Federal government employees have won protection under the Civil Service Reform Act of 1978, but protection under state laws or active support from the engineering professional societies is still spotty. Some farsighted companies have established the office of ombudsman or an ethics review committee to head off and solve these problems internally before they reach the whistleblowing stage.

15.10.2 Case Studies

Ethics is best taught by looking at real-life situations through case studies. From time to time major incidents occur that catch the public's attention, and these are recorded for posterity in the engineering ethics texts. Prominent examples are the space shuttle *Challenger* tragedy,[1] the Bay Area Rapid Transit (BART)[2] control system failure, and the meltdown of the Chernobyl nuclear reactor.[3] Entire areas of technology and society are the subjects of continuing ethical discussions, for example, genetic engineering. Environmental issues[4] and questions of scientific fraud and integrity in doing research[5] are also prominent areas for discussion.

While these major incidents and cutting-edge activities get most of the attention, the likelihood that the average engineer will be involved heavily in such cases is small. A more typical ethical situation would be:

- Should I authorize the release of production parts that are only marginally out of specification?
- Should I condone the use of pirated design software?

---

1. R. L. B. Pinkus et al., "Engineering Ethics: Lessons Learned from the Space Shuttle," Cambridge University Press, New York, 1997; C. Whitbeck, op. cit., Chap. 4.
2. S. H. Unger, "Controlling Technology: Ethics and the Responsible Engineer," 2d ed., Wiley, New York, 1994, pp. 20–25.
3. S. H. Unger, op. cit., pp. 77–91.
4. P. A. Vesilind and A. S. Gunn, "Engineering, Ethics, and the Environment," Cambridge University Press, New York, 1998.
5. C. Whitbeck, op. cit., Chaps. 6, 7, 9, 10.

A consulting engineer is hired by the county to investigate a bridge collapse. In the course of his investigation he examines a bridge of similar design and finds that it is only marginally safe. He contacts the county engineer to tell him about this discovery. The county official tells him that they know about this condition and that they hope to repair it in the next budget year. However, they must keep the second bridge open because to close it would increase the response time of emergency vehicles by about 30 minutes. What should the consulting engineer do?

He goes back to the marginal bridge and makes a more thorough investigation, taking photographs and measurements. He finds the situation more dangerous than he first thought. Back at the office he makes some calculations and prepares a brief report. He asks for a meeting with the county engineer and lays out the case for closing the bridge. The county engineer is impressed, but points out the political implications of closing the bridge. He suggests a joint meeting with the county supervisor. They meet with the county supervisor, who is impressed with the severity of the situation, and the spirit of civic duty shown by the engineer. They agree to post the bridge to forbid general traffic, but to leave it open to emergency vehicles. The county supervisor schedules a press conference to which he invites the consulting engineer as an honored guest.

- What should I do about the fact that my boss has inflated my credentials on the résumé that went out with the last proposal?

Fortunately, the number and diversity of case studies that deal with just such day-to-day ethical problems is rapidly growing. The NSPE Board of Ethical Review answers ethics questions submitted by members of the society. These have been published in their monthly magazine *Professional Engineer,* and currently in the monthly newspaper *Engineering Times.* Engineering case studies can be found on the worldwide web at a number of locations.[1]

15.11
SUMMARY

Engineers mostly work in the business world, and they are therefore required to perform their duties within the laws of the nation. But more than this, engineering is a profession that is critical to the advancement of society. How engineers do their jobs determines what kind of world future generations will enjoy. Thus, the practice of engineering without question will involve you in making ethical judgments. Most will be small in nature, involving your relationship with your management and your fellow engineers, but others could be momentous, affecting the safety of a city.

The law is a formalized code of conduct describing what society feels is the proper way to behave. Statutory law is created by a federal or state legislative body. Case law arises from the decisions of the courts. Ethics is the study of human con-

---

1. http://ethics.cwru.edu; http://ethics.tamu.edu/Nsfcases/; http://repont.tcc.virginia.edu/ethics/.

duct that lays out the moral ground rules based on society's values. Ethical conduct is the behavior that is desired by society and is separate from the minimum standards of the law.

Engineers should be familiar with contracts and liability, especially product liability. A contract is an agreement between two parties to do or not to do something. It consists of an offer, an acceptance of the offer, and a consideration, the exchange of something of value. A contract is discharged when the agreement has been performed to the satisfaction of both parties. A breach of contract occurs when one party fails to perform its part of the contract.

Liability means being bound or obligated to pay damages or restitution. Two common ways of incurring liability are breaching a contract or committing a tort. A tort is a civil wrong committed against a person, or the business, property, or reputation that causes damage. Common examples of torts are fraud, misrepresentation, negligence, and product liability.

Product liability is the legal action by which an injured party seeks to recover damages for personal injury or property loss from the producer or seller of a product. The law under which product liability is tried has evolved to a standard of strict product liability. Under this theory of law, the plaintiff must prove that: (1) the product was defective and unreasonably dangerous, (2) the defect existed at the time the product left the defendant's control, (3) the defect caused the harm, and (4) the harm is appropriately assignable to the identified defect. Previously, manufacturers were liable only when they could be proved negligent or unreasonably careless.

To protect against product liability suits, the design procedures described in Secs. 11.4, 11.5, 11.6, and 11.9 must be followed. In addition, documentation of these design methods and of testing and quality activities is vital. There should be an active product safety committee to see that every step is taken to ensure the design and production of safe products. Finally, it may be a wise business decision to obtain insurance protection for product liability suits and product recall expenses.

While the boundary between legal and illegal acts is generally well defined by the law, the distinction between what is ethical and what is unethical is much less well defined. Professional engineering societies provide guidance by means of codes of ethics. Different individuals respond differently depending on their value system. Engineering is a profession, and as such, you are bound by the ethical standards of the profession. It does not matter whether you have individually made that agreement. The profession expects you to behave in a certain ethical way. These rules of conduct are laid down in the code of ethics of each professional engineering society. The existence of a code of ethics is important to you because it gives you an authoritative standard to fall back on if you are engaged in a serious ethical conflict in the workplace.

Table 15.3 suggests typical ethical questions associated with different steps in the product design process.[1]

It is not inconceivable that you will be involved in a serious ethical conflict sometime in your career. This often arises from the competing value responsibilities that engineers have, such as loyalty and diligence to both their employer and the good of

---

1. M. W. Martin and R. Schinzinger, "Ethics in Engineering," 3d ed., McGraw-Hill, New York, 1996.

TABLE 15.3
Typical ethical questions associated with product design

Steps in product design	Possible ethical questions
Market study	Is the study unbiased or has it been embellished to attract investors or management support?
Conceptual design	Will the product be useful or will it be just a gimmick?
Embodiment design	Does the design team have sufficient expertise to properly judge whether computer programs are giving reliable results? Have any patents been violated?
Detail design	Has checking of results been done?
Manufacturing	Is the workplace safe and free of environmental hazards? Is enough time allowed to do quality work?
Product use	Is the product safe to use? Are users informed of possible hazards?
Retirement from service	Has the design allowed for recycling or reuse?

society. If such a conflict does arise, it is important to try to resolve the disagreement internally in your organization. Follow to the letter the prescribed appeal procedure, and document everything. If you must go outside of the organization, obtain competent legal counsel. While it may be necessary to be a whistleblower and release your story to the press, do this only as a last resort.

BIBLIOGRAPHY

Law and the Engineer

Blinn, K. W.: "Legal and Ethical Concepts in Engineering," Prentice-Hall, Englewood Cliffs, NJ, 1989.
Dunham, C. W., R. D. Young, and J. T. Bockrath: "Contracts, Specifications, and Law for Engineers," 3d ed., McGraw-Hill, New York, 1979.
"Engineering Law, Design Liability, and Professional Ethics," Professional Publications, Belmont CA, 1983.

Product Liability

Brown, S., I. LeMay, J. Sweet, and A. Weinstein, eds.: "Product Liability Handbook: Prevention, Risk, Consequence, and Forensics of Product Failure," Van Nostrand Reinhold, New York, 1990.
Hunziker, J. R., and T. O. Jones: "Product Liability and Innovation," National Academy Press, Washington, DC, 1994.
Smith, C. O.: "Products Liability: Are You Vulnerable?" Prentice-Hall, Englewood Cliffs, NJ, 1981.

Engineering Ethics

Davis, M.: "Thinking Like an Engineer: Studies in the Ethics of a Profession," Oxford University Press, Oxford, 1998.

Harris, C. E., M. S. Pritchard, and M. Rabins: "Engineering Ethics: Concepts and Cases," Wadsworth Publishing Co., Belmont, CA, 1995.

Martin, M. W., and R. Schinzinger: "Ethics in Engineering," 3d ed., McGraw-Hill, New York, 1996.

Unger, S. H.: "Controlling Technology. Ethics and the Responsible Engineer," 2d ed., Wiley, New York, 1994.

Whitbeck, C.: "Ethics in Engineering Practice and Research," Cambridge University Press, New York, 1998.

PROBLEMS AND EXERCISES

15.1. John Williams, a professional engineer, agrees to testify as an expert witness for the firm of Jones & Black in a court case. In return, the firm promises to pay Williams $1500 plus expenses for his services. (*a*) Is this a lawful contract? State the reasons for your decision. (*b*) Suppose Williams agrees to accept $2500 if Jones wins, but only expenses if Jones loses. Is this a lawful contract? State your reasons.

15.2. ABC Electric agreed by fax on Monday to buy 100 fractional-horsepower motors for $3000 from Amalgamated Electric. On Wednesday the purchasing agent from ABC calls and says he is canceling the order. Amalgamated says the motors have already been shipped and they want their money. (*a*) What is the legal responsibility of ABC Electric in this transaction? (*b*) Would it have been any different if the motors had not already been shipped?

15.3. A car designer specified steel bolts of the highest quality and strength when designing a connection for the front-end steering rods. The manufacturer of the bolts used an inadequate sampling plan for inspecting the bolts, and several defective bolts caused failure of the steering mechanism. Several deaths resulted and there was a major product recall. Discuss the liability of the designer, the auto company, and the bolt manufacturer.

15.4. Read the story of the failure of the General Electric refrigerator with the revolutionary rotary compressor (*Wall Street Journal,* May 7, 1990, p. A1, A5). What lessons does this teach us about product design? What implications does it have for product liability?

15.5. Aristotle put forth the precept that humanity should follow four virtues: (1) prudence, (2) justice, (3) fortitude, and (4) temperance. Define each virtue broadly and give examples of ethical behavior for each virtue.

15.6. Make a list of business practices that signal whether an organization is an ethical corporation. What role does the CEO of the corporation play in this?

15.7. We are in a period where the desire for steady increase in corporate earnings, driven to a large degree by the stock market, sometimes causes management to require layoffs even when profits are good. Discuss the ethics of this from the viewpoint of both corporate management and the individual engineer.

15.8. Imagine what it would be like if there were no codes of ethics for engineers. What would be the consequences?

15.9. A trend in sports equipment has been to improve the players' performance by introducing new products. Examples are the graphite-composite shaft and titanium head in golf drivers, lighter-weight composite tennis rackets with a larger "sweet" spot, and an aluminum baseball bat with built-in damping. Discuss the ethics of compensating for personal inadequacies in performance with technology in competitive sports.

15.10. Discuss the ethics of the following situation. You are a design engineer for the Ajax Manufacturing Co., a large multiplant producer of plastic parts. As part of your employment, you were required to sign a secrecy agreement that prohibits divulging information that the company considers proprietary.

Ajax has modified a standard piece of equipment that greatly increases the efficiency in cooling viscous plastic slurries. The company decides not to patent the development but instead to keep it as a trade secret. As part of your regular job assignment, you work with this proprietary equipment and become thoroughly familiar with its enhanced capabilities.

Five years later you leave Ajax and go to work for a candy manufacturer as chief of production. Your new employer is not in any way in competition with Ajax. You quickly realize that Ajax's trade secret can be applied with great profit to a completely different machine used for cooling fudge. You order the change to be made. Discuss the ethics.

15.11. Discuss the ethics in the following situation. You have been on the job for nine months as an assistant research engineer working with a world-famous authority on heat transfer. It is an ideal job, because you are learning a great deal under his sympathetic tutelage while you pursue an advanced degree part-time.

You are asked to evaluate two new flame-retardant paints A and B. Because of late delivery of some constituents of paint A, the test has been delayed and your boss has been forced to make a tentative recommendation of paint A to the design group. You are asked to make the after-the-fact tests "for the record." Much to your surprise, the tests show that your boss was wrong and that formulation B shows better flame resistance. However, a large quantity of paint A already has been purchased. Your boss asks you to "fudge the data" in favor of his original decision, and since there is reasonable possibility that your data were in error, you reluctantly change them to favor his decision. Discuss the ethics.

16

DETAIL DESIGN

16.1
INTRODUCTION

We have finally come to the last of the three stages into which we have divided the design process. As mentioned in the introduction to Chap. 6, the boundary between embodiment design and detail design has become blurred by the emphasis on reducing the product development cycle time by the use of concurrent engineering methods (Design for X), aided and abetted by computer-aided engineering (CAE). In many engineering organizations it is no longer correct to say that detail design is the phase of design where all of the dimensions, tolerances, and details are finalized. However, detail design, as the name implies, is the phase where all of the details are brought together, all decisions are finalized, and a decision is made by management to release the design for production. Poor detail design can ruin a brilliant design concept and lead to manufacturing defects, high costs, and poor reliability in service. The reverse is not true. A brilliant detail design will not rescue a poor conceptual design.

Figure 16.1 shows the stages of design by which we have organized this book. The numbers of the Chaps. 7 through 14 have been superimposed in order to show you where in the process this knowledge is generally applied. Detail design is the lowest level in the design abstraction hierarchy. Many decisions have been made to get to this point. Most of these decisions are very basic to the design and to change them now would be costly in time and effort. Thus, as the name implies, detail design is mainly concerned with filling in the details to ensure that a proven and tested design can be manufactured.

16.2
DETAIL DESIGN

We have defined the end of the design process to be detail design. Figure 16.2 shows the principal tasks to be completed in detail design.

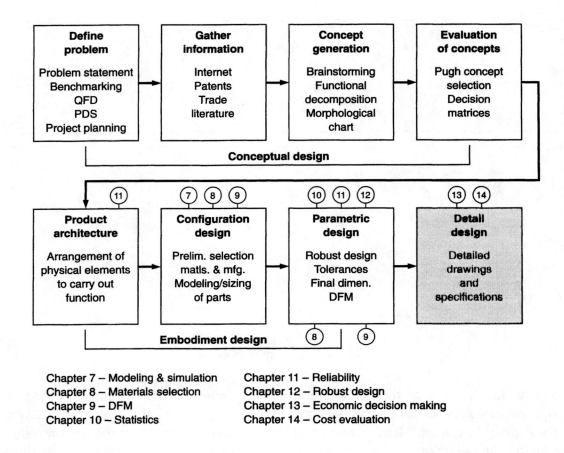

Chapter 7 – Modeling & simulation   Chapter 11 – Reliability
Chapter 8 – Materials selection   Chapter 12 – Robust design
Chapter 9 – DFM   Chapter 13 – Economic decision making
Chapter 10 – Statistics   Chapter 14 – Cost evaluation

FIGURE 16.1
Steps in the design process, showing where Chaps. 7 through 14 are chiefly applied.

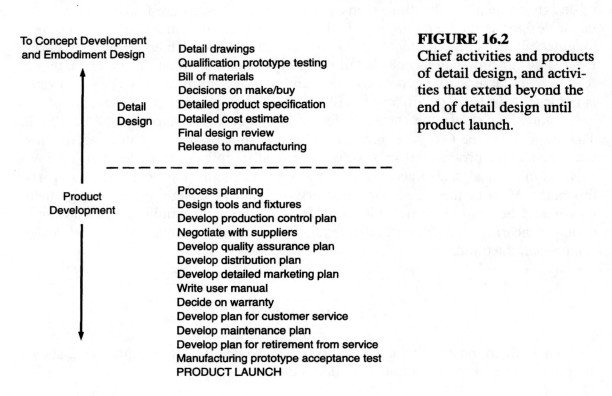

FIGURE 16.2
Chief activities and products of detail design, and activities that extend beyond the end of detail design until product launch.

258

The first task of detail design is to complete the detail drawings. Much of the technical analysis will have been done in embodiment design, but there will still be calculations to perform, questions to answer, and decisions to make. One important decision is to decide whether to make a component in-house or to buy it from an outside vendor. There will be many tests to run to assure that the components and assemblies meet the requirements laid down in the product design specification.

As each component, subassembly, and assembly is completed it is documented completely with detail drawings (see Sec. 16.3) and specifications. For individual parts the drawing and the specification are often the same document. The specification contains information on the technical performance of the part, its dimensions, test requirements, materials requirements, reliability requirement, design life, packaging requirement, and marking for shipment. The specification should be sufficiently detailed to avoid confusion as what is expected from the supplier.

If the product design is at all complex it most likely will be necessary to impose a *design freeze* at some point prior to completion. This means that beyond a certain point in time no changes to the design will be permitted unless they go through a formal review by a design control board. This is necessary to prevent the human tendency of always wanting to make a slight improvement, which unless controlled by some external means results in the job's never actually being completed. With a design freeze, only those last-minute changes that truly affect performance, safety, or cost get made.

Once the design is finalized, a final prototype is built and qualification tested to ensure that the design functions as required and is safe and reliable. Depending on the complexity of the product the qualification testing may simply be to run the product during an expected duty cycle and under overload conditions, or it may be a more elaborate series of staged tests. The detail drawings allow the calculation of detailed cost estimates. To make these calculations a bill of materials (see Sec. 16.4) is drawn up that lists all of the parts needed for making the product.

Once these steps have been successfully completed it is time to review the complete product design in a final design review (see Sec. 16.6). This involves top corporate management, the chief design personnel, the responsible manufacturing personnel, and the customer (if the product has a defined customer). The successful outcome of the design review is the release of the design to the manufacturing department.

While design release to manufacturing formally ends the detail design phase, as Fig. 16.2 shows, it does not end the product development process. There are many additional tasks, some carried out by engineers, some by other professionals, that must be done to achieve product launch. Most of these tasks are self-explanatory and do not require further elaboration.

Process planning and production control are related tasks. Process planning is the task of selecting the processes, and the individual steps that must be performed by each process in a prescribed sequence, to make each component. Ultimately, this information is needed to definitively calculate manufacturing cost. Process planning also includes laying out the production flow line. Production control is the task of scheduling the flow of work into production and providing the materials, supplies, and technical data needed for carrying out the manufacturing operation. One popular way of doing this today is *just-in-time* (JIT) *manufacturing*. With JIT a company minimizes inventory by receiving parts and subassemblies in small lots just as they are needed on the production floor. With this method of manufacturing the supplier is an extension of the production line. JIT manufacturing obviously requires close and harmonious relations with the supplier companies. The supplier must be reliable, ethical, and capable of delivering quality parts.

Just as successful testing of a qualification prototype ends the design phase of product development, the successful testing of the pilot runs from manufacturing ends the product development process. The proven ability to manufacture the product to specification and within cost budget makes possible the product launch in which the product is released to the general public or shipped to the customer.

16.3
DETAIL DRAWINGS

The historical goal of detail design has been to produce drawings that contain the information needed to manufacture the product. These drawing should be so complete that they leave no room for misinterpretation. The information on a detail drawing includes:

- Standard views of orthogonal projection—top, front, side views
- Auxiliary views such as sections, enlarged views, or isometric views that aid in visualizing the component and clarifying the details
- Dimensions—presented according to the GD&T standard ANSI Y14.5M
- Tolerances
- Material specification, and any special processing instructions
- Manufacturing details, such as parting line location, draft angle, surface finish

Sometimes a specification sheet replaces the notes on the drawing and accompanies it. Figure 16.3 is an example of a detail drawing. Note the level of detail contained in it. If the design is developed digitally in a CAD system, then the digital model becomes the authority for the component definition. In this case it is not necessary to include quite so much detail in the drawings since it resides in the computer and can be pulled up when needed.

Assembly drawings are part of the detail design. These are of two kinds. *Design layouts* show the spatial relationships of all components in the assembled product (the system). These have evolved from the rough sketches of conceptual design into often elaborate three-dimensional drawings. The solid model in CAD is a design layout. The design layout serves to visualize the functioning of the product and to ensure that there is physical space for all of the components. Design layout starts with the first glimmer of the concept and is developed more fully in the product architecture step of embodiment design. Design layouts serve as an input in the creation of detail drawings for each component.

Assembly drawings are created in detail design as tools for passing design intent to the production department, as well as the user. They show how the part is related in space and connected to other parts of the assembly. Dimensional information is limited to that necessary for the assembly. Reference is made to the detail drawing number for each part for this information. Also, the detail drawing will give the drawing

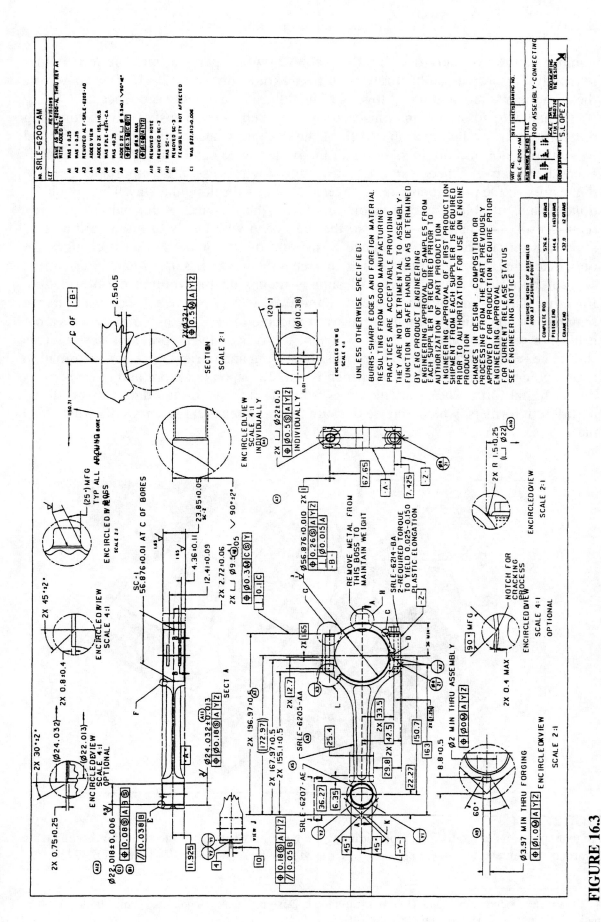

FIGURE 16.3

An example of a detail drawing. ("*ASM Handbook*," vol. 20, p. 227, ASM International, Materials Park, OH, 1997. Used with permission.)

number of the assembly drawing that shows how the part fits into the next higher assembly. Often an assembly drawing utilizes exploded views (Fig. 16.4) to show how the components are assembled together, including the assembly sequence.

When a detail drawing is finished, it must be checked to ensure that the drawing correctly portrays the function and fit of the design.[1] Checking should be performed by someone not initially involved with the project who can bring a fresh but experienced perspective. Since design is an evolutionary process, it is important to record the history of the project and the changes that are made along the way. This should be done in the title block and revision column of the drawing. A formalized drawing release process must be in place so that everyone who needs to know is informed about design changes. An advantage of using a digital model is that if changes are only made there, then everyone who can access the model has up-to-date information.

An important issue in detail design is managing the volume of information. Ensuring that design information can be retrieved is very important. For example, we may have made a design change that was expected to ease the assembly process, but it did not work as expected. Now, we want to go back to the previous design. This should be readily retrievable. The process of storing and retrieving design information is particularly complicated today. Much is still on paper, but more and more is moving to digital form. The problem comes from the fact that digital data may be stored in different formats, which may be difficult to be communicated across different CAD platforms.

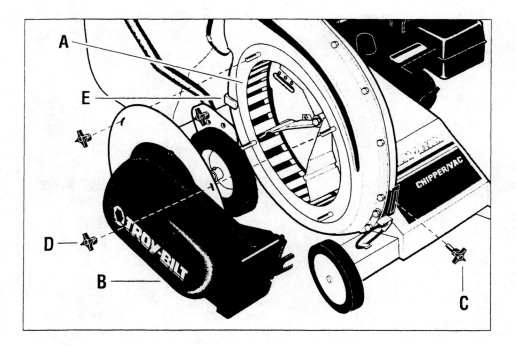

FIGURE 16.4
An example of an exploded assembly drawing showing how to replace the shredder screen (A) in a garden implement. (*Drawing courtesy of Garden Way Inc., 1 Garden Way, Troy, NY, 12180.*)

---

1. G. Vrsek, Documenting and Communicating the Design, "ASM Handbook," vol. 20, ASM International, Materials Park, OH, pp. 222–230, 1998.

Unfortunately, there is not a strong tradition of recording the decisions made during design so that the knowledge is not lost with the designer, and so that novices can learn from it. The place where this information is captured is the design notebook (see Sec. 17.2).

16.4
BILL OF MATERIALS

The bill of materials (BOM) or the parts list is a list of each individual component in the product. As Fig. 16.5 shows, it lists the part description, quantity needed for a complete assembly, part, number, the source of the part, and purchase order number if outsourced to a suppler. This version of the bill of materials also lists the name of the engineer responsible for the detail design of each part, and the name of the project engineer who is responsible for tracking the parts through manufacture and assembly.

The bill of materials has many uses. It is essential for determining the cost of the product. A bill of materials will be started early in the embodiment design phase, when the product architecture has been established, as a way of checking whether the product costs are in line with that called for in the PDS.[1] The bill of materials will be finalized in the detail design phase and will be used in the detailed cost analysis.

The bill of materials is vital for tracking the parts during manufacture and assembly. It is an important archival document for the design that needs to be preserved and be available for retrieval.

ENGINE PROGRAM PARTS LIST									
DOCUMENTING THE DESIGN									
Qty /		PART NUMBER					Delivery	RESPONSIBILITY	
Engine	PART DESCRIPTION	Prefix	Base	End	P.O. #	Source	Date	Design	Engineer
	PISTON								
6	PISTON (CAST/MACH)	SRLE	6110	24093	RN0694	Ace	11/17/95	S. LOPEZ	M. Mahoney
6	PISTON RING - UP COMPRESSION	SRLE	6150	AC	RN0694	Ace	rec'd FRL	S. LOPEZ	M. Mahoney
6	PISTON RING - LOWER COMPRESSION	SRLE	6152	AC	RN0694	Ace	rec'd FRL	S. LOPEZ	M. Mahoney
12	PISTON RING - SEGMENT OIL CONTROL	SRLE	6159	AC	RN0694	Ace	rec'd FRL	S. LOPEZ	M. Mahoney
6	PISTON RING - SPACER OIL CONTROL	SRLE	6161	AB	RN0694	Ace	rec'd FRL	S. LOPEZ	M. Mahoney
6	PIN - PISTON	SRLE	6135	AA		BN Inc.		S. LOPEZ	M. Mahoney
6	PISTON & CONNECTING ROD ASSY	SRLE	6100	AG				S. LOPEZ	M. Mahoney
6	CONNECTING ROD - FORGING	SRLE	6205	AA		Formall		S. LOPEZ	M. Mahoney
6	CONNECTING ROD ASSY	SRLE	6200	CI		MMR Inc.		S. LOPEZ	M. Mahoney
12	BUSHINGS - CONNECTING ROD	SRLE	6207	AE		Bear Inc.		S. LOPEZ	M. Mahoney
12	RETAINER - PISTON PIN	SRLE	6140	AC		Spring Co.		S. LOPEZ	M. Mahoney

FIGURE 16.5

An example of a bill of materials. (*"ASM Handbook," vol. 20, p. 228, ASM International. Used with permission.*)

---

1. K. T. Ulrich and S. D. Eppinger, "Product Design and Development," pp. 69–70, McGraw-Hill, New York, 1995.

For simple assemblies the bill of materials is placed directly on the assembly drawing. For more complex assemblies it is generated with a spreadsheet. Many CAD software packages allow for automatic generation of a bill of materials.

16.5
IMPACT OF CAE ON DETAIL DESIGN

Throughout this text we have tried to give a current picture of how computer-aided engineering (CAE) is impacting engineering design. Clearly the ability to make computer models and carry out computer-based simulation (Chap. 7) has greatly increased our ability to efficiently size parts and improve durability. The ability to design for robustness (Chap. 12) has increased the quality of what we design. But it is in detail design, where everything comes together, that CAE can have the greatest economic impact. Detail design involves the greatest commitment of personnel of the three stages of design because there is so great a volume of work to do.

The first CAE impact on detail design has already occurred in the drafting task of preparing detail drawings. The ability to make changes quickly in a CAD system has saved countless hours of redrawing details on vellum. Similarly, the ability to store standard details in a CAD system for retrieval when needed saves much drafting labor.

Many companies have a product line that is generic but requires engineering decisions to tailor the product to the customer's needs. For example, a manufacturer of industrial fans will change the motor speed, propeller pitch, and structural supports depending on the required flow rate, static pressure, and duct size. Typically this requires standard engineering calculations, a detail drawing, and a bill of materials (BOM) in order to produce a quote to the customer. Using conventional methods this might require a 2-week turnaround, but using modern integrated software that automates the computation, drawing, and BOM generation, the quote can be developed in 1 day.[1]

We are beginning to see the impact of modern information handling methods in detail design. Three types of software systems have evolved:[2] enterprise-requirement planning (ERP), product data management (PDM), and component and supplier management (CSM). ERP systems provide the bridge between manufacturing and procurement. They ensure that the procurement department is buying enough parts and materials at the right times, and supplying them to manufacturing at the right time to meet customer demand. ERP systems deal with order entry and purchasing execution, inventory management, MRP (materials requirements planning), and capacity planning.

PDM systems link design and manufacturing. They manage the product data and data structure and the engineering change process and ensure that the right design information is conveyed to manufacturing at the right time. The PDM system is linked with the CAD system.

The CSM system is the link between design and procurement. It is intended to help engineers select the best parts or reusable designs based on both technical and business

---

1. T. Dring, *Machine Design,* Sept. 26, 1994, pp. 59–64.
2. C. Palmer, *Mechanical Engineering,* April 1996, pp. 77–79.

criteria and to manage the supply chain better to reduce cost. For example, estimates by large manufacturers are that the cost to establish a new part, even if it is only a screw, is from $15,000 to $25,000.[1] This cost arises from the need to test the component, evaluate the supplier, obtain management approvals, and enter data on the new component into the internal data system. In a large, geographically distributed company it is not unusual for 2 to 5 percent of the total number of parts (often tens of thousands) to be exact duplicates or functional duplicates. Thus, CMS can have a big payoff.

16.6
FINAL DESIGN REVIEW

The final design review should be conducted when the production drawings are complete and ready for release to manufacturing. In most cases qualification prototype testing will have been completed. The purpose of the final design review is to compare the design against the most updated version of the product design specification (PDS) and a design review checklist, and to decide whether the design is ready for production.

The general conditions under which design reviews are held were discussed in Sec. 1.10. Since this is the last review before design release, a complete complement of personnel should be in attendance. This would include design specialists not associated with the project to constructively review that the design meets all requirements of the PDS. Other experts review the design for reliability and safety, quality assurance, field service engineering, and purchasing. Marketing people or the customer's representatives will be present. Manufacturing personnel will be in strong attendance, especially plant operating management responsible for producing the design, and DFM experts. Other experts who might be called in, depending upon circumstances, are representatives from legal, patents, human factors, or R & D. Supplier representation is often desirable. The intent is to have a group comprised of people with different expertise, interests, and agendas. The chairperson of the final design review will be an important corporate official like the VP of engineering, the director of product development, or an experienced engineering manager, depending on the importance of the product.

The formal meetings or reviews that will have preceded the final review include an initial product concept meeting to begin the establishment of the PDS, a review at the end of conceptual design to decide whether to finance the full-scale product development, and a review after embodiment design to decide whether to move into detail design. The latter may take the form of detailed partial reviews (meetings) to decide important issues like design for manufacturing, quality issues, reliability, safety, or preliminary cost estimates. Regardless of the review schedule, the final design review is the most structured and comprehensive of the reviews.

An effective design review consists of three elements:[2] (1) input documents, (2) an effective meeting process, and (3) an appropriate output.

---

1. C. Palmer, op. cit.
2. K. Sater-Black and N. Iverson, *Mechanical Engineering,* March 1994, pp. 89–92.

16.6.1 Input Documents

The input for the review consists of documents such as the PDS, the QFD analysis, key technical analyses like FEA and CFD, FMEAs, the quality plan, including robustness analysis, the results of the qualification tests, the detail and assembly drawings, and the product specifications, and cost projections. This documentation can be voluminous and it is not all covered in the final review. Important elements will have been reviewed previously and they will be certified at the final review. Another important input to the meeting is the selection of the people who will attend the review. They must be authorized to make decisions about the design and have the ability and responsibility to take corrective action.

Everyone attending the design review must receive a package of information well before the meeting. An ideal way to conduct a review is to hold a briefing session at least 10 days before the formal review. Members of the design team will make presentations to review the PDS and design review checklist to ensure that the review team has a common understanding of the design requirements. Then an overview of the design is given, describing how the contents of the design review information package relate to the design. Finally, members of the design review team will be assigned questions from the design checklist for special concentration. This is an informational meeting. Criticism of the design is reserved for later.

16.6.2 Review Meeting Process

The design review meeting should be formally structured with a well-planned agenda. The final design review is more of an audit in contrast to the earlier reviews, which are more multifunctional problem-solving sessions. The meeting is structured so it results in a documented assessment of the design. The review uses a checklist of items that need to be considered. Each item is discussed and it is decided whether it passes the review. The drawings, simulations, test results, FMEAs, etc., are used to support the evaluation. Sometimes a 1–5 scale is used to rate each requirement, but in a final review an "up or down" decision needs to be made. Any items that do not pass the review are tagged as action items and with the name of the responsible individual. Table 16.1 shows an abbreviated checklist for a final design review. A new checklist should be developed for each new product.

While the checklist in Table 16.1 is not exhaustive, it is illustrative of the many details that need to be considered in the final design review.

16.6.3 Output from Review

The output from the design review is a decision as to whether the product is ready to release to the manufacturing department. Sometimes the decision to proceed is tentative, with several open issues that need to be resolved, but in the judgment of management the fixes can be made before product launch.

TABLE 16.1
Typical items in a design checklist

1. Overall requirements—does it meet:
   Customer requirements
   Product design specification
   Applicable industry and governmental standards
2. Functional requirements—does it meet:
   Mechanical, electrical, thermal loads
   Size and weight
   Mechanical strength
   Projected life
3. Environmental requirements—does it meet:
   Temperature extremes, in operation and storage
   Extremes of humidity
   Extremes of vibration
   Shock
   Foreign material contamination
   Corrosion
   Outdoor exposure extremes (ultraviolet radiation, rain, hail, wind, sand)
4. Manufacturing requirements—does it meet:
   Use of standard components and subassemblies
   Tolerances consistent with processes and equipment
   Materials well defined and consistent with performance requirements
   Materials minimize material inventory
   Have critical control parameters been identified
   Manufacturing processes use existing equipment
5. Operational requirements
   Is it easy to install in the field?
   Are items requiring frequent maintenance easily accessible?
   Has serviceperson safety been considered?
   Have human factors been adequately considered in design?
   Are servicing instructions clear? Are they derived from FMEA or FTA?
6. Reliability requirements
   Have hazards been adequately investigated?
   Have failure modes been investigated and documented?
   Has a thorough safety analysis been conducted?
   Have life integrity tests been completed successfully?
   Has derating been employed in critical components?
7. Cost requirements:
   Does the product meet the cost target?
   Have cost comparisons been made with competitive products?
   Have service warranty costs been quantified and minimized?
   Has value engineering analysis been made for possible cost reduction?
8. Other requirements:
   Have critical components been optimized for robustness?
   Has a search been conducted to avoid patent infringement?
   Has prompt action been taken to apply for possible patent protection?
   Does the product appearance represent the technical quality and cost of the product?
   Has the product development process been adequately documented for defense in possible product liability action?
   Does the product comply with applicable laws and agency requirements?

The design review builds a paper trail of meeting minutes, the decisions or ratings for each design requirement, and a clear action plan of what will be done by whom and by when to fix any deficiencies in the design. This is important documentation to be used in any future product liability or patent litigation.

16.7
SUMMARY

Detail design is the phase of the design process where all of the details are brought together, decisions finalized, and a decision is made by management whether to release the design for production. It is the design phase where the greatest design cost is involved because the work to be done requires a heavy personnel contribution.

The first task of detail design is to complete the detail drawings and the assembly drawings. These documents, together with the design specifications, should contain the information to unambiguously manufacture the product. In order to finish the detail drawings, calculations and decisions not completed in the embodiment design phase need to be made. Often, in order to complete all these myriad details it is necessary to impose a *design freeze*. Once a freeze has been imposed, no changes can be made to the design unless they have been approved by a formal design control board.

The detail design phase also involves qualification testing of a prototype, the generation of a bill of materials (BOM) from the assembly drawings, a detailed cost estimate, and decisions on whether to make each part in-house or to obtain it from an outside supplier.

Detail design ends when the design is reviewed and accepted by a formal design review process. The review consists of comparing the design documentation (drawings, analyses, simulations, QFD, FAMAs, etc.) against a checklist of design requirements.

While detail design is the end of the *design process,* it is not the end of the *product development process.* Some of the tasks that must be completed before *product launch* are process planning, design of tooling, negotiate with suppliers, develop a quality assurance plan, marketing plan, distribution plan, customer service plan, maintenance plan, and a plan for retirement of the product from service. Product launch depends on the first batch of product from the production line passing a manufacturing prototype acceptance test.

BIBLIOGRAPHY

AT&T: "Moving a Design into Production," McGraw-Hill, New York, 1993.

"Detail Design," The Institution of Mechanical Engineers, London, 1975.

Hales, C.: "Managing Engineering Design," Wiley, New York, 1993.

Sekine, K., and K. Arai: "Design Team Revolution," Productivity Press, Portland, OR, 1994.

Vrsek, G.: Documenting and Communicating the Design "ASM Handbook," vol. 20: "Materials Selection and Design," pp. 222–230, ASM International, Materials Park, OH, 1997.

PROBLEMS AND EXERCISES

16.1. Examine the detail drawings for a product designed by a nearby manufacturing company. Be sure you can identify the actual shape, dimensions, and tolerances. What other information is contained in the drawing?

16.2. Look at an automotive mechanics manual. Identify a subassembly like a fuel-injection system or a front suspension. From the assembly drawings, write up a bill of materials.

16.3. Visualize the impact of CAE in a world that is even more electronic connected than it is today. How might the practice of detail design change?

16.4. Create a numbering system for use in drawing retrieval.

16.5. Prepare a final design review for your design project.

17

COMMUNICATING THE DESIGN

17.1
THE NATURE OF COMMUNICATION

You've completed your design, and you've come up with some innovative concepts and a cost estimate that predicts a nice healthy profit. What next? Now you must be able to communicate your findings to the people who matter. There is an old adage that a tree falling in a forest doesn't make a sound unless there is someone to listen. Similarly, the best technical design in the world might never be implemented unless you can communicate it to the proper people in the right way. To be successful with a design project, you must be able to communicate with your peers, your subordinates, and your superiors.

Communication can be simply described as *the flow of information from one mind to another.* Communication occurs through a common system of symbols, signs, and behavior that utilize one or more of the five human senses. We communicate by actual physical touch, as in a handshake or a pat on the back. We also communicate by visual movements of the body (body language), as with the wink of an eye or a smile. Sometimes we even communicate via taste and smell. In most technical communication, however, symbols or signs that are either heard with the ear or seen with the eyes are used.

The basic elements of all communication activities are shown in Fig. 17.1. The source of the communication arises somewhere in the organization: someone has information to communicate to someone else. An encoding process occurs when the information is translated into a systematic set of symbols (language) that expresses what the source wishes to transmit. The product of encoding is the message. The form of the message depends on the nature of the communication channel. The channel is the medium through which the message will be carried from source to receiver. The message can be a written report, a face-to-face communication, a telephone call, or a transmission via a computer network. It may or may not undergo a transformation in the decoder. When it reaches the receiver, it is interpreted in light of the person's pre-

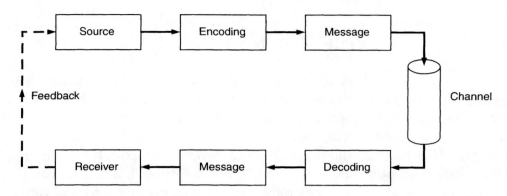

FIGURE 17.1
Basic elements of communications system.

vious experience or frame of reference. Feedback from the receiver to the source aids in determining how faithfully the message has been transmitted. Feedback gives the source an opportunity to determine whether the message has been received and whether it has produced the intended purpose.

Any communications system is less than perfect. Strong electric currents or atmospheric disturbances will produce some error in the transmission. These disturbances are called noise. In the same way, any communication between two persons will be subject to semantic noise and psychological noise. *Semantic noise* has to do with the meaning of words and ideas. In technical fields common words take on specialized meanings that can be completely unknown to the layman. *Psychological noise* arises from the particulars of the situation. A person who feels threatened by a new technology may have difficulty learning about it. Some people are intimidated by authority, and thus they have difficulty communicating with people above them in the organization. For communication to occur, the sender must have the authority of knowledge and a purpose for generating and transmitting the message. In addition, the recipient must be willing to receive the message and be capable of understanding it.

Studies of communication in business organizations have shown that geographic proximity is a major factor in enhancing communication. There usually is more information than the channel has capacity to handle. Sometimes selective filtration of information occurs. At any rate, the managements of many organizations make decisions on the basis of inadequate information. Communication in an organization is a multidimensional process. Many managers attempt to communicate only with the people under them and forget to communicate laterally with those who are assisting them. Lateral communication between project teams is particularly important in engineering organizations.

This chapter offers help and hints for communication of technical information. We deal first with written communication. Suggestions are presented for keeping a design notebook and organizing and writing a technical report, a technical paper, and a proposal for support. For oral communication, suggestions are made for giving successful presentations at business meetings and for presenting technical talks. Special emphasis is given to visual aids and electronic mail as enablers in effective communication.

17.2
THE DESIGN NOTEBOOK

We digress briefly from discussing communication of results to consider how ideas and experimental results should be recorded during the progress of the design project. If the recording task is treated with care and thoroughness, communicating the results of a design project will be made easier.

The chief tool for recording results is the design notebook. It should be an $8\frac{1}{2}$-by 11-in bound notebook (not spiral bound), preferably with a hard cover. It should be the repository for all of your planning (including plans that were not carried out), all analytical calculations, all records of experimental data, all references to sources of information, and all significant thinking about your project.

You should not use your notebook as a diary; but at the same time, you and your notebook should become an intimate communication system. Information should be entered directly into the notebook, not recopied from rough drafts. However, you should organize the information you enter in the notebook. Use main headings and subheadings; label key facts and ideas; liberally cross-reference your material; and keep an index at the front of the book to aid in your organization. About once a week, review what you have done and write a summary of your progress that emphasizes the high points. Whenever you do anything that may seem the least bit patentable, have your notebook read and witnessed by a knowledgeable colleague.

The following are good rules[1] for keeping a design notebook.

1. Keep an index at the front of the book.
2. Make your entries at the time you do the work. Include favorable and unfavorable results and things not fully understood at the time. If you make errors, just cross them out. Do not erase, and never tear a page out of the notebook.
3. All data must be in their original primary form (strip charts, oscilloscope pictures, photomicrographs, etc.), not after recalculation or transformation.
4. Rough graphs should be drawn directly in the notebook, but more carefully prepared plots on graph paper also should be made and entered in the book.
5. Give complete references to books, journals, reports, patents, and any other sources of information.
6. Entries should be made in ink and, of course, must be legible. Do not be obsessed with neatness at the expense of faithfully recording everything as it happens. Do not crowd your material on the pages. Paper is very much less expensive than engineering time.

A good engineering design notebook is one from which, several years after the project is completed, the project can be reconstructed. Critical decisions will be apparent, and the reasons for the actions taken will be backed up by facts. It should be possible to show where every figure, statement and conclusion of the published report of the project can be substantiated by original entries in the design notebook.

---

1. Adapted from T. T. Woodson, "Engineering Design," app. F, McGraw-Hill, New York, 1966.

17.3
WRITING THE TECHNICAL REPORT

In no other area of professional activity will you be judged so critically as your first technical report. The quality of a report generally provides an image in the reader's mind that, in large measure, determines the reader's impression of the quality of the work. Of course, an excellent job of report writing cannot disguise a sloppy investigation, but many excellent design studies have not received proper attention and credit because the work was reported in a careless manner. You should be aware that written reports carry a message farther than the spoken word and have greater permanence. Therefore, technical workers often are known more widely for their writings than for their talks.

17.3.1 Organization of Reports

Written communications take the form of letters, brief memorandum reports, formal technical reports, technical papers, and proposals. In terms of the communications model shown in Fig. 17.1, the source is the mind of the writer. The process of encoding consists of translating the idea from the mind to words on a paper. The channel is the pile of manuscript papers. Decoding the message depends on the reader's ability to understand the language and familiarity with the ideas presented in the message. The final receiver is the mind of the reader. Noise is present in the form of poor writing mechanics, incomplete diagrams, incorrect references, etc. Since there is no direct feedback, the writer must anticipate the needs of the receiver and attempt to minimize the noise.

The first principle of written communication is to know your audience so that you can anticipate and fulfill its needs. The purpose of engineering writing is to present information, not to entertain. Therefore, the information should be easy to find. Always when writing your report, keep in mind the busy reader who has only a limited amount of time for your report and may, in addition, not be familiar with your subject.

Memorandum reports

The memorandum report usually is written to a specific person or group of persons concerning a specific topic with which both the writer and recipient(s) are familiar. For example, it may be a report of a trip you took to observe a competitor's new product, or it could be a disclosure of a new idea you have for an improved product. It is written in memorandum form.

- Date
- To:
- From:
- Subject:
- Introduction (brief and indicating why the study was carried out)
- Discussion (includes data and its analysis)
- Conclusions (includes what was concluded from the study and recommendations made on the conclusions)

Memorandum reports are short (one to three pages). Sometimes a report that is more than one page has a summary section before the introduction so the reader does not have to read the entire memorandum to get its message. The purpose in writing a memorandum report is to get a concise report to interested parties as quickly as possible. The main emphasis is on results, discussion, and conclusions with a minimum of writing about experimental details unless, of course, those details are critical to the analysis of the data. Very often a more detailed report follows the memorandum report.

Formal technical reports

A formal technical report usually is written at the end of a project. Generally, it is a complete, stand-alone document aimed at persons having widely diverse backgrounds. Therefore, much more detail is required. The outline of a typical formal report[1] might be:

- Covering letter (letter of transmittal)
- Title page
- Summary (containing conclusions)
- Table of contents, including list of figures and tables
- Introduction (containing background to the work to acquaint reader with the problem and the purpose for carrying on the work)
- Experimental procedure
- Experimental results
- Discussion (of results)
- Conclusions
- References
- Appendixes
- Tables
- Figures

The *covering letter* is provided so that persons who might receive the report without prior notification will have some introduction to it. The *title page* provides a concise title and the names, affiliations, and addresses of the authors. The *summary* is provided early in the report to enable the busy reader to determine if it is worth the effort to read the entire report or send it to someone else who may be interested in the topic. It is generally less than a page in length and contains three paragraphs. The first briefly describes the objective of the study and the problems studied. Paragraph two describes your solution to the problem. The last paragraph addresses its importance to the business in terms of cost savings, improved quality, or new business opportunities.

The *introduction* should contain the pertinent technical facts that might be unknown to the reader but will be used in the report. It sets the stage in the same way as the summary, but in greater detail. The *experimental procedure section* is usually included to indicate how the data were obtained and to describe any nonstandard types of apparatus or techniques that were employed. The *experimental results sec-*

---

1. The contribution of Professor Richard W. Heckel for much of the material in this section is acknowledged.

tion describe's the results of the study. Data in the form of tables or figures are usually placed at the end of the report and are referred to by number in the results section. This section should also indicate any uncertainties in the data and possible errors in their sources. The *discussion section* is normally concerned with analyzing the data to make a specific point, develop the data into some more meaningful form, or relate the data to theory described in the introduction. All arguments based on the data are developed here. The section may also be used to discuss the effects of experimental error on the analysis of the data. The *conclusion section* states in as concise a form as possible the conclusions *that can be drawn from the study. No new information should be introduced here.* In general, this section is the culmination of the work and the report. The conclusions are directly related to the purpose in undertaking the study. *Appendixes* are used for mathematical developments, sample calculations, etc., that are not directly associated with the subject of the report and that, if placed in the main body of the report, would seriously impede the logical flow of thought. Final equations developed in the appendixes are then placed in the body of the report with reference to the particular appendix in which they were developed. The same procedure applies to mathematical calculations; the results are used in the report and the proper appendix is referenced.

Technical papers. These usually have an outline similar to this:

- Abstract
- Introduction
- Experimental procedure ⎫ These may be combined in a single section
- Experimental results ⎭
- Discussion
- Summary and/or conclusions
- Acknowledgments
- Appendixes
- Tables
- Figures

The content of the above sections is the same as for a formal technical report. The *abstract section* is similar to the formal report summary except that it doesn't contain reference to orientation of the work to particular company problems. A technical paper often contains a *summary* at its end that allows the writer to "assemble" the paper prior to making *conclusions*. Some papers omit the summary section if it is not felt to be necessary and if it would be essentially the same as the abstract.

Proposals. A proposal is a report written to a sponsor in solicitation of financial support. The object of a proposal is to convince the sponsor of the value of your idea and to convince him that your organization has the capability (laborpower and facilities) to deliver the expected results. A typical proposal to a federal agency might be organized as follows:

- Introduction
- Purpose and objectives

- Technical background
- Program approach (your ideas and approach)
- Statement of work
- Program schedule
- Program organization
- Personnel qualifications
- Facilities and equipment
- Summary
- References
- Budget (often submitted as a separate document)
- Appendixes

The secret to writing winning proposals is to align your interests with those of the sponsor. Be sure the proposal carefully indicates the magnitude of the expected gain from doing the proposed work. It usually is helpful to know who will evaluate the proposal and what their standards for performance and excellence will be.

17.3.2 Steps in Writing a Report

The five operations involved in the writing of a high-quality report are best remembered with the acronym POWER.

P	Plan the writing
O	Outline the report
W	Write
E	Edit
R	Rewrite

The planning stage of a report is concerned with assembling the data, analyzing the data, drawing conclusions from the data analysis, and organizing the report into various logical sections. The planning of a report is usually carried out by considering the various facets of the work and providing a logical blend of the material. The initial planning of a report should begin *before* the work is carried out. In that way the planning of the work and planning of the report are woven together, which facilitates the actual writing operation.

Outlining the report consists of actually formulating a series of headings, subheadings, sub-subheadings, etc., which encompass the various sections of the report. The outline can then be used as a guide to the writing. A complete outline can be detailed to the point at which each line consists of a single thought or point to be made and will then represent one paragraph in the report. The main headings and subheadings of the outline are usually placed in the report to guide the reader.

The writing operation should be carried out in the form of a rough draft using the maximum technical and compositional skill at the command of the writer. However, do not worry about perfection at this stage. Once you get going, don't break stride to check out fine details of punctuation or sentence structure.

Editing is the process of reading the rough draft and employing self-criticism. It consists of strengthening the rough draft by analyzing paragraph and sentence structure, economizing on words, checking spelling and punctuation, checking the line of logical thought, and, in general, asking oneself the question "Why?" Editing can be the secret of good writing. It is better for writers to ask themselves embarrassing questions than to hear them from their technical readers, a supervisor, or an instructor. In connection with editing, it has often been said that the superior writer makes good use of both ends of the pencil.

It is generally good practice to allow at least a day to elapse after writing the rough draft before editing it. That allows the writer to forget the logical pattern used in writing the report and appear more in the role of an unbiased reader when editing. Many mistakes or weak lines of thought that would normally escape unnoticed are thereby uncovered. The rewriting operation consists of retyping or rewriting the edited rough draft to put it in a form suitable for the reader.

17.3.3 Word Processing Software

Word processing software is a very useful tool for the engineer. The ability to move sections of a report by "cut and paste," to insert or change words, to check spelling and grammar, and to increase the readability by changing the format or size of type have made writing easier. Most engineers in industry function today without major secretarial support because they have mastered simple typing and editing skills.

However, there are two pitfalls to watch out for.[1] *Nice-output syndrome* occurs when engineers are so enthralled by the beautiful printed pages coming out of the laser printer that they fail to do a proper job of editing and rewriting. The *hurry-up-and-wait disease* occurs when writers are composing at the keyboard and are such good touch typists that they can easily outrun the speed at which they can think. This interrupts the natural flow of ideas in writing. It is far better to match the flow at which the ideas are put to paper with the speed at which they are generated by the mind. Some writers purposely write the first draft by hand to achieve this synchronization.

17.3.4 Mechanics of Writing

The following suggestions are presented as a guide to writing and an aid in avoiding some of the most common mistakes. You also should avail yourself of one of the popular guides to English grammar and style.[2]

Title
The title should be a meaningful description of what you have written.

Basic ideas
State basic ideas early; give the reader an overview of your study at the beginning. Enough background must be given to allow the least-informed reader to understand

---

1. D. E. Goldberg, "Life Skills and Leadership for Engineers," chap. 2, McGraw-Hill, New York, 1995.
2. W. Strunk and E. B. White, "The Elements of Style," 3d ed., Macmillan, New York, 1978; S. W. Baker, "The Practical Stylist," 8th ed., Addison-Wesley, Reading, MA, 1997.

why the design was undertaken. The reader must be able to fit whatever is being reported into a context that is meaningful.

Whole vs. part

Describe the whole before the part; be sure you present the reader with the whole picture before you lead into the details. You should describe the essence, the function, and the purpose of a device, process, or product before you go into details about the parts.

Important information

Emphasize important information; beware of the common error of burying it under a mass of details. Put the important ideas early in your writing; use appropriate capitalization and underlining; and relegate information of secondary importance to the appendix.

Headings

Use headings liberally; headings and subheadings are signposts that help the reader understand the organization of your ideas. If you have prepared a good outline, the headings will be self-evident.

Fact vs. opinion

Separate fact from opinion. It is important for the reader to know what your contributions are, what ideas you obtained from others (the references should indicate that), and which are opinions not substantiated by fact.

Paragraph structure

Each paragraph should begin with a topic sentence that provides an overall understanding of the paragraph. Since each paragraph should have a single theme or conclusion, the topic sentence states that theme or conclusion. Any elaboration is deferred to subsequent sentences in the paragraph. Don't force the reader to wade through many sentences of disconnected verbiage to arrive at the conclusion in the last sentence of the paragraph. The reader should be able to get an understanding of the report by reading the first sentence of each paragraph.

Sentence length

Sentences should be kept as short as possible so that their structure is simple and readable. Generally a sentence should not exceed about 35 words. Long sentences require complex construction, provide an abundance of opportunity for grammatical errors, take considerable writing time, and slow the reader down. Long sentences are often the result of putting together two independent thoughts that could be stated better in separate sentences.

Pronouns

There is no room for any degree of ambiguity between a pronoun and the noun for which it is used. Novices commonly use "it," "this," "that," etc., where it would be better to use one of several nouns. It may be clear to the writer, but it is often ambiguous to the reader.

In general, personal pronouns (I, you, he, she, we, my, mine, our, us) are not used in technical reports. The only exception is when the writer *must* be involved personally in the report, as when writing a report to be used as a basis for a patent. In that instance, the writer must state definitely that he or she was the inventor.

Tense

The choice of the tense of verbs is often confusing to student writers. The following simple rules are usually employed by experienced writers:

Past tense: Use to describe work done in the laboratory or in general to past events. "Hardness readings *were* taken on all specimens."

Present tense: Use in reference to items and ideas in the report itself. "It *is* clear from the data in Figure 4 that strain energy *is* the driving force for recovery" or "The group recommends that the experiment be repeated" (present opinion).

Future tense: Use in making prediction from the data that will be applicable in the future. "The market data given in Table II indicate that the sales *will continue* to increase in the next ten years."

Spelling and punctuation

Errors in these basic elements of writing in the final draft of the report are inexcusable.

Appendixes, tables, and figures

Appendixes, tables, and figures are placed at the end of a report to speed the reading of the text and to allow separate preparation of tables and figures without having to bother with leaving the required space in the text. The following numbering conventions are often used:

Appendix A, B, C, D (capital letters)
Table I, II, III, IV (Roman numerals)
Figure 1, 2, 3, 4 (numbers)

Each appendix, table, or figure should have a title and should be self-explanatory. For example, the reader should not have to refer to the text for an understanding of the variables plotted on a graph. Graphs should be drawn on suitable graph paper (linear, semilog, loglog, etc.), and the axes should be properly labeled (including units). If data points are labeled by code numbers, the code should appear on the graph, not in the text. The independent and dependent variables are usually placed on the abscissa (x axis) and ordinate (y axis), respectively. Generally, only one table or figure is placed on a page. However, several small photographs may make up one figure.

Reference to data in tables and figures is often a cause of difficulty. The statement "It is obvious from the data that . . ." is used much too often when nothing is obvious before the data have been explained properly. The statement given above should be used *only* when an obvious conclusion can be made, not when it is the hope of the writer that the reader thinks something is obvious.

The *initial* reference to a set of data in a table or figure as: "The data are given in Table III" exerts an extreme hardship on readers and in many instances forces them to grope unguided through the data. In such instances the reader must digest the data in a few minutes, whereas the digestion may have taken the writer days or weeks. (The writer also runs the risk of the reader's reaching an "improper" conclusion before being biased by the text.) It is better form to first describe what a set of results shows *prior* to telling the reader where the data can be found. This saves the reader's time by indicating what to look for when exposed to the data.

References

References are usually placed at the end of the written text. Those to the technical literature (described as readily available on subscription and included in most library collections) are made by author and journal reference (often with the title of article omitted) as shown by the following example. There is no single universally accepted format for references, but many journals follow the style given here.

Journal article
   R. M. Horn and Robert O. Ritchie: *Metall. Trans. A,* 1978 vol. 9A, pp. 1039–1053.

Book
   Thomas T. Woodson: "Introduction to Engineering Design," pp. 321–346, McGraw-Hill, New York, 1966.

A private communication
   J. J. Doe, XYZ Company, Altoona, PA, unpublished research, 1981.

Internal reports
   J. J. Doe: Report No. 642, XYZ Company, Altoona, PA, February 1980.

Be scrupulous about references as you acquire them. A few minutes spent in recording the full reference (including the inclusive page numbers) can prevent hours of time being spent in the library when you are finishing the final report.

17.4
MEETINGS AND PRESENTATIONS

The business world is full of meetings which are held to communicate on a variety of levels and subjects. Most of these involve some kind of prepared oral presentation.

At the lowest level of this hierarchy is the design team meeting. Those present are focused on a common goal and have a generally common background. The purpose of the meeting is to share the progress that has been made, identify problems, and hopefully, find help and support in solving the problems. This is a group discussion, with an agenda and probably some visual aids, but the presentation is informal and not rehearsed. Detailed tips for effectively holding this type of meeting were given in Sec. 3.5.

Next up in the meeting hierarchy would be a design briefing or design review. The size and diversity of the audience would depend on the importance of the project. It could vary from 10 to 50 people, and include company managers and executives. A design briefing for high-level management must be brief and to the point. Such people are very busy and not at all interested in the technical details that engineers love to talk about. Usually you will have only 5 to 10 min to get your point across to the top executive. If you are speaking to technical managers, they will be more interested in the important technical details, but don't forget also to cover information on schedule and costs. Generally, they will give you 15 to 30 min to get your points across. A presentation similar to the latter type of design briefing is a technical talk before a professional or technical society. Here you will generally have 15 to 20 min to make your presentation before an audience of 30 to 100 people.

At the top of the pyramid is a formal speech. A speech is carefully scripted and discussion often is not allowed. It is one-way communication from the speaker to the audience, as when the President of the United States gives the State of the Union address. As a young engineer you probably will not be asked to give speeches, but as you advance in your career such opportunities may appear, e.g., on giving the major lecture at your professional society annual meeting or a speech via satellite video as corporate VP to all members of your division on winning a major contract.

17.5
ORAL PRESENTATIONS

Impressions and reputations (favorable or unfavorable) are made most quickly by audience reaction to an oral presentation. There are a number of situations in which you will be called upon to give a talk. Progress reports, whether to your boss in a one-on-one situation or in a more formal setting to your customer, are common situations in which oral communication is used. Selling an idea or a proposal to your management budget committee or a sponsor is another common situation. In the more technical arena, you may be asked to present a talk to a local technical society chapter or present a paper at a national technical meeting.

Oral communication has several special characteristics: quick feedback by questions and dialogue; impact of personal enthusiasm; impact of visual aids; and the important influence of tone, emphasis, and gesture. A skilled speaker in close contact with an audience can communicate far more effectively than the cold, distant, easily evaded written word. On the other hand, the organization and logic of presentation must be of a higher order for oral than for written communication. The listener to an oral communication has no opportunity to reread a page to clarify a point. Many opportunities for noise exist in oral communication. The preparation and delivery of the speaker, the environment of the meeting room, and the quality of the visual aids all contribute to the efficiency of the oral communication process.

17.5.1 The Business-Oriented Technical Talk

The purpose of your talk may be to present the results of the past 3 months of work by a 10-person design team, or it may be to present some new ideas on computer-aided design to an audience of upper management who are skeptical that their large investment in CAD will pay off. Whatever the reason, you should know the purpose of your talk and have a good idea of who will be attending your presentation. This information is vital if you are to prepare an effective talk.

The most appropriate type of delivery for most business-oriented talks is an *extemporaneous-prepared talk.* All the points in the talk are thought out and planned in detail. However, the delivery is based on a written outline, or alternatively, the text of the talk is completely written but the talk is delivered from an outline prepared from the text. This type of presentation establishes a more natural, closer contact with the audience that is much more believable than if the talk is read by the speaker.

Develop the material in your talk in terms of the interest of the audience. Organize it on a thought-by-thought rather than a word-by-word basis. Write your conclusions first. That will make it easier to sort through all the material you have and select only the pieces of information that support the conclusions. If your talk is aimed at selling an idea, list all of your idea's strengths and weaknesses. That will help you counter arguments against adopting your idea.

The opening few minutes of your talk are vital in establishing whether you will get the audience's attention. You need to "bring them up to speed" by explaining the reason for your presentation. Include enough background that they can follow the main body of your presentation, which should be carefully planned. Stay well within the time allotted for the talk so there is an opportunity for questions. Include humorous stories and jokes in your talk only if you are very good at telling them. If you are not, it is best to play it straight. Also, avoid specialized technical jargon in your talk. Before ending your presentation, summarize your main points and conclusions. The audience should have no confusion as to the message you wanted to deliver.

Visual aids are an important part of any technical presentation; good ones can increase the audience retention of your ideas by 50 percent. The type of visual aid to use depends upon the nature of the talk and the audience. For a small informal meeting of up to 10 or 12 people, handouts of an outline, data, and charts usually are effective. Transparencies used with an overhead projector are good for groups from 10 to 200 people. Slides are the preferred visual aids for large audiences. The important subject of visual aids is discussed at greater length in Sec. 17.6.

The usual reason a technical talk is poor is lack of preparation. It is a rare individual who is able to give an outstanding talk without practicing it. Once you have prepared the talk, the first stage is individual practice. Give the talk out loud in an empty room to fix the thoughts in your mind and check the timing. You may want to memorize the introductory and concluding remarks. If at all possible, videotape your individual practice. The dry run is a dress rehearsal before a small audience. If possible, hold the dry run in the same room where you will give the talk. Use the same visual aids that you will use in your talk. The purpose of the dry run is to help you work out any problems in delivery, organization, or timing. There should be a critique following the dry run, and the talk should be reworked and repeated as many times as are necessary to do it right.

When delivering the talk, if you are not formally introduced, you should give your name and the names of any other team members. You should speak loudly enough to be easily heard. For a large group that will require the use of a microphone. Work hard to project a calm, confident delivery, but don't come on in an overly aggressive style that will arouse adversarial tendencies in your audience. Avoid annoying mannerisms like rattling the change in your pocket and pacing up and down the platform. Whenever possible, avoid talking in the dark. The audience might well go to sleep or, at worst, sneak out. Maintaining eye contact with the audience is an important part of the feedback in the communication loop.

The questions that follow a talk are an important part of the oral communication process; they show that the audience is interested and has been listening. If at all possible, do not allow interruptions to your talk for questions. If the "big boss" interrupts with a question, compliment him for his perceptiveness and explain that the point will be covered in a few moments. Never apologize for the inadequacy of your results. Let a questioner complete the questions before breaking in with an answer. Avoid being argumentative or letting the questioner see that you think the question is stupid. Do not prolong the question period unnecessarily. When the questions slack off, adjourn the meeting.

17.5.2 The Technical Society Talk

It is an honor to be asked to present the results of your work at a national meeting of a professional society, but you may be surprised to find that you have only 15 or 20 minutes in which to present your work. That calls for good planning and organization. Frequently an abstract of your talk will be available in the meeting announcement or printed book of abstracts that is available to registrants of the meeting. However, that does not absolve you from the responsibility for starting your talk with a good introduction, which should set forth the scope and objectives of the talk. It may deal with the history of events leading up to the work to be discussed. Any coauthors of the work described should be mentioned, and acknowledgments should be made to sponsors and those who may have given special help.

The main body of the technical talk covers the following items:

- Experimental or analytical procedure
- Results and observations
- Discussions and conclusions
- Ongoing research and/or future studies

The talk should end with a summary that repeats the main information given in the body of the talk. A good scheme for the organization of a technical talk is to:

1. Tell them what you are going to tell them.
2. Tell them.
3. Tell them what you told them!

No matter what kind of talk you give there are two factors that will control your success. The first is to be in complete command of your facts. Know the material cold. The quickest way to lose an audience is if they think you are faking it. Second, show enthusiasm. We don't mean to "go ape," but neither should you be a deadpan "cold fish." For your talk to succeed you must command the attention of the audience. You do this by being enthusiastic and knowledgeable.

17.6
VISUAL AIDS

Except in a small meeting, visual aids make the difference between effective and ineffective oral communication. The selection of the visual aid medium will depend upon the size and importance of the audience and the number of times the talk will be given. Not only are good visual aids important in transmitting the message, so that the dual senses of hearing and seeing are employed, they also assist greatly in reducing the nervous tension (psychological noise) of inexperienced speakers.

The chief purpose of a visual aid is to improve and simplify communication. There should be no intention to have a slide or viewgraph stand alone, unsupported by oral communication. The spoken word should complement the limited information that can be contained on the visual. On the other hand, it is a waste of time for the speaker to read the words on the slide to the audience.

The three most commonly used visual aids are handouts, overhead transparencies, and 35-mm slides. There are advantages and disadvantages to each. A photocopied handout is inexpensive, does not require much lead time for preparation, and provides a take-away from the presentation. However, it has the disadvantage that it can serve as a distraction from the presentation as people page through the handout at a pace that differs from the pace of the presentation. Handouts are most commonly used at small, informal presentations. The other types of visual aids are discussed below.

17.6.1 Graphics Presentation Software

The preparation of transparencies and slides has been greatly facilitated by the development of graphics presentation programs (GPP) for use with the personal computer. Perhaps the best-known GPP is Microsoft PowerPoint. Not only does this software provide great versatility in available fonts, styling, and colors, but it provides advice in graphic design through on-line help screens and tutorials. GPPs can be used to produce professional-level black-and-white transparencies, 35-mm slides, and full-screen projected electronic color slides. The outlining feature built into the software assists in preparing the presentation, and the ability to print out reduced-scale copies of the slides gives a take-away note-taking capability.

17.6.2 Overhead Transparencies

Transparencies used with an overhead projector provide a flexible visual aid system for groups up to about 100 people. This is the most common way of presenting visual material. Because transparencies can be used in a semilighted room, they permit the speaker to face the audience and maintain eye contact. They can be made quickly and inexpensively with a standard office copier. Color transparencies can be made with a color laser printer or color copier, but at greater expense. Paper copies of the transparencies can be used as handouts for small groups. The chief disadvantage of transparencies is that they are not as good as slides for reproducing photographs.

17.6.3 35-mm Slides

Slides prepared from 35-mm transparency film (2- by 2-in size) are the standard visual aid for presentations given to large audiences since they can be projected with a large distance from the projector to the screen. Photographs are reproduced sharp and clear. The preparation of slides generally requires several days of lead time. Proper viewing of slides requires a darkened room.

17.6.4 Computer Projected Slides

A modern alternative to 35-mm slides is computer projected slides. The text material is prepared with a GPP, like PowerPoint, and copied to a floppy disk. The disk is loaded into the computer attached to the projection system, and a mouse is used to click through the slides, line by line. This system not only provides vivid color and graphics, but it has the feature of advanced visual effects. For example, you can build each slide line by line, as the words fly in from the side, or you can transition from slide to slide with eye-catching dissolves.

17.6.5 Other Visual Aids

There are several other kinds of visual aids that may be appropriate. A *flip chart,* a large pad of paper mounted on an easel, can be effective in a small meeting of up to 12 people. Each page is flipped over to reveal the neatly lettered message.

Video tapes are often used to display group dynamics or high-speed motion. These work well in small groups but are difficult to manage with large groups because of the small size of most TV monitors.

It is common to bring small pieces of hardware or test specimens for the audience to view and touch and feel. It will be distracting to your talk if these are passed around during the talk. It is better to have them on display for viewing after the talk.

17.6.6 Tips on Talks

1. Limit slides (or transparencies) to *no more than* one per minute.
2. Each slide should contain one idea.
3. Slides that present more than three curves on a single graph or 20 words or numbers on a slide are too complicated.
4. The first slide in the presentation should show the title of your talk and the names and affiliations of the authors.
5. The second slide should give a brief outline of your talk.
6. The last slide should summarize the message you delivered.
7. If you need to show a slide more than once, use a second copy so the projectionist will not have to back up, and in the process distract the audience.
8. Avoid leaving on the screen a slide that you have finished discussing while you go on to something else. Put in a blank slide, which will allow the audience to turn their attention to your words.

9. Prior to the presentation, make sure the slides are in order and oriented properly.

10. Place a blank sheet of paper between each pair of transparencies to avoid sticking. The sheet of paper also enables you to read the transparency prior to placing on the overhead projector.

11. If a transparency includes a number of unrelated items, such as a list of conclusions, use a piece of paper to conceal those you have not yet discussed. Move the paper down the transparency to reveal the items as they are discussed.

12. When making your presentation, do not stand in a place that blocks the audience's view of the screen. A good place to stand is to the right of the screen, facing the audience.

13. Do not try to use notecards when working with transparencies. They should contain sufficient clues for you to make a smooth talk—with practice.

14. Stay with one type of visual aid if possible. If you must switch between 35-mm slides and transparencies, arrange the talk to do this only once.

It is important to remember that the projected area of an overhead projector is square. When preparing the transparencies, position the letters in a square format, not in long lines across the page. Make the letters as large as possible, at least 18 point. Use no more than seven lines on a transparency. A combination of upper- and lowercase letters is easier to read than all uppercase letters. Also, fonts with serifs are easier to read than sans-serif fonts. Give each transparency a title at the top. Use a horizontal format with a height-to-width ratio of 4:5 and a maximum area of 7.5×9.5 in. If a vertical format must be used, keep the text in the upper two-thirds of the transparency. Otherwise it will be out of focus.

17.7
USING ELECTRONIC MAIL

No form of communication has grown so rapidly as electronic mail (e-mail). It is estimated that Americans will send four trillion e-mail messages in 1998 and that this will grow to seven trillion by 2000. Electronic mail has proved to be invaluable for scheduling meetings, communicating between engineers at different plant sites, communicating with the office while on a trip, or just keeping up with the activities of the relatives.

Because e-mail is so instant and personal there is a tendency to treat it differently from other written communication. People feel free to write and send things they would never put in a business letter. E-mail seems to free people from their normal inhibitions. It is so easy to hit the reply key without thinking about the consequences. There are many documented instances of two business friends "having fun" in their e-mail exchange, only to discover that the message inadvertently was given mass circulation.

Electronic mail also can easily lead to information overload. Top management, in their desire to communicate with those below them, can easily dilute the message by overuse. It is all too easy to invite unwelcome advertisements into your e-mail address. And, there are those coworkers who just cannot resist the temptation to share the latest joke with you.

17.7.1 E-mail Etiquette

There are easy things you can do to help your colleagues cope with the mass of messages coming over their computer screens. Following these suggestions will also give a professional tone to your business messages.

- For formal business correspondence, write as you would in a business letter.
- For communications to close friends or colleagues, write as you would speak.
- Use both upper- and lowercase letters, as you would in a business letter. If you type all capitals it means you are angry and shouting.
- Don't use tabs. Use spaces for indenting.
- Be very careful in using the "redirect" key. Be sure you know who will be on the receiving end.
- If you think formatting will be a problem, send the message first to yourself.
- Always treat the person you are writing to with respect. But remember, that person might forward your message to someone else.
- Keep your messages short.
- Realize that deleting a message by sending it to the trash bin probably means that it is still retrievable, since most companies keep backup tapes on e-mail.
- If you write a message in anger or frustration, wait 24 hours before sending it. This gives you time to cool down and possibly rethink your action. This also is good practice in ordinary nonelectronic communication.

17.7.2 Business Issues

Many technology companies view their open e-mail environment as conducive to creativity. They are reluctant to regulate its use by their employees in any way. However, more companies are beginning to realize that e-mail communication can be a time bomb. Electronic messages are not secure. For example, e-mail messages have become important evidence in sexual harassment suits and antitrust suits. Many companies are developing strict e-mail policies so they can limit their exposure to lawsuits. These typically involve company monitoring of e-mail and prohibition against using company e-mail to share jokes, photographs, and nonbusiness information of any kind.

17.7.3 Groupware

The popularity of e-mail as a communication medium has led to its widespread use managing group projects. However, most e-mail systems are not well suited for interactive discussion because messages can only be seen in the order in which they were written. Thus, a response to a question may be separated from the original query by a large number of unrelated messages. Generally, the responder will reply to the messages in serial order, losing the continuity of the discussion. Also, there is difficulty with the transfer of documents in arbitrary formats, using many e-mail systems.

A class of software called *groupware*[1] has been developed to deal with these issues and make electronic mail a smooth tool for communication within large project teams. Groupware provides methods for viewing documents as a discussion hierarchy or topic-centered organization. Such software also provides security for messages not generally found in ordinary software. Those who have used groupware say it significantly improves communication, but at the expense of a rather strong learning curve to become proficient.

17.8
SUMMARY

Ability to communicate in both written and oral formats often is the most important factor in determining a professional's success in the business world. Engineers, who are proud of their technical accomplishments, may not like to hear this advice—but it is true. Most people can learn to be good communicators with a little knowledge and lots of practice.

For both written and oral communication the most important rules for success are: (1) understand your audience, and (2) practice/practice/practice. In writing a technical report this means understanding the various audiences that will read the report, and organizing it accordingly. It also means working the original draft into a polished communication by the hard work of several rewrites. In making an oral presentation it means understanding your audience and organizing the talk accordingly. It also requires the hard work of practice until you have mastered the talk. Computer software now available aids in increasing the efficiency and quality of reports (word processing) and presentations (graphics presentation programs).

Business and personal communication have been greatly facilitated by the advent of electronic mail. In business situations, treat this medium with respect. Resist the temptation to regard it as your personal vehicle for communication and realize that it is not a secure medium. Remember, anything untoward that you might write in e-mail could come back to haunt you.

BIBLIOGRAPHY

Written Communication

Brusaw, C. T. (ed.): "Handbook of Technical Writing," 5th ed., St. Martin's Press, New York, 1997.
Eisenberg. A.: "Effective Technical Communication," 2d ed., McGraw-Hill, New York, 1992.
Ellis, R.: "Communication for Engineers: Bridge the Gap," Wiley, New York, 1997.
McMurrey, D., and D. F. Beer: "A Guide to Writing as an Engineer," Wiley, New York, 1996.
Patton, D.: "Communicating Technical Information: A Guide for the Electronic Age," Prentice-Hall, Upper Saddle River, NJ, 1997.

---

1. Perhaps the best-known example is Lotus Notes, available from IBM.

Oral Communication

Goldberg, D. E.: "Life Skills and Leadership for Engineers," McGraw-Hill, New York, 1995, chap. 3.

Hoff, R.: "I Can See You Naked: A Fearless Guide to Making Great Presentations," Andrews and McMeel, Kansas City, MO, 1988.

Wilder, L.: "Talk Your Way to Success," Simon and Schuster, New York, 1986.

PROBLEMS AND EXERCISES

17.1. See whether your library has copies of the notebooks of Leonardo da Vinci and Michael Faraday. Use the notebooks to discuss the proper recording of experimental ideas.

17.2. Carefully read a technical paper from a journal in your field and comment on how it conforms with the outline discussed in Sec. 17.3.

17.3. Write a memorandum to your supervisor justifying your project being 3 weeks late and asking for an extension.

17.4. Prepare a PowerPoint presentation for the first design review of your team project.

17.5. Prepare a technical talk based on the paper you studied in Prob. 17.2.

17.6. Prepare a poster session from this technical talk or for the final presentation for your design project. A poster session is a large visual display, with a series of graphics, containing text, mounted on a large sheet of posterboard. The display should be self-contained, such that a technical person will be able to understand what you did.

Editing for Style and Usage

Outline

Changing from Writer to Editor

When you switch from being the *writer* of the report to the *editor*, you'll change your focus from *composing* (actually shaping your thoughts) to *editing* what you've written (making important changes in the wording of the report).

Of course, you probably thought about the wording of your sentences as you were composing the report, but to fine-tune your wording effectively, you'll find it useful to dedicate an hour or two after you've finished the rough draft solely to this editing task.

Editing is the subject of Chapters 4 and 5. When you are the editor, you return to the report with the perspective of an outsider, casting a cold eye on the text, and then selecting, trimming, and focusing the language so that your message is as clear as possible.

In the matter of style, Chapter 4 addresses these issues:

- Insertion of definitions, abbreviations, and acronyms into the narrative.
- Governing verb tense in each section of the report.
- Use of *I* and *we* (first-person pronouns) in the narrative.
- Use of *he* as the governing third-person singular.
- Representation of numbers in figures or words.
- Consistency and precision of language in technical text.

In the matter of usage, Chapter 4 discusses the small choices in language that writers make (for instance, between *affect* and *effect* or between *imply* and *infer*), the treatment of Greek and Latin terminology in science, and other confusibles like *adverse* versus *averse* and *expect* versus *anticipate*.

Matters of Style

Definitions, Abbreviations, and Acronyms

When should you stop to define a term you are using?

- When you think the term may be unfamiliar to the reader.

- When you think the reader may know the general use of the term, but not the narrow or specific way in which you are using it.
- When the term is easily confused with another term.
- When the term is a governing one (that is, when it's crucial to the underlying argument that you are making).

Whether you insert definitions in your text depends on the background of your readers—on how much they know before you begin, and how much more you decide to tell them.

If you are an electrical engineer writing for other electrical engineers, you are safe using the abbreviations of your field—other EEs will know what an IC is. (But if you are not an electrical engineer, you may wonder whether IC means, for instance, integrated circuit or ion chromatography.)

Often you will be writing your report not just for people in your field, but for people with a variety of technical backgrounds. If so, you'll need to write out unfamiliar terms in full on first use and then follow with an abbreviated form and a definition.

Sometimes the definition is just a synonym or short explanatory phrase enclosed in parentheses. For instance, in one report in Chapter 2, the author defines surfactant this way:

[I]t is possible to determine if the molecules are surfactants (molecules localized to the particle surface).

Sometimes the definition of a term will include etymological information (information related to the origin of the word).

The modem (for modulator-demodulator) is a device that can be attached to convert the computer's digital signals into signals for transmission over telephone lines.

Bits (short for binary digits) are units describing the information contents of any message.

If you are using an abbreviation or acronym, it should follow the first use of the term and be enclosed in parentheses.

In its current form as an aerosol particle fluorescence microscope (APFM), the microscope is affixed with optical filters and polarizers for recording images in inelastic fluorescence scattering.

Abbreviations (for example, IC) are pronounced as letters; acronyms (for example, LASER) are pronounced as words. On first reference, use full spelling of the term followed by the shortened form in parentheses. For subsequent references, use the shortened form.

At one time, periods or points were used after each letter in abbreviations or acronyms but today more and more style sheets permit you to represent abbreviations without periods.

Most abbreviations, including abbreviations for units of measure like *amp*, *Hz*, *cal*, *cm*, *hr*, *hp*, *sec*, and *rad*, no longer use points.

One exception to this is abbreviations that might be misread as words. Thus, the abbreviations for the units of measure *at.*, *gal.*, and *no.* have points, as otherwise they might be construed as the words *at*, *gal*, and *no*.

Note that if the abbreviation falls at the end of a sentence, one period is enough. Do not add a second one.

Example 1 An introduction with undefined terms

In the past year only a trickle of money on the World Wide Web has actually made its way toward consumer goods such as books, flowers, and airline tickets. But the Web has actually produced a bona fide financial hit—intranets.

Intranets (and extranets) are the emerging bourgeoisie of the Internet—stable, productive money earners that are becoming the economic bedrock of cyberspace.

[What are intranets?]
[What are extranets?]

Example 2 An introduction with new terms defined

In the past year only a trickle of money on the World Wide Web has actually made its way toward consumer goods such as books, flowers, and airline tickets. But the Web has actually produced a bona fide financial hit—intranets. Intranets are networks that are generally accessible only to select users and that rely on the rules of the Internet that permit computers to "talk" to one another.

Intranets (and extranets, or networks extended to branches and business partners) are the emerging bourgeoisie of the Internet—stable, productive money earners that are becoming the economic bedrock of cyberspace.

[The author decides to define intranets, *a relatively new term for readers, but not* World Wide Web, *as the term is very familiar to readers.]*

[The author inserts a definition of extranets, *a new term, but does not define the extremely familiar* cyberspace.*]*

In your English classes, you have probably been taught to "stay in the same tense."

This is good advice. However, in technical and scientific reports, this good advice has a special twist, for the rules for tense are slightly different in science than in English classes.

The difference is that the governing tense—the main tense in which you tell the story—may change from section to section of a report. That means that even though the report is a whole, in the same way that an essay is a complete document, the tense in which you tell the report is not continuous—it varies according to what you are saying within the report.

The governing tense of the introduction is the present tense. In this section you are telling the reader what the problem or issue is that you are addressing. You may also use the present perfect tense if your work started in the past and extends into the present.

Here is the introduction from the example used in Chapter 2, slightly shortened, with the verbs italicized.

Introduction

Microparticles in air, such as biological spores or other aerosol particles, *partake* in biological reproduction and in the dissemination of disease [1]; *provide* small "test tubes" for brewing acid rain; and *are* a subject of continual environmental monitoring. [2] Although such particles *are* commonly investigated by collecting the particles on filter paper for spectrochemical analyses, this method *can* corrupt the particles in several ways. Contact *can* easily lead to chemical contamination, physical distortion, and charge transfer.

We have *introduced* a means for investigating a single aerosol particle "in situ," through microphotography on a levitated particle. [4] In addition to contributing to the construction and design of the microscope, our work *has expanded* into fluorescence microphotography. By spectrally resolving microphotographs of levitated microdroplets containing fluorescent molecules, it *is* possible to determine if the molecules *are* surfactants (molecules localized to the particle surface).

In what follows we *describe* our aerosol particle fluorescence microscope (APFM), *discuss* the preparation of individual particles, *present* results on the fluorescence microphotography of surfactant chromophores, and *discuss* these results in terms of the physics of fluorescence and the physical chemistry of molecules at a liquid's surface.

While the governing tense of the introduction is the present, the governing tense of the procedure is the past, for in this section you are telling what you *did* during the experiment. Use the simple past tense unless you are describing an action that happened before another action in the past. In this case, use the past perfect. (We *examined* the oscilloscope after it *had been subjected* to a severe shock.)

Here is a selection from an example used in Chapter 2, slightly shortened, with the verbs italicized:

Experimental Work

In the first part of the experiment, a function generator *was connected* directly to the oscilloscope to obtain an image on the scope. Afterwards, the point-to-point voltage of the image *was measured and converted* to RMS voltage.

In the experiment, the voltage on the function generator *was set* to 2 V RMS, and then the DMM *was used* to determine the voltage output of the generator more accurately. After the signal *was measured* with the DMM, it *was confirmed* with the oscilloscope, which measured the peak-to-peak voltage from the image of the sine wave on the oscilloscope screen.

The second part of the experiment *tested* the accuracy of the frequency of the sine waves generated by the signal generator. To do this, the trigger *was set* to Line, which is 60 Hz. The frequency of the function generator was then *changed* to observe the settings for which one could observe a stationary image. Afterwards, a short table comparing actual frequencies with the dial setting on the generator *was prepared*.

In the third part of the experiment, the advantages and disadvantages of the two modes of operating the oscilloscope *were compared:* dc and ac coupling modes. Once a sine wave *was displayed* on the oscilloscope, the dc offset of the function generator *was varied*. That *added* a constant voltage to the sine wave. The change in the image using dc vs. ac coupling modes *was* then *observed*. A square wave *was* then *substituted* for a sine wave, and the comparison of dc and ac *made* again.

The governing tense of the discussion is the present, for in this section you are arguing for what you think is so.

Since the transition moment of ORDB *is known* to lie in the plane of the three aromatic rings, our measurement for the direction of the transition moment *is consistent* with the plane of the rings being parallel with the plane of the particle's surface.

The results *show* that it *is* possible to estimate the orientation of a surfactant molecule on a liquid's surface through long-term fluorescent imaging of doped aerosol particles.

The author of the report quoted above and in Chapter 2 also used the *past tense* in the discussion when he spoke of actions in the past, and the *future tense* to suggest applications of the research.

First-Person Pronouns

Can you use the pronouns *we* and *I* in the reports that you write? Is it correct to say, "I observed" or "we observed," or must you say "It was observed that" to avoid using *I* or *we*?

Whether to use first-person pronouns *(I, we)* or a passive cliche like "it was observed that" has been a controversial issue in technical and scientific writing since the turn of the century.

It may surprise you to learn that at one time all scientists used *we* and *I*. In fact, from the Renaissance to the early twentieth century, *we* and *I* were entirely acceptable words in scientific discourse. In 1615, for instance, Harvey wrote in *An Anatomical Disquisition on the Motion of the Heart-Blood in Animals*.

I finally saw that the blood, forced by the action of the left ventricle into the arteries, was distributed to the body at large and its several parts, in the same manner as it is sent through the lungs, impelled by the right ventricle into the right pulmonary artery, and that it then passed through the veins and along the vena cava, and so round to the left ventricle in the manner already indicated, which motion we may be allowed to call circular.

In 1869, first person was still alive and well when Joseph Lister reported to the British Medical Association that "In the course of an extended investigation into the nature of inflammation, and the healthy and morbid conditions of the blood in relation to it, I arrived, several years ago, at the conclusion that the essential cause of suppuration in wounds is decomposition."

But in the early twentieth century, the first person fell out of favor among those who decided they would sound "more objective" if they did not include references to themselves. To do this, they removed the first person, and substituted for it what is called in grammar *passive voice*—that is, they substituted "it was observed" for "I saw," and "it was demonstrated that" for "we demonstrated."

What is the difference between active and passive voices? The active voice emphasizes the subject of the sentence:

Smith examined the spectra.

The passive voice emphasizes the object:

The spectra were examined.

The passive is formed by a combination of the verb *to be* and the past participle *(were + examined)*. It may contain a "by" clause if the writer wishes *(by Smith)*.

The spectra were examined by Smith.

In the 1980s, a second trend reinforced the use of passive voice in science and technology. U.S. companies developed a strong belief in the importance of teamwork, and when they did, the use of *I* fell completely out of favor. It was considered an egocentric, highly inappropriate pronoun for team-driven efforts. *We*, however, was acceptable.

Today it is possible to use *we* if you work for a company, but less possible to use *I* because of its historical associations.

Scientific journals are fighting for the use of *I* and *we*—or at least *we*—urging their readers to use the first person when appropriate, particularly in the introduction and conclusion to a paper, where the author's voice is most clearly heard discussing and interpreting.

However, *I* remains suspect, so most people working in science and technology find themselves opting for the old-fashioned, very useful passive voice when the choice lies between the passive and the forbidden *I*.

As a rule of thumb, use the passive when the performer is irrelevant to, or less important than, the object; avoid it when the focus belongs on the subject. Thus, use "The engineering staff assessed the damage" to accent the staff, but "Damages were assessed" if you don't know who did the assessing, if you don't care who did the assessing, if who did the assessing doesn't matter, or if the damage is the most important element in the sentence.

When you do use passive voice, you'll probably have to disregard the disconcerting warnings from the grammar checker on your word processor; most grammar programs include alerts on overuse of the passive voice.

He as the Governing Third-Person Singular

While English offers a third-person plural pronoun that includes both masculine and feminine *(they, them)*, it lacks such a pronoun for third-person singular *(he, she, him, her)*. This leads to a problem when the writer uses a term like *everyone, everybody, each person,* or *one,* for these words all require a singular pronoun. The historical solution has been to use a masculine pronoun:

Each person in the lab should maintain his notebook carefully.

This sort of sentence, though, excludes females. One solution to this exclusionary language is to change singular antecedents to plurals:

Students should maintain their notebooks carefully.

Another solution is to recast the sentence:

Notebooks should be maintained carefully.

Some writers use *he or she,* although others find the phrase cumbersome.

Representing Numbers—Figures versus Words

When should you write out numbers as words, and when may you simply represent them in figures? This is a confusing issue, for numbers are written out far more often in literary writing than in technical fields. Still, there are some occasions in technical text when numbers should be represented as words rather than figures. Here are guidelines:

1. Use figures
with units of measure:

0.40 mg, 4 sec

in a mathematical or chemical context:

5 orders of magnitude, a factor of 8

> for items and sections:

Sample 1, Unit 3

> for figures and tables:

Figure 1, Table 1

> for all numbers in a series, even if a particular item in the series might ordinarily be spelled out:

Panels 1, 2, and 3 included 2, 4, and 8 subjects, respectively.

2. Use words
for numbers below 10, both cardinal and ordinal, unaccompanied by a unit of measure:

three pipettes but 30 pipettes

fifth trial but 30th trial

> for numbers below 10, even when accompanied by a unit of measure, if the use is not technical:

Last year I worked on the project for two months.

> for numbers that begin sentences:

Twenty-one students participated in the project.

(You can also, of course, recast the sentence to avoid spelling out *twenty-one:* Participating in the project were 21 students.)

> for common fractions:

One-fourth of the sample

> If you use two consecutive numerical expressions, either spell out one expression or recast the sentence:

Fourteen 5-part packets accompanied the set.
(not 14 5-part packets).

> These rules also apply to adjectival forms:

A five-year-old sample

A 30-hour trial

Consistency and Precision in Technical Language

Whether you are speaking or writing, certain constraints in the rhetoric of scientific and technical writing will influence how you present your ideas.

Literary writing is the search to create what poet Marianne Moore calls "imaginary gardens with real toads in them"—to present a flashing, psychologically correct setting in which readers suddenly come upon their own experiences with the shock of recognition.

Scientific writing does not speak in this tongue. Instead, one finds an avoidance of impressionistic detail, of language that is obviously emotive or suggestive. In other words, the writer struggles to reduce the emotional involvement of the reader's response rather than to evoke it.

Elaborate prose is rare. The author attempts to transmit information as objectively as possible, with language the admitted enemy in this endeavor. Language can be rife with ambiguity; emotional associations cluster around words. It is the technical professional's job to cut away at this ambiguity. Precision and consistency are hallmarks of the style.

As an aid, scientists often invent words that are not in everyday use and therefore not likely to evoke irrelevant associations in the reader's mind. For example, when Faraday finished his work on electrolysis, he visited William Whewell (at that time a professor of moral philosophy at Cambridge University in England) to have an untarnished set of words coined for his results. That is how the terms *anode* and *cathode* came into existence.

The people who coin technical and scientific terms specifically to limit their connotations often watch, aghast, as the public embraces these words and in so doing corrupts their meanings.

The broadening in popular use of the term *quantum* (plural, *quanta*) is a good example of this process. Used by Planck, Einstein, and Bohr, the term had a distinct meaning. It referred to small, discrete amounts of energy. The term, when adopted by the public, soon became *quantum leap*, meaning a large amount. A television show used the expression to refer to the weekly leaps of a hero trapped in a time machine. While the term bears some vestiges of its original definition, the precision of its meaning is gone.

The rigor and consistency of scientific and technical vocabulary distinguish it from the vocabulary of more general writing. For example, in many types of literary writing, students are taught to avoid repeating words and instead to find synonyms. In technical and scientific writing, consistency—rather than switching from one term to a possible synonym—is highly valued, whether in a report for the Food and Drug Administration or instructions for using a machine. Changing terminology can confuse the reader of the document.

Color in technical and scientific writing is rare, and for good reason. Consider, for instance, this letter that Charles Babbage (inventor of the precursor to the modern computer) wrote to Tennyson, the English poet:

Sir,

In your otherwise beautiful poem there is a verse which reads

Every moment dies a man,
Every moment one is born.

299

It must be manifest that if this were true, the population of the world would be at a standstill. In truth the rate of birth is slightly in excess of that of death. I would suggest that in the next edition of your poem you have it read

> *Every moment dies a man,*
> *Every moment 1 1/16 is born.*

Strictly speaking this is not correct, the actual figure is so long that I cannot give it into a line, but I believe the figure 1 1/16 will be sufficiently accurate for poetry.

Babbage takes issue with the poet Tennyson for figurative use of the expression, "every moment dies a man." The accuracy of language in poetry is very different from the accuracy of language in scientific and technical literature. True, it is possible to find an occasional figure of speech in technical text. For instance, R. W. Wood describes spectra as "furrowed," and Woodward in the *Journal of the American Chemical Society* once described the strychnine molecule as a "tangled skein of atoms." In general, though, the language of science and technology is remarkably austere. Figurative language is infrequent. Narrative voice is scant. And humor is very rare. Usually, the speaker is shoved firmly into the background, and organization and logic become the mainstays of explication.

The one form of figurative language used by both poets and technical writers is comparison, although often it's used in its plainest forms rather than in metaphors or analogies.

Thomas Edison wrote in his notebook, "I am experimenting upon an instrument which does for the Eye what the phonograph does for the Ear, which is the recording and reproduction of things in motion."

Comparison is often used to bring numbers to life on a page. Here is Richard Feynmann, explaining tests of the theory of quantum electrodynamics:

> I'll give you some recent numbers: experiments have Dirac's number at 1.00115965221 (with an uncertainty of about 4 in the last digit); the theory puts it at 1.00115965246 (with an uncertainty of about five times as much). To give you a feeling for the accuracy of these numbers, it comes out something like this: If you were to measure the distance from Los Angeles to New York for this accuracy, it would be exact to the thickness of a human hair. That's how delicately quantum electrodynamics has, in the past fifty years, been checked—both theoretically and experimentally.

There are some cases, though, where comparison is not the right technique. "Make measurements in centimeters, not in fruits, vegetables, or nuts," a medical textbook advises. "Pea-sized, lemon-sized and walnut-sized lesions vaguely convey an idea, but make accurate evaluations and future comparisons impossible. How big were the lemons or peas? Does the walnut have a shell?" Walnuts come in different sizes; the comparison is not useful for the audience that needs not a flash of insight, but specific dimensions.

Matters of Usage

When you are involved in writing a report and therefore very busy struggling with the content, the finer points of language like usage are best put aside. But later, when you revise your document, you'll want to think about how you use each word within a sentence.

Correct usage plays an important part in clear language. Readers respond to the small, careful choices in language good writers make. Did you say "affect" when you meant "effect"? Of such small distinctions as those between *affect* and *effect* is language made.

Questions of usage perplex students, in part because guidelines for what does and does not constitute correct usage (linguistic propriety) change fairly quickly in the United States, where no official group or academy opposes the introduction of, say, the expression "Author the report" to mean "Write the report."

English adapts to change—in fact, some linguists speculate that this openness to the new or the adapted—such as from *floppy disc* to *software* to *menu*—is one of the reasons English has become the international language of science.

Such rapid change means that some usages we were taught were unacceptable at age 12 may be perfectly proper within five or six years. In the 1950s, for example, usage handbooks advised students to use *contact* only as a noun, never as a verb.

Some changes, like using *contact* as a verb, are settled by gradual academic capitulation to popular speech. Today, *contact* is a perfectly acceptable verb—you can *contact* your instructor by e-mail whenever you wish—but the jury is still out on *aliquotting* your samples or *portholing* your data.

Many changes that are popular in speech have only marginal acceptance in formal discourse. Thus we have a new group of people who intend to *author* their reports, although traditionalists still prefer to *write* them.

Some usage changes are inevitable. Arguing against them, as the linguist Geoffry Nunberg once commented, is like a landscape gardener arguing with continental drift.

Other changes, though, are fended off by spirited argument. *Irregardless* is still rejected as a proper word by many dictionaries at this writing, although it will probably gain currency in the future. (It is already in *Webster's*.) Using *data* as a singular was disputed hotly as early as 1900; the use of "the data is" remains controversial even today. While most academics still construe the term as a plural ("these data are . . ."), many popular writers now routinely use "data" as a collective singular.

Sometimes the fight is over loss of a distinction (as in the confusion of *imply* and *infer*, or *respectively* and *each*); other issues are strictly grammatical, as in using *impact* as a verb.

5

Editing for Grammar and Punctuation

Outline

Close Editing

Close editing for grammar and punctuation is often done late in the writing process rather than at the beginning, when writers have to maintain their impetus by getting ideas down and organizing them coherently.

Chapter 5 presents basic troublespots in grammar and punctuation that you are likely to confront as you edit your reports.

In matters of *grammar*, the classic pitfalls for students proofreading their reports often involve

- Agreement in number of subject and verb.
- Errors in parallel structure.
- Misplaced or dangling modifiers.
- Use of collective nouns.
- Use of pronouns.

Punctuation problems in reports usually concern the use of the apostrophe, the colon, the comma, ellipses, hyphens, parentheses and brackets, and semicolons.

Some errors, such as misplaced modifiers, are the same as those examined in English class; others, like rapid changes in hyphenation for technical terms, are different.

Here are some guidelines for each of these areas.

Matters of Grammar

Agreement in Number of Subject and Verb

This sentence has a grammatical error:

> The microscope and associated apparatus consists of an electrodynamic levitator trap equipped with lateral-centering electrodes, a homemade microscope, and a cooled integrating CCD camera.

The error is in the verb *consists*. It should be *consist*. Why? Because the subject of the sentence, "microscope and associated apparatus," has two parts, making it a plural subject. (The technical name for subjects joined by *and* is *compound subject*.)

Plural subjects require plural verbs, as singular subjects require singular verbs. Another way to say this is that verb and subject have to agree in number.

Errors in subject–verb agreement are common in reports. Why does this happen? Sometimes the problem lies in sentences so long that the subject is no longer in shouting distance of the verb. Sometimes, though, the error has to do with the writer's ignorance of the many tricky conventions that govern subject–verb agreement. Here is a brief review:

1. Compound subjects (subjects joined by *and*) are usually plural. Not

mpilation of technical information for the report and its use graphics and tabular material *is* very important.

ut

The *compilation* of technical information for the report *and* its *use* with graphics and tabular material *are* very important.

The exception is when the compound subject is thought of as one unit:

Research and development *is* in this wing of the building.

If the compound subject is modified by *each* or *every,* the verb is singular:

Each computer and printer *is* available.

2. *Each, either, neither, one, anybody,* and *somebody* are always singular when they are pronoun subjects:

Neither of the instruments *works* well.

3. Ignore objects of prepositions and compound prepositions such as *along with, in addition to, together with,* and *accompanied by* when determining the number of the verb:

The *head* of the team, as well as all the other members, *is* responsible for writing a report.

As can be seen from the table, *substitution* of the benzene ring with electron donating groups, as well as some electron withdrawing groups, generally *has* no effects on final product purity.

4. Collective nouns are usually construed as singular:

The engineering staff *has* voted on the matter.

Collective nouns may be construed as plural, though, if each member of the group is acting individually:

A number of engineering majors *are* choosing electrical engineering as a major.

But

The number of engineering majors *is* increasing.

Note that units of measure are usually regarded as collective singulars and therefore take singular verbs:

30 ml *was* added (not *were* added).

5. In *either–or* and *neither–nor* constructions, use a singular verb when both subjects are singular. If both are plural, use a plural verb. If one is singular and the other plural, the verb agrees with the nearer subject:

Neither the device nor the chemicals *have* arrived.
Neither the chemicals nor the device *has* arrived.

6. Noun clauses that are the subject of the sentence take a singular verb:

What this report needs *is* more proofreading.

7. Linking verbs *(am, is, are, was, were, seems, appears)* take their number from the subject (the words before the linking verb), not the complement (the words after the linking verb):

Repeated absences *were* the reason he failed.
The reason he failed *was* repeated absences.
The rigorous calculations *are* the only difficulty with the method.
The only difficulty with the method *is* the rigorous calculations.

Errors in Parallel Construction

In parallel construction all the items joined in a series or comparison have the same grammatical form. For instance, in the sentence, "He often navigates files by moving to the beginning of the line and search for text," the words *moving* and *search* are not parallel. One is an -ing form and the other is an infinitive.

To correct the sentence, try "He often navigates files by *moving* to the beginning of the line and *searching* for text."

In parallel form, adjectives are linked with adjectives, prepositional phrases with prepositional phrases, infinitives with infinitives. In a list, too, all items should be parallel.
Not

Jones made two recommendations:
1. The installation of new mounting blocks to reposition the valves.
2. Add a pneumatic control loop.

But either

Jones made two recommendations:
1. The installation of new mounting blocks to reposition the valves.
2. The addition of a pneumatic control loop.

Or

Jones made two recommendations:
1. Install a new mounting block to reposition the valves.
2. Add a pneumatic control loop.

Here is an error in parallel elements taken from a procedure:

Procedure:
1. Check with safety coordinator to confirm all waste was transferred and accounted for before any burning takes place.

2. Check to see if ash and water effluent-drums are staged.

3. The induction fan on the caustic water system is operational.

The first two items are commands, but the third item is a regular sentence. Therefore, item 3 is not parallel with items 1 and 2.

Corrected, the sequence might read

Procedure:

1. Check with safety coordinator to confirm all waste was transferred and accounted for before any burning takes place.

2. Check to see if ash and water effluent-drums are staged.

3. Make sure the induction fan on the caustic water system is operational.

Misplaced or Dangling Modifiers

Readers expect introductory phrases to modify (explain) the subject of the main sentence. Introductory phrases that fail to do this are said to dangle.

For instance, this sentence has a classic misplaced or dangling modifier:

Once captured and balanced in the electrodynamic trap, we irradiated the particle from below with a circular polarized beam from an Argon ion laser.

In the sentence, it sounds as though the authors ("we"), rather than the particle, were captured and balanced in the electrodynamic trap.

This error occurs became the words "once captured and balanced in the electrodynamic trap" are in the wrong place—next to "we" rather than next to the words they modify, "particle." To fix the sentence, place "particle" next to the phrase modifying it:

Once captured and balanced in the electrodynamic trap, the particle is irradiated from below with a circular polarized beam from an Argon ion laser.

Some sentences are best corrected by adding a logical subject. Not

To alter screen position, the blue key must be depressed.

But

To alter screen position, *you* must depress the blue key.

Not

If thought about a while, most people might agree with that statement.

But

If *they* thought for a while, most people might agree with the statement.

Some sentences must be recast to avoid ambiguous modification. In a sentence like "At the meeting, our team joined the mostly French chemists," the meaning of "mostly" is unclear. Try "At the meeting, our team joined the chemists, many of whom were French."

Use of Pronouns

Pronouns must have a noun or pronoun that the reader is sure is the antecedent (the word the pronoun stands for). If the reader must pause to decide on the probable antecedent, you need to recast the sentence to prevent any momentary jolt, ambiguity, or misunderstanding.

Not

> After the *Challenger* accident, NASA engineers, acting on the prodding of an investigatory committee, presented a series of design changes for the O-rings, *which* pleased the committee.

The antecedent of "which" could be "design changes for the O-rings" or the fact that the engineers responded to prodding. To make the sentence clearer, you might change the "which," depending on meaning, as follows:

> After the *Challenger* accident, NASA engineers, acting on the prodding of an investigatory committee, presented a series of design changes for the O-rings, *changes that* pleased the committee.

Pronouns should agree in number with the words they replace: singular antecedent, singular pronoun; plural antecedent, plural pronoun. Therefore, this sentence has an error:

> *Each* person in the group should submit *their* report.

Each, the antecedent, is singular, but *their*, the pronoun, is plural. The pronoun does not agree with its antecedent.

To correct the sentence, try

> Each person in the group should submit a report.

Note that the indefinite pronouns *each, either, everyone, everybody, anybody, anyone, either, neither, one, no one, someone,* and *somebody* are construed as singular:

> Neither of them *is* correct.

Several, both, few, and *many* are construed as plurals:

> Several of the instruments *have* arrived.

All, any, some, most, and *none* are singular or plural depending on meaning or referent. (Look at the prepositional phrase that follows *all, any, some,* or *most.* If its object is plural, use a plural verb.)

All of the *reports have* been submitted.

All of the *substance remains* in the container.

Punctuation of pronominal possessives *(yours, its, his, hers, ours, theirs)* poses other problems. The common error is to confuse *its,* a pronominal possessive that does not take an apostrophe, with *it's,* the contraction of *it* plus *is.*
Not

Its standard procedure to stack the boxes that way.

But

It's standard procedure to stack the boxes that way.

Not

It's cost is high.

But

Its cost is high.

Note that pronominal possessives do not take *'s.*
Not

The report is *her's.*

But

The report is *hers.*

Use of Collective Nouns

In daily conversation outside the laboratory, you may have heard confusing sentences like this:

The couple *is* married.

The couple *are* divorced.

Which is correct? Is the couple a singular ("is") or a plural ("are")?
Actually, both sentences are correct. The verb depends on whether the couple is acting together as a collective singular. Once divorced, they are no longer a collective singular.

Collective nouns are very common in technical writing. For instance, *series*, *variety*, and *combination* are collective nouns used frequently in technical and scientific texts. So long as you view the members of the group as a unit (a collective singular), use singular verbs and pronouns to refer to the group:

The series *demonstrates* important features of spectroscopic perturbation.

But when you are dealing with individual items use plural verbs and plural pronouns:

The series of spectra *were transferred* onto transparencies using a laser printer.

Units of measure are collective singulars, and therefore take singular verbs:

Six quarts *was* added.

In general, plurals of quantity and extent take a singular verb so long as they are viewed as a unit:

Thirty percent *is* a good response rate.
Fourteen dollars *is* the unit price.

Apostrophes

Use the apostrophe to show possession *(Feynmann's lectures)*, to indicate a contraction *(won't)*, and to form plurals of letters, symbols, and words referred to as words:

Repetition of q's and r's was common.

In general, you needn't use an apostrophe in all-capitalized abbreviations or acronyms, or for numbers:

ICs, during the 1990s

Use an apostrophe and *s* to form the possessive singular, including for most nouns ending in *s (Sweiss's notebook)*, but note some famous historical exceptions:

Gauss' law, Bayes' theorem, Stokes' law

Use an apostrophe to form the possessive of plural nouns ending in *s* or *es:*

the teams' reports

For all other nouns, add *'s*:

> Freshmen's choice

For more than one owner, add the apostrophe to the last name:

> Pauling and Wilson's book on quantum mechanics

Pronominal possessives use no apostrophe:

> his, hers, its, ours, theirs, yours

Note the apostrophe in expressions such as a *month's delay*.

Colons

Use a colon

1. To introduce a list:

The rank order of activity from the most to the least active agent was as follows: ceftizoxime, ceftriaxone, norfloxacin, and imipenem.

2. To introduce a restatement or explanation. You will hear the words *namely* or *as follows*. If you wish, you may capitalize the initial letter of the restatement or explanation:

Thomas Edison had an inviolate procedure in keeping his laboratory notebooks: He made sure all entries were signed, dated, and properly witnessed.

Commas

Use a comma

1. To set off introductory clauses and phrases:

Because of problems we were having with the equipment, we postponed collecting the data.

To follow up on this lead, we tried changing phase ratios from 60:60 to 45:55, 50:50, and 35:65 to determine the right mix.

2. To set off parenthetical words and phrases:

Some of the materials were too light. *For example,* foam was inappropriate for the container. (The words *for example* are parenthetic.)

Particles are generated using a device similar to an ink jet; *however,* the device developed at the lab acts more like a pipette than an ink jet. (The word *however* is parenthetic.)

The maximum and time-weighted average concentrations, *as predicted by GENEEC,* are below all acute and chronic levels of concern. (The expression *as predicted by GENEEC* is parenthetic.)

The hydrophilic portion of the molecule remains in the polar solvent while the nonpolar portions, *which are hydrophobic,* are pushed into the air. (The expression *which are hydrophobic* is parenthetic.)

3. To separate three or more items in a series. The conjunction before the last item *(and, or, nor)* may be preceded by a comma (the serial comma). Most technical publications prefer the serial comma:

The instrument is equipped with lateral-centering electrodes, a homemade microscope, and a cooled CD camera.

4. To separate coordinate adjectives (adjectives that could logically be linked by *and*):

We added a large, crumpled piece of aluminum to the container.

In contrast, notice that you would not use a comma in an expression like *early warning system* because the word *early* explains *warning.*

A common error is to link independent clauses with a comma:

Load waste material into the autoclave, please do not overstuff the chamber.

To correct the sentence, either

• Place a period between the two independent clauses:

Load waste material into the autoclave. Please do not overstuff the chamber.

Or

• Link the two clauses with a semicolon:

Load waste material into the autoclave; please do not overstuff the chamber.

Ellipses

In text, use three points (. . .) to represent deleted material within a sentence:

Medewar comments that "a lecturer can be a bore . . . because he goes into quite unnecessary details about matters of technique." .

Use four points for omissions at the end of a sentence.
Show changes in capitalization with brackets:

As Medewar comments, "[P]eople with anything to say can usually say it briefly."

Hyphens

What is the matter with these phrases?

> long term storage stability
> solvent free binder
> a six day two week period
> applications on an 11 to 16 day schedule
> a time weighted average
> water based neoprene

The answer is that they are all missing a necessary punctuation mark, the hyphen.

> long-term storage stability
> solvent-free binder
> a six-day two-week period
> applications on an 11- to 16-day schedule
> a time-weighted average
> water-based neoprene

Hyphens are a popular punctuation mark in technical text; you are likely to run into them at every turn, from *on-line documentation* to *menu-driven systems*.

Hyphens perplex students because they often appear between words in one example and then disappear in the next. For instance, you may see *on-line* on one page, but *online* on the next.

The reason is that hyphens are a very fluid, fast-changing part of English punctuation. Often when they are introduced in new compounds like *on-line*, they gradually disappear, and the two parts of the compound fuse: *online*. Many prefixes that used to be hyphenated, too, are vanishing. *Pre-test* has gone to *pretest, co-operation* to *cooperation*.

Some hyphens, though, remain, at least for now. There are two types of hyphens: soft hyphens and hard hyphens.

Soft hyphens are those inserted by the author to divide a word into two parts between the end of one line of text and the start of the next line. Avoid soft hyphens when possible, but if a division is unavoidable, break at the syllable, after the prefix, or before the suffix. Do not divide contractions, acronyms, abbreviations, or one-syllable words.

Hard hyphens are those used to separate the bases of a compound word *(work-station)* or to separate prefixes or suffixes from a base *(a cell-like configuration)*. Use hard hyphens.

1. For numbers between 21 and 99 when written as words except for multiples of 10:

twenty-one, fifty-six

2. For fractions used within the narrative:

one-third of the container

3. For compounds beginning with a single capital letter:

O-rings

4. For coordinate compounds:

English-Chinese version

5. For premodifying expressions of age, weight, time, size, and quantity that are written open (no hyphen) when they are not premodifiers:

an apparatus that is five years old

but

a five-year-old apparatus

6. For ad hoc premodifying compounds:

a signal-to-noise ratio
a what-you-see-is-what-you-get system

7. For adjective compounds in which the second base is a participle, an adjective, or a noun:

menu-driven
polynomial-based descrambler
a blue-gray mixture
a rock-hard substance
a high-frequency measurement

8. To separate a prefix or suffix from a base:
  • If the base begins with a capital or figure:

pre-1990

  • To avoid doubling an *i* or tripling a consonant:

anti-inflammatory, wall-like

  • To avoid ambiguity:

re-cover the container,

but

recover from a catastrophe

  • After *half, quasi,* and *self:*

half-finished

Don't use a hyphen if the first base in the compound ends in *ly:*

a poorly constructed apparatus

Parentheses and Brackets

Parentheses have an established place in technical prose, particularly for asides like table and figure citations and definitions of terms. Here are some of their common uses:

1. For figure and table citations:

Using this presumed alignment and other aspects associated with symmetry, it is possible to explain the anisotropy observed in the analyzed image (Figure 5).

2. To introduce abbreviations and acronyms:

An aerosol particle fluorescence microscope (APFM) is described for characterizing impurity chromophores within an aerosol particle.

3. For interpolations and asides, particularly of subsidiary information clarifying procedures or results:

By applying a voltage pulse to piezoelectric strips in the particle injector body, a small droplet (about 20-um radius) is squeezed from the orifice at the end of the tip.
It should be pointed out that no particular polarization state (i.e., x or y) is impressed on the surface by the incident radiation.

4. To enclose the numbers of items in lists that are run into text, rather than displayed. (In a displayed list, each item begins on a new line.):

These commands work (1) to reply to messages, (2) to forward messages to other addresses, and (3) to mark for deletion.

Use either brackets or parentheses for citations:

Several reports describe the value of magnetic resonance imaging (MRI) in visualizing the damage [1,3,7].

Microparticles in air, such as biological spores or other aerosol particles, partake in biological reproduction and the dissemination of disease, according to *Spread of Viral Infections of Aerosols* (1987; 17;89–131).

Use brackets

1. For interpolations within quotations. The brackets show the reader that the material within was added by the writer or editor, and was not spoken by the person quoted:

Feynmann comments in this context that "the phenomenon of colors produced by the *partial* reflection of white light by two surfaces is called iridescence [italics added]."

2. For parentheses within parentheses. For chemical and mathematical notation, use parentheses for the innermost item, followed by square brackets and then braces.

$$\langle I(\phi; \theta_m) \rangle \propto \mu^2 (a_{per})^2 \{[\cos(\theta_m)\sin(\phi)]^2$$
$$+ (1/2)(a_{par}/a_{per})^2 [\sin(\theta_m)\cos(\phi)]^2\}$$

Semicolons

Semicolons are useful when you want to connect independent clauses tightly:

> The homogeneal light and rays which appear red, or rather make objects appear so, I call Rubrifick, or red-making; those which make objects appear yellow, green, blue, and violet, I call yellow-making, green-making, blue-making, violet-making, and so of the rest.
>
> *Isaac Newton*

A common error in writing is to link independent clauses with a comma:

> Solid samples are not homogeneous, a great deal of care has to be taken to melt the material completely.

If you want to join two independent clauses, you can, of course, use a coordinating conjunction *(and, but, for, or, nor, so, yet)*.

> Solid samples are not homogeneous, so a great deal of care has to be taken to melt the material completely.

A closer link is provided by the semicolon:

> Solid samples are not homogeneous; a great deal of care has to be taken to melt the material completely.

Use a semicolon to separate items in a list when the items themselves are punctuated:

> Members of the panel included Teresa Wong, representing Team 1, Georgetown, Washington, D.C.; George Sinclair, representing Team 2, Silver Spring, Maryland; and Herbert Singh, representing Team 3, Chevy Chase, Maryland.

Use a semicolon, not a comma, to link independent clauses joined by a conjunctive adverb *(however, therefore, thus, then, still, hence, indeed, instead, nonetheless, otherwise)*.

Not

> Solid samples are not homogeneous, therefore, a great deal of care has to be taken to melt the material completely.

But

> Solid samples are not homogeneous; therefore, a great deal of care has to be taken to melt the material completely.